Spanish Culture
behind Barbed Wire

Argelès-sur-Mer, by Mariano Aguayo. Photo courtesy of Marina Aguayo and Salvador Gómez, Archivo Gráfico Gómez-Aguayo.

Spanish Culture behind Barbed Wire

Memory and Representation
of the French Concentration Camps,
1939–1945

Francie Cate-Arries

Lewisburg
Bucknell University Press

© 2004 by Rosemont Publishing & Printing Corp.

All rights reserved. Authorized to photocopy items for internal or personal use, or the internal or personal use of specific clients, is granted by the copyright owner, provided that a base fee of $10.00 plus eight cents per page, per copy is paid directly to the Copyright Clearance Center, 222 Rosewood Drive, Danvers, Massachusetts 01923. [0-8387-5546-1/04 $10.00 + 8¢ pp, pc.]

Associated University Presses
2010 Eastpark Boulevard
Cranbury, NJ 08512

The paper used in this publication meets the requirements of the American National Standard for Permanence of Paper for Printed Library Materials Z39.48-1984.

Library of Congress Cataloging-in-Publication Data

Cate-Arries, Francie, 1956–
Spanish culture behind barbed wire : memory and representation of the French concentration camps, 1939–1945 / Francie Cate-Arries.
   p. cm.
Includes bibliographical references and index.
ISBN 0-8387-5546-1 (alk. paper)
1. Spain—History—Civil War, 1936–1939—Literature and the war.
2. Concentration camp inmates' writings—History and criticism.
3. Spain—History—Civil War, 1936–1939—Prisoners and prisons.
4. Spain—History—Civil War, 1936–1939—Concentration camps—France.
5. Concentration camps—France—History—20th century.
6. World War, 1939–1945—Concentration camps—France.
7. Memory—Political aspects. I. Title.
    DP269.8.L5C38   2004
  946.081'1—dc22   2003019368

PRINTED IN THE UNITED STATES OF AMERICA

For Jonathan, always

Contents

Acknowledgments 9

Introduction: Re-membering Spanish History 13

Part I. Recovering Common Ground: The Camps as Places of Memory

1. Marking Refugee Territory: Barbed-Wire Borderlands and the Birth of the Exiled Nation 21
2. Sacrifice and the Nation: The Death and Resurrection of Antonio Machado 34
3. A Commemorative Memory Album of Exile: *Campos de concentración, 1939–194 . . .* (1944) 53

Part II. The Politics of Remembering the Camps: Grounds for Moral Authority

4. Max Aub's *Morir por cerrar los ojos* (1944): The Drama of Seeing Clearly on a World Stage 85
5. Imagining Paris: Spanish Refugees Caught between the Camps and the Capital 100
6. Luis Suárez's *España comienza en los Pirineos* (1944): World War without Borders 129

Part III. Creative Transformations: The Camps as Construction Sites of Cultural Resistance and Continuity

7. Manuel Andújar's *St. Cyprien, plage . . . campo de concentración* (1942): A Survey of History 145
8. Celso Amieva's *La almohada de arena* (1960): Exile Identity as Buried Treasure 167
9. Agustí Bartra's *Cristo de 200.000 brazos (Campo de Argelès)* (1943): Resurrection, or the Redemptive Beauty of Fraternity 189

*Part IV. The Camps as Battlegrounds of Emigration:
The Struggle for Liberation*

10. Telling Stories of Getting Out: The Politics of Emigration — 211
11. Manuel García Gerpe's *Alambradas* (1941): Performing the Politics of Identity — 235
12. Eulalio Ferrer's *Entre alambradas* (1987): A 1939 Diary of the Quixotic Spectacle of Exile — 260
Epilogue: Haunted History: Replacing the Specter of Exile — 285

Notes — 290
Works Cited — 326
Index — 338

Acknowledgments

I WAS ABLE TO WRITE THIS BOOK THANKS TO TWO GRANTS, PROVIDED by the National Endowment for the Humanities (1999–2000) and the College of William & Mary (2000–2001). I am indebted to these two institutions for their generous support of my work. Leonor Sarmiento Pubillones, president of the Ateneo Español de México, has provided invaluable assistance to me during my research trips to Mexico City over the past six years. I am grateful for her many kindnesses to me, as well as her outstanding stewardship of the fine archival collection of the Ateneo. I thank the center's past and present librarians, Alejandro Yustiaza and Belén Santos Hernández, for their cheerful assistance. Cyndi Mack and the staff at the College of William & Mary's excellent Interlibrary Loan Office have tracked down books for me that I thought I would never hold in my hands; I thank them for their wonderful efficiency. Mike Blum's expert preparation of the text illustrations, as well as all his advice on computer-related matters, were very much appreciated. My dear friend Eileen Morales of Elon University was always available to answer my questions regarding points of translation.

It was a great joy for me to make contact with former refugee camp internee-authors examined in this book, or with surviving family members. My unforgettable meeting in Mexico City with Luis Suárez was a highlight of this project. I am particularly grateful for the time I spent in Guanajuato in the company of the indefatigable Eulalio Ferrer, and I thank him for his cooperation and support. I express special appreciation to Celso Amieva's gracious niece María Teresa Alvarez Posada for the materials she so generously provided, and to Bernice Bromberg de Bartolí and Jaume Canyameres for their expert assistance in my investigation of Josep Bartolí's work. My sincerest thanks to the following individuals or institutions for permission to quote material in this book: Paloma Altolaguirre; Ananda Velasco de Andújar; Elena Aub; Roger Bartra; Bernice Bromberg de Bartolí; Eulalio Ferrer; José Miguel Herrera Soler; Luis Suárez; Geneviève Dreyfus-Armand, director of Bibliothèque de documentation international contemporaine of Nanterre; Salvador Gómez and Marina Aguayo; and Eliane Lavaud, president of *Hispanística XX* of Dijon. I thank Alfonso Alcocer of the Museo Iconográfico del Quijote for his indispensable help with the artwork for the book cover. My work was frequently facilitated by the notices, news, and information posted by fellow scholars of Spanish exile on the REDER listserve, a research instrument that I have found to be immensely valuable.

I am fortunate to have written this book surrounded by good friends, generous colleagues, and a loving family. I am grateful for the collegiality and many years of friendship that I have enjoyed with my fellow faculty members in the Department of Modern Languages and Literatures at the College of William & Mary. I offer a special word of thanks to two colleagues in the Hispanic Studies Program, Carla Buck and Teresa Longo, who good-naturedly took on additional administrative duties and teaching responsibilities while I was on research sabbatical. My three boys Gabriel, Nathan, and Caleb, models of boundless energy and delightful humor, furnished endless distractions while I was working on this project. I am lucky to live in a house where their imagination, infectious enthusiasm, and lively personalities (quite literally) run wild. I thank my parents Hollis Lanier Cate and Mary Boone Cate for sharing with me their love of language and for teaching me the power and beauty of the story well told. Finally, I thank my husband Jonathan Arries for providing the kind of "life support" that has made this project possible, and made everything else worthwhile.

Spanish Culture
behind Barbed Wire

Introduction: Re-membering Spanish History

> Quizá la historia entre en vía de razón cuando la conduzcan hombres dotados de larga memoria y hondo sentimiento, que conserven vivo, como si ellos lo hubiesen vivido, el recuerdo—la experiencia—de todas las derrotas.
>
> [Perhaps history will be on the right path when it is written by men who have a long memory and deep compassion, who keep alive, as if it were their very own, the memory—the experience—of all defeats.]
> —María Zambrano, "Sentido de la derrota"

> Y si no puedo verme,
> si de mí quedan sólo las raíces,
> si los pájaros buscan vanamente
> el lugar de sus nidos
> en las tristes ausencias de mis brazos,
> entonces, desde el fondo,
> con el silencio de una primavera,
> brotaré de la tierra como llanto
> insinuaciones de verdor y vida.
>
> [And when I can no longer see myself / when only my roots remain, / when the birds look in vain / for where their nests once were / held in the sorrowful absence of my arms, / then, from the very depths, / with the silence of springtime, / I will spring forth from the earth like a sob / verdant promises of new life.]
> —Manuel Altolaguirre, "Ultima muerte"

IN THE SPRING OF 1975, JUST MONTHS BEFORE THE DEATH OF THE SPANish dictator Francisco Franco, the well-known writer Manuel Vázquez Montalbán penned a short preface, "Perder la historia" (A Lost History), for a collection of essays written by the longtime Republican exile Carlos Sampelayo, *Los que no volvieron* (The Ones Who Never Returned). In his remarks, Vázquez Montalbán reported that, almost forty years after the end of the Spanish Civil War, the Spanish state would at long last implement a program to grant pensions for the disabled veterans who had fought to defend the democratically elected Spanish Republic against the Franco-led military insurgency in 1936.[1] Unlike their counterparts who had been wounded in the name of a Nationalist victory, the so-called *Caballeros mutilados por la Patria* [gentlemen maimed in service to the homeland], the former Republican combatants had waited for decades to be remembered by the government with monetary compensation.[2] Vázquez Montalbán points out that the state-sanctioned oblivion to which the invalid *vencidos* of civil war had been relegated was replicated in the truncated pages of the official history of post–civil war Spain that omitted their story of loss, displacement, and struggle: "If it has taken thirty-six years to inadequately resolve the problem of those who were maimed in the war, how long will it take to alleviate the pain of the crippling wounds that one can't see? . . . I speak of the mutilations of History. I speak of the traumatic psychological scarring of those who lost the war and History without so much as losing a little finger. I speak of the darkened recesses of trauma inherited by the 1940s generation, born of the losers' womb, a womb full of fissures, shadows, loss."[3] The shadowy space of national amnesia that the dictator's regime would accord specifically to the Spanish Republican exiles of 1939 was alluded to by José Esteban Vilaró in his December 1939 book, *El ocaso de los dioses rojos: Barcelona, Perthus, Argelès, París, Méjico* . . . (The Twilight of the Red Gods), one of the very few accounts to appear in early postwar Spain about the war refugees living in France. Here the fervently pro-Franco author consigns the newly displaced Spanish nationals to a precarious place in history; the Republican "Reds" will live on only in infamy before quickly disappearing from the collective imaginary and the annals of history altogether: "Heroes of terror, legendary names that will be recorded in history in order to frighten children as the tangible expression of a terrifying thing. At this very moment begins the decline of their existence. They will wither away without glory in the most remote reaches of the globe. It is, when all is said and done, the history of all emigrants . . . The history of all emigrants is one of a slow disappearance without glory."[4] The vanquished will be banished, the vanquished will simply vanish from national memory. The 1950 edition of the Espasa-Calpe dictionary published in Franco's Spain failed to include an entry for the word *exilio*. As the Cuban writer Guillermo Cabrera Infante has noted, "For Franco, there was no exile. Exiles simply didn't exist. There were only enemies rapidly running for cover."[5]

But Franco's beleaguered *perdedores* who lost their place in the homeland did not lose their memory; they carried their stories and experiences like the bundles on their backs with which they crossed the border into exile. Wounded by war like Franco's *Caballeros mutilados por la Patria*, they too bore the marks of history and memory like gashes on the body. The exiled memoirist Avel·lí Artís-Gener recalls one such companion in 1975. His war buddy Claudio Fournier, nicknamed El

Muerto after being badly wounded and left for dead among a pile of cadavers in the Plaza de Cataluña on the very day the war started, was famous for his miraculous revival. During Fournier's subsequent long exile in Mexico, on every anniversary of the military uprising for three days before *el 18 de julio* and three days afterward, his deeply disfigured face became impossibly inflamed and swollen.[6] Fournier's scarred expression insistently bespoke a language of memory that for so many years was inaudible among the Spanish *pueblo* that the exiles had left behind the nation's borders. But with the spate of civil war publications from "the other side" that followed Franco's death, these exiles have claimed their piece of history. In his 1985 memoir, Zurita Castañer speaks for an entire community when he states categorically, "We too are History."[7] Perhaps one of the longest forgotten chapters of all of civil war exile history belongs to the Spanish Republicans who were interned in hastily constructed French concentration camps, the largest of which were located along the open shorelines of France's southernmost beaches. This book chronicles the rich cultural memory of a war refugee population whose stories as camp inmates in 1939 and the early 1940s have not been as widely disseminated nor received the same critical attention as the literature and testimony of the survivors of Nazi death camps.[8] The "hidden history" of France's seaside camps for thousands of refugees spawned a rich legacy of cultural works that dramatically demonstrate how a displaced political community began to reconstitute itself from the ruins of war, literally from the sands of exile. Combining close textual analyses of memoirs, poetry, drama, and fiction with a carefully researched historical perspective, this book investigates how the most significant literature of the early post–civil war exile period appropriated the concentration camp as a discursive vehicle. Beginning with the oral testimonies and memoirs that depict the massive exodus across the French border in the winter of 1939 as an annihilating moment of cultural rupture, dispossession, and mutilation of the body politic, I explore the process of cultural reconstruction that begins behind the barbed-wire perimeter of the camps themselves. I focus on the constitutive function of the refugee camps as figured in the symbolic terrain of the exiled national imaginary during the years when world war raged: as a place of collective memory; as grounds for political legitimacy and moral authority; as the site of creative resistance and cultural renewal.

In "Part I. Recovering Common Ground: The Camps as Places of Memory," I draw on the French cultural historian Pierre Nora's concept of *lieux de mémoire* in order to suggest that the barren place of the camps is transformed through discourse as a fecund "place of memory" that grounds the Spanish exile community's initial processes of nation-building. Nora's field of research is based primarily on those forms of public memory that have been sanctioned or certified by the state. But as Benedict Anderson has commented in his classic study of national identity as an imagined community, contestatory versions of national history simultaneously erupt along the periphery of the dominant official discourse. A significant portion of the marginalized memory of post–civil war Spanish history belongs of course to the exiled community, and the place that will first engender the seeds of their collective consciousness is necessarily located at the physical limits of the nation-state, the periphery of the border itself. The profound connections among collective memory, historical trauma, and the representations of the nation, a line of inquiry that has been particularly fruitful in the area of Holocaust studies, inform the three chapters of Part I. In my analysis of the textual construction of the French border town of Collioure—both the burial ground for Spain's most famous exile, the great poet Antonio Machado (1875–1939), as well as the location of one of the most brutal prisons for Republican soldier-refugees—I note how this place of suffering, sacrifice, and commemoration functions as a generative matrix for the cultural codes and values of the nation in exile.

The exiled writers that I examine in "Part II. The Politics of Remembering the Camps: Grounds for Moral Authority," including Max Aub, José Herrera Petere, Luis Suárez, and Victoria Kent, appropriate the concentration camps in order to build a persuasive case for an international audience that defends their community's own moral authority and legitimacy. A recurring theme in these texts is the idea that the true squalor of these catastrophic times resides not among the dirty, malnourished Spanish internees, but rather with the collaborationist activities of French government officials and the blitheful ignorance of the French citizenry who turn a blind eye to encroaching disaster. These writers share a language in which the literary allusions to the camp inmates serve to express in idealistic terms the Spanish *pueblo* in exile as the harbinger of passionate ideals, spiritual and moral fortitude, and indomitable resistance. In contrast, the society of France of 1939–40 as seen on the other side of the barbed wire is construed in these accounts as a spineless world on the brink of collapse, a self-deluded enclave on the verge of destruction by the outside forces of war, betrayed by cowardice and hypocrisy from within. In the three chapters of "Part III. Creative Transformations: The Camps as Construction Sites of Cultural Resistance and Continuity," I argue that the camps are frequently configured as a kind of construction site for the nation in exile, a place where the survivors of civil war begin to inscribe a new national history as well as reassemble their political identity as fighters for social justice. I explore how the inmates who inhabit and represent in writing the unfamiliar physical space of the camps of France ultimately encode these sites as places of subversion, resistance, and agency. The internees' ability to crudely transform the material limitations of their world into a more habitable environment in turn prepares the terrain for symbolic representations that skillfully inscribe the concentration camps as an emergent place capable of sustaining the Spaniards' being-in-exile.

The final three chapters of "Part IV. The Camps as Battlegrounds of Emigration: The Struggle for Liberation" consider how the inmates are chosen by official relief agencies for liberation, and how their story of the struggle among the internees vying for selection is told in the camp literature. I examine the extent to which the increasingly fractured relationships among the Republican groups in exile play a role in the politics of camp emigration. Additionally, I explore how "Mexico"—the object of desire for thousands of Spaniards in the camps of France—is constructed in the exile imaginary. A central question that unifies my readings in this section pertains to how the exiles who successfully escaped the barbed wire—both those who write from the privileged position of Paris as well as Mexico City—represent and remember those unlucky thousands who remained on the beaches of France and the shores of world war. Their memories of these comrades "left behind" significantly inform the story of exile that begins to take shape in Mexico during the early post–civil war years, a period that likewise coincides with the violent onslaught of World War II. Like the fallen soldiers on the battlefields of Spain, the abandoned refugees in the camps of France are idealistically portrayed in the pages penned by the liberated exile-survivors as the true martyred heroes and frontline fighters of a Spanish people who waged a war in the name of justice.

The recovered voices of the internment camp refugees express the language of history's most dispossessed, and the trope of the wounded, mutilated body that continued to speak from its fractured position is a recurring motif in this literature. The earliest memoirs written in the camps themselves express the hope that the broken body of the Spanish Republic will soon be resurrected. Eulalio Ferrer recalls in his camp diary that on the occasion of Bastille Day in 1939, fellow inmates took advantage of the festive atmosphere among the French guards and soldiers stationed in the camps in order to express their own solidarity and faith in the future of the Spanish Republic. Supported by the makeshift staff of a *mutilado*'s crutch, a tricolored Republican banner waved in the wind.[9] Eight years later, from the shores of exile in Mexico, the editors of the short-lived exile journal *Ultramar* published a civil war photograph of a horribly disfigured survivor who smiles up at the camera despite his missing limbs; part of the caption reads: "Wounded, torn apart, his Spanish eyes are still ablaze. You can see into his soul and hear his cries in every wound. Maimed and crippled? Yes, so he is, one of our own, who gave pieces of his flesh and heartbeats of his blood for the good of his country. But just like Spain, the nation for which he fought and suffered, he's only partially immobilized. One day, armed with a spirit of steel and holding on by his teeth if he has to, he will embrace victory. . . ."[10] Still hopeful in the early postwar years that the democratic nations that fought against Hitler, Mussolini, and Hirohito would similarly seek to topple the totalitarian regime of Franco, the exiles expressed the belief that soon an ideal body politic of justice, freedom, and equality would be assembled on Spanish soil. Clearly such imagined wholeness remained a fantasy, and many exiles would not live to see Spain's transition to a democratic state in the late 1970s. But their conviction that "We too are History" is realized in the stories they left behind of a time and a place forgotten for too long. To re-place the pieces of this missing history, to re-member these shattered lives, are the objectives that have guided the writing of this book.

Part I
Recovering Common Ground: The Camps as Places of Memory

1

Marking Refugee Territory: Barbed-Wire Borderlands and the Birth of the Exiled Nation

> L'exil est une maladie secrétée par l'histoire et la raison d' Etat. L'exil, c'est une prison.
>
> [Exile is an illness hidden away by history and the State. Exile is a prison.]
>
> —Paco Ibáñez, Spanish exile in France

IN DECEMBER OF 1983, THE PALACIO DE VELÁZQUEZ DEL RETIRO IN Madrid opened its doors to a special exhibition entitled El exilio español en México (Spanish Exile in Mexico), an exceptional sample of the cultural legacy of the twenty-five thousand exiled Spaniards living in Mexico after the Spanish Civil War. This collection, the first and most complete of its kind ever assembled and displayed in Spain, included more than a thousand objects: paintings, drawings, literary works, sculpture, historical documents, and personal effects. It is interesting to note that in the catalog that accompanied this exhibition, over half of the images of place that were represented were neither those of Spain, the lost homeland, nor of Mexico, the adopted *patria*, but rather those of either the French border crossing or the refugee border camps in France. What first strikes the viewer of the photographs, drawings, and oil paintings of these camps, "home" to some 275,000 Spaniards by the middle of February 1939, is their depiction of a "nowhere," a location paradoxically defined by its lack or absence as a place.[1] In one of Julián Oliva's series of photographs recorded in the camp of St. Cyprien, a sleeping man has sought a place of shelter where there is none; his inert body lies huddled against his suitcase, an improvised headboard, surrounded by a broad expanse of frozen sand. Another image shows in the foreground a couple of men squatting beside a makeshift hut, a jumble of sticks and blankets; in the background open sky meets miles of beach, dotted with the diminutive figures of inmates exposed to the elements. In a photograph from Bram taken by Agustí Centelles, the site of the camp's "pharmacy" is located on a single table.² Even the "walls" of the camps that imprison thousands of Spaniards allow the viewer, as well as the inmate, to see the empty spaces stretching through open air; ubiquitous rows of barbed wire crisscross along slender posts, emerging in the black-and-white photographs of St. Cyprien and Bram like shapeless strings.³

The majority of the literature written about the camps similarly recreates the place of the camp through tropes of the void, as an unnameable nowhere whose dehumanized and demoralized inhabitants are constantly threatened by the brute forces of both Nature and Man. In his 1940 memoir, Jaime Espinar refers to the place of the Argelès-sur-Mer camp as an absolutely vacuous space of death: "It wasn't even a 'camp' . . . A spot on the Mediterranean coast, an inhospitable place, where the February winds whipped their lashes into Spanish flesh. For a cemetery, any place on earth will do."⁴ The images of death and dissolution, insinuations of negation and nothingness, are the most pervasive figures in the barren landscape. Wind, water, and sand all seem to conspire to annihilate the Spanish refugees. The narrator of Agustí Cabruja's 1947 *La ciudad de madera* (The City of Wood) awakes in St. Cyprien to find a suicide's cadaver floating in the waves of the ocean. Antonio Sánchez Barbudo—a former camp inmate and later a longtime professor at the University of Wisconsin—recalled that before the *barracas* were finally constructed it was necessary to take turns standing sentry over sleeping companions, to make sure that one wasn't entombed in the night by the wind raging through the sand. But disease still took its toll: "Every morning, several dead bodies turned up nearby."⁵ Countless memoirists describe a process of bodily dissolution mediated by the same sand and water. For a time the water pumped in for drinking comes directly from the sea and results in chronic, severe dysentery. The constant close contact with the inescapable sand, with filth, results in massive infestations of lice. The body invaded, the body voided, it is easy to understand critic José Naharro-Calderón's observation in a 1998 article that "the camp for its inhabitants is a nonproductive space *par excellence*; it only generates pain."⁶

The border campgrounds seem to be, both literally and theoretically speaking, a negative space, an empty transitional zone between the place of home (Spain) and the place of exile (Mexico). This notion of the camp as a nonproductive space, a nowhere, is belied however by the very presence, even excess, of the images that dominate the collection assembled for the 1983 exhibition. This pictorial instance of the "persistence of memory" of the place of both border and camps in the space of the exile imaginary introduces their function as foundational sites of an emerging exilic identity. Rather than spaces of transit and dissolution that are analytically devoid of place value in the story of Spanish exile from Spain to Mexico, I suggest that the barren place of the camps is transformed through discourse into a fecund "place of memory" that grounds the exile community's initial processes of nation-building. Pierre Nora first coins the phrase *"lieux de mémoire"* in his 1984 introduction to his ambitious multivolume collaborative history of French culture in order to describe the material manifestations of collective memory—with their attendant symbolic and emotional connotations— that a nation uses to represent itself. He identifies the *"lieux de mémoire"* as sites such as architectural landmarks, war memorials, commemorations, and public festivals that serve to "codify, condense, anchor . . . national memory."[7] I propose to examine the makeshift camps, located primarily along the French border, as just such an enduring, archival site within the exilic consciousness where, in Nora's words, "memory crystallizes and secretes itself."[8] Nora's field of research is based primarily on those forms of public memory that have been sanctioned or certified by the state; the triumphant Spanish Nationalist regime's early postwar tribute to her war dead, the architectural behemoth of the sprawling necropolis the Valle de los Caídos (Valley of the Fallen) would perhaps more closely serve as an example of such an "official" site of memory. But as Benedict Anderson has commented in his classic study of national identity as an "imagined community," contestatory versions of national history—and, I argue, alternative "sites of memory"—simultaneously erupt along the periphery of the dominant official discourse; referring specifically to Spain's war in his 1991 chapter "Memory and Forgetting," Anderson observes: "At the state's margins, a 'memory' was already emerging of a 'Spanish' Civil War."[9] A significant portion of this marginalized memory belongs of course to the displaced exiled community, and the place that will first engender the seeds of their collective consciousness is necessarily located at the physical limits of the nation-state, the periphery of the border itself. The notion of a "border-place" as a meaningful discursive site is key to my reading of the border camps as formative spaces in the fledgling Spanish collective consciousness in exile.

Losing Ground: Images of Border Crossings

In his 2000 article "Invention, Memory, Place," Edward Said reflected on the interrelationship of imaginative geography and national consciousness, pointing out the profoundly generative role of space and memory in the shared historical experience of a national group: "Collective memory is not an inert and passive thing, but a field of activity in which past events are selected, reconstructed, maintained, modified, and endowed with political meaning."[10] For a nation under siege, for the half million war-weary Spaniards who cross the French border and the quarter million of them who end up in refugee camps, its collective memory will be predicated first and foremost on a very real deterritorialization, a radical loss of ground, a forfeiture of place. Amy Kaminsky's provocative 1999 book *After Exile: Writing the Latin American Diaspora* reminds us that this crucial feature of absence and lack is constitutive in the formation of the exilic conscious: "Identity as a national subject depends on friction and is often tied to loss, lack, and longing."[11] The sense of placelessness that most radically defines the condition of exile is poignantly expressed by one of Max Aub's theatrical characters, the German antifascist exile Berta Gross in the prolific Spanish writer's 1946 play *El rapto de Europa*: "Firm ground no longer exists for me. It's all gotten so soft and unsteady, so shaky. A world made of cotton, muddy earth, slippery and dirty. A world of enormous exhaustion, because the hope of victory begins to wane. Where to put our feet? There's no longer a world for us."[12] The story of a people's collective dislocation and forced internment in camps begins at the very moment of losing their ground, of leaving their land behind. The first stage of exile, the massive exodus across the French border, is represented in oral testimonies and memoirs as an annihilating moment of cultural rupture, dispossession, and mutilation of the body politic.

I inscribe my reading of the apocalyptic border crossing into France alongside an illuminating essay by Giuliana Di Febo in which the author defines the border, both a literal place of national demarcation and a metaphorical marker of separation, as "a fundamental part of the collective imagination and the historical memory of Spanish exile."[13] Di Febo locates the border as a place of memory in the narration of the history of exile ("a memory zone present in the stories of the exiles") that serves as an important bridge between the long journey's first two key geographical sites, the final bloody battlegrounds of Spain and the inhospitable concentration campgrounds of France. The juxtaposition of these first two sites of memory—the military and civilian flight from war into France, the crossing over into the camps—as figured in various exile texts uncovers a defining feature that inheres deep within a displaced population borne into exile: the radical lack or void, the "ground zero" on which they must paradoxically lay the foundations for a new cultural identity.

The exodus out of Cataluña in late January and early February 1939 is comprised of entire battalions of Republican soldiers in retreat and masses of panic-stricken civilians fleeing the encroaching Nationalist army. Thousands escape Spain via every conceivable mode of transportation: in military vehicles, cars, wagons, bicycles, horses, donkeys, and ambulances. Most of the refugees actually make the arduous trip on foot; Vicente Barona (who three years after crossing the French border as a teenager ended up as a slave laborer for twenty-six months in Nazi-operated French concentration camps such as Hennebont) recalls his mother's question that set his and his siblings' two-hundred-kilometer journey in motion: "Kids, are your legs ready to do some walking?"[14] All of the war victims who trudge toward France suffer from the freezing temperatures, steady rainfall, and the relentless aerial bombing campaigns by the enemy. The sheer terror and physical hardship have certainly been amply documented in the survivors' memories of those days of chaos and confusion. In addition, the Spanish Republicans' stories of the French border crossing illustrate in a dramatically poignant manner the state of radical placelessness that lies at the core of the condition of exile. Di Febo has referred to the complete disorientation that the witnesses report; the loss of the familiar terrain of the homeland is accompanied by a loss of a sense of direction. Numerous accounts chronicle the passage into exile as a surreal entry into a no-man's-land, a shadowy realm without familiar topographical markers that can ground and orient the traveler. Thirty-five years after making his exhausting trek over the Pyrenees with a group of fellow soldiers, veteran Avel·lí Artís-Gener sits with a map and compass in hand, trying to retrace the serpentine route of his exodus that he experienced as a "a kind of dream" upon crossing the border at "the phantasmagoric Coll Pregon"; the unearthly quality of the passage into this ghostly border place is exacerbated by the fact that even today the author can't locate the site on the map: "It doesn't show up on any map and therefore it seems made up."[15] Another account, by fellow author-veterans Antonio Tellado Vázquez and Antonio Sánchez-Bravo Cenjor, recalls the retreat out of Figueras—where the last assembly of the Spanish Republican *Cortes* gathered on February 1, 1939—as an absurd comedy of errors in which the driver of their military vehicle is repeatedly given bad directions. Three times the vehicle maddeningly ends back up in Figueras, until the occupants give up and abandon the truck. The frustrated travelers, lost in meaningless circles before they even begin the journey, set off on foot for the as yet totally inconceivable, vague end point of all the refugees, the border: "Limbo or something like it. Because it sure wasn't paradise."[16] Clemente Cimorra evokes a poignant figure against the backdrop of the dramatic exodus, a bewildered old woman who doggedly continued to advance toward parts unknown: "An old woman, still respectable-looking in spite of her disheveled appearance from the long journey, approached a commander: 'Is this the road to France?' 'Yes, ma'm. But . . .' The old woman continued on her weary way, alone, without a bit of luggage, without knowing what France even was."[17] In his 1939 book *El éxodo, por un refugiado español*, Solano Palacio recalls overhearing a woman on the road to Figueras encouraging her small, exhausted child to keep walking, urging him toward a fanciful, fairy-tale kind of destination: "'Come on, son, over there' (and she pointed to the distant horizon), 'Grandmama is waiting for you with sweets and coffee.'"[18]

The exiled poet Manuel Altolaguirre's memories of the border crossing are driven by a double dynamic of loss; geographical displacement and topographical confusion generate a concomitant loss of identity. In his autobiography *El caballo griego* (The Greek Horse), he recounts in painful, deliberate detail his nervous breakdown and incarceration in a hospital shortly after arriving in a camp in France. There he feels literally separated from self ("I prayed . . . as if it wasn't me who was praying"; "I manage to get outside of myself, losing myself") as he remembers his recent journey in which he is incapable of identifying place names: he leaves Spain at night, traveling blindly along "a rugged path, without knowing exactly when we would arrive"; his arrival in France takes place in an anonymous French village with a Cervantinely unspoken name, "whose name I don't wish to recall"; his wanderings in Perpignan occur "in I don't know which street."[19] Unable to name where he is, the exiled writer is a lifetime removed from the street in Málaga where he lived as a child, "Manuel Altolaguirre Street." The poet had nostalgically recalled this safe place of childhood, a street named for his father, just two years before in an autobiographical piece published during the war, "De mis recuerdos" (From My Memories).[20] The reassuring coincidence of place and name—the home of the self—is wrested from the refugee, leaving him in uneasy limbo, both mentally and physically.

Shortly after his harrowing entry into France, Altolaguirre tore up his own valid passport and identification papers in a crazed display of solidarity with fellow Spanish refugees, the majority of whom lacked the necessary legal documentation for immigration. A unifying thread running throughout the recollections of the exodus out of Spain are similar images of shredded signs of identity, both personal and national. Silvia Mistral, pen name for Hortensia Blanch Pita, published one of the very first memoirs of exile to Mexico in early 1940, inscribing the evacuation of Barcelona as a series of holocausts; all around her she witnesses hasty scenes of book burnings, fiery destructions of political party credentials, and widespread "personal *autos da fe*."[21] Mistral closes the introductory chapter of her book with the first such episode of Republican identities in tatters. On January 24, 1939, the eve of the Nationalist army's takeover of Cataluña, Mistral arrives at her place of work, a film distribution company. There, ironically situated under the publicity poster for the Russian war movie *Marinos del Báltico*, fellow employees are shredding all kinds of potentially incriminating records of the identities of employees and business contacts. Mistral joins in, spending four hours methodically destroying all records. Walking through a working-class neighborhood later that night, she observes the sky in flames, due not to the familiar enemy bombings, but rather to the multiple bonfires alit on rooftops and in city squares. Fragments of book titles—torn pieces of liberal political viewpoints, of earlier calls for economic justice and social reform—swirl through the streets: "There are works by Marx, Bujarin, Roisseau [*sic*], Blasco Ibáñez, Pío Baroja, Remarque, Barbusse, and the whole collected works of José Martí."[22] The burning piles of pages remind a friend of Mistral's, an antifascist journalist, of a comparable moment of political upheaval in his native Germany, "the days that followed Hitler's take-over, after the Reichstag fire."[23] Mistral, amid her fellow Republican supporters frantically preparing to leave Barcelona, sees in the pieces of papers, these scraps of identity, the physical proof of a nation-state in ruins: "Receipts, letters, posters, reports, everything is thrown out into the street, like a stark white symbol of an organization that is falling apart."[24] Fellow exile in Mexico Juan Renau has similarly described Barcelona on the eve of its capture as a ghost town dotted with the torn traces of its former inhabitants: "Streets and city squares were blanketed with I.D. cards and documentation in shreds."[25]

As the Republican military units undertake the retreat, a disheartening sight reported by Mistral, further evidence of a government reduced to ashes litters the road to the border. Four days after the events documented in Barcelona by Silvia Mistral in her diary, the ex-combatant Enrique Rioja witnessed other fires also designed to erase the traces of Republican identity. Years later, in 1963, he remembers leaving Cerviá de Ter: "At the moment of departure we were able to see in the twilight shadows, under the bough of an ancient tree, how some peasants prudently began to burn Republican and Catalonian flags."[26] A photograph taken at the French border in February 1939 shows an intact Republican flag that survived the retreat but was confiscated by the French border guards, who in the snapshot curiously inspect the crumpled emblem; the gendarmes unfurl the dirty banner from out of a mess of scattered firearms, similarly confiscated from their refugee owners.[27] Other war materials originally destined to fight the Nationalist insurgents had been torched by the retreating soldiers themselves, in order to avoid falling into enemy hands; fireballs of intermittent explosions form part of the landscape of the exodus. One of the veterans interviewed for Antonio Soriano's 1989 book of oral testimony, Joan Martorell, was in charge of blowing up reserves of abandoned ammunition and recalls detonating heaps of explosives all along the route of retreat: "We blew up the stores of ammunition that we found in isolated houses."[28] Tellado Vázquez and Sánchez-Bravo remember seeing the twisted metal of burning military transport vehicles, forever immobilized along the road's ravines by the soldiers who realized they could not advance due to the sheer numbers of refugees clogging the way: "All of them, without fail, ended up in a ravine. Piled up one upon another, now without owners or guides, they ended their life twisting about in the bonfire."[29] But clearly, the most horrific memories of the border crossing as a vision of flaming apocalypse are engendered by the Nationalist bombs dropped by low-flying aircraft. Franco's pilots strafe the ground in a hailstorm of firepower as thousands of defenseless civilians push toward France. In her posthumously published memoir, the writer Concha Méndez summarizes her nightmarish journey across the border in a few sentences, a passage in which the tragedy of the violent death scene she survives is heightened by the succinct, matter-of-fact tone of the painful account. She remembers traveling by car in the company of her three-year-old daughter Paloma Altolaguirre and the family of a Belgian diplomat: "We went along, and the bombs fell on the people going on foot; they fell on entire families, on children and old people who were trying to get to the border; it was a long way and not everybody made it. Along one stretch of the road we stopped the car. A bomb had just fallen on a family; all of them were dead, except an infant. The Belgian girl, seeing that the child was moving, picked him up to take with us; as soon as she did, he died. We made it to France."[30]

In the face of such physical misery and widespread destruction, it is understandable that the stories of the refugees' traversal into France coalesce around images of fragmentation and mutilation. Many of the refugees are, quite literally, emigrating with wounded bodies and missing body parts; throngs of amputees and the severely injured form part of the massive exodus. But even the able-bodied describe themselves as torn pieces of spirit and flesh. Pedro Serra states that everyone who traveled with him in the caravans out of Spain shared the same broken spirit, "They came as we did: weak . . . broken . . . dragging their feet . . ."[31] In his 1941 memoir *Alambradas: Mis nueve meses por los campos de concentración de Francia*, Manuel García Gerpe recalls his movement toward the border in a truncated style that captures the sense of fragmentation that defined this moment of impending exile: "Behind us, Spain. Pieces of our life. Remnants of our dream."[32] Pieces of people's most prized personal possessions also start the journey of exile with their recently uprooted owners. The image of thousands of refugees carrying their belongings on their backs like slow-moving snails is one of the most pervasive figures in the landscape of the border crossing recorded in the survivors' testimonies. Even more poignant is the memory of many of the same objects strewn along the road, abandoned by the worn-out proprietors who cannot carry them another step. Jaime Espinar describes the chaotic jumble of belongings that litter the way to France, sad reminders of the homes left behind and of the owners' new status as refugees. Espinar opens his 1940 memoir of the border and the camps with the inaugural vision of heaps of now useless possessions, piled in unlikely, meaningless juxtaposition: "From a luxury automobile to that stub of a candle lost in the jumble of the forgotten drawers of home, an entire world of objects."[33] Joan Puigverd witnesses the border crossing at Port-Bou, "a gigantic pandemonium," as an emblematic scene of the overwhelming loss and separation that brands forever the emigrating Spaniards as exiles; in the masses of grief-stricken refugees, among the parents who frantically look for lost children and amidst other family members searching the crowd for their friends and loved ones, says Puigverd, the value of the individual pieces of their scattered personal effects reaches the level of a quasi-totemic object: "In the midst of that infernal mess, they had lost a suitcase and it seemed that their whole future depended on finding it, because for them it was the most important thing in the world. When I say suitcase imagine a blanket, a canary and its cage, or a coffee grinder. Any absurd and unexpected thing. That's what the terror's like, it makes you lose your perspective and your sense of priorities goes to hell; people's attitudes are simply insane."[34] The loss of personal belongings is one of the material markers that divides forever the exile's life into the two distinct temporal realms of "before exile" and "after exile"; Silvia Mistral reports in her diary on the day she crosses the border: "I can't find my books, my articles, my little knick-knacks, and this loss seems to separate my life into two stages."[35] Certainly the motif of misplaced manuscripts, of irreplaceable personal papers (a diary, old letters, newspaper clippings, a beloved book, etc.) forever separated from their owners as well as the life experiences that engendered these texts, is one of the most recurring images in the literature that recounts the border crossing. New owners recall their "rescue" of these pages as an effort to maintain a tenuous tie with a past time and place that are quickly receding from the exile's reach. Solano Palacio, for instance, utilizes the vehicle of the "found manuscript" as a narrative device in his 1939 novel unsuccessfully submitted for publication in Paris shortly after his own trek across the Pyrenees. The narrator of his *Entre dos fascismos: Memorias de un voluntario de las Brigadas Internacionales en España* (Between Two Fascisms: Memoir of a Volunteer in the International Brigades in Spain) explains that the story in his reader's hands was discovered in a knapsack amidst the mounds of confused objects scattered along the evacuation route out of Spain; buoyed up by the spirited account of the struggle of "a heroic nation" that he rapidly reads, the Spanish soldier carries a fellow *vencido*'s version of civil war history with him across the border: "When I finished reading this narrative that I judge to be the truth about an indisputable reality, I started walking straight ahead with the manuscript under my arm, towards Junquera, where a teeming crowd had gathered in hopes of crossing the border."[36]

The Republicans are forced to assume the inescapable exilic condition of radical otherness at the very moment of passing through the official border checkpoints under the fierce scrutiny of French gendarmes. As stated earlier, the majority of the war refugees do not have passports or valid papers for emigration. In addition to the personal possessions that these Spaniards have left behind or lost in transit, their scant belongings are further diminished as the French border guards illegally confiscate many items. Fountain pens, cameras, typewriters, and timepieces are the most frequently cited articles ceded to the guards' greedy pockets, a transfer that deprives the refugees of their most basic tools for recording reality and communicating their experiences. One witness bitterly reports that some disoriented travelers are even separated from the fistfuls of Spanish soil that they still clutch in their hands: "When I saw one of the *gardes mobiles* forcibly open one of these clenched hands and scatter the soil in disdain I knew that the soldiers of France did not understand the meaning of the word 'home,' and I wished that one day they might pay for it."[37] As they give up the signs of self and identity, and lose touch with any secure sense of place and home, the refugees are obligated to recognize the condition of alterity that the French soldiers and civilians assign to them. Di Febo has referred to the initial moment of linguistic and emotional estrangement that the Spaniards experience as many receive harsh, even brutal treatment from the border guards, punctuated with a constantly repeated official refrain: "The gendarmes' *'allez/allez,'* recalled obsessively . . . is the first sign of linguistic and territorial alterity registered with all of its intensity."[38] The same guards are the first French citizens to confer with their gaze upon the ragged, weary emigrants the latters' newly minted status as the other. The veteran Antonio Miró states: "France received us alright, but we were already reduced to nothing. I understood this immediately upon meeting the gendarme's indifferent gaze."[39] This painful realization that as the refugees trudge across the border, they will collectively step into an unwelcome new identity, is recorded by Pedro Foix: "We were a huge crowd, with dirty shoes and with pants covered to the knees with mud, manure, and automobile oil, with clothes soaked from the persistent light rain, empty stomachs, dead-tired from the kilometers traveled and the lack of rest, blistered feet and nerves on edge. We focused all our attention on the uncertain passage into France that everybody hoped for; with fists and teeth clenched in rage, we thought: 'We are the defeated.'"[40] Curious onlookers, newspaper accounts in the conservative French press, the French police and border guards will receive the Republicans with shouts and murmurs of *"rojos/rojos."* Jaime Espinar, who reports this frequently heard chant ("'Reds, reds.' A curse upon us"), immediately contextualizes this designation of mistrust and suspicion within a wider political context, increasingly uneasy and unstable in February 1939: "European politics, as hesitant and contradictory as ever. And with us in the role of 'the commie emigrants' . . ."[41] The frankly hostile reception of the defeated Republican population by the officials of a conservative French government is the clearest manifestation of the latter's political position of nonintervention. With such a policy France distanced itself from the Republican cause during the two and a half years of civil war, frequently dismissing it as the work of rabble-rousing *rojos*. The emigrants who cross the border realize the extent of the demonization of Republican Spain through the responses of French onlookers, many of whom line the streets to see the public spectacle of crowds of refugees passing by. Rose Duroux, who as a baby in the arms of her mother formed part of the bedraggled group of emigrants passing through Prats-de-Molló, has recorded the maternal testimony: "The townspeople had their windows half-opened so that they could see us. The newspapers had said so many things about the refugees that people must have been scared of us. What an awful memory!"[42] In one of the first book-length historical accounts of Republican exile in France, David Pike reports questions raised in the conservative French press about the impact of these so-called red hordes, fearing they would turn *la France* into "the manure pile of the world"; similar journalistic laments predicted such contamination as leading to a widespread conversion of French soil into "the world's garbage dump."[43] In an article published on March 2, 1939, a French journalist describing the area around the most massive concentration camp for refugees "Argelès-sur-Mer," bitterly complains that thousands of displaced civil war survivors are a bad business for the local leisure economy: "Today the whole area stinks. . . . Our beach will be unusable this summer. . . . The red invasion has killed tourism . . . since international clientele are not willing to deal with the filthy riffraff that we have received in such record numbers."[44]

Benedict Anderson has stated that one cannot pinpoint the moment that a nation comes into being: "Nations have no identifiable births."[45] In the case of the exiled nation, however, their collective sense of deterritorialized identity may be located at the place of this crisis scene of the border crossing. A striking commonality shared by the group of informers that Soriano interviews in his book of testimony is the precision with which they remember the exact date, often the exact time, that they crossed the border; they report the moment like an hour of birth. Manolo Valiente describes the moment he passes through the two markers that separated Spain from France under the watchful eye of the French guards: "I stuck out my right foot, at 2:30 on the dot, and I told them, 'Good-bye! See you later!'"[46] In a 1967 conversation with Nancy Macdonald, Francisco Bardes Font recalled the time on the clock almost three decades earlier when he stepped into exile: "At one on the night [*sic*] of February 6th, 1939, I crossed the frontier at Cerbère."[47] In a 1939 letter written from the Bram camp, Miguel Giménez Igualada pinpoints the moment of crossing over: "At 3:00 in the afternoon on February 10, 1939 we entered France."[48] Federica Montseny, in an account originally published in France in 1950, represents the passage into exile as the end point of a painful labor; it is a devastatingly traumatic birth: "It was like being ripped apart, worse than the moment of birth. All of a sudden, in a matter of minutes, we cut the umbilical cord that had joined us to twenty generations: connecting us to the furniture that had been our grandparents', to the familiar landscape ... to the toys we had played with and that our children still played with. We lost perhaps forever the right to be the children of somewhere."[49] Interestingly, even the Republican general Vicente Rojo borrows the trope of a violent separation from the *madre patria* to initiate his early exile text published just eight months after fleeing Spain in March of 1939. In the opening paragraphs of his account of the final months of the Spanish Civil War, the well-known military commander remembers losing his mother many years earlier in a tiny town of the Valencia province. That moment of intense personal grief is the first image rendered in his tale of civil war and eventual exile: "That same image, still incomplete, is replayed today on a much larger scale, among the hundreds of thousands of members of Spain's family who, complete orphans, without a country and without a home, remain imprisoned in concentration camps — euphemism used nowadays in all countries to cover up the new jails of modern society — in refuges, and in squalid, poorly maintained housing."[50] Similarly, Montseny's overwhelming grief occasioned by the death of her own mother just days after crossing the French border at Perthus, is symbolically reconfigured in the author's narrative as an emblem of the exile's plight: the paradoxical condition of being irrevocably torn away from the Motherland ("Meanwhile, my mother was dying. Meanwhile, exiles were dying by the thousands; meanwhile, I had no father, no husband, no home, no future. And sharing my fate, thousands of women and children, thousands of men, thousands of families") as an instance of a new, however unwanted, beginning in life: "Out of that gut-wrenching process, another woman would have to be born: that woman who I had been, died with my mother and was buried with her. The other, the one being born, tragically and painfully, would carry forever in her soul an unquenchable thirst for the fountain now run dry."[51]

Carrying forever the signs of exilic identity, the Spanish exiles initially tell their story of displacement through the tropes of loss, orphanhood, dispossession, and death. It will be their task to reconfigure, to recreate the signs of a political and cultural identity in exile, in order to establish new symbolic ground capable of nurturing and sustaining the expression of a collective memory and a national history outside of Spain.[52] This book examines how Spanish Republicans in exile begin to construe a shared sense of nationhood through the unlikely discursive vehicle of the French concentration camp. Throughout the ensuing chapters, I explore the complex, constitutive function of the camps in exile literature as either a key commemorative place of remembrance; as grounds for moral authority and political legitimacy; as the site of creative resistance and cultural renewal; or as an arena for a polarized, embattled struggle for emigration to America.

2

Sacrifice and the Nation: The Death and Resurrection of Antonio Machado

> La guerra civil—e incivil—de España agonizaba en esta forma: con gentes semiprisioneras, acumuladas por aquí y allá, metidas en fortalezas, hacinadas durmiendo en el suelo sobre la arena. El éxodo rompió el corazón del máximo poeta don Antonio Machado. Apenas cruzó la frontera se terminó su vida. Todavía con restos de sus uniformes, soldados de la República llevaron su ataúd al cementerio de Collioure.
>
> [The civil—and uncivil—war of Spain gave its dying gasp like this: with people living like prisoners in groups here and there, stuck in fortresses, packed onto beaches where they were forced to sleep on the ground. The exodus broke the heart of Spain's greatest poet, Antonio Machado. No sooner did he cross the border than he died. Still wearing what was left of their uniforms, the soldiers of the Republic carried his coffin to the cemetery in Collioure.]
>
> —Pablo Neruda, *El* Winnipeg y *otros poemas*

THE COMPLEX PROCESS OF PIECING TOGETHER THE FRAGMENTED, UP-rooted exile identity, of transcending separation and dispersal, will be founded on the transformation of the real acts of death and destruction into new symbolic codes for the nation in crisis. The profound connections between collective memory, historical trauma, and the representations of the nation have increasingly been the object of recent critical attention among scholars in the fields of history, literature, and cultural studies. Homi Bhabha's inclusion of Ernest Renan's 1882 essay "What Is a Nation?" in his 1990 volume *Nation and Narration*, publicized Renan's early meditations on this subject, which has since been energetically interrogated, especially during the past decade. Renan highlights the role of sacrifice and its remembrance as crucial for the consolidation of the nation: "Suffering in common unifies more than joy does. Where national memories are concerned, griefs are of more value than triumphs, for they impose duties and require a common effort."[1] More recent theorists' work continues to develop the interrelationship of crisis, memory, and national identity formation introduced by Renan; this line of inquiry has been particularly fruitful in the area of Holocaust studies. Dominick LaCapra, building on Pierre Nora's work on the *"lieux de mémoire,"* makes the claim in his *History and Memory after Auschwitz* that "A memory site is generally also a site of trauma."[2] Daniel Sherman's suggestive book *The Construction of Memory in Interwar France* focuses on World War I as the site of trauma that the author examines in his study of French commemorative culture. Sherman refers to the constitutive role of these types of memory sites: "Commemoration seeks to reinforce the solidarity of a particular community. . . . It does so by forging a consensus version of an event or connected series of events that has either disrupted the stability of the community or threatened to do so."[3] Similarly, in his essay "Memory, Sacrifice and the Nation," Michael Rowlands emphasizes the function of cultural continuity that is derived from the discursive and material sites associated with warfare and cataclysmic historical events. These markers of the past are "part of a monumentalising discourse of the political and emotional construction of national identities through the remembrance of acts of human sacrifice and the redemption of those who survive. This is particularly so at times when the inchoate nature of the nation state either in its formation or the internal divisions that risk achievement of identity [*sic*]."[4] Certainly the condition of forced exile itself results from just such a moment of upheaval, as Angel Loureiro points out in his study of the Spanish exile María Teresa León: "Exile always bespeaks some form of national convulsion and thus necessarily imposes the reconstruction of the nation by means of figures that would presumably embody its essence."[5] It is my thesis that the formation of the exile identity of *la España Peregrina* that eventually settles in Mexico, takes root in the fertile imaginative terrain stimulated by the remembrance and representation of the place of the French border/camps inhabited by Spanish refugees. The textualization of camps like Argelès-sur-Mer, Collioure, St. Cyprien, Vernet, or Barcarès in the numerous versions authored by former inmates, including memoirs, testimonial narrative, poetry, plays, and novels, transforms the places of suffering, sacrifice, and trauma into powerful, enduring sites of memory, thereby creating a generative matrix for the cultural codes and values of a nascent nation in exile. In this study I have limited my analysis primarily to those books or accounts of life in the French camps that were published in Mexico within the first few years after the end of the civil war, as the events of World War II were dramatically unfolding. The reception and circulation of these early stories among the members of the growing exile community in Mexico were a significant source of the community's collective sense of identity, and functioned as a key master text in this group's shared narrated history.⁶

I open this discussion by initially situating my analysis in a specific geographical location, the border town of Collioure, which I read as a foundational site in the emerging exile narrative of *los vencidos'* heroic sacrifice and martyrdom. First, it is here on February 22, 1939, that the Spanish Republic's most beloved poet, Antonio Machado, died just weeks after crossing the Pyrenees with thousands of his compatriots. Secondly, Collioure is also the site of the most infamously inhumane concentration camp in France, which exclusively imprisoned combatants of the bloody civil war who had all been united in the military fight against fascism and Franco. In the earlier cited article on sacrifice and the nation, Rowlands has explained that in moments of danger for the nation, the collective consciousness is shaped around "diagnostic iconic images"; these are, Rowlands says, "precisely those acts of sacrifice, the creation of heroes and martyrs around which conviction of the just cause and longevity of a national identity is forged. Within the materiality of long term cultural continuity and repetition, erupts the memory of disruptive events after which nothing was the same."⁷ Antonio Machado and the Republican soldier-prisoners of Collioure are just such examples of Rowlands's martyred heroes. I introduce the concept of the camps as sites of memory by examining how the inscription of the border place of Collioure, richly imbued with sacrificial suffering, functions in the exile imaginary as a wellspring of strength and political conviction in a historical moment of significant instability and uncertainty.

Joaquin Xirau's "Por una senda clara": Making One's Way in Exile

The idea that Antonio Machado is the most significant symbol of exiled Spain is as old as the civil war diaspora itself. Cristóbal Ruiz's famous life-size portrait of Machado has overseen the cultural activities sponsored by the exiles' Ateneo Español in Mexico City since its founding more than fifty years ago in 1949. So did Machado's life, poetic legacy, and moral integrity preside over the exiled intellectuals' cultural endeavors in Mexico, as the critics James Valender and Gabriel Rojo Leyva have ably demonstrated in their exhaustive 1999 study of one of the most important Spanish exile journals in Mexico, *Las Españas*.⁸ Teresa Férriz has similarly traced the powerful presence of Machado in another exile journal published in Mexico, *Romance*, suggesting in her short but informative article how the poet is transformed into "the honorary exile and symbol of all displaced Spaniards."⁹ According to the writer Manuel Andújar, former inmate of the St. Cyprien camp and longtime resident of Mexico City, the legacy of Antonio Machado provided the displaced defenders of the Spanish Republic with an important bridge of continuity connecting the period of civil war and the period of exile: "Don Antonio Machado's poetry could be found nestled in the backpacks and in the hopes of commanders and soldiers alike—peasants, workers, good people, loyal to their oaths, without a cent to their names—who fought for the Republic. His volumes of fluid verse and wise and elegant prose (Oh, Juan de Mairena!) have been—throughout exile, relocation, and return—our most beloved books."[10] In 1945, on the occasion of the official presentation of a newly configurated Republican government-in-exile in Mexico City, the recently appointed prime minister José Giral concluded his lengthy remarks before the *Cortes* by citing the work of Antonio Machado: "I conclude my remarks on this date of November 7, a date that for the past nine years has been a symbol of faith and of invincible heroism for all Spaniards who keep Madrid in their hearts. Our thoughts are with Spain, with that Spain, as the great Antonio Machado said, which was 'sold out, river by river, mountain by mountain, sea by sea,' but there our hearts remain, because as the poet added, 'there we were born to life and to love.' On this day, the Government sends warmest greetings to its representatives."[11] Once again, the invocation of Machado's name and the memory of his civil war writings inaugurate a new phase of the Spanish national identity in exile. It is interesting to note that thirty years after these remarks, in the very first full-scale history of the Spanish exile of 1939 published in Spain—José Luis Abellán's 1976 six-volume *El exilio español de 1939*—José Giral's son Francisco described the plight of the hundreds of thousands of refugees that crossed the border into France specifically in terms of Machado's example, using words written by Machado. The younger Giral oddly inserts a paragraph-length lyrical tribute to Machado squarely within the carefully documented history of political events that he chronicles; he interpolates italicized fragments primarily from Machado's own civil war articles (including the exact line cited by his father José Giral in 1945, "All of Spain sold out, river by river, mountain by mountain, sea by sea") with his own commentary, which begins: "To cite just one example: Antonio Machado, who *knew how to rise to the occasion, no matter how difficult it was*, whose *heart was broken by one of the two Spains* that February in the south of France. That heart, that mind and that pen, *that were always on the side of the Spanish Republic*, that Republic that he had *helped to proclaim five years earlier with a few die-hard Republicans by raising the tricolored flag in the City Hall of Segovia*, that Republic *that maintained its legitimacy as long as the will of the people, freely expressed, did not denounce it.*"[12]

Machado's painful border crossing and death in February 1939 in Collioure continue to be recalled in histories of the Spanish exodus to Mexico as primordial scenes of the birth and genesis of the entire exile community itself. In 1999, as part of a commemoration of the Spanish exile of 1939, an ambitious series of twelve conferences was held throughout Spain between March and December of 1999, entitled Sixty Years Later: The Spanish Exile of 1939. The enumeration of the sites of the dozen meeting places effectively outlines a map of Spain: Madrid, Toledo, Valencia, Barcelona, Granada, Huesca, Oviedo, Santander, León, Logroño, Vizcaya, Santiago de Compostela. The closing ceremony of this massive anniversary of Spanish exile held on December 18, 1999, was, however, celebrated where it all began, just past the Pyrenees, on the other side of the French border, in the little French town of Collioure, the site of Machado's grave. Commenting in early 1999 on the proposed location for the conclusion of the yearlong commemorative symposia, the conference series organizer Manuel Aznar Soler referred to Collioure as "the mythical place of our collective memory where Antonio Machado is buried."[13]

Joaquín Xirau's moving personal remembrance of accompanying Machado into exile in France, "Por una senda clara" (Along a Clear Path), also concludes in Collioure. The essay was written one month after the poet's death there and partially published in Mexico in a February 1940 issue of *España Peregrina* on the occasion of the one-year anniversary. A subsequent publication of the article in 1983 was illustrated with a series of ink drawings of anonymous Republican soldiers, thus figuring through the juxtaposition of text and image the ties that bound together Machado and the legacy of the Republican struggle for democratic ideals that survived in exile. Decades after Xirau wrote the article, yet another reprint in a special 1999 issue of *La Gaceta del Fondo de Cultura Económica* published in Mexico introduced the series of articles commemorating the sixty-year anniversary of the end of the war and the beginning of exile. So insistently has Xirau's version of Machado's last days in Spain and first hours in exile been told in successive editions that it will be instructive to examine this document more closely; I read Xirau's text as a canonical account of how the figure of Machado has been inscribed in the exiles' cultural history as an exemplary, inspiring role model for the Republican community in exile.

The multiple, ever-changing venues of Xirau's tale — Machado's home in wartime Barcelona, the road to France, the border crossing, and the French border town of Cerbère — are presented as a series of communal spaces that the poet shares in solidarity with his fellow Republicans. Machado's last residence in Barcelona also houses on the first floor entire families who sought refuge there during the Ebro campaign. In one of the old mansion's largest rooms, Machado meets with a constant stream of visitors, including friends, soldiers from the front, students, foreign humanitarian aid workers; they are united together through the recitals of popular poetry, informal performances of folk songs and music, and discussions of the finest exponents of Spanish culture, names that Xirau wistfully lists as he remembers in exile this scene, "the great figures of Spanish genius—Ramón Llull y Cervantes, San Juan de la Cruz y Ausias March, Lope de Vega and Luis de León."[14] Frequently subjected to blackouts due to bombing raids, the activities within the circle of compatriots continue undeterred: "The light was restored and the poetry reborn" (59). Xirau's portrait of the poet's last days in Barcelona paints a picture of stoic dignity and spiritual fortitude in the face of certain defeat. Recognizing Machado's feeble physical state, Xirau contrasts his infirmity with a strength of spirit that never wavers. Machado is depicted here as the consummate patriot, the loyal son of the Republic who rejects all offers to emigrate until the bitter end, proving with the example of the courage of his convictions the legitimacy of what his people are fighting for: "He endured in that corner of Spain because of human dignity and especially—he said it himself over and over—because of patriotism. His deeply rooted patriotism, quiet but genuine, is what joined his fate to that of his beleaguered nation suffering at the hands of treacherous invaders. . . . He knew that a life consecrated to an ideal is the only life worth living" (59). Occasionally the author inserts Machado's own voice into his memoir, a technique that serves to highlight and unify thematic threads that run through the account. Xirau underscores Machado's indignant reactions to the destruction of his beloved Republic by, on the one hand, the constant bombings—"Scoundrels! Scoundrels!" (58)—and on the other, the European democracies' failure to assist Spain: "They are going to play a filthy trick on us" (58). Writing this account from Paris in March of 1939, as the French government imprisons thousands of Spanish refugees in concentration camps, Xirau effectively uses Machado's ominous words of foreboding to posthumously condemn the continued mistreatment of the exiled Republic at the hands of foreign nations.

Xirau's ensuing description of the exodus itself chronicles the now familiar trajectory of physical hardship, panic, and chaos: bombs explode in the night sky (60); the refugees stumble along in the blinding rain, numbed by exhaustion and hunger (63); they cross the border with nothing ("We didn't have passports. We didn't have money" (64). Machado suffers the identical fate of thousands of his fellow Republicans who make the same arduous journey, says Xirau, with characteristic dignity: "He didn't once complain" (64). In the conclusion of the essay that pays solemn homage to the exiled author of "Caminante, no hay camino / se hace camino al andar" [Traveler, there is no path / you make your path as you walk], Xirau juxtaposes a cluster of tropes that fittingly allude to paths, roads, and possible directions, all of which intersect in the space of memory that recreates the last time the author ever saw Machado. In a crowded café in the train station of the border town of Cerbère, jammed at a table among throngs of other refugees, says Xirau, Machado joins in a conversation about exiled Spain's future. One interlocutor refers to the heady possibility of starting fresh, blazing new trails; Xirau uses Machado's response to emphasize the message of collective perseverance and cultural continuity for the audience to whom he addresses his essay: "The important thing isn't to embark upon a path but rather to keep going, to stay the course" (64). Xirau goes on to recall his last glimpse of Machado from the window of a train as he leaves the poet behind in Collioure, "on the road to the town" (64), the road to his final resting place, a place of memory in the exile imaginary that begins to take shape even as Xirau completes his article. Finally, to close his memoir, the author borrows a line from Machado's famous 1915 elegy written in remembrance to his own beloved mentor, Don Francisco Giner de los Ríos, "Sólo sabemos que se nos fue por una senda clara" [All we know is that he departed along a clear path] (64). The ensuing verses of this well-known poem, "Vivid, la vida sigue, / los muertos mueren y las sombras pasan" [Live! Life goes on, / the dead die and the shadows pass], are not cited in this text, but echo in their absence in the memory of Xirau's reader.[15] Once again, Xirau uses Machado's voice, both spoken and remembered, in order to inspire the community of Republicans left behind in exile, urging them to continue the struggle, to move forward with hope, energy, and optimism.

An unlikely convergence of the spaces of Machado's border crossing and of the burgeoning concentration camps appears in the concluding paragraphs of Xirau's "memory text." Due to the absolute lack of available accommodations in Cerbère, the author explains that Machado and his family are forced to spend their very first night in France in a stationary train car designated for Spanish refugees. Early the next morning the weary group descends from the car because of the train's imminent departure: "At six in the morning the train was supposed to leave with refugees to deliver them to the concentration camps" (64). Earlier, Xirau had alluded to the threatening presence of the camps: "In Cerbère the police went through the streets and picked up undocumented Spaniards to take them to the concentration camps. It wasn't possible to leave the station" (64). Certainly, the story of Machado's exile and death is inseparable from the story of the Republicans' experience of the French concentration camps. Less documented in the history of Spanish exile than the privileged status of Machado as intellectual and spiritual mentor has been the reception of the news of Machado's death by fellow exiles within the barbed-wire confines of the camps in France, and the inscription of this seminal event into the earliest pages of exile.

Agusti Cabruja's *La Ciudad de Madera*: Mourning Spaces

La ciudad de madera (The City of Wood) by Agustí Cabruja Auguet (1911–83) is a representative text that suggests how Machado's death at Collioure nurtured the spirit of the surviving exiles in the camps and was appropriated by them as an emblem of humanity, solidarity, and continuity. Published in Mexico City in 1947, the fictionalized memoir consists of sixty-seven brief vignettes of the fourteen months that the author spent in the camps of Argelès-sur-Mer and Saint-Cyprien. The central trope of the book is the mutilated body: the protagonist is a war amputee, and the opening sentence as well as the first illustration of the work introduce the narrator, accompanied by an orphaned child, hobbling across the French border on one leg. A significant space in the text, beyond the camp, is a French hospital for badly injured *mutilados*, decimated pieces of human flesh, "truly wasted human specimens, pieces of shattered, ruined lives"; almost a year later, still in the camp, the only men who remain, we are told, are the old, the infirm, the disabled, "the throwaways."[16] A fiery image of a textual corpus in disintegration is also figured in one of the many flashback memories that the protagonist recalls while in the hospital. Just prior to crossing the border into exile, he writes to his mother, "Burn all my papers. And also the books in the library" (33). He grieves for the incineration of these beloved books and pages like one more death: "Many times I've cried over the death of those dreams of mine" (33). The body politic is also presented in terms of a radical dismemberment, a body diseased. After spending fourteen months in the camp, he refers to the group of invalid exiles that remain as ravaged flesh, "locked away on that isolated, dirty, contaminated beach like awful lepers whom people avoided and reviled, we waited, indifferent, cynical, apathetic" (133).

Toward the very middle of these pages is a central chapter called "Antonio Machado," fully twice as long as any other section, in which the narrator reports the poet's burial a few days earlier in "that cold and harsh cemetery in the little town of Collioure" (88). In contrast with the bleak burial ground, the author juxtaposes an unexpectedly warm and cozy scene in this overwhelmingly inhospitable camp, Saint-Cyprien. A motley, disparate crew of campers have gathered for a poetry recital and lecture on the life and work of Machado: "boys, soldiers, and workers, people of all ages and professions, gathered in the warm embrace of fellowship" (89). The sense of community and solidarity is engendered by the communal act of homage that is rendered in quasi-religious overtones: "It is the simplest, the most emotional and loving tribute—intimate and humble like the prayer of children or of Christ's apostles, in the woods or in the desert—that has ever been offered to a poet" (89). The ragged representatives of the Spanish Republic, earlier referred to by Cabruja as "a shattered, abandoned nation" (133), form here a rare image of wholeness, cohesiveness, and continuity in a text that otherwise is expressed through figures of fragmentation and loss. In Cabruja's version of the days after the burial in Collioure, the poet is represented first and foremost as the people's poet, and offered up to the campers who mourn his death as their first cultural legacy in exile to which the author forcefully lays claim. Cabruja refers to the young *falangista* Dionisio Ridruejo's earlier call published in Madrid to "rescue" Machado from the Republicans in exile. Cabruja passionately repudiates the legitimacy of any claim on Machado's legacy that would wrest him away from the *pueblo* that he accompanied into exile: "From the moment the exodus began, he refused to abandon us" (89). The insistent use of the possessive form is striking throughout this section: "Antonio Machado . . . is ours. . . . His word, his spirit, his whole existence, belong wholly to our cause" (89). A second passage, wedged between two fragments of Machado's poetry, grammatically mirrors the *pueblo* with its *poeta*, finally fusing the two together: "The people have always loved their poets. Their verses are their own, their songs and their tears are theirs too; the people understand them and feel them, they are a slice of their very life" (90). The long-suffering narrator and his nation, *los vencidos*, will insist on this: Machado is ours.

Celso Amieva's "Corona de Espinas": Poetic Communion

Celso Amieva, pen name for the Asturian writer José María Alvarez Posada, spent more than three and a half years interned in the camps of Argelès, Barcarès, and Saint-Cyprien before eventually emigrating to Mexico in the 1950s. In the opening pages of his memoir *Asturianos en el destierro (Francia)* (Asturians in Exile (France)), he recalls the day he learned of Machado's death while an inmate at the Argelès camp: "*L'Indépendant*, a newspaper in Perpignan that took sadistic pleasure in our suffering, published a line that it believed to be contemptuous but seemed to me to be immortal: 'In Collioure the Spanish poet and soldier *(miliciano)* Antonio Machado has died.' And I ran away to seek solace alone, throwing myself face down in the sand."[17] Amieva channels his grief into a poem of homage to Machado, "Corona de espinas" (Crown of Thorns), that serves as the inaugural text in his book of concentration camp verse published in Mexico in 1960, *La almohada de arena* (Pillow of Sand). The history of the camps and the memory of Machado are skillfully intertwined throughout the poem, mimicking the creative act of weaving together resistant strands that is undertaken by the central figure of the poem, "El Loco": "Está entretejiendo el loco / sentado en el arenal / una corona de alambre / de púas, frente a la mar" [Seated in the sand / facing out to sea / The crazy man is weaving / a barbed-wire crown of thorns].[18] Both Amieva and his protagonist painstakingly transform the harsh material reality of the camp into an emotional tribute to a fallen martyr: "Sangre brota de sus dedos / y la viene a restañar / la ruda caricia helada / del huracán" [Blood spurts from his fingertips / the flow of blood is frozen / kissed by the coarse caress / of the winter wind's icy touch]. Amieva's use of El Loco allows him to connect the physical place of the camp (thrashed by freezing wind; surrounded by barbed wire and indifferent French guards) with poetic spaces from Machado's own work, which function indirectly as intertext in "Corona de espinas." The "crazy man" was in fact an all-too-familiar face among the thousands of Spanish internees, so much so that the problem of trauma-related insanity in the camps was declared by medical personnel to be one of the most urgent health concerns.[19] Additionally, this figure serves as a link with Machado's verses, frequently populated by such vulnerable individuals—among other common, simple folk—who are treated with equal sympathy. In the best-known poem of this type, "Un loco" (A Crazy Man), published in 1913 and included in revised editions of *Campos de Castilla*, the title character wanders through a stark landscape eerily analogous to the barren spaces of Amieva's camp, indistinguishable in appearance from his counterpart in the camps: "El loco vocifera / a solas con su sombra y su quimera / . . . / flaco, sucio, maltrecho y mal rapado" [The crazy man screams / alone with his shadow and his chimera / . . . / skinny, dirty, ill-shaven, and ill-treated].[20] Machado's character occupies a fringe position as he flees a corrupt society; Amieva's Loco is likewise a marginalized member of an already doubly marginalized community (on foreign soil at one remove from Spain, the Spanish refugees are further alienated within kilometers of barbed wire).[21] As the most disenfranchised of Machado's *pueblo*, it is he among the thousands of pent-up Spaniards who is their mouthpiece: "—Tejiendo estoy la corona / de un muerto que es inmortal" [I'm weaving the crown / of a dead man who is immortal]. Addressed simply as "Español," he speaks in response to

the narrator's question, "—Español, ¿qué estás haciendo? / ¡Te vas a helar! . . .—" [Spaniard, what are you doing? / You're going to freeze! . . .]. Both the form of address as well as the use of the verb *helar* also allow the reader to detect echoes of Machado's most famous verses from his "Proverbios y cantares" directed to yet another innocent victim of conflict: "Españolito que vienes / al mundo, te guarde Dios. / Una de las dos Españas / ha de helarte el corazón" [Little Spaniard born / into the world, may God protect you. / One of the two Spains / is going to chill your heart].[22]

The central locus in the poem is of course the bleak physical terrain of the windswept beach itself, the no-man's-land of no return, "en la linde de la playa / de Irás y no Volverás" [at the outer limits of the beach / of You-can-enter but You-can-never-leave]. Fellow internees who inhabited Argelès-sur-Mer when Amieva was there have described the desolate landscape: "Two huge tracts of deserted, barren land, sandy, inaccessible, wet, and hard."[23] Another exiled writer to Mexico, Agustí Bartra, opens his 1943 novelized memoir *Xabola* (Hut) (translated from the original Catalan, revised, and republished in 1958 as *Cristo de 200.000 brazos*) with a series of lyrical meditations on the place of Argelès: "City of defeat. Sand, wind, rain. Sand under your fingernails, sand in your hair, sand in your eyes. Ocean"; it is an empty place, devoid of history, laments Bartra: "City of defeat. Its history can't even find a stone on which to inscribe itself."[24] In such an unstoried environment of loss, the steady transformative labor in the busy hands of Amieva's Loco gains significance. Reference to his creative handiwork initiates the poem; the repetition of his weaving activity ("está entretejiendo"; "tejiendo"; "teje que teje") fills the verses, as do a series of gerunds that highlight the energetic process of creation. By utilizing the barbs from the wire fences, instruments of the Spaniards' physical confinement and dehumanization, Amieva's humble protagonist transgresses the limitations imposed from without; this subversive act is echoed in the narrator's caustic reference to the despised French guards at the outer boundaries of the camp, "La Guardia Móvil se ríe, / crustáceos faltos de sal" [The members of the Mobile Guard laugh, / crustaceans without wit (salt)]. Ultimately the dangerously sharp barbs that the fingers of the resourceful "Español" piece together serve as a tool used to *grabarse su historia*. The memorial to Antonio Machado, an improvised *corona* befitting a Christlike poet laureate of a vanquished nation, leaves its bloody traces in the shifting sands: "Teje que teje está el loco / su trágico canevá / La corona goteante / ya ensangrienta el arenal. / Un minuto de silencio / gravita con fuerza tal, / que las cabezas se inclinan / al pasar" [The crazy man is weaving, weaving / his tragic canvas / The dripping crown / now bloodies the sandy ground. / A moment of silence / hangs so heavily, / that heads are bowed / as they pass by].

Memorializing Machado

The sense that the Spanish concentration camp inmates' story of exile will be inscribed under the long shadow of Antonio Machado's memory, or stimulated by it, is reinforced in countless memoirs and testimonies. Editor Antonio Soriano, a civil war veteran and camp survivor, prefaced his interviews with eleven ex-Republican combatants, many former camp internees among them, with two epigraphs from Machado's poetry.[25] Eulalio Ferrer, a well-known public relations executive and philanthropist featured in a 1998 profile of successful Spanish emigrants to Mexico, kept a diary of his internment in Argelès-sur-Mer, Barcarès, and Saint-Cyprien, which he published in 1987 as *Entre alambradas*. In revised as well as newly published excerpts of the diary reissued in 1999, Ferrer penned a new title for the very first entry, "Entre Antonio Machado y Don Quijote."[26] He acknowledges in this way the two cultural giants that helped sustain his spirit during the period of his internment after literally accompanying him into exile. Ferrer slept with a treasured copy of Cervantes's novel under his head, a 1902 edition that he bartered for as he crossed the border at Port-Vendres in exchange for a pack of cigarettes. The young soldier recalls that just before acquiring his copy of *Don Quijote* upon entering France, that he had occasion to pay a small tribute and bid farewell to Antonio Machado himself. Passing through Cerbère, he meets up with Machado and his ailing mother seated on a bench, waiting to be taken to Collioure. In an impulsive act, says Ferrer, he offers his heavy military overcoat to the frail poet, "as if to pay some kind of tribute to this great poet whom I admire so much; his voice is hushed, an almost inaudible whisper."[27] Later, in the camps, Ferrer and his compatriots will observe improvised acts of commemoration honoring all of the Republic's dead, both famous and anonymous. On July 19, the third anniversary of the beginning of the civil war, the campers of Barcarès construct symbolic sculptures honoring the Republic fashioned out of tiny pebbles, sand, and seashells. Ferrer describes the most impressive among them as "a kind of tomb, with an image made of clay of a Spanish soldier and a wreath of flowers with this inscription: *in memory of the fallen*."[28] The wind, the rain, and the ocean tides will dissolve these commemorative memorials, but the sites of these memories remain engraved in the collective consciousness of the Spanish exiles.[29]

Silvia Mistral devotes a separate diary entry entitled "The Death of the Poet," dated March 3, 1939, in order to pay homage to Machado, juxtaposing his fate to that of thousands of Spaniards suffering in refugee camps, a connection that will be constantly emphasized in the exile accounts recalling the poet's death. Living with other Spanish women in the small town of Les Mages, Mistral is in close contact with her *compañero* who is an inmate in Argelès-sur-Mer; she, like other memoirists and even some historians, reports Machado's death as in fact having occurred after his internment in a concentration camp: "Human indifference killed this poet, who despite the burden of his sixty-four years, was cast out into exile and subjected to physical and moral hardships; he was forced to suffer the humiliation of the barbed-wire refugee camp."[30] Mistral is not the only early chronicler of exile who records this erroneous fact. Three thousand miles away, Juan Ramón Jiménez establishes a fund to help evacuate Spanish intellectuals imprisoned in the camps, and in a notice published in *La Prensa* made an appeal for monetary donations: "A large group of our contemporaries, Spanish writers, artists, and scientists, are experiencing hunger, cold, and the most absolute destitution in the concentration camps that France has set up along its southern border for the Spaniards who fled Cataluña. Antonio Machado, our great poet, supreme symbol of all of them, has died there; his death casts an enormous shadow over us all."[31] Several years later, in a 1945 interview in Paris, the French writer and ardent defender of the Spanish Republic, Albert Camus (himself the son of a Spanish mother), denounced his government's role in the great poet Machado's death: "Franco killed García Lorca, but it was France that allowed Machado to die upon his release from a concentration camp"; in 1946, Camus repeats his accusation that the nation of France was a poor protector of one of Europe's greatest poets: "We were responsible for Machado—and one day Europe will be able to take the measure of this great man—, as we were for all of his people, targeted with insults by a large segment of our press. Meanwhile, our Republican government cordoned them off, surrounding them with hateful gendarmes."[32] Camus's belief that Machado was interned in a camp ("We just locked away the poet Antonio Machado in a concentration camp from which he left on the eve of his death") was circulated among the camp inmates, many of whom believed the oft-repeated reports that the poet had also died there.[33] In a fourteen-page September 1939 issue of the newsletter prepared by interned members of the Profesionales de la Enseñanza (teaching professionals) of the Barcarès camp, the article "Machado" appears. Seven months after the fact, the unsigned notice announces the poet's death: "The poet Antonio Machado—no adjectives are necessary—has died on the sands of one of dear France's beaches, in a camp for Spanish refugees. As he had foreseen in his 'Self-portrait,' his last journey found him traveling light, almost naked, like the children of the sea."[34] Machado, states the author, has left a legion of poetic voices in his wake ("the Albertis, the Garfias, the Altolaguirres, the Hernández and so many other young poets") that will continue to sing of his beloved Spanish *pueblo* in exile, as a much-needed antidote to the Nationalists' pernicious rhetoric: "With their best verses, they have all sung of the heroic deeds of the Spanish people. In the name of black Spain sings a chorus of nightingales without a voice of their own—Quevedo would call them *poetas hebenes* [hybrid poets]—presided over by Marquina and Pemán. In the face of brave, democratic, republican hispanism, with its genuine poetry, is the new vulgar style of the non-essential anti-Spain." Machado's camp eulogist concludes like Joaquín Xirau by invoking the poet's own life-affirming verses written years before for Giner de los Ríos: "But, let us not posthumously honor maestro Machado, as we wait for the moment to return his remains to his country, with a mourner's plaintive tribute. Let us honor him as he wanted to honor Giner; may the bells be silent and let the anvils ring."[35]

Even excepting those accounts that literally place Machado within the barbed-wire confines, the shared memory of the exodus out of Spain and of exiles' earliest victims will forever unite Machado and the camp internees. Cesáreo de la Cruz y Gómez, who as an adolescent was interned in several camps with his mother and sister, recalls the letters written from his father, who once spent an extended period in solitary confinement in one of the French labor camps. The son reports his father's explanation of how he kept his sanity and his spirits up during the difficult separation from everyone and everything dear to him: "He thought about so many Spaniards who died in the land of *fraternité*, some from hunger, others from the cold or from both. And he often remembered Antonio Machado, our poet, who [like the father himself] had been a professor in Soria and Segovia and who died in Collioure, a small French town on the coast."[36] For Juan Rejano, an editor of the exile journal *Romance* and prolific journalist during his years in Mexico City, hearing as an inmate in Argelès-sur-Mer of the death of Machado is forever inscribed as the moment Spain-as-Memory was born. Concomitantly, he says, an exile history came into being that day as it registered its first foundational event: the death in Collioure. Writing for a homage edition on the twentieth anniversary of the poet's death, Rejano recalls the day in February in Argelès-sur-Mer when images of Machado's verses—and the painfully fresh memories of the places of Spain—came to life in exile:

> I was dragging my bones from one place to another in the anxiety-ridden sands of the Argelès-sur-Mer concentration camp, when one morning as a

north wind shook the huts and barracks, I learned of Machado's death. I don't know if I read it in a newspaper or if someone told me. I don't know if I heard on the 22nd, or the next day. What I do remember is that the loss of don Antonio struck a dull blow to my heart; it resounded like the first terrible blow that exiled Spain would receive. Overwhelmed by despair, it was as if his death gave new life to the beloved ghosts still so nearby, because before my mind's eye paraded the images of the frozen fields of Castilla, Andalusian olive groves, provincial little squares with the bubbling sound of fountains and children's laughter, the silent orchards of lemon trees, of blackbirds, the Guadalquivir and the legendary language of the Duero . . . All that world of the senses that we had just lost, recreated by the poet with magical simplicity.[37]

One year after the events recalled by Rejano, on the very first anniversary of Machado's death, a group of intellectuals in Mexico City (including Spanish exiles José Bergamín, Joaquín Xirau, José Puche as well as Mexican writers Xavier Villaurrutia, Carlos Pellicer, and Alfonso Reyes) presented a program in honor of the fallen poet. Excerpts of the speakers' remarks were published in the March 1940 issue of the journal *España Peregrina*; in an increasingly common pattern in exilic homages to Machado, these commemorative texts were directly followed by a call to remember those other anonymous compatriots in concentration camps who shared the fate of the Spanish Republic's greatest poet, to suffer in exile:

In memory of Antonio Machado, victim of exile, may we not forget our many comrades and friends who have been suffering in unspeakable ways for more than a year in the concentration camps of France or who are scattered through its towns and cities, if they are not enlisted in the arduous work companies. They would like nothing more than to join us in our honorable activities. But let us not be satisfied with an emotional tribute. May all of us, especially those of us already settled here, do everything in our power and more to help any one of these men who fought so unselfishly and bravely in our ranks; let's help them make the trip over and get settled here. This is our moral obligation that we must fulfill. May our American friends do their part to help us in this just, beneficial, and truly humanitarian cause.[38]

Collioure, The Camps, and Memories of Martyrdom

The tomb of Machado in Collioure, paradoxically a vessel of vitality and affirmation in the exilic consciousness, is not the only space at the French frontier that incubates a nascent collective memory that in turn informs a sense of national identity. The legendary maximum security prison for refugees located in a crumbling castle in Collioure is the source of origin for some of the most notorious horror stories of all of French concentration camp history. The prisoners, all Republican combatants of the war including veterans from the International Brigades as well, are transferred into this *campo de castigo* [punishment camp] from other camps, having been deemed by French authorities to be particularly dangerous or criminal; each is labeled an "international undesirable."[39] Generally such designations are politically based and often accorded to military officers and selected rank-and-file soldiers affiliated with the Communist Party. Survivors' testimonies about life in Collioure read like tales of a house of horrors; certainly Collioure's reputation as the most inhumane place where a refugee could end up was well known among the communities of Spaniards residing both in and around the other camps. In her diary-memoir *Éxodo* published just months after arriving in Mexico in July 1939, Silvia Mistral tells of her chance encounter in May 1939 in the French town of Les Mages with a half-dead escapee from "the infernal camp" of Collioure: "He speaks of this place of punishment as something impossible for human reason to comprehend. Isolation, solitary confinement, insults, beatings, hunger strikes—in protest against such inhumane treatment—and every kind of hardship. A little Guayana nestled in the Eastern Pyrenees."[40]

Gómez Burón's detailed account of the last weeks of Machado's life in Collioure reveals an intriguing conflation of the superimposed spaces of suffering between the iconic figure of the dying poet and the brutalized Spanish prisoners, both of whom are figured as national martyrs in the early history of exile disseminated in Mexico.[41] According to Gómez Burón's (possibly apocryphal?) version of events, Machado not only could see from his hotel room balcony the medieval castle of San Telmo, where the Spanish prisoners were kept; he actually could hear shouts and sounds emanating from the prison. Gómez Burón reports statements made by the Frenchman Jacques Baills and the hotel owner Madame Pauline Quintana (who both attended to Machado in his final days in Collioure), indicating that the week before the poet's death he asked them about the loud noises that were audible from the fortress. Visibly shaken when he was told that they were Republican prisoners being punished at the hands of French officials, he asked, "When will this be over?"[42] Agustín Vilella was taken as a prisoner from Saint-Cyprien to Collioure for protesting the harsh treatment in the camps; he recalls his arrival at the site that he later realizes was shared by Machado: "They gave me a beating. Handcuffed, I was put in a van that took me to the fort at Collioure. Just meters away from that hell, our poet Antonio Machado was drawing his last breath."[43] Fittingly, the pallbearers who carry the coffin bearing Machado's body to the cemetery in Collioure arrive from the Collioure castle. Celso Amieva refers to the event in his "Corona de espinas": "Esta madrugada misma / lo llevaban a enterrar / dos veteranos de Líster" [That very dawn / two of Líster's veterans / carried him to his grave].[44] Monique Alonso explains in her detailed account of the poet's burial on February 23: "The most moving part of the burial was, without a doubt, the presence of those soldiers from the Second Cavalry Brigade of the Spanish army. They were prisoners from the castle of Collioure who came out to pay their respects to the poet."[45] The poet is finally buried in the company of a large contingent of Spanish refugees, according to eyewitness Jacques Baills: "The funeral was worthy of Machado. It was a simple affair and with the greatest simplicity everyone came. Well, I refer especially to the Spaniards, fellow exiles and lots of them, who were in Collioure. First they had come to pay their respects and later for the removal of the body. The hotel was absolutely overrun with Spaniards...."[46] Antonio Machado, who helped raise the Republican flag at the town hall of Segovia on the day of the Republic's proclamation, was laid to rest draped in the same banner, accompanied by the men whom he had followed into exile fighting for it. Twenty years later the remains of the poet were transferred to their final resting place in Collioure, a different tomb constructed with donations made to the Asociación de Amigos de Machado. Monique Alonso, who helped found in 1977 the Collioure-based Fundación del Premio Internacional de Literatura Antonio Machado, concludes her exhaustive anthology *Antonio Machado, poeta en el exilio* with a final passage joining together the shared destiny of Machado and his fellow Spanish refugees who grieved, suffered, and died in neighboring concentration camps: "Close by the beaches of Argelès and St. Cyprien that had been transformed into concentration camps when the poet arrived in Collioure, Antonio Machado sleeps his last sleep. Don Antonio is yet another exile who rests near the ocean in the south of France. He is a symbol for all; a symbol of so many anonymous Spaniards who rest in French soil after having to abandon their country: *I'm sure that foreign lands / would mean death for me...*"[47]

Exactly one year after Machado's death in Collioure, a book of harrowing testimony called *Los de Collioure* appeared in Mexico City with a fervent prologue written by Margarita Nelken. Comprised of the detailed accounts by four former inmates about the utterly dehumanized existence they were forced to endure in the infamous prison, the book constitutes an impassioned plea to the conscience of the exile community in Mexico. The message of unity and solidarity—the leitmotiv of the Republican groups in exile—is here formulated as a powerful act of memory: not to forget those exiles left behind who are still languishing in the camps. The book closes with the words of the survivor-witness

Agapito Perujo Echevarría, who remembers "the true antifascist fighters" who still wait for freedom: "Ever since arriving in Mexico, as I think about so many comrades who did not have the good luck of gaining freedom, I feel it is my duty to work tirelessly for the rescue of fellow comrades who suffer in France."[48] The place of the camps is in fact constantly invoked in the earliest texts of exile, particularly by the small minority who had the good fortune to be evacuated from them. Almost every single memoir is written in the name and dedicated to the memory of those left behind in the camps. In his *Caravana nazarena (Exodo y odisea de España, 1936–1940 y . . .)*, "a fictionalized history" published in Mexico in 1945, Angel Samblancat solemnly enumerates the places of the camps like a commemorative list of war dead: "The camps of death of Argelès-sur-Mer [Argelès-by-the-sea] or rather by-the-shit [merde] . . . , Barcarès, Septfonds, Saint-Cyprien, Bram, Recebedou, Vernet, Colliure [*sic*]: Spain will never forget you! . . . Each refugee earned there his or her halo of blessed saintliness, the martyr's palm. For the immense majority of the prisoners behind the barbed-wire fence, those times were their harshest trial by fire."[49] Fellow Spaniards, former internees, remember those that still remain with grief and guilt. Solano Palacio writes in 1939 as he is bound at last for America on board ship: "Everyone feels something akin to the bitterness of defeat: the memory of the companions that remain behind in the concentration camps and in the homeland now lost to us."[50] The plight of the thousands of Spaniards who continue to live behind barbed wire — Javier Rubio estimates that 140,000 exiles still are imprisoned in French camps in December 1939 — must not be forgotten by the rest of the world.[51] Manuel García Gerpe explains in the foreword to his 1941 *Alambradas* that he is motivated to bear witness on behalf of the enormous contingency of exiled Spaniards that two years after the war remain in the camps: "I am moved and motivated solely by the suffering of my compatriots: their suffering is my own. More than 150,000 Spanish refugees, who have spent two long years of confinement behind barbed-wire, remain today prisoners of this pain. They endure all kinds of illnesses, they fight with death, they are just as deprived of hope, as alienated and forgotten by the world, as they ever were in the first days of our martyrdom. At that time the immense suffering of an enslaved nation still hadn't reached the four corners of the earth. They are the cream of the crop of Spain . . . and of the world."[52] The idea that the long-suffering Spaniards who continue as internees represent the best of Spain, that they are emblematic of the true *pueblo* in whose name the Republic was founded and defended to the death, is a key concept in the early exilic literature. Writing the conclusion of his memoir *Argelès-Sur-Mer* as a freed man in Santo Domingo in 1939, Jaime Espinar states: "More than four hundred thousand Spaniards paid the price of unnecessary suffering and death on the beaches of France. What did we half a million Spaniards stand for? We stood for and still stand for something beyond the dangers and vicissitudes of civil war, beyond the economic causes of our war. We represented, along with a small minority still in Spain, the reserves of a nation, its creative element, its remains.... The masses of Spanish emigrants represented something else: the life force that never stops flowing, just like the river's currents. The Spain that proves itself in its people and makes history."[53] In the earlier cited article by Michael Rowlands, the author refers to the memorializing discourse that characterizes commemorative monuments erected in honor of war dead as a form of speech that emphasizes "the idea that the deaths were not wasted but were constitutive of a collective sense of nation."[54] Such is the language of memory expressed in the concentration camp memoirs themselves as well as in the words that extend the length of a large stone monument completed in 1979 in the original Septfonds camp cemetery; the memorial's designer, Angel Hernández, was himself a concentration camp survivor of Mauthausen.[55] Each word in large block capital letters occupies its own separate line of the message: "NO / SOIS / LA / MUERTE / SOIS / LAS / NUEVAS / JUVENTUDES" [YOU / ARE / NOT / DEATH / YOU / ARE / THE / NEW / GENERATION].[56] Survivors of Septfonds like García Gerpe not only identified himself with his former companions still living in the camps as the most "genuine" core of the *pueblo* ("Here are the real Republicans, we who have fought in anonymity. But, for this very reason . . . we will have to suffer in anonymity, and die in anonymity as well"); they speak as well of their dead as the fertilizing agent for the resurrection of the collective spirit that will carry on the struggle against tyranny. García Gerpe pays tribute to those who have died in his camp of Septfonds: "Praise to the hundreds of unknown heroes who died outside of their country, for the freedom of Spain! They fought for freedom; for freedom they died. . . . They have opened the gates for the resurgence of Spain, true Spain, the Spain of free men."[57] The memoirist insists that the fighting spirit of those who will return triumphantly to reconquer Spain "on tomorrow's morn" will in fact be the reincarnation of the camps' fallen, "the resuscitated dead from the cemetery of the Septfonds camp."[58] Deprived of the privilege of consecrating the place of their war dead on the actual battlegrounds or cemeteries of Spanish territory, the exiles claim as theirs the alien terrain of their captivity in France. The camps, then, are inscribed in the history of Spanish exile as the first terrain of collective memory, the commemorative grounds for national regeneration.

3
A Commemorative Memory Album of Exile: *Campos de concentración, 1939–194 . . .* (1944)

> Lo que jamás podrán robaros será el recuerdo de lo que fuisteis y la voluntad que os anima de volver a ser hombres.
>
> [What they can never take from you is the memory you have of who you once were and the will that inspires you to live again as men.]
> —Molins i Fábrega, *Campos de concentración*

THE EARLIEST TEXTUAL AND PICTORIAL EXPONENT OF A COMMEMOrative "memory album" of the concentration camp experience is Narcís Molins i Fábrega's and Josep Bartolí's *Campos de concentración, 1939–194 . . .*, published in Mexico City in 1944. A trilingual volume (in French, English, and Spanish) copiously illustrated with more than sixty-five drawings by Bartolí, the book is an intriguing document from the period of World War II when the Spaniards in Mexico campaign tirelessly to spread the word to an international audience about the justness and moral legitimacy of their political cause in exile. The preface is replete with many of the same themes disseminated by other Republican writers and sympathizers writing in the early 1940s: Spain was but the first battleground in the fight against fascism ("No one remembered then that the world's first front line of defense of freedom against fascism was formed in Irún, in Madrid, in the trenches of Aragon, on the plains of Extremadura and Andalusia"); the urgent alarm raised by Republicans about the threat of fascism fell on deaf ears: "Upon rising up to defend what they had paid so dearly for, they sounded an alarm to all that few wanted to heed."[1] Furthermore, the phenomenon of the concentration camps has revealed the two faces of France: a corrupt, collaborationist government ("Some politicians sacrificed those wretched souls in the name of internal political expediency, without realizing . . . that this paved the way for others who would later hand their country over to a common enemy" [17]), in contrast with the French people, the "true France" (16) that passively tolerated immoral official policies too long for their own good ("But, unfortunately, there were fewer of them among the powerful or else they were too weak as a group" [17]). The author's preface is inscribed between Bartolí's three initial drawings that call attention to the international posturing that helped contribute to the tragic circumstances of the French concentration camps specifically, and the disastrous spread of fascism generally. The first illustration depicts six ridiculous-looking politicians, elegantly dressed in top hats and tails, five of whom are balanced precariously like clownish acrobats on top of the cigar-chomping central figure who wears a French medallion of honor; a caricature of Lord Neville Chamberlain dangles his infamous umbrella on the foot of his hiked-up leg. The buffoonish circus act daintily holds up an ironically emblazoned banner, COMMITTEE OF NON-INTERVENTION, which is encircled by a menacing serpent and sustains two white peace doves who collide headlong into one another. The second illustration, which is placed on the facing page at the end of the preface translated into French, portrays a lone Spanish militiaman in full military gear; the five-pointed star emblazoned on his helmet and belt buckle identify him as a member of the Ejército Popular de la República.[2] An armored tank and a dangerously low-flying airplane are behind him; barbed-wire fencing and the peaks of the Pyrenees are placed in the foreground. Bartolí's handwritten dedication reads: "To the militias, to all the soldiers of the Popular Army and the International Brigades, to the refugees of the entire world, to those who are still rotting in concentration camps, in forced labor camps, in prisons and . . ." (31). The final drawing that marks the conclusion of the prefatory remarks features the backside of a faceless politician, who has a hole in his head, caught with his pants down. He is held up to a public podium by two outstretched hands (with the Chamberlainesque umbrella hanging from the sleeve), and attached by the cranial hole to the cord of a prerecorded message emitted by a phonograph. The audience he addresses from this world stage is, literally, all ears. This time the Bartolí autograph writ large signs the following statement: "To the politicians of our country and abroad responsible for our defeat in Spain and for the tragedy of exile" (33). The rest of the 165 pages eulogize the "tragedy of exile" through the authors' visual and lyrical history of the concentration camp experience.

My interest in this work is twofold. On the one hand, I argue that the elegiac function is the fundamental organizing principle that informs the thirty one vignettes presented in the book. This volume, perhaps more than any of the other publications from these early post–civil war years in Mexico, seeks to consecrate the place of the concentration camps in France as hallowed ground, sacred soil because it is the final resting place for so many exiled Republicans and the site of so much suffering. However, before reading *Campos de concentración* as a memorial to the war dead, I first propose to examine the heavily illustrated book as a kind of collective scrapbook or "memory album"; it essentially takes a snapshot of the day-to-day existence in the camps as well as records what I call the prevailing "camp mythology," stories that were widely circulated among the refugees in many different camps and later preserved in documentation as part of the collective memory. At no point in the text of *Campos* is an individual camp mentioned by name; the experiences that are committed to memory are painted with a broad, quasi-allegorical brush in order to express a common, general moment of exilic history. I have selected key "memories" represented in the book that are also chronicled repeatedly in other published accounts; I use the authors' references in *Campos de concentración* as a point of departure to discuss the mutual language of memory of life in the camps that is shared by countless other memoirists.

THE VOLUME OF VOICES: SHARED MEMORIES, COMMON STORIES

> La arena como suelo, el cielo como techo y el mar como puerta, ése es el refugio provisional que se les ofrece.
>
> [The sand was our floor, the sky our roof and the doorway out was the sea, that's the temporary shelter that they gave us.]
> —Juan Carrasco, Argelès-sur-Mer

First and foremost among all of the textual and pictorial configurations of the concentration camps are the pervasive initial references to the physical environment, a state of primitiveness exacerbated by the prevailing climatological conditions of these seaside locations at the foot of the Pyrenees. In one of the first entries of the 1944 book, Molins i Fábrega writes, "Wind, rain, and cold. Cold, rain, and wind. Piercing darts that the adverse heavens hurl down upon the frozen prisoners, starving and half-naked" (51); Bartolí's accompanying illustrations insistently portray the driving rain that drenches the shabbily dressed inhabitants in and around the flimsy *barracas* (51). The early days of the camps in February 1939 to which these opening pages of *Campos* refer are similarly documented in fellow inmates' versions of events. In his 1941 memoir *Ombres entre tenebres (L'exode de Catalunya)* (Men among the Shadows (The Exodus from Catalonia)), Manuel Valldeperes documents his memories of the unbearably frigid temperatures of Argelès-sur-Mer: "The cold is terrible on that beach, exposed as it is to the wind and inclement weather. . . . The cold is so intense on those solitary plains that the majority [of internees] use their suitcases as firewood to keep the fire going through the night."[3] Silvia Mistral reproduces a fragment of a letter she receives from her companion in the same camp, commenting on the unbelievably strong, gale-force winds that punish the campers: "The wind hammers on, without let up, and we've gotten so used to it that when we go inside a hut, we lose our balance."[4] The sense that even Mother Nature is in cahoots with the despised French officials in order to torture the refugees is a constant refrain in survivor accounts. The prologuist to Miguel Giménez Igualada's 1946 memory of the camps, *Más allá del dolor*, Adolfo Ballano Bueno remembers Argelès-sur-Mer: "The geography itself was an accomplice in human suffering: mountains, clouds, and sand fenced in the Spanish emigrants, and there hope did not always triumph"; Ballano Bueno goes on to elaborate detailed commentary about the natural forces that were witnesses and, more often than not, complicit partners to crimes committed against the internees: the sea, the wind, the rain.[5] He describes a catastrophic flood that occurred in the camp in October 1939 in biblical terms of a cataclysmic event from the Old Testament. Dr. José Pujol, who spent more than three years in various concentration camps, recalls in similar language another deadly storm in the same camp in January 1941 when "even the elements turned against us": "The wind, the rain, and the sea joined forces. The howling waves advanced on the camp, torrential rains beat against the barracks and gale-force wind gusts tore off the roofs, blowing them far away. The sand, stirred up by the storm, beat against the unprotected barracks, burying people. Terrified, the guards—gendarmes, Senegalese soldiers, officers, and camp personnel—fled the camp. For three days the wretched refugees fought against the elements. A lot of people drowned, especially women and children. And for three days, abandoned by everyone, at the mercy of the violence of nature, beaten by the sea, by the rain, by the wind, they didn't have food to eat or water to drink. . . . All of us who lived through those hours will never be able to forget them."[6] Pujol's testimony recorded by Federica Montseny in 1949 is clearly motivated by his directly stated desire that this event (consequence of natural disaster coupled with political betrayal) form part of the record of world history, permanently inscribed in public memory: "All the great collective disasters: the sinking of the *Medusa*, the shipwreck of the *Titanic*, the torpedo attack against the *Lusitania*, the great Chicago fire, the earthquakes of Yokohama, the terrible monsoons of India, all this and much more is evoked in the tragedy of January '41 in Argelès, a tragedy we will always remember."[7]

The Guards

Nos trataban como a perros, nos robaron, apalearon, empujaron, pues para ellos éramos sólo unos elementos indeseables de los que había que desembarazarse lo antes posible sacándoles antes, claro, todo el jugo posible.

[They treated us like dogs; they robbed us, they beat us, they pushed us around. For them we were just a bunch of undesirables whom they needed to get rid of as soon as possible, but only after, of course, they had bled us dry.]

—Antonio Vilanova, St. Cyprien

According to the text and images of *Campos de concentración*, even the savage forces of the natural world wane in comparison with the fierce dominion exercised over the refugees by the French gendarmes. Of the fifty-plus drawings specifically of the camps themselves (among others of Spain, the border, Paris, or other French locales) that Bartolí produced for this volume, more than a dozen feature the guards; all of them appear under the same guise: fat, hairy creatures, more beast than human, armed with the ubiquitous bayonet and pistol, they are the very picture of depravity and violence. Using these monstrous figures, Bartolí is able to give a face to the French government that has created and maintained for the Spanish Republican exiles a network of concentration camps that are unfit for human habitation. The very first drawing that fully focuses on the "infame cancerbero del infierno" [monstrous gatekeeper of hell] (71) within the camp is replete with all the trappings of official France. Two hideous guards, one morbidly obese, loom in the window of their quarters as they stand sentry over tiny stick figures of half-dressed inmates. Both sport fancy uniforms heavily decorated with military medallions presented by a grateful nation. The names of French officials like General Weygand adorn the walls; a copy of the right-wing French newspaper *Gringoire*—reportedly Marshal Pétain's favorite weekly—lies on the desk. A sleek government car, identified with the French flag, is parked outside; on one wall the ever-present slogan *Liberté, fraternité, egalité* is tightly juxtaposed with a signed photograph of a naked prostitute. The giant, hairy hands of the gargantuan guard stroke the fur of a miniature lapdog, an image that recalls a famous exhibit of the 1937 II Congreso Internacional de Escritores para la Defensa de la Cultura held in wartime Valencia in which Franco was represented as a minuscule *perrito faldero* panting at the feet of an oversized Hitler and Mussolini. This guard, in fact, bears a striking resemblance to the only depiction of Hitler in the book, a hulking, war-

Infame cancerbero del infierno [Monstrous Gatekeeper of Hell] (Bartolí, *Campos de concentración*; permission for use granted by Bernice Bromberg de Bartolí)

mongering thug named Attila who makes his effortless way through France due in no small measure to finding kindred spirits all along the way: "He found like-minded individuals everywhere he went. The powerful of the earth smoothed the way for him" (135). Attila, like his mustachioed, colossal counterpart in the French concentration camp guard station, is also the proud possessor of a nude that he displays nearby;

De nuevo venció Atila [Attila Has Conquered Again] (Bartolí, *Campos de concentración*; permission for use granted by Bernice Bromberg de Bartolí)

this one is a Venus de Milo from the hallowed halls of an Occupied Paris now directly placed under his jackbooted foot. The dreadful warrior, resting his arm on a swastika-emblazoned shield that prominently features *España*, also has a lapdog seated at his feet: Mariscal Pétain.[8]

Throughout the pages of the book the French guards are represented much as is this first repellent gendarme, huge and ugly, always lurking, filling the space of the camp with their odious presence. In one drawing a loutish guard peers around the doorway of the *barraca*, constantly vigilant even as the prisoners sleep (77). The suffocating, watchful shadow of the officers as well as the Moorish *spahi* and Senegalese soldiers are a fact of life in the camps, frequently remarked upon by other witnesses.[9] Juan Carrasco complains sarcastically in the photo caption he writes for one of the images of his own 1980 bilingual *album-souvenir* record of events: "A gendarme stands guard over a team of potato peelers. You never know when one of them might stick potatoes in his pockets . . . or he might eat them! We're up to our ears in gendarmes!, the refugees complained. And it was true: the man in uniform was always lurking around, his constant presence caused us annoyance, disgust, and shame."[10] Artís-Gener recalls with bitterness that the prisoners were often deprived of the most elementary level of privacy; the guards, he says, "also spied on us when we had a bowel movement, which for man, a defecating animal, is unavoidable."[11] This sense of being stood over and stalked even to the outer reaches of a sleeping refugee's dreamworld explains the curious drawing that portrays a batlike winged guard, rifle in hand, that flies high above what Pedro Serra has neologistically called the *barracópolis*; Molins i Fábrega's accompanying text reads: "The gendarme who insulted you during the day, who treated you like a Spanish pig, and who beat you to get your weak body up and moving, has robbed the devil of his wings and flies silently, but vigilantly. He flies between you and the spaces of infinity, ready to open fire against your very thoughts if you dare to escape in dreams, fleeing towards what you love or where you become free again . . ." (59).[12] Indeed, it seems that one of the most recurring nightmares shared among the refugees was that of being pursued by a French guard, a Spanish Civil Guard, or a strange composite persecutor into whom the two hated assailants have merged. The fugitive's terror of being pursued, represented in numerous Bartolí drawings, was a very real fear for those who escaped from the camps, merely contemplated escape, or imagined their fate if sent back to Spain. Most Republican refugees did not feel safe in France, a nation that publicly recognized Franco's government even before the civil war's end and aggressively repatriated thousands of refugees. Even the civilian Silvia Mistral details in one of her May 15th, 1939, diary entries the feverish thoughts that come to her in sleep: "When I manage to fall asleep, as the sun peeps from behind the lofty Provencal mountains, all I see is a parade of crimes, persecutions, and hunger. I dream that I'm walking barefoot, that the black capes of the Civil guards wrap me in their folds and that I run away until I fall to my knees, like an exhausted horse. It's always the same haunting vision."[13] Soon after crossing the border, Manuel García Gerpe was also plagued with nightmares of being chased by French-Spanish guards shortly before he was in fact apprehended by French officers and sent to the concentration camp of Septfonds. While working for a French baker in exchange for meals and a bed of straw in a woodshed, García Gerpe experienced a particularly vivid dream in which the present time and place in France (as the baker attempts to wake him) is confused with a frightening return to Franco's Spain: "I was back in Spain . . . ; the sinister Civil Guard 'hunted' me down in my hiding place between the stacks of firewood; he was getting ready to blindfold me before pumping me full of lead. A loud voice from the shadows echoed in my ears . . . *'espagnol, rouge';* but I could only focus on the criminal explosion of gunfire . . . *'espagnol, rouge,'* the *patissier* repeated, closer. . . . I woke up from my horrible dream."[14] Agustí Cabruja recounts in his concentration camp memoir a dream of going home to Spain only to meet a violent death at the hands of faceless men who come for him. In a section entitled "Sueños negros" (Black dreams), he inserts a recurrent dream-sequence return to his *pueblo*: he emotionally embraces his mother and then hears the knocks at the door. He flees amid his mother's shouts ("It's them . . . Yes, it's them! . . . They're coming to arrest you. . . . Run . . . For the love of God, run, get away! . . .) and awakes only after his alter ego has been shot: "Then shots are fired and I find myself on the ground, wounded, drenched in blood. And then I wake up."[15]

The Lorca-like allusions to an ominous armed unit that threatens from the other side of the door are fully exploited in the concentration camp poetry of Celso Amieva, who writes the second poem of his collection *La almohada de arena* as a reinscription of Lorca's famous "Romance de la Guardia Civil Española." The superimposition and fusion of two hostile locales (Daladier's France and the Civil Guards' Spain) and two tormentors (the camp gendarme and the Civil Guard) provide the setting and the antagonists in Amieva's text "Romance de la Guardia Móvil Francesa," in which a common target (the Republican Spaniard) suffers at the hands of a brutal police force. The temporal and geographical dislocation alluded to earlier by García Gerpe is acknowledged by the concentration camp protagonist of another Amieva poem; "dreaming of civil guards" ("El Tricornio" [The Three-Cornered Hat], v. 11), the narrator confesses: "Yo ya no sé en dónde estoy, / si en

Francia estoy o en España, / si allí ya ha pasado todo / y aquí no ha pasado nada. / He perdido la noción / del tiempo y de la distancia" [I no longer know where I am, / if I'm in France or Spain, / there where everything has already happened / and here where nothing has. / I have lost all sense / of time and of space]. Dreaming or wakeful, the campers feel unprotected, in danger. In one of his most vivid visual depictions of this obsessive fear of reprisal and retribution from either Spanish or French authorities, Bartolí has shown how the refugees imagine being mercilessly hunted down by packs of wild dogs. More than a dozen and a half of the horrid uniformed dog-guards, jaws snapping and tails flailing, give chase to the barefoot refugees fleeing between two skeleton-filled jail cells: "Cemeteries and graveyards are still hungry for more. . . . And the man is chased by packs of ignoble hounds" (107). This image of the primitive manhunt is referred to as well by Luis Suárez in his 1944 camp memoir *España comienza en los Pirineos*; the author cites a 1939 newspaper article that describes the figures of the hunters that incongruously dot the coastal landscapes of France: "Ten kilometers outside of Saint-Cyprien, on their little Arabian horses, nervous and skittish, military riflemen make a sweep of the road. Now and then they examine the horizon: they're on a manhunt."[16]

Nightmare Visions of Franco's Spain

—¡Hijo mío, no vengas todavía, / que ronda en las noches la Guardia Civil!—
[My son, don't come back yet, / the Civil Guard makes its nightly rounds!]

—"Voces" (Voices), Celso Amieva, Barcarès

The exiled inmates may achingly long for the familiar corner of earth that was theirs—wistfully represented in these dreams through nostalgic references to hearth and home: *el pueblo, la madre, la casa*—but by and large España is now configured in the refugees' imagination as a wasteland of death, murder, and persecution. One of Bartolí's most elaborate drawings in *Campos de concentración*, and one of the few that shows a space outside of the barbed-wire perimeter, is the sole picture of postwar Spain (145). The sketch was originally published in Mexico City on the cover of the September 1943 issue of *Mundo: Socialismo y libertad*, an issue that included references to other infamous European concentration camps in articles like "Tremblinka [sic]: Death Camp in Poland." The illustration's central character is an enormous grinning skeleton, coquettishly outfitted in a floral mantilla and an arrow-filled belt of the Falange insignia, who offers a welcoming embrace to the

Franco's Spain (Bartolí, *Campos de concentración*; permission for use granted by Bernice Bromberg de Bartolí)

porcine French guards who drag a massive group of half-dead concentration camp exiles across the border. Franco's dreaded *guardia civil*, indistinguishable in appearance from the monstrous French guards elsewhere in the book, stands shoulder to shoulder with a Falange soldier. The twin figures dominate the foreground of the drawing as they raise their weapons in firing squad formation, an action that is redeployed twice more in the drawing. In fact, every motif in the full-length panel represents some version of death: dozens of graveyard crosses are sprinkled behind the specter's head like ornamental spangles; a cadaver hangs from a buzzard-topped tree; hollow-eyed faces crammed into a jail cell gaze vacantly at the viewer; bodies litter the ground like so much trash; a farm is engulfed in flames. The city of Burgos, seat of the Nationalist government during part of the civil war, is spotlighted under the spire of its imposing Catholic cathedral; as the site of one of Franco's most infamous prisons (indeed, the drawing's jail is positioned just across the river), it witnessed few acts of Christian charity and forgiveness but plenty of the most brutal postwar scenes of horror.[17] The only images in this complex collage that do not allude to physical death and destruction all refer to the empty symbols of the *españolada* that dot the barren cultural landscape of Franco's Spain: the bullring, the guitar player, the flamenco dancer. One cannot help but discern in this instance the echoes of Machado's damning 1913 portrait of the spiritually and politically inert, enervated Spain that the poet's Republic would eventually attempt to reform and replace: "La España de charanga y pandereta/ . . . / Esa España inferior que ora y bosteza, / . . . / esa España inferior que ora y embiste" [The Spain of the military brass band and the tambourine / . . . / That inferior Spain that prays and yawns, / . . . / that inferior Spain that prays and charges like a bull].[18] Instead, as Bartolí mercilessly shows, nothing remains of the now exiled Republic's dreams except the bitter fulfillment of a Machadian warning: "el vacuo ayer dará un mañana huero" [the vacuous past will yield to an empty tomorrow].[19]

The forced repatriation depicted in this drawing is located historically in the early 1940s following the Nazi occupation of France: "Today they worship Attila. You all are the holocaust's sacrificial lamb" (143). Molins i Fábrega's accompanying text refers to the French government's stepped-up efforts to empty out the camps of *bocas inútiles* that could not—or could no longer—provide cheap manual labor in the work crews or serve in the French military: "You left the fruit of your labor in camps, woods, and factories. You lost your companions in Alsace, the Netherlands, Norway, and Dunkirk. . . . Your bones have gone soft. You don't have any sweat left on your brow or blood in your veins. . . . They are sending you back across the border, where you know that suffering and death await you" (143). In a vignette ironically entitled "Navidad" (Christmas) in Agustí Cabruja-Auguet's 1947 *La ciudad de madera*, the invalid narrator describes the pressure to repatriate that the group of *mutilados* like him experienced in the Argelès-sur-Mer camp in late December 1939. The head of the camp ("ugly, pudgy, near-sighted . . . with an air about him like a wounded, raging boar, always with his whip in his hand, like a circus lion tamer") commands the group of the elderly, the infirm, *mancos*, and cripples ("There's nothing left in the camp but the trash; the able-bodied have been all used up, rowing the ships of State like galley-slaves") to pointlessly stand or march for hours in military formation; many collapse in the freezing cold from exhaustion and malnutrition. The refugees understand the jefe's motives: "He wants us to go back to Spain. . . . And so he dreams up the most far-fetched maneuvers imaginable to bore us and wear us down. Today they didn't even feed us."[20] The certainty that only greater pain and probably death await the Republicans who do return to Spain is one of the most powerful beliefs that circulates among all of the refugees in all of the camps. A 1939 letter written in the very early days of exile from the camp of Argelès-sur-Mer explains, "I don't dream about the sun of Spain, since I don't believe we can go back there no matter how many guarantees Franco gives us. . . . I'm in a cage and I dream about the sun of the world."[21] A letter dated April 14, 1939, from the women's refugee camp in Carolue alludes to the same fate of execution that Bartolí illustrated with his firing squad unit at the border; referring to a group of refugees who opted to return to Spain, Esperanza Panadero Caballero relays what she has heard about their treatment: "Many were shot right at the border where the *'falange'* of well-to-do young men and the Civil Guard waited for them."[22]

Perhaps the most obvious common denominator that links the memories from the earliest days of exile in the camps is the almost pathological fear the refugees share of being forcibly returned to Franco's Spain. Typically the camp inmates who were transported from one camp to another or from a camp to a work crew locale had no idea of where they were being taken; their absolute disorientation generally leads to a state of panic as they assume a worst case scenario: their imminent deportation to Spain. This terror is recalled in detail by each of the four informants whose individual narratives comprise the testimony published in Nelken's 1940 edited volume, *Los de Collioure* (The Men of Collioure). As Angel Sánchez Ramírez was being moved from St. Cyprien to the horrifying prison of Collioure on March 14, 1939, he was able to see only a tiny patch of countryside out of the back of the vehicle. His testimony recreates through two entire pages of text the agonizing uncertainty he suffered as he watched a series of kilometer signs indicating the diminishing distance to the border pass menacingly by: "51 kms. to the border. . . . 49, 48, 45 kms. to the border. . . . 43, 42, 37 kms. to the border. . . . 36, 35, 31 kms. to the border. . . . 26, 24, 23 kms. to the border. There could be no doubt: my final destination was the border." Convinced that he was being sent back to Spain, feeling completely desperate, he devised an almost delirious plan of action as his most logical recourse: "When they take me out of the car, I'll throw myself down an embankment if I'm still hand-cuffed, and if not, I'll attack a guard, I'll hit him, I'll try to get his weapon. That way I'd have committed a crime in France, and the French courts would have to indict me. That would make it impossible for me to be sent to Spain. As a last resort, I would fight however I could, with my arms, with my feet, with my teeth, whether tied up or free, anything not to fall in the hands of the Civil Guard."[23] Cándido Souza, future coowner of the famous photography agency in Mexico, the Hermanos Mayo, was seventeen years old when he was taken from St. Cyprien to the Collioure prison on March 6, 1939. He, like Sánchez Ramírez, recalls nervously watching the roadside kilometer markers ("It gave us quite a scare to see that each marker showed we were drawing closer to the border"); the French guards serving as escorts taunted Souza Fernández's group with the refugees' deepest fear: "The whole way the guards threatened to hand us over to Franco."[24] Manuel López Rodríguez was taken from the camp at Prats-de-Molló on March 13, 1939, with an unlucky group of companions who had been told they were going to a "better camp"; the passengers despair as they surmise they are headed for the Spanish border: "We started to get scared, since the route we took was towards the border, and we feared we had been tricked and were being taken back to Spain."[25] The final witness-narrator of *Los de Collioure*, Agapito Perujo Echevarría, arrived on April 30, 1939, after having been threatened in the Septfonds camp with the worst punishment the French authorities could invent: "They were giving me back to Franco, and so on."[26] A year after these hand-wringing transfers to Collioure, Celso Amieva was one of a 750-member *compañía de trabajo* leaving Argelès on February 1, 1940, for an undisclosed work site in France. Once the train is underway, a familiar scene ensues: "At one stop, a companion climbed up to the peephole and fell back in fear. 'Those bastards have got us in Spain!' Generalized panic. 'What do you mean in Spain?' 'We're in Cáceres!' 'That's impossible!' 'I'm telling you we're in Cáceres!' 'Where we are is screwed.' 'OK, OK, somebody else get up there and look for the name of the station.' They helped me climb up . 'We're not in Cáceres, we're in Cazeres, close to Toulouse.' "[27] Relief floods the car as the badly oriented passengers discover their topographical error.

Stories of this type abound in the camp memoirs. One of the incidents reported in the French press at the time and later transmitted through the exile community in Mexico as well concerned trainloads of Spanish women and children who were supposedly being transported from one refugee center to another: "Some fifty refugees, mostly women and children, were escorted by mobile guards towards the international bridge of Hendaye. When they realized that on the other side of the Bidasoa flew the blood-red and gold flag of Francoist Spain, they stopped, refusing categorically to take another step that would lead them into rebel Spain. In spite of the military French authorities' insistence, the refugees stubbornly refused to go any further. They were taken to Hendaye, and later taken to Revel."[28] Different versions of these basic facts appear in various iterations. According to Antonio Mije, in September 1940 two trains originating from Grenoble were going toward the south, one supposedly destined for Hendaye, the other for Cerbère. When the passengers going to Hendaye realize they in fact are being deported to Spain, they pull emergency alarms attempting to force the train to stop, and some jump off the train. Mije reports that one youth was killed on the tracks and several women were injured; all were deported. As the second train bound for Cerbère prepared to leave from Perpignan, the women similarly sounded the alarms, threw their belongings out of the window, got off, and refused to remove themselves from the tracks. These rebellious women were taken to Argelès instead.[29] Rosa Laviña reports an almost identical eyewitness account: "In Le Mans they put us on a train without telling us where they were taking us"; the women realize they're headed for Spain when they stop in Perpignan. They activate the alarm and are allowed to stay in Spain.[30] But she reports the date as September 1939. Yet another aborted deportation? A confusion of dates? Celso Amieva refers to refugees from the camps being deported (men, now) in the fall of 1940: "I heard about some people who, before reaching Cerbère, threw themselves off the train that was taking them to Spain. With their head split open, or with a broken leg, they would then be transferred to a hospital in Perpignan."[31] Hearsay? Fictitious versions? What is not in dispute is the status of the stories as camp lore that deeply informs the collective memory of the early exile experience and is freely cited as proof of the exiles' determination to vigorously act, to rebel, before allowing themselves to be subjected to Franco's dominion. As refugees residing in Les Mages, Silvia Mistral and her companions were threatened in late March 1939 with repatriation. Mistral, who ultimately was not deported, details a plan of fantastic resistance in her diary that recalls the earlier cited testimony of Sánchez Ramírez, the former prisoner of Collioure: "We put the finishing touches on our plan. If [the guards] should show up right away with the orders for repatriation, we'll throw ourselves to the ground, we'll scream, we'll climb out on the roof and pretend to want to kill ourselves. If they don't come right away, we'll set up a vigil close to the mayor's office and at the first sign [of deportation] we'll head for the mountains. If we fall into the gendarmes' hands, at whichever train station, we'll ask them to take us to a concentration camp."[32] Similarly, the memoirist Miguel Giménez Igualada explains that on one occasion when he feared imminent repatriation to Spain, he covertly armed himself with a razor blade, preferring to take his life at the border rather than fall captive to the forces of tyranny: "All the cosmic forces of destruction and all the moral forces of liberation converged in my hand, which I would hold steady, and in that insignificant little blade, which would do my bidding. On the way to the Spanish border, if that is indeed where we were going, I thought, I would spill my own blood, and the killers that hoped to take pleasure in torturing another man, would receive in their clutches the man's cadaver. And so you see, I smiled with satisfaction. . . ."[33]

Horror stories of Franco's incarceration and mass executions of Republican Spaniards spread through the camps like wildfire. Early newspaper articles in France, to which the campers eventually had access, published items like the following report of a session of French parliament: "House of Representatives: 'At 9:30, with Mr. Herriott presiding, Mr. Nogueres, Socialist, took the podium and pointed out the fact that many refugees who had returned to Spain, had been shot.'"[34] Sometimes the news from Spain was furnished in first person accounts from fellow Republicans who had managed to sneak across the border into France. Eulalio Ferrer writes in a Saint-Cyprien diary entry dated September 29, 1939 about his meeting with "Jacinto," a compatriot from his native Santander who had recently escaped from prison where he was awaiting a death sentence: "He tells us that we occupy a privileged position compared to that of thousands of Spaniards in jail."[35] The condemned man explained to Ferrer and his companions the deadly routine that took place each night in the jail: "I was in a group of 80 men condemned to death. Each night they took four or five of us, and the cruel uncertainty of the wait made it even more terrifying. In addition, the jailers read the list of *the chosen* slowly, with a highly refined sadism. They would read the first name. If it was a José, imagine the state of mind of all the people with that name. With the same slowness the first surname was read. When it was a Pérez, a Rodríguez or a Solana, the desperation mounted. Some resignedly stepped forward, before they heard the second surname."[36] Manuel García Gerpe includes the testimony of a camp companion who had returned to Spain from the Argelès camp, only to confront the harsh reality of his future as an ex-Republican combatant under Franco's rule: "The deal was that those of us who returned were divided into three groups. Our companions in the first group were granted safe passage to get them to the town where they had lived most recently; the second group, including yours truly, was to be taken to the outskirts of Ripoll, where the Francoists had set up a Concentration Camp; the third and largest group, were kept some distance away from us, and they were hand-cuffed and closely guarded by the Civil Guard, and beaten by the *señoritos* of the 'Falange.' We had just begun our march toward the new Camp, when we heard gunshots, as the Civil Guards, under orders from the officers of the Falange, finished off the gullible believers in the justice of Franco."[37]

Direct eyewitness accounts of events in Spain were far less common than news received by mail from family and friends who remained at home. Cabruja-Auguet watched his cousin voluntarily leave the camp to go back to Spain, only to learn later that he had killed himself in the Burgos prison: "Burgos—voice and specter of the old Spain. . . . (uniforms, convents and bell towers). It's the feudal castle and a millennium of the sword and the cross. . . . And at dawn that day this student of the humanities committed suicide, throwing himself from a window onto the jail's courtyard."[38] Silvia Mistral includes a fragment of a letter received from home in an entry dated April 1, 1939, the official date of the end of the Spanish Civil War: "If I told you stories, they would sound like some of Edgar Allan Poe's."[39] Because of the vigilance of Spanish censors, most personal correspondence from Spain was composed in a curiously encoded communication. Celso Amieva offers examples from the camp in Barcarès of this special secret language in his memoir: "One time Comi showed up with a letter from his family. He needed to decipher a few clues. Like so many other anguished missives, it was full of euphemisms and periphrasis, ingenious turns of phrases and murky references: 'Ramón now lives with Grandmother.' And since the grandmother died eleven years ago, Ramón also is six feet under. One more victim of the firing squads."[40] Similarly, Enric Yuglá Mariné describes letters from home that he and his companions received in the Bram camp: "In answer to our question about whether we could return to Spain, it said: 'Come as soon as you can; you can go live with your uncle, he's expecting you.' (The uncle had been dead for some time, which meant: don't move a muscle)."[41] The scrambled messages from home were not limited to those directed to concentration camp recipients, but were widely disseminated among the entire refugee community residing in France. Ramón López Barrantes, living in Paris immediately after crossing the border, recalls the first letter he receives in 1939 from his elderly mother in Madrid: "they were expecting me, without fail, for my niece Mariví's wedding. She was seven years old at the time! A cryptic way of telling me to not even think about coming back, but to get used to the idea of a long wait."[42] Regardless of the cryptic phrases employed, the exiles in France all comprehended the common message they were being given: You can't come home now. Look for liberty somewhere else.

Walking on Water: Dreams of Freedom

> —¿A dónde vas?—le preguntaron. —A México, a México . . . —contestó alegre. E iba, hacia el mar, adentrándose en el agua. Los amigos corrieron hacia él. Marchaba a México, por el mar, como Jesucristo, sobre las olas.
>
> ["Where are you going?" they asked him. "To Mexico, to Mexico . . ." he answered happily. And off he went toward the sea, wading out into the water. His friends ran after him. He was going to Mexico, by sea, like Jesus Christ, walking on waves.]
> —Silvia Mistral, Argelès-sur-Mer

One of the very smallest of the sixty-five Bartolí drawings in *Campos de concentración* depicts an array of miniature objects scattered on the sand: a chessboard, game pieces, a rowboat, an intricately carved ship (67). These small artifacts of the imagination—carefully crafted out of pieces of driftwood, bones, or soap—helped the internees pass the interminable hours: whittling away the time, playing rounds of chess.[43] The tiny seafaring vessels—the magnificently mounted sailboat, the unfinished hull of another nearby—conjure up visions of voyages that fill the hearts and minds of the thousands of inmates who wait and wait and wait for release. Bartolí juxtaposes the wistfully fashioned creations on one page with two idle campers languishing at the water's edge on the next. The haggard man seated in the sand delouses his filthy clothes; the man leaning against the barbed-wire fence faces away from the camp itself. He stares out at a ship passing by, faraway and free, a dot on the distant horizon (69). The text that the drawings accompany is representative of one of the most widely disseminated narratives of the "camp mythology": that of the refugee who, in a crazed act of desperation, packs his bag and walks slowly out into the sea, seeking liberation: "And the captive dared to do it. The sea was the only way to get to freedom from the world of the dead. The sea! The sea! First his bare feet, frozen stiff. Then his skinny legs. Gradually, with the joy of knowing he's on the shining path to freedom, he advances step by step, in search of the Sun that pulls him onward. He did it! He disappeared among the waves. Now he's free! His brothers, less motivated, think he was crazy. But he, in his cold, drifting tomb, knows he's not" (67). Certainly no anecdote is more often repeated in the camp memoirs; eyewitness reports indicate that the stories are not always apocryphal, but it is the power of the message—the exiles' intense yearning for freedom at any cost—that explains the pervasiveness of the account. In some versions the fantasized destination is *la patria*; the man is going home to Spain. In their *El peso de la derrota*, Tellado and Sánchez-Bravo cite the case of "Manolo" who packed up his shabby wooden suitcase one day and walked into the sea, repeating mechanically, "I'm going home, I'm going by sea." Manolo, whom the authors and their companions were able to pull back to shore, exemplifies the fierce (albeit irrational and dangerous) desire for freedom shared among the Spanish *pueblo*: "The idealistic insanity of some of the peasants revealed a pureness of spirit that had steadfastly refused to accept the loss of liberty."[44] Most of the incidents that are recounted refer to the *loco*'s fixation not on home but abroad, and respond to dreams of escaping to America. Juan Carrasco, whose previously cited photo album of the camps echoes so many of the same images and stories as Molins i Fábrega's and Bartolí's volume, is reminded of the story when looking at one of the photographs he publishes in his book of memories: "The now classic picture of the concentration camps by the seashore: the refugees' obligatory leisure time on the beach, the unavoidable gendarme charged with making his report about the behavior of the internees . . ." His pictorial image, like Bartolí's drawing of the two bored campers, contrasts the material reality of confinement (here, the guards; in Bartolí, the barbed wire) with the tempting seas of liberation: "Looking at this picture brings back the memory of one refugee's insanity (today it's hard to pinpoint the name of the camp where it happened), who with his suitcases in hand walked out to sea, shouting: 'I'm going to Mexico!' . . . The sea swallowed up the crazy man, and his suitcases, afloat for a few minutes, returned to the point of departure, the beach. Some refugees watched the death of their compatriot like impotent spectators."[45] The concluding lines of the originally cited story in *Campos de concentración* transform the death of the desperate refugee seeking liberation through the sea into an image of resurrection and inspiration for those he has left behind: "Be strong! They will not defeat you! Beyond the sea, next to the light, is freedom" (67). All of the memories that inspire Bartolí's illustrations and Molins i Fábrega's text ultimately seek to pay tribute to the camps' victims, whose deaths in exile in France are heralded from Mexico as a life-affirming sacrifice for tomorrow's Spain.

Commemorating the Dead: The Memorializing Discourse

> Al pie de la carretera, antes de llegar al pueblo, se encuentra un campo sembrado de hierbas altas y espigadas, y de cruces. . . . Es

> un cementerio de exiliados españoles. Jamás se ve un alma triste y enlutada por aquellos alrededores. Ni un ramo de violetas—tiernas o marchitas—, ni una inscripción humilde—nombre o recuerdo—acaricia esas tumbas.
>
> [At the end of the road, before you get to the town, there's a field full of weeds and crosses. . . . It's a cemetery of exiled Spaniards. You never see a single soul, not one mourner in these parts. Not a single sprig of violets—neither fresh nor wilted—nor even the most humble inscription—a name, a memory—grace those graves].
>
> —Agustí Cabruja-Auguet, Argelès-sur-Mer

The survivors' memory of the concentration camps in France is by definition a memory of the dead; thousands of Spanish internees died of disease or war-related injuries between 1939 and 1944, and their bodies filled the hastily constructed cemeteries that grew up around the place of the camps. The transient nature of the refugees and the fact that the camps were impermanent sites that would disappear without apparent traces one day were of course highly desirable conditions for those who sought release from their barbed-wire fences. But the fact that many refugees would find their final resting place on these grounds, in unmarked graves on foreign soil, caused those who survived them to seek ways to commemorate their dead comrades. Adolfo Ballano Bueno, survivor of Argelès-sur-Mer, wrote from Mexico in 1946 that the sands of the camps themselves threatened to eradicate any memory of those who had lived and died there: "That carpet of shifting sand was where all the great and profound human tragedies played themselves out. Footprints were erased and blood was soaked up like water. That's why it looked so innocent."[46] The need to engrave, to literally make a lasting mark upon the place of the camps in the name of the deceased, is the primary impetus and greatest unifying theme in *Campos de concentración, 1939–194 . . .* , the book I have first analyzed as a collective memory album. I now turn my attention to the text and illustrations in order to show how the authors offer up their words and images as an inscription against erasure, oblivion, and anonymity. They create a memorial to the dead against forgetting.

The protagonist of *Campos de concentración* is introduced in the opening pages of the preface as a kind of divine prophet in the guise of a *pueblo* seeking refuge, the most humble of all possible messengers who first brings the news of Fascism's fury to the world.[47] The voice of "a few outcasts" goes unheeded by "the great powers of the world" (14). Throughout his book, Molins i Fábrega will develop a fundamental narrative tension that obtains between the humble role of a suffering figure, the bearer of news that can save the world, and the antagonistic, authoritative forces of power, wealth, and political self-interest that conspire to kill the messenger. The Christlike allegory that the author adopts as a vehicle to tell the story begins and ends in the same place: at the tomb of the murdered messiahs. The first reference to the "asylum of the death shroud" (16) that the refugees are offered in France describes "las fosas de más amplios cementerios" "grave sites of vast cemeteries" (14) that masquerade as their sanctuary. Molins cites Vichy government statistics that reveal that as of May 1942, seventy-two thousand Spaniards had died in France (16). He goes on to acknowledge the renowned practice in France of commemorative ceremonies, landmarks, and public monuments erected to its war dead, and bitterly contrasts this tradition with the ignoble treatment of Spanish exiles in France: "Cemetery-sanctuaries where no monuments are erected and which will never stand as a hallmark of glory for France. Instead they will be an embarrassment for the politicians who created them, the nation that tolerated them, and the world that caused them to happen" (16). Similarly, at the very end of the book, in the final vignette, Molins concludes his narrative at the site of the tomb; he addresses his buried hero: "You lie buried in oblivion. . . . In your tomb you feel forgotten by the world and its men" (155). Throughout the pages in between, the author Molins i Fábrega and the illustrator Bartolí construct a heartfelt memorial to commemorate the concentration camps' victims and, more broadly, the war dead left behind in Spain. The prevailing message of the book is one of redemption and resurrection; Republican Spain in exile in Mexico is nurtured and sustained by the example of sacrifice of her fallen heroes not only on the battlefield of Spain but in the camps of France.

The analogy alluded to in the preface between a biblical Christ-figure's passion, cruxifixion, and resurrection, and Molins i Fábrega's protagonist of his epic tale of civil war and exile, is firmly established in the very first vignette of the book. Following the opening two lines of text ("Long ago and far away, men created God from a fellow man, because of the message of redemption that he shouted to the world. The men crucified him" [35]), the humble Republican "Everyman" soldier, Juan Español, is introduced as the modern incarnation of the voice of hope and redemption that is similarly sacrificed: "He hangs from the cross, he rests on the ground." Bartolí's illustration, the book's only picture of wartime Spain, depicts the martyred victims and the ravages of war with brutal intensity: a naked, Goyaesque figure hangs horribly from a tree, the face of the dead man hidden under a Falange-emblazoned hood; another mangled cadaver lies contorted on the ground; a rubble of ruins rest under the swastika-shaped aerial formation of Nazi bombers. Two other ghostly characters, their translucent garments betraying their otherworldly condition, form part of this devastated Spanish landscape of violent death and absolute destruction. This image of the unconsecrated ground of Spain where the remains of the exiled Republicans' fellow soldiers are unceremoniously scattered is the vision that the refugees carry with them across the border. This tragedy of the postwar nation in exile, the inability to properly bury and memorialize its war dead, informs and motivates every page of the book. In addition to the collective tribute to the Republican nation's dead generally, Bartolí often offers individual elegies to specific war companions through a series of personal inscriptions that accompany various images. The ghastly image of wartime Spain, for example, is dedicated to the memory of a friend, "Jaume Girabau," executed by members of the Falange. This remembrance of the dead, the constant presence in exile of absent comrades, is emphasized in the second entry describing the border crossing into France by the war's survivors. Their passage into new territory, the land of exile, is represented as a journey shared with those left on Spanish soil by way of the unbreakable bonds of memory: "The brothers that stayed behind, whose blood is spilled on the soil that these comrades must abandon, follow them on their sad journey" (39). The merging of yesterday's dead with today's survivors into a single spirit of tomorrow's Spain—a kind of powerful process of transubstantiation enacted by memory and desire—is introduced in the third piece. Here the former Republican war combatants assume their awful new identity, that of concentration camp inmates, stripped bare of any vestiges of human dignity: "They torture your bodies" (43). As Bartolí's illustration of two campers carrying a stinking, sloshing vat of human excrement shows, the Republicans have been reduced to the basest levels of existence. But it is the painful communion with the recent tragic events of death and war ("You knead your bread with bitter tears"), the recollection (the reconnection) of the past, that will provide the grounds for national reconstruction: "What they can never take from you is the memory of who you once were and the will that inspires you to live again as men" (43). This promise of a new birth, a reemergence from the ashes of destruction, was introduced in the first vignette, closely paralleling the Christ narrative of death and resurrection through an image of a star of hope buried in the tomb of Juan Español: "In order to be born again one day, with blood and with light to show the way for other men who are less blind and more human" (35).[48] This shining star, first visible on the helmet and belt buckle of the Republican soldier featured in Bartolí's drawing for the preface, is in subsequent drawings replicated by the dozens in the skies that witness the suffering of the beleaguered camp inmates. Against all odds, the twinkling sparks of memory and hope flickering like so many tiny fireflies fail to be extinguished.

3: A COMMEMORATIVE MEMORY ALBUM OF EXILE

The urge to pay homage to Republican war veterans like the aforementioned soldier of the Ejército Popular is reflected in the fourth piece; this section juxtaposes France's solemn, elaborate commemoration of her own war veterans and war dead, on the one hand, with that same nation's inhumane treatment of the former combatants that fought in the Spanish Civil War. The narrator of the text addresses two interlocutors, both maimed and crippled by war: the French war veteran and the Republican internee. The former is outfitted with a fine wheelchair, boasts a chest full of medals, and receives a crown of laurels for his duties performed; the latter is simply left to die in oblivion: "You have nothing. Your living, breathing carcass rots in a dung heap" (47). Bartolí's drawing not only draws a contrast between the two veterans, but highlights the absence of any sort of gesture of respectful acknowledgment of Republican service and sacrifice made in the name of freedom and justice. Bartolí's weighty monumental structure erected behind the crippled French veteran by the Legion des combattants is a sprawling conglomeration of official pomp and circumstance: an enormous fleshy emblem of Lady France teeters atop a statue of a French soldier standing tall; the huge stone base supports giant French flags as well as branches and wreaths of laurel. Three bearded bureaucrats (one suspiciously bearing the Chamberlain umbrella from the earlier "nonintervention" meetings) raise a one-armed salute to a gesticulating demagogue who energetically addresses his audience from a raised podium. In contrast, the Republican *mutilado* hunched on the ground is surrounded only by the dreary landmarks of the concentration camp: the sharp barbs of the fencing and the flimsy boards of an unsturdy *barraca*. But in a pattern that becomes increasingly more insistent in the book, this text concludes the sad portrait of the Spanish veteran not with despair, but with a rousing shout of encouragement: "What difference does it make! One day you will rise up, your burden will be lifted, you will recover the use of your legs, and with a smile on your face, you will march through the world that you conquered with your own blood" (47).

This kind of shimmering image of redemption and rebirth is sprinkled along the pages of the book like a smattering of the stars in the night skies that alternate with dark and hopeless depictions of anguish. The central trope used in this book to represent the space of the concentration camp is the cemetery: "sad cemetery of shifting sands"; "the cemetery of the living"; "the very tomb of living men." The guards, then, are referred to as "the keepers of your tombs." The internees, though survivors of a war, are now wasting away and themselves transformed into specters of the dead; an array of terms that emphasizes the campers' status as zombie creatures, "the living dead," fills the book:

War heroes (Bartolí, *Campos de concentración*; permission for use granted by Bernice Bromberg de Bartolí)

"how you suffer in graves and cemeteries"; "bones of the cemetery"; "the cemetery of living creatures."⁴⁹ The text's frequent linguistic juxtaposition between the verb *encerrar*, to confine thousands of refugees, and *enterrar*, to bury many of them, reminds the reader that the distinction between the two states is minimal; the book's homage to the camp and its martyred living inhabitants, a kind of hallowed "holy ground"/*campo santo*, stresses the small space that separates one field of activity from another: the *campo santo*/"cemetery" filled with graves. The literal deaths of many of the refugees or their family members are recorded in the book as well, and these references again include illustrations with personal dedications to specific individuals. A lyrical elegy describes the poignant death of the camper who clutches his mother's letter in his hand; Bartolí's portrait of this man, erect, gazing clear-eyed at the viewer, respectfully accords him at the moment of death his former individuality, health, and humanity (87). Another piece announces the death in the women's camp of another inmate's three children (103). In yet another, a full page-length drawing occupying the very center of the book shows a picture of the sick and dying in the foreground. In the background, placed squarely above the primitive hospital structure, a leering skeleton with scythe bustles busily about the campgrounds, ready to receive his next victim; an inert man on a stretcher is being carried toward death's grasp by two round-shouldered camp attendants. The text refers to the grave digger, whose job is never done: "Death kept you company. The eternal Grim Reaper [Gravedigger Joe] worked night and day to bury your flaccid bodies, already rotten before they died" (91). In a later installment, the author Molins i Fábrega will use his elegy of another unnamed camp inmate in order to render homage to all the anonymous dead of the camps whose bodies rest in unmarked graves of France. Using his dying victim as his mouthpiece, the author ascribes a quiet dignity to the modest "tomb of the unknown soldier" that he creates in his postwar tribute: "Tomorrow, on the rugged rock you use to cover my tomb, don't inscribe any name. . . . That way, some day, the mother who lost her son, can imagine that in death he returned to her" (115).

Even as the authors paint a pathetic picture of the dead and dying in the concentration camps, in keeping with the dynamic inherent in the biblical master narrative, Molins i Fábrega and Bartolí also warn their readers that a Day of Judgment will follow the deaths of the heroic "demigods" (63, 75, 83, 87, 151) chronicled in the book. Those responsible for the pain and suffering of thousands of Spanish Civil War refugees in France—government officials, guards, a passive public—will in turn one day soon be held accountable for their crimes against humanity. The same government that today sanctions the inhumane treatment of the campers at the hands of the sadistic guards will tomorrow be implicated in their henchmen's testimony in the court of public opinion: "But this beast doesn't realize that after his service as an executioner, a vile and despicable job, it will be his turn to testify, a lofty and noble task, no less so even when the individual chosen by destiny to perform it is disgusting and cruel. If the powerful of the earth knew what was coming, they would already be shaking in their boots" (83). In one of the most starkly violent images of *Campos de concentración* that focuses on the measures used to punish so-called "lawbreakers" within the camps, a pigtailed guard brutally clubs a hapless prisoner. Bartolí's illustration represents the beating as a kinetically charged nightmare; he achieves a sense of movement and frenzy by reproducing over and over the same inert, half-dressed victim, turned topsy-turvy, upside down, by the sheer force of the blows he receives. The frame of the picture is filled with raised arms bearing wooden batons, all belonging to the same savage guard sketched repeatedly from every possible angle. The blows that rain down upon the defenseless man are set against the threatening words that the narrator addresses to the criminal assailant: "Not even the blood you see flowing from the wounds is really blood. Each drop will be transformed into a new being, stronger than ever. One day they will form an army that will destroy your stinking hide, which will end up like those of the lords and masters you have served" (111).

From this point onward, about two-thirds of the way through the narrative, the fantasies of vengeance and retribution become increasingly pronounced. In one of the pieces that refers to the issue of rape of refugee women by French guards, the woman's tormenter is warned that even the distant stars, the tiny symbols of the refugees' flickering hope, will bear witness against him: "It's useless to try to hide your sickening crime under the cover of darkness. The stars saw you. They will guide the avenger to wherever you are. Nothing can save you from the punishment you deserve" (119). The following vignette describes how a group of campers turn the tables on their adversaries when they execute a savage attack against one of the guards: "Even the banished can rebel. . . . The ones who beat him up know that their actions avenged the shame and suffering of each and every one of their brothers in captivity" (123). While the Spanish historian Javier Rubio has questioned whether such attacks on guards widely reported in camp inmate testimony are anything other than purely apocryphal "myths of resistance" or "fantasies of power and revenge," the cathartic significance of these accounts is indisputable.[50] In the context of the topoi of death, resurrection, and retribution of *Campos de concentración*, the anecdote of revenge forms part of a narrative crescendo that leads the reader toward the final chapters of resolution. Not surprisingly, the penultimate full-sized illustration is finally of the concentration camp cemetery itself. Although constantly referred to throughout the book primarily in metaphorical terms, the cemetery is not directly represented by the authors until they close their volume of commemoration: "From the cemetery where you lived like exhausted shadows, you crossed over to the cemetery where the flesh disappears" (151). Bartolí's drawing depicts four skeletal bodies that await interment; under the ever-watchful eye of a guard, two refugees labor among the grave sites behind the coffins as they prepare to bury their dead (153). The accompanying text eulogizes these deceased specifically, and all of the camps' fallen generally, solemnly announcing the transfiguration of the flesh into the guiding spirit for future generations of Spaniards: "In death you will one day be the spiritual core of mankind, its true communion" (151). It is, the authors make clear, the conversion of the tragic history of war and exile into the stuff of collective memory—its stories and myths, heroes and martyrs— that will be the source of new life and new identity: "You lived like restless souls in deserted lands. On your graves, roses and carnations will bloom one day. And in the distant future, when you all are no more than a terrible, mysterious legend, a child, happy at last, will gently pick the red flower that found its home in your great, good heart" (151). Bartolí's final two images that illustrate the very last entry in the lengthy memorial to the Republic's dead are tied together by the motif of "marking the ground," of inscribing presence in the place of the camps. The penultimate drawing shows a lone camp survivor, standing tall, approaching the horizon of a new beginning; the footprints that he leaves behind inscribe a path toward tomorrow that has its point of origin in the camp itself (155). Once again, this traveler walking toward new lands of exile, like the earlier Spaniards who crossed the border into France, carries with him the sustaining memory of those who remain behind, either figuratively or literally "buried" in oblivion in the camps. The last drawing before the short epilogue similarly depicts the one who leaves and also the one who stays. The tiny retreating figure in the top of the frame has almost disappeared from view. The dominant image in the foreground represents a single bony arm protruding from the sandy soil, clutching in its hand a piece of bowed barbed-wire fencing; it sticks out of the earth like an unsteady cross (157). These exiled Republicans—those who have died in the camps, those who await release, those who have gone on to other places—will forever be reunited in the collective memory of a nation that dreams of again reclaiming its sovereignty: "Bearing your cemetery's crown of thorns, you and they will one day soon march radiantly towards victory" (155). Three thousand miles away from the site of the camps, the community of Spanish exiles in Mexico has already begun to remember, to relive and retell the stories of the battlegrounds of Spain and the campgrounds of France as they watch the world war and expect to soon go back to their *patria*.

Campos de concentración, 1939–194 . . . concludes with a brief epilogue, "To France" that was written in March 1944 as the war raged in Europe. The author makes the characteristic distinction between the hated

Otros se fueron: tú quedaste [The Others Left: You Stayed Behind] (Bartolí *Campos de concentración*; permission for use granted by Bernice Bromberg de Bartolí)

3: A COMMEMORATIVE MEMORY ALBUM OF EXILE

"official" France ("a reactionary bourgeoisie that tried to imprison a free nation behind thick barbed wire. The persecutors of these people were the same ones who betrayed France and handed it over to Hitler" [159]) and the "true France" of the Resistance that has finally joined the Republicans' struggle against fascism. Now brave Spanish combatants in France's resistance movement fight shoulder to shoulder with their French counterparts united at last in a common cause: "Hundreds of Spaniards, former guests of the Concentration Camps, struggle alongside the French people who fight and die. . . . Thousands of them suffer the same fate of captivity as the French prisoners of war in the factories, labor camps, and work houses of Germany. . . . The common bonds of suffering have created communion. The fraternity of the struggle creates the basis for a future, prosperous collaboration between the two nations" (159–60). The Republican exiles living in Mexico in 1944 share the *Campos de concentración* authors' hope and conviction that a Europe free of fascism in the near future will include not only France ("the new France that is resurrected from the ashes of defeat" [160]), but their own beloved, long-suffering Spain as well: "We have spilled so much of our blood, victims of the same enemy who betrayed and sold out the French people" (160). Shared memories of the past and shared dreams for the future sustain the national imagination of a community that awaits in exile the chance to go home.

Part II
The Politics of Remembering the Camps: Grounds for Moral Authority

4

Max Aub's *Morir por cerrar los ojos* (1944): The Drama of Seeing Clearly on a World Stage

> [Argelès-sur-Mer] era la fofez moral, intelectual, física, cívica, de un momento de la historia que quería la paz a todo trance al precio que fuera. Era el más total y elemental no querer saber nada, ni intentar nada. Se trataba desde todos los puntos de vista de la hora cero de la ignominia.
>
> [(Argelès-sur-Mer) was moral, intellectual, physical, and civic turpitude personified, from a time in history when peace was to be protected at all costs. It was an exercise in complete and utter ignorance, of total inaction. It was, no matter how you look at it, the ground zero of ignominy.]
> —Antonio Tellado and Antonio Sánchez-Bravo (Bravo-Tellado), *El peso de la derrota*

IN HIS DISCUSSION OF THE POLITICS OF COLLECTIVE MEMORY, Edward Said has highlighted the crucial function of the stories that members of a nation-group tell themselves and others about their shared experiences, a role that Said defines as the "power of narrative history to mobilize people around a common goal."[1] For political exiles, one of the primary goals of the community, in fact the "paramount issue" according to Yossi Shain, is to establish and maintain legal and official authority.[2] In their introduction to a 1998 collection of essays entitled *Borders, Exiles, Diasporas*, the editors summarize the characteristic features of the exile identity, which include "the cultural stamina of the exiled, their constant loyalty to the historical memory of the communal life . . . and struggle for authenticity and sacrifice."[3] The Spanish exiles in Mexico will utilize the powerful narratives of the concentration camp experiences in order to build for an international audience a persuasive case that defends their own moral and legal authority as the only legitimate Spanish political entity still standing after the civil war.

Perhaps the most renowned Spanish writer exiled to Mexico who experienced firsthand the "freedom, equality, and fraternity" of the concentration camps in France was Max Aub (1903–72). The critic José

Naharro-Calderón's 1999 in-depth study of the events that inform Aub's allegorical version of camp life in Vernet d'Ariège, *Manuscrito Cuervo*, is introduced under the ironic header so frequently cited with derision by the camp survivors themselves: "Liberté, égalité, fraternité."[4] Naharro relates Aub's arrest in Paris on April 5, 1940 (he was denounced anonymously as a "Jew, a communist and revolutionary activist"), and subsequent internment in a series of French prisons and camps as casualties of a xenophobic, collaborationist French government that would soon passively submit to Hitler's occupation of the country. He characterizes the Third Republic in its waning days: "That society was obsessed with its own self-sufficiency and harbored a fearful suspicion of everything that was different or foreign."[5] The literary work that most directly interrogates the relationship between this French nation and its treatment of the foreign "Other" in concentration camps is Aub's ambitious drama *Morir por cerrar los ojos* (Death by Blindness), published in 1944 in Mexico two years after the exiled author's arrival to the capital city. In many important ways the issues that Aub represents theatrically mirror those that had been vigorously addressed two years earlier in the 1942 diary-memoir *Ballet de sangre: la caída de Francia* (Ballet of Blood: The Fall of France), published by the Mexican ambassador to France, Luis I. Rodríguez, a tireless advocate in the early 1940s for Spanish refugees like Aub interned in French camps.[6] In their respective texts, both men detail scathing accounts of circumstances that inform the political scene of a faltering French nation on the eve of the Nazi invasion of Paris: official France's cowardice (or worse, collusionist actions) in the face of fascism; the petty self-interest of a passive French people who turn a blind eye to neighboring nations suffering at their doorstep; the political scapegoating of war refugees—especially the Spanish Republicans—in French concentration camps. Rodríguez's diary, with its little-known preface by Pablo Neruda, carefully documents the events that begin in Paris on June 1, 1940, and concludes in the south of France on July 10, 1940. The first part of Aub's loosely autobiographical six-act play begins in Paris on May 10, 1940 (the day the Germans invaded Belgium); subsequent acts of the second part are dated June 5, 1940, and June 16, 1940; the final scene takes place on July 10, 1940, in the notorious camp of Vernet d'Ariège. The epigraphs that frame each writer's work also are closely linked by the motif of fighting with honor, a virtue seen as inherent to the Spanish Republican struggle and tragically absent in the French response to Hitler's aggression. Rodríguez had initiated his narrative under the quotation: "Los que mueren con honra, siempre viven. Los que viven sin honra, son los muertos" [Those who die with honor, will live forever. Those who live without honor, are already dead]; for his part Aub cites a fragment of Quevedo's *Marco Bruto*, which echoes an identical sentiment: "To forfeit freedom is to live as an animal; to allow another to take it away, is to live as a coward. He who lives as a slave just to survive, doesn't realize that living in bondage is not living; he dies of fear rather than face the enemy who would kill him. We believe that it's an honorable thing to die of an illness, and yet will we refuse to die because of the illness that plagues our republic? Whoever does not see the beauty in sacrificing his life in order to preserve his honor, has neither life nor honor."[7] Rodríguez's entire book in fact praises Spanish Republican efforts to live and die with honor, and bitterly reproaches a France that in June 1940 gives up without a fight. The author had described the massive evacuation of Paris on June 11, 1940, as the sad retreat of a spiritless nation that lacked the guiding force of its own ideals: "The caravan of the exodus relentlessly continues on its way, without food, without shelter; without God or country. It is a remnant of a democracy that exists now only in the yellowed, forgotten pages of the history books of the past, along with its freedom of thought, the rights of man, and the concept of universal brotherhood. When seen in the light of the resplendent future's bright new day, this image will serve as a living, burning reminder of a time of the shame and suffering of man, of failure and humiliation. And all because this nation committed the ugly crime of not knowing how to honor the ideals of democracy" (68). Max Aub's play expresses a similarly damning indictment against the French government as well as the citizens who tolerated or often supported the massive internment of European refugees fleeing the onslaught of fascism. In a climactic moment of the drama that represents the French flight itself from Nazi invasion, a high-ranking French army officer will confess with intense shame and disillusionment that for the sake of protecting economic gain and material comfort, French leaders have spinelessly sold their souls to the highest bidder: "And all for what? It was fear. Fear of losing their savings! So they sacrifice everything just so they won't lose ten per cent of their profits! They give up their honor for the sake of a healthy checking account! They are capable of handing over Córcega, Alsacia, and the bellies of their daughters . . ." (144). Echoing Rodríguez's admonition to the French people ("Your cruelest enemy is the one you carry inside" [65]), Aub's lieutenant ruefully concedes that the blame for the current crisis lies squarely with France itself: "It's a betrayal without traitors, due to an incalculable sum of small acts of cowardice. A traitor is someone who deceives, and no one here has tried to deceive anybody. Everyone was always in agreement about settling for a false sense of security that would let them die in peace and allow them to enjoy the crumbs that they were given" (143). And the crime of course, is not without victims;

the concentration camps of France are overflowing with them. They are the international antifascists that fill the ranks of Aub's cast, who for the playwright are the legitimate voices of liberty, equality, and fraternity.

The year before the publication of *Morir por cerrar los ojos* in 1944, Max Aub had addressed a group of writers at a meeting of the P.E.N. Club in Mexico City. Describing his most recent places of residence before arriving in America the year before, "the prisons and camps that France's blindness created for us Spaniards," Aub refers for the first time to France's establishment of the barely habitable refugee camps, exploitative work companies, and brutal prisons as the act of a myopic nation.[8] In his play, the dramatist will develop this central motif of political blindness through the manipulation of theatrical spaces—both onstage and offstage—that he structures according to their proximity to or distance from a wider world arena of international events. Part 1 introduces the world of Paris in May 1940 as the place of chauvinistic, self-serving complacency; most of the scenes are staged in the confined interiors of a comfortable apartment building inhabited by middle-class French families. The well-appointed home of a Spanish small-business owner, Julio Ferrándiz, twenty-year resident of France, and his French wife, María, provides the setting for much of the first half of the play. Part 2 opens up this insulated domestic dwelling and stages the remaining three acts in public places established by the state that fully expose the characters to the winds of political change and turmoil: the prison of Roland Garros, the concentration camp of Vernet. The citizens of the Third Republic are forced to open their eyes to the role they may have played in fascism's increasing power, and confront the disastrous effects of their own political shortsightedness and lack of clear moral vision.

Before analyzing Aub's use of dramatic space as a vehicle to develop his critique of official France's reactionary politics and his support for the committed struggle against fascism, I will briefly summarize the plot of the play. Julio Ferrándiz, a thirty-five-year-old Spanish immigrant owner of a radio shop in Paris, and his French wife María maintain correspondence with Julio's half brother Juan, a fellow long-term immigrant resident of Paris who recently returned to France after fighting for the Spanish Republic during the civil war. Interned in the concentration camp of Vernet d'Ariège for the past six months, Juan escapes unbeknownst to his family and is making his way to Paris to see Julio and María, his own former girlfriend. Meanwhile, the French authorities pay a visit themselves to the Ferrándiz home and initially arrest Julio in a case of apparent mistaken identity, believing him to be the brother Juan. In his analysis of the play, the critic Donald Shaw has pointed out that the Julio-María-Juan love triangle allows Aub to more satisfactorily dramatize the tensions of the historical events of the summer of 1940 in Paris.[9] Indeed, from the outset of the play Aub aligns his character Julio with the sector of French society whose principal priority is to protect personal property, capital, and comfortable living above all other concerns: "I'm satisfied with what I've got and I plan to keep it" (197). As a veteran of the Spanish Civil War, the brother Juan is in the now-familiar role of warning the world of fascism's threat and impending danger, especially for Spain's neighbors. As the play's mouthpiece, Juan serves the testimonial function of all good historical dramas, according to Aub's definition of them in his 1944 prologue: "They denounce evil, they warn 'This is how it is, every man for himself': they are the raw truth" (67). María, as the French wife of one immigrant and ex-girlfriend of the other, essentially mediates the two ideological worlds that the protagonists represent. It is María's journey from the shuttered space of her husband Julio's narrowly centered world to the broader vistas of Juan's internationally informed position that furnishes the central dramatic movement of the play.

Belying the turbulence of the European scene in May 1940, the stage is set in act 1 of part 1 for a life of ease and comfort; the first lines of the opening stage directions situate the drama in Julio Ferrándiz's neat and tidy home. Creature comforts and the signs of good living are pointed out by the nosy *portera* Madame Meunier who visits with María and Julio: this envious neighbor admires a brand-new top-of-the-line radio (74); she inquires about a fancy vase supposedly from the Louvre (75); she exchanges tasty recipes with the lady of the house who just last night enjoyed a leisurely evening at the cinema (77). The shiny radio set connects the onstage setting with an important offstage space at the center of Julio's existence, the store where he sells high-frequency radios capable of receiving signals from around the world; ironically, he and María listen to international news broadcasts from abroad without understanding a word (74). Throughout the entire first act the business owner Julio, typecast as a kind of "everyman" member of a merchant class ("neither tall nor short, neither fat nor thin, neither foolish nor clever" [76] will constantly fret and fume about his shop. Even when confronted by the imposing Inspector and the Policia who come to take him to the police station for questioning ("you're a red. . . . you were against Franco" [78]), Julio's obsessive concern is first and foremost financial. Insisting that he absolutely did not intervene in the recent Spanish Civil War, he assures the French authorities that his sole interest is commercial: "I have never bothered anybody about anything. All I care about is my business" (78). Over and over he nervously asks what's to become of his store; his one request of María as he is being taken away is for her to collect payment due from his customers (81).

The offstage space so crucial to Julio's identity, the shop, is juxtaposed in act 1 with a second offstage dramatic space tightly connected to his brother Juan's existence: the concentration camp in Vernet d'Ariège. This threatening, highly politicized environment is "home" to all those refugees that French citizens like the *portera* denounce as "reds" (90), "foreigners . . . , communists" (75); she laments the presence on French soil of so many strange foreign mouths to feed that are responsible for the hike in the price of a decent bottle of wine: "And who's to blame? All those blood-sucking foreigners!" (91). The unpleasant reality of the camps, and by extension the political arena of world war, begins to insinuate itself into the orderly Ferrándiz abode within the very first moments of the play; Madame Meunier delivers the newspaper along with a letter that Juan writes from the camp, a location that initially appears as a mere return address on an envelope examined by the snooping Meunier: "Looks like he's still in the same place. . . . Doesn't seem like such a bad arrangement to me" (74, 75). For his part, Julio pays scant attention to his brother's plight, interned now six months in the infamously brutal camp. In fact, in his haste to open his store on time, he neglects to even read the letter; in the next breath he breezily dismisses other news of European war quickly skimmed in the newspaper: "Looks like that business in Norway finished badly" (77). He considers his brother's current fate in the camp as a consequence of Juan's misguided involvement in the Spanish Civil War, an affair that for Julio has nothing to do with the world past the Pyrenees. Later in act 1, when María faces the camp escapee Juan in her own apartment, she heatedly accuses his wrongheaded affiliation with Spain's war as the source of her family's current troubles with the police; Juan responds by urging María to see that the acts of suspicion, betrayal, and self-interest that have resulted in Julio's arrest are the effects of a poisonous political atmosphere that extend far beyond Spain's national borders:

María. Look where your beloved politics have gotten us!
Juan. You should say, look where everybody's politics have gotten us.[10]

Julio and María, like all members of French society in 1940, are fully implicated in the course of the turbulent international political events that take place all around them. Julio's stubborn refusal to see his brother's antifascist struggle as his own, to act in solidarity with his fellow man, provides the dramatic tension that develops through the remaining five acts of the play. This tension is exacerbated by his wife María's concurrently emerging position as a committed believer in the universal fight being waged against the forces of tyranny.

The change of setting from a private apartment in act 1 to the streets of Paris in act 2 allows Aub to more fully establish the parallels between the familial conflict and the crisis on a national and international scale. The act begins and ends with the words of French soldiers, the voices of official France. Initially two guards discuss Hitler's increasing acts of military aggression against France's neighbors, bragging nonetheless of their country's impenetrability against invasion: "You've seen how they don't dare with the Maginot Line" (92); the act concludes with the very same character making way for a drunkard who passes by, shouting his slurred words like a caricature of a government spokesperson: "They shall not pass! *(Adopting an orator's stance, speaking in a grandiloquent tone to the guards)* I am the Maginot Line!" (100).[11] In between the boastful posturing of the *Guardias* and the drunken delusions of the *Borracho*, Juan talks as he strolls with María, establishing the place of Spain in the fight taking hold of Europe. The topography of the war in Spain is superimposed with the streets of Paris, highlighting the common ground that the Spanish and French Republicans share as fascism advances; national history and personal history merge in Juan's memory of the recent past:

> *Juan*. I remember one night in Brunete when there was a moon just like tonight, I saw all this that surrounds us now. I was walking with you on my arm, just like now, and you put your head on my shoulder. [*María puts her head on Juan's shoulder; he puts his arm around her waist.*] María, where are we?
> *María*. In Brunete, Juan.
>
> (99–100)

This intimate moment in which María shares the space of Juan's memories of his fight in Spain ("As I lay there on the ground at night, as the bombing got worse, I told myself, as if on the edge of an abyss: You're here because you want to be; right now you could be at home, with María in your arms. But at that very moment I heard another voice, telling me I was right to be there" [97]) comes after his impassioned exhortation to María to listen to her own inner voice of moral certitude. He urges her to open her eyes and see clearly that the French nation cannot continue with its head in the sand, cowering behind a wall of fear: "The bad thing is you don't have faith. You want peace as a lesser evil, out of selfish convenience, out of fear. Your own complacency prevents you from seeing the world, you're shut inside of yourself. . . . You all will die in the tempest that your own cowardice has unleashed" (97). The personification of the Maginot Line in the figure of the dazed drunk closes act 2 by lending credence to Juan's words of warning to María.

The conclusion of part 1 in the same place where it began, back in the Ferrándiz apartment, enables the reader/spectator to appreciate the futility of a nation's efforts that originate without the impulse of solidarity with others, that act by doing nothing. France's self-serving, even morally corrupt actions are enacted by the character of Julio, who never makes a selfless gesture or commits an altruistic act for the good of another. Released from police custody the same day of the arrest, he retreats to the false haven of a home exposed in act 1 as a violated space invaded by nosy, gossiping neighbors who resent his successful immigrant status; by police who ruthlessly hunt down "enemies of the state"; by a half brother whose very presence reminds him of his adopted country's ugly treatment of foreigners and refugees. Julio's blind rejection of these truths in act 3 now approaches epic proportions. Back in his apartment, Julio identifies not with the other detainees held by the police, but with his captors: "They're not as bad as they seem, they have their reasons for what they do. They're well-mannered people, like you and me" (101). Instead of being moved to outrage by the affront to his personal liberty and civil rights, he is resolutely determined to retreat behind the walls of his small business: "To do my job and be left in peace" (106). When he hears gunshots fired in the street after Juan leaves the apartment, he refuses to go outside to assist his fugitive brother; he states impassively to María: "Whatever happens, there's nothing we can do. Why get involved? Don't you think I've been through enough?" (110).[12] Turning a deaf ear to the sound of violence that comes from beyond hearth and home, turning a blind eye to the injustices committed by the French government against its own citizens as well as refugees in the name of "law and order," does not however save Julio. His inaction, comparable to that of like-minded French citizens and officials denounced by so many Spanish Republican writers and supporters, leads to his own tragic fall by the end of the play.

The three acts of part 2 completely open up the world of the play to an international stage: act 1 takes place in the prison for political detainees housed in the Roland Garros Stadium of Paris; the first scene of act 2 takes place in a farmer's home along the route of the evacuation of Paris following Hitler's invasion; the second scene of act 2 and the entire act 3 are situated in the concentration camp of Vernet. In accordance with the transference of location from largely private spaces in part 1 to sites under the state's purview, the personal story of the Ferrándiz family becomes secondary to the larger drama of the men and women who were history's witnesses to the fall of France in June 1940 and to the fight for the Spanish Republic immediately before. The saga of the Ferrándiz brothers of course continues; the Cain-and-Abel pair meet again as prisoners first at Roland Garros and later in Vernet. Julio has an infamous reputation among his fellow camp internees as a hated *chivato*, a snitch who at the play's end betrays to the authorities even his own brother's plans to escape. The antagonist Julio himself falls victim to a bungled escape plot and is shot dead by a concentration camp guard in the closing moments of the last scene. But the true protagonists of the second half of the play are the inmates of the concentration camp, men from all over the world who have joined the fight against fascism and totalitarian systems of social injustice, and now languish in camps at the hands of the French government. Aub first introduces his audience to his large cast of players in the Paris prison of Roland Garros just as they are being prepared for transport to the camp at Vernet. His characters represent a wide array of nationalities united by a common fate, that of simply being "other," targeted as subversives or undesirables: the German antifascist writer Gerhard von Ruhn, who, as the Nazis approach Paris, cuts his own throat before being moved to the concentration camp;[13] the Spanish Republican and civil war fighter for liberty Villanueva, who laments the irony of his imprisonment in so-called free France; the Yugoslav national who has resided in France for the past forty years and fallen victim to a hysterical, anti-immigrant frenzy. The extent of France's chauvinism and vitriolic xenophobia, introduced in part 1 in the person of the racist, small-minded *portera*, is fully revealed by the end of this first act of part 2, complete with the devastating evidence of its harmful effects on humanity.

Before finally turning the dramatic spotlight onto the space of the concentration camp where these Roland Garros prisoners end up in act 3, the longest and most central section of the play, Aub first represents the collapse of Paris from the point of view not of foreigners, international refugees, or immigrants, but of the French people that the dramatist blames for the evacuation that he reenacts. In act 2, María and Juan's wife Emilia join the hordes of Parisians who flee the capital and seek refuge in a farmer's house. Here Aub stages a climactic scene, a dialogue between a Swedish antifascist exile, the painter Stroholm, and an officer of the French army, Lieutenant Bernard. The vehement condemnation of France's sorry state of affairs that has resulted in the nation's massive capitulation to the Nazis comes not from Stroholm, but Bernard; Aub makes his mouthpiece a Frenchman, "right-wing and Catholic" (144), so as to lend greater weight to the force of this criticism expressed from within the system itself. Aub's words in the *Teniente*'s mouth echo like a refrain the same fierce denouncements made by so many spokespeople for the Spanish Republican community in exile in Mexico. The body politic of France is described as an organism infested with a diseased growth: "France had a cancerous tumor and nobody knew, or rather, nobody wanted to know" (143). Recalling Bartolí's drawing of a nude French prostitute tacked onto the *Liberté, egalité, fra-*

ternité slogan inside the guards' quarters in *Campos de concentración*, Aub's Lieutenant curses the French leadership: "I'm talking about those who handed the French over, like a prostitute, for one dark night of peace" (144). He identifies as at least one of the reactionary French government's motivations for selling out to the fascists the excuse to no longer have to make concessions to the demonized working-class Left: "Truthfully, in spite of the stupefying surprise of defeat, for them it's not all bad, because they are lulled by the thought that strikes and paid vacations are over, now that the Left is crushed. . . . They prefer a humiliated France to a France that is more or less Socialist. So closed-minded about anything different from themselves. Social order first and foremost, and then and only then, all the rest. All because of the suicidal myopia of the politicians. They saw the specter of revolution in the smallest labor grievance, in any criticism. He's a red!, they would say, as if trying to associate the term with the fires of hell, with the devil himself" (144–45). The final accusation that the French officer lodges against his nation connects his fervent critique to the initial image of a complacent society that Aub had condemned in the first scenes in the Ferrándiz apartment; he damns a country that will sacrifice its ideals in the name of material gain and comfort, and that only acts when the latter is threatened: "We don't care about anything other than eating and drinking to our hearts' content—until we lose it" (146). Aub concludes the Lieutenant's tirade by focusing on the rapt attention given to it by María; she timidly approaches the speaker, but when he asks what she wants, she cannot say. María's experience of heightened political consciousness, first stimulated by the Spanish civil war fighter Juan in part 1, is encouraged in part 2 by none other than a fellow French compatriot who has finally begun to see the light himself.

The last scene before the climactic act 3 behind the barbed wire within the Vernet concentration camp moves the action to the fringes of the internees' world; the setting is the main administrative office of the camp, where the *chivato* Julio freely comes and goes. The purpose of this short scene is to lay the groundwork for the play's denouement. María has arrived to share with both Julio and Juan the details of her plan for their escape; she has bribed a guard with five hundred francs who will permit their flight from Vernet that very night, July 10, 1940. It is clear from the closing lines of the scene that Julio will betray his brother to the camp authorities: "Sergeant sir, please inform the commander that I want to speak with him as soon as possible. It is urgent" (156). The stage is now set for a rapid conclusion of dramatic events, and yet the last act is the very longest and most dynamic of the six acts. The final, culminating setting of the play is the camp: "The front of a cabin in the Vernet Concentration Camp"; the unlikely heroes of the act are a motley crew of ragged men: "Behind the barbed wire, in single file, the prisoners pass large stones down the row, from one hand to another, from right to left. They are dressed in rags, practically barefoot. . . ." (157). Among the internees we recognize the faces of the earlier prisoners from Paris and the non-French national evacuees from the farmhouse; now they are all joined together in forced labor. The first speakers who introduce the act are the painter Stroholm, the French lieutenant Bernard's Swedish interlocutor from act 2, and the Professor, a German antifascist first seen in Roland Garros. The absurdity of the fact that the French government, witness now to the invasion of the Nazis, has interned thousands of antifascists in concentration camps, is the opening commentary that frames act 3: "They've locked us up for defending what the Government that has arrested us is supposedly defending. They take revenge on us out of their own uncertainty, out of a lack of faith" (157). Foreshadowing the events of the climax, the camp's commander makes an appearance to warn the group that prisoners who try to escape will be shot. What follows this admonition, excepting the very final scenes, has nothing to do with advancing the story's plot. Instead, Aub turns the spotlight onto individual inmates, allowing the audience to catch snatches of conversation that illuminate various dimensions of life in the camps, of the ideals that guide the fighters' struggle, or of their memories of other places and dreams for the future. The dramatist Aub, interned in Vernet himself only a few years earlier, devotes most of act 3 to the creation of a series of tableaux that function like moving portraits taken from a memory album or a sketchbook of images. The parallels in theme and content between Aub's animated, theatrical tribute to the long-suffering inmates and Molins i Fábrega and Bartolí's text and illustrations of *Campos de concentración* are striking. Together these two artistic works published in Mexico in the same year, 1944, provide poignant documents of the earliest Spanish exile experience mired in the campgrounds and politics of France.

Aub stages an energetic, fluid sequence of dialogues among the prisoners who constantly pass to and fro onstage, as the directions explain: "The majority of the others begin to walk by in groups of two, three, or four. We will hear their conversations in succession as they appear from the right; other groups in the middle don't speak" (159). This technique—of recording a flow of voices, a stream of memories, oral snippets of testimony—is used as well in Aub's numerous short stories of the concentration camps.[14] Refusing to allow his audience to passively, voyeuristically detach itself from the spectacle of the camps, Aub fully implicates his spectators as witnesses to a historical reality (particularly in the year of publication, 1944) that must not be ignored. Throughout this entire sequence he places a character, El Internado (the Internee), facing toward the audience, looking out through the barbed-wire fence: "Standing at the far right, an internee holds on to the barbed wire; he stares vacantly out over the audience" (159). This mute witness forces the spectator to return his gaze, to see him because he never goes away, to ask the question: Why is he, why are they, there? El Internado himself bears witness to each and every scene and conversation that transpires (165, 166, 168), even though he is constantly threatened by the guards (A fellow inmate warns him, "Get away from there, if a guard sees you, he'll shave your head" [165]; the stubborn witness, we learn later when he removes his cap, is indeed "totally bald" [168]). Aub in turn records the history and tells the story that the silent Internado can't. In the drama, fragments of scenes and scraps of stories from the author's concentration camp past are re-presented, replayed onstage like the picture of memories focused through the mind's eye.

The vivid *cuadro de costumbres* that comes to life in the theater captures many of the same observations that inform the vignettes of *Campos de concentración*, especially the difficult living conditions: lack of food ("I tell you I got just three pieces of turnip and two slices of carrot" [165]); massive infestations of lice ("You have to conduct a scientific search: you start with the blankets, you continue with your clothes and you finish up with your underwear. Especially the seams; once you've done this six times a day, you cover yourself with naphthalene powder" [161]); the demoralizing burden of their own excrement (*"several internees go by, loaded down with huge vats; they can't manage them. The Guards that escort them give them a shove"* [162]). Both texts also share damning indictments of a corrupt French government. The embezzlement and theft by French camp officials of humanitarian aid (food, clothing, medicine) sent by various international relief agencies is one of the first topics of discussion introduced by two characters in the play:

> Loefel *[to his Companion]*. Out of the fifty cartons of bottles of milk sent by the Quakers, thirty-five have disappeared.
> *Companion.* Javier told me that the mobile guards that left last night took them.
> *Loefel.* And out of the one hundred pairs of sandals that the American Committee sent, they are going to hand out thirty, and just to the people picked by the barrack chiefs: guess where the rest of them will end up?
> (159)

Likewise, Molins i Fábrega's narrator sarcastically wonders what happened to the medicine promised by the ladies of the Red Cross: "The ladies of high society, with fear and loathing in their eyes and promises on their lips, may have ordered medicine that could've saved your lives.

In any event, the medicine never made it to your stinking sickbed. Did it get lost in a mix-up at the border? Did it get lost in the offices of your guards, perhaps ending up in the hands of unscrupulous pharmacists, in exchange for a few coins destined for idle pleasures? Unfathomable mystery!" (*Campos de concentración*, 91). The brutality and violence of the guards is, of course, a constant. In a scene with a single speaker, the Spanish Republican Villanueva, the murder of an inmate who attempts to escape is recounted to a small group of listeners: "Rodríguez died. They caught him three kilometers from here. A bullet in the belly" (*Morir*, 160). Bartolí depicts a similar moment; four fat guards, rifles still smoking, approach the cadaver of an escapee tangled in the barbed-wire fencing (*Campos de concentración*, 117). The accompanying text reads: "You dreamed of freedom; but you forgot about the angel of death who watches over your cemetery. The eyes of this night bird of prey discovered your plan. His poisoned arrow cut your life short, when you had almost managed to reach the light" (115). But the most egregious forms of corruption and brutality are those committed not by individual guards, but official programs fully sanctioned by the French government. The atrocities against Spanish Republicans and other war refugees interned in the labor camps and work prisons of the French Sahara are, not surprisingly, referred to by both Aub and Molins i Fábrega, each of whom was a survivor of the African camps.[15] One of Aub's most elderly characters obliquely recalls his recent internment in Africa: "I had to take refuge in Gibraltar. I was working on The Line. The Arabs were all over us, and wouldn't let us get out" (164). The references in *Campos de concentración*, on the other hand, are painstakingly detailed. The central motifs of Bartolí's illustration are the train tracks of the trans-Sahara railroad that the forced camp labor constructs, and the mercilessly blazing sun and equally fierce guards that torture the workers. The words of the text lament yet another exile cemetery on foreign soil: "Later, day after day, the slave paved the road of Commerce with the blood, sweat, and tears of his hide. Soon North and South would join hands over an enormous cemetery" (147). The French government responsible for this inhumane treatment of war refugees, notes one of Aub's Spanish exiles derisively, is the same that abandons its own capital to the Nazis without a flicker of resistance; the French, says Luis, are now themselves the most recent victims of their own weak-willed position of nonintervention: "How did you expect them to win a war they didn't want to fight? What happened is that as far as they're concerned, 'nonintervention' still continues. That's how they destroyed us and now they've destroyed themselves. Since the officers were fascists, and the people watched them imprison antifascists, what did you expect? They say that the Germans had 149 divisions, and the French had 110. Don't you think that should have been enough for the French to stand their ground and fight? If we . . ." (163–64).

The implied comparison that Luis makes between the French capitulation to fascism and the Spanish battle to the death against it ("If we . . .") is by now an easily recognizable contrastive pattern that assigns legitimacy, dignity, and honor to the Spanish Republic. As is so often the case in these early postwar texts, throughout the scenes of Aub's play the echoes of the Spanish Civil War reverberate in the space of the camp; memories of past bravery, camaraderie, and resistance nurture the spirit of the imprisoned exiles. The very first conversation that Aub introduces is between two civil war veterans, Luis and Villanueva, who remember vividly the events of August 1936; Villanueva remembers with satisfaction the fear that his troops inspired in the enemy, even when they were woefully underarmed: "We met up with the fascists. There were more than a thousand of us, with fifty rifles. . . . Later we heard that they came running into Granada shouting: 'Reds, reds!'" (159). Elsewhere a Belgian soldier from the International Brigade recalls wartime Spain as an idealized space of goodwill, vitality, and fraternity; in the monologue of his single appearance, the Belgian reminisces: "I've been to Indochina, India, all over the world. I just want to go back to Spain. To Almansa; the white-washed streets, the plaza. We were in uniform, and we said stuff to the girls. Until I went to Spain I didn't know what love was. Everywhere they make love, there they feel it. . . . *(He takes out a photograph; he stops)* See?, that's me. There they respect a man; now that was living . . ." (163).[16] Later, María is raped just outside the camp by the Sergeant she has bribed as part of the escape plot for Juan and Julio. The offstage act of violence is juxtaposed with the sounds of invisible camp inmates singing one of the most famous Republican civil war songs, "Ay Carmela." Despite the criminal actions associated with the camps, the lyrics of this anthem about the committed struggle against fascism suggests that the fighting spirit that sustained the Republicans through their war will not soon be broken.

The final scene of Aub's play focuses on the figure of María, symbolically violated by her own government, who now stands strong and firm in the face of the death and destruction that surrounds her. The body of her murdered husband Julio at her feet, she demonstrates that she has learned well the earlier lessons taught her by the Spanish war veteran Juan and the disillusioned French officer Lieutenant Bernard. Her eyes have been opened at last: "Traitors! Murderers! This is how you defend France! I also once believed this was the way and it's cost me my life. By keeping my eyes shut, I lived like a blind person, like a dead person" (177). María's enlightenment, and that of all of the brave sectors of France that emerge from behind the facade of the complicit government, will be responsible for that nation's rebirth. As María is being apprehended by camp guards to be herself interned, she raises her voice against her captors, in the name of her dead loved ones, "Your death will nurture a new France . . . !" (178). The play concludes as María tentatively begins to sing the French national anthem, "La Marseillaise"; immediately the heterogeneous group of camp inmates join her in a rousing refrain against tyranny. The well-known tune of this hymn, a favorite marching song of the soldiers of the International Brigades, is transferred out of the trenches of warfare in Spain and repositioned behind the barbed-wire lines of a new battleground. With their eyes wide open and their voices strong, the international mix of concentration camp internees sing out their shared commitment to the struggle against fascism as the curtain falls.[17]

5

Imagining Paris: Spanish Refugees Caught between the Camps and the Capital

> Me parece que cada ventana es un ojo, cada pared un oído. Cuando suena un timbre o se abre una puerta, pienso, sin remedio, en la policía.
>
> [I imagine that every window is an eye, every wall an ear. When a doorbell rings or a door opens, I can't help but think, it's the police.]
> —Max Aub's Berta Gross, *El rapto de Europa* (1946)

IN A LITTLE-KNOWN PROLOGUE TO THE *FALANGISTA* JOURNALIST Marcial Retuerto's 1941 collection of essays about the Spanish immigrant communities of Paris, *Cómo viven los españoles en París* (The Life of Spaniards in Paris), Gregorio Marañón writes an emotional meditation on the legacy of Spain's long history of war and exile. He laments the debilitating consequences for the nation of so many bloody cycles of internecine strife and subsequent displacement of large groups of Spanish citizens; each civil war throughout the ages, says Marañón, "ushers in the sad and sorry aftermath of emigration; a massive, all-too-familiar bloodletting that would deplete the reserves of a country even greater than ours. . . . Will this never end? Will this relentless flow of blood, this hemophilia on a national scale that periodically wastes the talents of Spain's best and brightest, ever cease?"[1] Referring sympathetically to the most recent massive exodus of Spanish civil war refugees, the author notes a distinctive feature that separates the experience of this group of exiles from that of their predecessors: "For the most part, the world lived in peace. One could work anywhere and it was almost feasible to be happy, even in another country. Compare that with the current situation of the concentration camps, whose tragic story will horrify the world when it is finally told. And it's not just the lack of monetary aid—that's the least of it!—but it's being watched by the police, occasionally being hunted down by them, always living in fear and on edge, this just exacerbates the exiled people's anguish and tragedy."[2]

Marañón's 1941 allusion to the world of Spanish refugees in Paris as a place of police persecution, a kind of first-stage stopover on the way to the concentration camps, drew a picture of reality initially unknown for the Spanish civil war immigrants. By and large, the earliest references to Paris written in 1939 by refugees who had never been there express a positive vision of the city not only for its reputation as a dynamically modern place, but by virtue of being the seat of relief agencies for the Republicans. In an April 4, 1939, diary entry written from her refugee center in Les Mages, Silvia Mistral writes that she has received a letter from Paris: "I try to imagine what such a city must be like with all of its sounds, its bright lights shining at night, the crowds and the cars." The letter informs her of a new development there, "the creation of a Relief Agency"; she immediately adds that all the women confined with her are certainly desperate to get out: "Hopes of getting out abound, but the truth is that time goes by and no one manages to get out of Les Mages."³ Elsewhere she states more categorically that although the desire for escape is all-encompassing in the refugee community, the chances of successfully eluding the French authorities and attaining liberty are minuscule: "Escape is impossible. You wouldn't get further than two or three stations without a proper passport. . . . Escapees from the concentration camps hide in local hotels, hotels whose doors you expect to fly open to the shouts of 'Police! Police . . . !'"⁴ One concentration camp inmate who dreams day and night of sneaking past the armed guards is Eulalio Ferrer; a diary entry dated July 5, 1939, indicates that the first stop on his way to freedom would be Paris: "Paris is our first destination. After that, the open sea. . . ."⁵ Throughout the summer months that he spends in the Argelès and Barcarès camps, Ferrer refers constantly in his diary to his plans for a Parisian adventure: "I don't hide my dream of going to Paris, a place of adventure full of attractions for me"; "I keep dreaming about Paris."⁶ Only when France teeters on the brink of world war with Germany do the hopeful images of Paris as a haven begin to disappear from his daily entries. On August 28, just days before Hitler's invasion of Poland and France's subsequent declaration of war on Germany, Ferrer writes that two new arrivals to his camp arrested and sent straight from Paris have given the "old timer" internees a discouraging report from Republican headquarters: "Panic has taken hold of the Spanish leaders and every one of them is worrying about how to get out of this rattrap that France has become."⁷

In the novels set in Paris written by Spanish exiles that I examine in this chapter (José Herrera Petere's 1940 *Niebla de cuernos*; Victoria Kent's 1947 *Cuatro años en París (1940–1944)*; and Manuel Benavides's 1942 *Los nuevos profetas*), the Spanish characters that emerge are constructed in such a way as to showcase a central fact: the true squalor of their times resides not in the dirty refugee camps of the so-called *rojos*, but rather in the corrupt ministerial offices, the brutal police jails, and the wealthy *salons* that line the sparkling streets of prewar Paris. These writers share a language in which the literary allusions to the concentration camp internees serve to encode in idealistic terms the *pueblo* of the Spanish Republic now in exile as the harbinger of passionate ideals, spiritual and moral fortitude, and indomitable resistance. By contrast, the world the authors observe in the renowned capital city, beginning in these early days of exile on the eve of France's declaration of war on Germany, is represented as a deceiving mirage of a civilized society. Despite its appearance as an urban oasis of tranquility and abundance, Paris is figured in these accounts as a spineless world on the brink of collapse, a self-deluded enclave on the verge of falling open to the outside forces of war, betrayed by cowardice and hypocrisy from within.

José Herrera Petere's *Niebla de Cuernos*

On May 10, 1940, the very day that the German campaign to advance against France began with the invasion of Belgium (the same date Max Aub chose to inaugurate the dramatic events of his play *Morir por cerrar los ojos*), José Herrera Petere (1909–77) published in Mexico his novelized account of a Spanish refugee's life in prewar Paris between February and September 1939, *Niebla de cuernos (Entreacto en Europa)*.[8] In his review of the work that appeared in *Letras de México* the following month, fellow exile Antonio Sánchez Barbudo refers to the "deceivingly tranquil situation" that the civil war veteran protagonist discovers in the famous French city: "*Niebla de cuernos* showcases Europe in the period following the Spanish war and prior to the current conflict. A series of sketchily developed scenes inscribed within the anguish of the void, an intimate look into a hidden catastrophe, unacknowledged and unexplored, is the basis of this book in which 'nothing happens.' Or almost nothing. Nothing visible, except for the empty-headed frivolity of a dense fog of horns [*de cuernos*, of cuckolds], since everything else takes place in the soul of a suffering, frightened, humiliated man. And preserved like a relic are the memory and the hope of one day clearly seeing a promised horizon, when the suffocating fog that makes the world banal, blind, and indifferent, is finally lifted."[9] Sánchez Barbudo alludes to the book's ironic evocation of the rarefied world of Paris between wars as a place where "nothing happens" as its defining feature. Indeed, the author José Herrera Petere, an officer in the Republican army (like his famous father, Gen. Emilio Herrera), member of the Spanish Communist Party and eventual internee in St.

Cyprien, places his unnamed narrator (likewise an ex-combatant who arrives in the city via the trenches of Spain and the concentration camps of France) in a series of opulently insulated Parisian settings in which the sounds of war are discernible only as the muted murmurs of idle party chitchat. The explosive events on the other side of the Pyrenees as well as Hitler's ominous military maneuvers on this side of Europe barely make a ripple in the superficially calm waters of the highbrow circles in which the Spanish protagonist moves. Throughout the novel the author plays with the contrast between the ugly "sound and fury," the strident, messy realities ushered in by the winds of war, and the carefully controlled, well-modulated tones of a superciliously polite society that refuses to speak the truth of war or turn their eyes toward the specter of violence that casts an increasingly long shadow on the venerated capital of culture. The novel is perhaps the first fictionalized depiction of 1939 Paris as seen through the eyes of a Spanish Republican; in the opinion of book reviewer Juan Rejano, writing in July 1940, the work incisively portrays "the moral landscape of France, clouded by betrayal" that stands in direct contrast with "the unflagging spirit, the renewed faith of the Spanish people, already thinking about the next battle from the throes of defeat."[10] *Niebla de cuernos* underscores a message that will be echoed in subsequent works by civil war exiles like Max Aub, Manuel Benavides, and Luis Suárez. Herrera Petere, who in a 1944 article presented himself by means of a sardonic reformulation of Cartesian ontology ("First I exist as an enraged, insatiable fighter. Then I think"), introduces the notion that the weary, ragged civil war refugees, specifically former or future inmates of French concentration camps, are in early 1939 the only Western Europeans capable of prophetically seeing the face of the future, the visage of world war hiding behind the mask and cloudy haze of business-as-usual: "With a real feline suspicion derived from combat, we the defeated, the hunted, the dishonored, observe the goings-on of life. We see the inner workings of things, the hidden machinery that manipulates the smiles and the stories in the press, from behind the scenes we see the schemes that launch battleships. We guess the meaning of the secret meetings of the gentlemen who smile on the outside and rage on the inside."[11]

The novel's opening sentence places the narrator in "a cold night in Paris," besieged by anguished memories of a home recently left behind, "I was writhing in pain at the memory of Spain's destruction" (9). The superimposition of the two topographical spaces of home and exile, of memory and lived reality, so characteristic of the literature of exile generally, sets up the jarring juxtaposition of the refugee's harrowing epic tragedy with the local's quotidian, soothing routines.[12] In one chapter after another, the author inserts his protagonist in an environment made surreal by its stubborn impenetrability to the horrors of warfare looming just outside the national borders. The first setting is a spectacularly lavish ball hosted at the castle home of a wealthy French friend, Jehoel du Bois Sanglant; the elegant halls are brimming with the rich and powerful, "English diplomats, ministers, bankers, high-ranking journalists and men of influence" (13), who are surrounded by gigantic papier-mâché masks of famous Frenchmen.[13] Stuffing themselves on fine food and eighty-year-old cognac, occasionally the partygoers take note of the ill-at-ease Spanish guest whose discomfited presence vaguely reminds them of something unpleasant. A journalist from a well-known news agency learns that the narrator is Spanish, and beats a hasty retreat away from him "as if he'd been told his house was on fire" (14). A French diplomat in Daladier's government makes polite conversation with the exile, incongruously offering touristic tips to the war refugee ("Paris . . . is very beautiful, people here really enjoy themselves; they have a great time. It's the city of lights, the city of joy and wit, of kindness and *esprit*. Have you seen the Tulleries?" [16]). With a voice thick with alcohol, this Antoin mumbles concern for his interlocutor's country before disappearing to the bar: "Ah yes, Spain! . . . I really love the Spanish people and I'm so sorry for what's happened to them. What a tragedy!" (16). When Hitler's name is invoked, it is merely to comment favorably on a recent headline about the Führer's upcoming writing projects: "Hitler's going to write about the will as the basis of social interactions. . . . He's got a point there. Don't you agree?" (19). Before leaving, the protagonist is introduced to an aristocratic Frenchman who is anxious to host the newcomer at his estate at Confilans de Sainte Honorine, certain that Spain's war will be a fascinating and entertaining luncheon party topic: "It would be a real pleasure if we could chat over lunch about the tragedy of Spain" (20).

Subsequent scenes reinforce the notion that these Parisians—of the Old World, old institutions, old money—believe they have the power to hold war at a safe distance, no matter what the cost. A studied facade of discreet decorum and the hushed tones of detached good manners meet the Spaniard wherever he goes. Even the sleek, shiny train that takes him to the country seems to mimic the maddeningly muted sounds of so-called "civilized" living: "a hushed train that didn't utter one word louder than another" (25). At a restaurant outside Paris, the narrator observes wealthy patrons who have come from far and wide to enjoy the establishment's star attraction, an orchestra expertly led by a Jewish German refugee. As the well-fed customers serenaded by Hitler's outcasts debate the quality of the condiments ("There's no smoother mustard anywhere" [29]), the Spaniard pensively chews on an empty cigarette holder "that he'd managed to rescue from the war in Spain," noting with irony that the surrounding countryside was the site of World War I battles: "How the artillery shells must have whistled through these places! They would've sounded like the long and deadly caresses of a *cocotte* or of a snake!" (31). These phantasms of war not only follow the protagonist wherever he goes, but will slowly encroach upon the Parisian environs whose inhabitants try so hard to remain blissfully oblivious to them. For now, the only sounds the narrator hears above the plaintive strains of the Jewish conductor's music ("It was like the protest of a great, embittered human heart, subjected to irreparable misfortunes . . ." [27]), are the sounds of silence: "No one objected, not a leaf, not a fly. You couldn't hear the roar of a cannon, nor the burst of machine-gun fire" (33). Later, at the pretentious country home of Camile Giroflax Saint Saens, the gentleman the narrator met at the party, the Spanish visitor gets a couple of perfunctory questions ("So you were actually in the war in Spain? [38]; "You say the war in Spain was a war of independence?" [41]), before the host, wife, and two grown children Renato and Ursulette distractedly drop the topic altogether. They live behind the four walls of their ostentatious home as if in a cocoon cushioned from unwelcome sights and sounds from the outside world. The guest is led into a cluttered *saloncito* "heavily draped with thick curtains" (37); the wife, son, and daughter are huddled together under a blanket, explaining that the heater is broken: "You must be surprised to see us so wrapped up" (37). Any allusion to violence, despite the narrator's repeatedly thwarted efforts during the meal to explain Spain's devastation and suffering at the hands of fascist invaders, is contained and controlled as aesthetic object in a gilded picture frame: "In the dining room I sat facing a portrait of a wild boar being attacked by several dogs, two of whom lay torn apart with their entrails exposed" (40). Reeling from the disconnection between his hosts' mindless chatter ("[Renato] is getting a job in a perfume company" [39]) and his own anguished thoughts ("Meanwhile in Spain, the blood of her young people was flowing freely. . . ." [42]), the dinner guest again resigns himself to silence: "Meanwhile, I ate politely in civilized society. And no one could fathom what I was going through" (43).

The turning point in the narrative is marked by the introduction at the novel's midpoint of one of the narrator's civil war companions, the crude and loutish Saturnino Fragoso, who, like Aub's Juan Ferrándiz, makes his way to Paris after escaping from a concentration camp. In contrast to the well-heeled, soft-spoken "group of empty suits" (85) of the capital whose haughty disdain and scornful dismissal of Spain's plight specifically, and world events generally, never ceases to amaze the refugee protagonist ("Must be nice not to know anything about anything!" [85]), Saturnino's coarse, earthy, and very vocal presence among the chic Parisian elite will be ignored with difficulty: "He was badly spoken, even more badly dressed, he bragged obnoxiously and did the grossest things in public. . . . He got worked up over the least thing, he smacked his lips when he chewed. . . . He was particularly infamous for making unbelievable grunting sounds like a pig which completely exasperated his listeners" (119, 120). The author represents Saturnino as the well-mannered protagonist's alter ego; whereas the narrator wonders if the gendarmes in the *Barrio Latino* can tell he's Spanish ("I had the feeling that everybody knew I was Spanish" [86]), the character Saturnino's refugee status is highlighted by his initial appearance in the foreign affairs division of Paris's police headquarters. Here in this austere official space, the dirty world of the French government's primitive concentration camps is mentioned for the very first time; the impatient police chief, surrounded by crowds of desperate Spanish refugees seeking documentation, shouts his orders: "Listen up, all of you: it's either the concentration camp or Franco! If you'd been braver, none of this would have happened to you!" (118). Unlike the self-conscious narrator who in the past has bitten his tongue to avoid screaming his impatience ("I clenched my teeth and stuffed my fists in my pockets. Tears sprang to my eyes" [47]), the uncouth Saturnino will make himself seen and heard in disquieting ways, forcing his French neighbors to acknowledge his disruptive proximity to them. He belligerently draws attention to himself in response to the police officer's disrespectful treatment of his fellow Spaniards: "Immediately he started to badmouth the chief of police, using words that were so foul it's impossible to record them. The least offensive were: *chulo, soplapitos* and *cabronazo*" (121). Upon presenting a letter of recommendation from an influential French society matron, the narrator obtains his and Saturnino's coveted *récépissé* that allows them to stay in Paris. Regardless of the narrator's powerful connections and the official documentation, however, both of these temporarily "legal aliens" straight out of Spain's death-filled trenches and France's inhumane concentration camps, continue to carry the marks of their political alterity through the streets of "gay Paris," embodying a threat to the "mindless *status quo*" (33) so jealously guarded by their French counterparts in the summer of 1939.

The second half of this novel reinforces the above-cited sense that "nothing's happening" by essentially redeploying the narrator's earlier movements at fancy parties, country estates, and luxurious banquets, repeated now in the company of the ill-spoken, unkempt Saturnino. The discrepancy between the sharp, painful immediacy of the refugees' experiences of war in Spain and the foggy-headed persistence of the Parisians' pursuit of pleasure and self-gratification is heightened by Saturnino's obnoxious presence in "polite" society. The two men celebrate receipt of their *récépissé* by feasting in a fine restaurant; Saturnino's stories of Spain (memories from his peasant childhood of the local *terrateniente*'s abuses; graphic details of the battle of Teruel), loudly recounted as he shovels in mouthfuls of mayonnaise, pollute the refined atmosphere of this exclusive eatery, off limits to "the vulgar newspapers" (124). The dreaded base realities of the outside world nonetheless materialize in the flesh-and-blood form of Saturnino; the outraged diners lament the invasion of Franco's outcasts: "Oh! . . . without a doubt they're Spanish refugees. . . . All of Paris is full of these good-for-nothings . . . you can't even go out anymore!" (128). On the very eve of France's entry into war with Germany, the narrator and Saturnino join the aristocrat Jehoel du Bois Sanglant and the latter's friends on a weekend excursion to his country estate. Surrounded by haughty blue bloods, Saturnino makes a fool of himself as he joins in the leisure activities (a jaunty game of tennis, horseback riding, an early morning hunt) of a landed gentleman. His relentless reminders of the world of war exasperate his host and fellow guests to the breaking point. In the chapter ironically entitled "Let's Enjoy Life," while the group relaxes with a particularly fine French wine brought directly by train from Bourdeaux, Saturnino embarks on a lengthy description of the battle of Ebro, an account that occupies almost half of the chapter. The civil war veteran recalls with expert attention to dramatic detail the audacity of the Republican offensive, the combatants' bravery despite their ill-equipped units, and the terrifying encounter with violence and death. Even as his bored listeners lose interest, Saturnino explains with powerful poignancy the simple heroism and shining spirit of the common soldier in battle: "What stands out at times like these isn't the tragedy, it's the joy, the simple things, the songs that people sing in these circumstances and the jokes that they still tell, or at least they did in Spain" (159).[14] His memories of the battle against fascism, like the narrator's own stories, clearly fall on deaf ears ("No one was listening to him anymore. . . ." [161]), but the sounds of France's own war will be in earshot soon enough. The narrator, when earlier confronted with his French interlocutors' uncomfortable mumblings of pity for what happened "over there," had thought to himself, "Don't cry for me, Frenchmen, cry for yourselves, for your women, for your children" (48). Now, as he and Saturnino prepare to leave the thoroughly unpleasant events of the strained weekend behind, the narrator summarizes the effect that they, like all Spanish refugees, have had on their European neighbors cowering for months on end at the prospect of war: "We Spaniards fear nothing, because we've lost everything. Survival is just a stroke of luck or comes through cowardice. That's how we came to watch the show with our eyes wide open, not like some dopey American tourist, but with a passionate, creative sense of vengeance. Europe has treated us like the scourge of the earth; we've provoked disgust and revulsion and even fear in European gentlemen" (185).

The last chapter of the novel, "Lost in the Fog," inaugurates a climactic scene that will play itself out time and again in subsequent texts that represent the war refugees' experiences in Paris during this period: police arrest and internment in France's concentration camps. The narrator refers to the outcome as an inevitable denouement, "eventually everything concluded in perfect synch with the times in which we live" (208). He recounts the final events that precede his return to the St. Cyprien concentration camp where he had escaped six months earlier, like a prelude to the Calvary: the police knock three times the first evening that they come for him; the narrator enjoys a ceremonious last supper before his ultimate arrest; a fellow exile reminds him that the recent sacrifice of democratic Spain will prepare the resurrection ("there will be a new resurrection, not of the flesh but of blood. And the color of blood is red, especially the blood of men who are thirty-three years old in every sense of the word" [212]); he remembers the camp that awaits him as the quintessential site of suffering: "One lost one's very identity as a human being as well as one's ideas. We had no voice, no knowledge of anything" (215). One thing the narrator and his fellow camp inmates do know is the precise moment that war finally comes for France: "We knew when war was declared because they put up electric fences for us" (215). From the punishing sidelines of the concentration camp, thousands of prophetic Spanish martyrs watch the spectacle of world war that blows over the Pyrenees into the rest of Europe: "Like dead men, like philosophers, millions of us young people watched the human tragedy, with the accursed knowledge of having seen it all before. The exiles keep quiet while the perennial loudmouths and speculators keep blathering on" (211–12).

The day the police came for the narrator, he bid an emotional farewell to Rochelle, the French laborer and ex-combatant in Spain's war who had housed the Spaniard in his Parisian flat. Rochelle's words of solidarity accompany the narrator into the concentration camp of Saint Cyprien: "Above all else, you mustn't lose hope" (214). The novel's narrator, along with the tens of thousands of Spanish refugees who remain in concentration camps when France wakes up to war, waits and hopes behind the barbed wire. The novel's author, now watching world events from the shores of Mexico, publishes *Niebla de cuernos* on the very day, May 10, 1940, that Hitler's army invades Belgium, initiating in earnest the offensive against France. The fog covering *la belle France* has been lifted; her myopic native sons can now clearly see her betrayal and realize that it is they who wear the horns.

5: IMAGINING PARIS

Remedios Varo's Portraits of Persecution

Just before the protagonist of *Niebla de cuernos* is arrested and returned to the camp of St. Cyprien ("I already knew that I was a goner and that nobody could liberate me from the concentration camp" [213]), he reflects on the fact that his status of Spanish refugee in Paris confers upon him a highly undesirable role in an anxious game of cat-and-mouse; the police circle his residence "with the certainty of a cat that plays with a rat" (210). One of Max Aub's characters of *El rapto de Europa* likewise refers to antifascist refugees as eventual captives in France's gigantic "mousetrap."[15] The notion that France's legendary beautiful city of lights has been transformed into a hunting ground for the "vermin" of Spain's refugees is represented by Spanish artists who themselves fell in the clutches of the French authorities. Josep Bartolí, longtime inmate of Argelès and illustrator of *Campos de concentración, 1939-194...* , shows a trio of images of Paris among the book's very few depictions of space beyond the barbed wire. In one of the two full-page references to the city, he focuses on the flight of a refugee, hotly pursued by a quartet of armed police mounted on bicycles. As the wheeled brigade overtakes its prey dashing toward the top of the frame, a frightened rat simultaneously darts down a hole in the bottom corner of the picture (57). A subsequent drawing, with the same Eiffel Tower in the background and the same brick pavement in the foreground, also shows four guards, now peering malevolently around the corner of a building; one hideous face cranes atop another to form a monstrous kind of totem pole. A half-opened window located above them reveals the object of their furtive search: the hiding place crammed full of the terrified faces of the hunted (95). If there was any doubt about the identity of the persecuted, Molins i Fábrega's two-line text dispels the uncertainty: *"Sale étranger! / Espagnol de merde!"* [Dirty foreigner! / Shitty Spaniard!].

The atmosphere of fear and dread that the *Campos de concentración* sketches evoke are replicated in selected paintings by Remedios Varo (1908–63), the Spanish émigré who lived in Paris and Marseilles until her 1941 voyage on the *Serpa Pinto* to Mexico. Varo, according to her biographer Janet Kaplan, had been able to arrange the release of her former husband Gerardo Lizarraga from a concentration camp after spotting his face purely by chance in a newsreel shot of Argelès-sur-Mer shown in a Parisian cinema. Later, she watched as her companion, the French surrealist poet Benjamin Péret, was arrested in Paris and taken away by a group of French police; once both were safely in Mexico, in 1942 Péret wrote of Varo's frightened state of mind: "I knew she was menaced both by internment in a French camp and by expulsion—

Paris 1939–1940 (Bartolí, *Campos de concentración*; permission for use granted by Bernice Bromberg de Bartolí)

which would have meant a concentration camp. I could not forget the expression of terrified distress which I had seen on her face when I left her, eight or ten days before in Paris. She was standing on the platform of the Gare Montparnasse when I, handcuffed and surrounded by an imposing escort of policemen, had boarded the train for Rennes."[16] He

Sale étranger! [Dirty Foreigner!] (Bartolí, *Campos de concentración*; permission for use granted by Bernice Bromberg de Bartolí)

remembers how much he hoped that his companion would stay "free, out of reach of the dastardly police."[17] According to her husband in Mexico Walter Gruen's 1966 recollection, Varo did not in fact escape arrest: "Remedios is imprisoned, possibly for having hidden a deserter from the French army. Very little is known about this unfortunate incident, because she never spoke about it. Paris is occupied by Hitler's troops. Péret and Remedios, like many other artists, flee to Marseilles...."[18] Varo may never have spoken or written about the years she and Péret spent running, hiding, and eventually falling into the hands of French authorities, but it is clear that the artist most certainly did document these days in her paintings. Just as Bartolí evoked the streets of Paris as peopled with ominous uniformed officials and half-hidden, panic-stricken faces, so too does Varo devote a series of her canvases to the portrayal of shadowy alleyways, darkened thresholds, and curtained windows; in each picture the same frightened figure of a woman with wide, startled eyes attempts to elude the grasping reach of the band of men who search for her. I include commentary of a series of Varo paintings below in order to argue that many of this well-known Spanish artist's paintings (completed during her long exile in Mexico City) in fact recreate the same Parisian milieu of persecuted Spanish refugees and the French police who pursue them that is found in the written testimony of the artist's Spanish compatriots. The Parisian police's frequent mode of locomotion, Bartolí's bicycle, is also ingeniously represented in paintings like Varo's *Locomoción capilar* (Hairy Locomotion), originally entitled *Detectives*. Three men in suits maneuver their own beards as wheeled contraptions that transport them into the path of the woman hiding around a corner; she in turn is captured by the flowing whiskers of a fourth man spying from a window above. Of the painting, Varo herself has written: "These men are detectives disguised so as to go unnoticed: their beards also serve as their means of locomotion. The man looking out the window uses his beard to kidnap the poor, frightened girl who is just around the corner" (*Remedios Varo*, 57).[19]

In the work aptly entitled *Angustia* (Anguish), another woman in another darkened corridor falls victim to a menacing band of winged insects who wrap her body in the strands of a tangled web that visually echo the threads of the hairy human captors (91). In *Caza nocturna* (Nocturnal Hunt), completed one year before *Locomoción capilar*, other flying creatures (owls this time) emerge from windows and doorways along a dark street; their larger-than-life cohort, a giant owl, wraps its prey within its cloak as the kicking legs and shoeless feet of an unseen woman flail beneath the folds of the fabric (154); the image recalls Silvia Mistral's recurring nightmare (cited in chapter 3), "I dream that I'm walking barefoot, that the black capes of the Civil Guards wrap me in their folds." In *Fenómeno* (Phenomenon), the woman fares better; watching furtively from the temporary safety of a curtained window, she observes a stern man in a suit who casts a realistically detailed shadow that inches its way ominously toward her hiding place (215).

In contrast to the dangerous public street scenes, other "memory portraits" completed during this same period of feverish artistic activity (especially the years 1958–60) show the solitary woman seated within the four walls of a private room, apparently seeking refuge from the outsiders' persistent pursuit and threatening vigilance. In the well-known painting *Mimetismo* (Mimetism), a Remedios lookalike seems to try to literally blend into the background; the skin of her face matches the fabric of the chair, and her own extremities have taken on the shape of the chair's arms and feet (189). By appropriating nature's weapon of self-protection against one's predators, this human chameleon (like her feline companion peering up from its hiding place beneath the floorboards) attempts to make herself invisible to outside attackers. A helpful matching chair in the background stealthily conceals in the wardrobe drawer potentially telltale signs capable of incriminating the woman to her enemies who may come for her at any time. The fear and anxiety of nervously waiting for the terrifying knock on the door, a terror widely shared according to European exile memoirists living in Paris during 1939–40, is powerfully expressed in Varo's *Presencia inquietante* (Unsettling Presence). Here in the same room as before—denoted by the same fleur-de-lis patterned chair, the woman's distinctive hairdo, and the jumble of threads that the woman creatively transforms in both paintings—the protagonist is haunted by a nightmarish feeling of dread. The spine-chilling sensation of doom is represented in the form of a horrible visage that ambushes her from within the very upholstery of the chair that had earlier camouflaged her; the mocking face announces its presence by licking the back of her neck in a repellent greeting (175). This foreboding of danger is realized in *Visita inesperada* (Unexpected Visitor). Here the woman appears again in a domestic interior scene (159). A candlelit table is set for two; the cat that keeps her company in so many scenes is at her feet. The now naked figure of the woman, which signals that unlike in *Mimetismo* she has been momentarily caught off guard with her defenses down, is shocked by the appearance of an extraordinary visitor; his arrival is heralded by a band of buzzing accomplices, identical to the flying insects of *Angustia*, who now seem to come out of the very woodwork. The man's partially visible face (reminiscent of that of the *Presencia inquietante*) hangs upside down inside a mobile unit on wheels whose ostentatiously plumed adornment would seem to denote that it has come for her in an official capacity. For support, the surprised woman tightly grasps behind her the hand of someone else sharing the space of either her room or of her memory. In Varo's commentary of this painting, she emphasizes the great fear of the woman: "This woman was expecting a guest, but not the one that has arrived, and she is quite terrified. Upon reaching behind her, probably in an attempt to elicit help, her wish comes true and a hand comes out of the wall, which she clasps in hers." In this version of the hapless woman who once again must confront unfriendly forces from the outside, Varo paints a fantasy of revenge; the lady who draws strength from contact with an invisible comrade harbors a secret weapon to punish unwanted intruders: "Underneath the table is a hidden pit where she usually casts her victims. But she can't throw this one into the pit, for he wouldn't even fit. The animal in the right foreground was made out of a bunch of leaves" (*Remedios Varo*, 57). The prescience of death (the dead leaves now covering the once safely hidden cat were blown in with the awful *visita*) is not easily held at bay. The fact that the unwelcome visitor could not be easily disposed of through a magical trapdoor perhaps explains the specter of its recurrence in the work painted one year later, *El visitante* (The Visitor). The same red apparatus trailing a beast's furled tail is, excepting its enlarged size, completely identical to the earlier one of *Visita inesperada*; both have swinging doors that open to reveal the spookily inverted face as well as a vase of flowers (164). Deceptively bearing gifts like a Trojan horse, the vehicle and its occupant are a reminder of life in Paris more than a decade before when police raids and armed roundups of "suspicious" foreigners ruled the times.

Victoria Kent's *Cuatro Años en Paris (1940–1944)*

A literary text that closely parallels the refugee world in Paris of fear and police persecution that Remedios Varo documents pictorially is *Cuatro años en París (1940–1944)* (Four Years in Paris) by Victoria Kent (1897–1987).[20] Kent's male protagonist Plácido (whose novelized voice in the first three sections gives way to the author's own autobiographical diary entries and essays in the last) opens the narrative from within the claustrophobic space of an apartment in Nazi-occupied Paris. In fact, the entire first part, aptly titled "The Four Walls (1940–1941)" is written as a kind of interior monologue comprised of this refugee's quasi-philosophical meditations on war and exile, solitude, struggle, and solidarity as he hides in virtually complete isolation for ten months behind barred doors. As a fugitive running from authorities with orders for his extradition back to Spain, Plácido is plagued by thoughts filled with vivid images of the hunter and the hunted; he succinctly summarizes the plight of the Spanish refugee in 1940: "The others, that's us, we are the undesirables, animals that are to be hunted down" (73). At one point anxiously believing he hears his persecutors on the other side of the door, he flings it open, hoping to put an end to the nerve-racking uncertainty once and for all: "He heard voices outside and he made up his mind to go out; he decided to be the one who would meet them face to face. He was ready. He opened the door. No one, no one was there. He had been ready to end the uncertainty, once and for all, no matter what unpleasant reality awaited him" (15). Plácido imagines the scene when a seven-man corps of military police did come for him, appearing in his mind's eye like a band of Remedios Varo's monstrous apparitions: "At dawn's first light seven rifles came through the door; fourteen arms, fourteen legs, seven bodies: not a single soul. They didn't find him; that night he hadn't slept there" (41). His self-imposed period of solitary confinement began then, a period of long days and nights when he thinks incessantly of his less fortunate fellow refugees who suffer in prisons and concentration camps, or worse, are deported to face certain death at the hands of Franco. A radio broadcast from Spain announces that two well-known Republicans, friends of his arrested during the same police sweep that he escaped, have been shot upon their return. A new breed of criminal, sanctioned by the state, crosses national borders to ferret out its defenseless prey: "This strange police force of the dictatorship that crosses the border in a sleeping-car, well-guarded by other police; they carry out their business in a foreign country, aided by their local counterparts that know the layout of the land. Then, under the shadow of darkness, everything is put into place to trap the individual who's leading a normal life; that's when they make their move" (54–55). The dreaded moment when this armed force moves in on its target plays itself out in Plácido's head like a shadowy scene of film noir: "They set a trap for a man in his pajamas or a woman in her nightgown. After the surprise passes, the man or the woman gets dressed in front of loved ones, they go down the stairs: two or three cars are waiting in the street. They get in and so begins the free ride of no return" (55).[21]

In part 2, "In the Street (1941–1942)," as the section header indicates, the protagonist begins to tentatively move out of the "four walls" and into a circumscribed perimeter of Occupied Paris. He observes that the French citizens themselves, who for so long were deaf, dumb, and blind to the rumblings of world war that first shook Spain, now share his own loss of liberty: "The others, the 'free' French, are more or less just like me: locked-up in this prison that Europe has become" (86–87). Later, the narrator will clarify that there are levels of oppression, and not everyone occupies the same circle of hell: "Yeah, sure, we're all prisoners, but there are prisoners, and then there are prisoners; there's a difference between the prisoner in solitary confinement and the one who can make chairs or sandals and plan his escape; there's a difference between the ones who can get around on bicycle taxis, and those who depend on the black market, who sleep in a different place every night, who flee even as they forget there's no escape, the ones who keep still because they know sooner or later they'll end up behind barbed wire . . ." (127). The spaces of greatest deprivation and oppression, according to Plácido, are not the streets or even the hiding places of Paris, but rather those venues of the refugee community inhabited by its most marginalized members: "It's happening everywhere: concentration camps, jails, deportations and the disappeared among the living. The same spectacle, the same anguish, the identical tragedy. In exile, the Spaniard is subjected physically as well as spiritually to all kinds of violent acts, to all kinds of outrage. In addition to the police pursuits and concentration camps, there are deportations, jobs in the mines of Bou-Erfa, which the locals want nothing to do with; and you can't forget the forced labor in the desert sands that builds the *transaharien*" (87–88). What is striking about Kent's enumeration of the sites of suffering and victimization of the Spanish *vencidos* in exile, a sorrowful litany centrally situated between the book's first section, "The Four Walls," and its last, "Towards Freedom," is that the invocation of these Republicans is used to make a powerful statement about hope and triumph. Immediately juxtaposed with the references to the miserable status of these dispossessed ("The Spanish refugee can hope for no relief during this war"; "we are cannon fodder" [88]), is Kent's assertion that her Republic's spirit of struggle and conviction of ideals are in fact most fully embodied in these mistreated and despised freedom fighters. In a rousing conclusion to this lengthy passage, Kent's words rise on an emotional crescendo: "We are now and always will be the enemy of all tyranny, because we are the fighters for a free Spain, because we are combatants left powerless by circumstances: because we are Spanish fighters, which means we are fighters full of faith and determination" (88).

The motif of Spanish Republicans' spiritual fortitude and political resistance in the face of overwhelming adversity and brutality in fact presents a unifying thread throughout Kent's text, which obliquely traces a parallel evolution of the French Resistance movement itself. Even from Plácido's impotent position as a wanted man initially hiding for almost a year in a locked room "in an empty city" (29), he still is able to affirm his belief that one must always be prepared to act. His French contact person with the outside world, El Encargado, expresses his own pessimistic views regarding the outcome of any organized French resistance to the German occupation troops: "Things get worse every day. Now they're talking about warrants for searches and arrests. Sure, there are people who refuse to turn themselves in, who won't give in. But they don't realize that there's nothing to be done against this kind of power. These guys are so strong, they can do anything. This country has been defeated, and they can do whatever they want with it" (43–44). The Spanish Civil War veteran vigorously disagrees: "I believe, and I've got reason to believe it, that every kind of abuse, every kind of violent attack may be possible, but you still have to defend yourself. Sitting back and doing nothing is simply unacceptable" (44). It is the sixty-year-old refugee living hand-to-mouth on the foreign soil of France who offers encouragement and comfort to his cowed protector: "I understand your fears, but I don't agree with you. Don't worry, there's always a way out; the world's a big place, even if it's full of barbed wire; let's keep hope alive" (45). Later in part 2, immediately following the aforementioned passionate speech on the refugee identity, Plácido notes with pleasure that the German barracks located near his own room have suffered a terrorist attack that has killed seven soldiers (91). In part 3, the circles of Paris he now moves in bring him together with members of the French Resistance, including a famous fighter pilot. Later, in part 4, "Towards Freedom (1943–1944)," the spotlight on heroic Resistance fighters is turned on Antonio Alfonso, a Spanish refugee who is executed for his subversive activities in the Movement: "The newspapers published photographs of the condemned men before they were taken before the firing squad: the only one who calmly smiled was Alfonso. I must admit that the newspaper that day did him justice with its commentary: 'They are all defeated. The only one who looks calm, who even smiles, is Alfonso'" (151–52).

Elsewhere, with similar motives of connecting Republican Spain's ongoing struggle with the one now waged by its sister nation, the narrator cites in its entirety a 1943 letter written to Marshal Pétain by a group of French students from the University of Paris. After more than two years of living in a country occupied by Nazi Germany, these students state unequivocally to the leader of Vichy France that they will no longer keep silent about the betrayal of the French people. They vigorously denounce the forced deportation of thousands of French workers to Germany and speak up in solidarity with their working-class brothers: "Because we are willing to share the fate of our deported brothers, because we are determined not to abandon the cause of the doomed French nation, we feel free to proclaim to our country and to the world what we students of the University of Paris and the *Grandes Escuelas* have silently been thinking for some time now" (121). Most significantly, the protesters recognize with deep admiration the efforts of their fellow patriots who have been active in the Resistance and announce their plans to join the fight: "There are plenty of woods and mountains to hide us as we wait for the future time when we will take our place in the French liberation army. Those of us who can, will not hesitate to join forces with the leaders of the resistance movement of our France, leaders who deserve our gratitude and faith for their role in this resistance" (122). The young intellectuals sign off their lengthy document by linking their committed struggle for freedom with that undertaken by other student activists far and wide: "We will fight, we will suffer, thinking of our heroic brothers at the universities of Prague and Varsovia, of Belgrade and Ljubliana, of Oxford and Cambridge, Harvard and Montreal, Lovaina and Leyde, we will fight for the triumph of our common ideals of humanity and Christianity" (123). The Spanish narrator, while praising the letter writers' idealistic fervor and enthusiasm, takes them to task for omitting mention of the University of Madrid students who already seven years earlier had left their classrooms and joined the trenches as their campus was literally transformed into the front lines of the war against fascism, "They were the first heroes who came to the defense of the common ideals of freedom and justice, who paved the way for all the intellectuals of this war. It's time to realize that totalitarianism's campaign against freedom began in Spain, that our war, which for some was just a civil war, *was the beginning of this war*, that it represented the resistance to the mandates and the power of totalitarian states" (124; emphasis in the original).

In the fourth and final section, "Towards Freedom," Kent drops the use of her male protagonist Plácido, a literary masking device that Shirley Mangini has compared to Kent's recourse to a real-life disguise as "Madame Duval" during her own years in hiding.[22] But the new first-person narrator similarly champions the exemplary actions of sacrifice and courage performed by the Spanish refugees who continue to wage war in France. In yet another significant passage about what it means to be a Spanish refugee in France during the world war, Kent is careful to assign subjectivity and purposeful agency to her fellow Republicans. She rejects group labels like "emigrant" or "exiles" in favor of a term that denotes a more decisive and proactive assumption of the refugee status, *"renunciadores."* Kent's notion of the Republicans' "emigration" is not predicated first and foremost on a sense of loss and a search for comfort, but rather in terms of the journey's guiding ideological objective, the moral values for which the odyssey of sacrifice was undertaken. For the Republicans, says Kent, all roads out of Spain are traveled for freedom's sake:

> We aren't emigrants, we aren't the children of a poverty-stricken country that can't support us, we didn't leave Spain looking for sanctuary, a shelter that we knew we otherwise couldn't have. We are *renunciadores* [the ones

who said no]. We said no to material possessions in order to play a part in a struggle of a higher order, in freedom's crusade. This story must be told, because only by telling it over and over can we Spaniards take the credit that we deserve. A refugee is not a man who crosses the border and joins another country's army in order to continue the fight for freedom. There are already Spaniards buried in many lands where the fight for freedom continues; they are buried in France, in the desert sands of Africa, in the camps of Germany, they died fighting for France's freedom, because the freedom of France was their own. Wherever there's a struggle for liberty, Spaniards will be there: Freedom is the only right we did not renounce, because for a Spaniard, freedom and life itself are one and the same thing. (150)

The last view of Paris in Kent's book belongs to the eve of the Allied liberation of the city in the last days of August 1944. The narrator's voice, once heard as whispers and murmurs "behind four walls" in part 1, now shouts gleefully from a bicycle shooting through the streets of the city. The narrator hails her male alter ego, Plácido ("Ride, ride with me on the bicycle, let's take a spin for freedom" [181]) and the two join forces for a joyride along the avenues that once only housed a primitive fear, "that fear of death, fear of my death, of my imminent death just like the others who fell during those times" (182). Word that the Allies are just days away from entering the Champs-Élysées has transformed the sight of the city sprawled before the narrator: "Isn't Paris gorgeous? Paris is so beautiful when freedom is in the air" (184). The only thing that could make the breathtaking view of liberty more splendid is the final scene that unfolds on August 26, the day of the liberation of Paris. Spanish Republican volunteers in the Leclerc Division's tank squadron, each vehicle adorned with the tricolored Spanish Republican flag and named for a famous civil war battle ("'Guadalajara,' 'Teruel,' and they're the first to parade down the great avenue" [189]), usher in at least one country's long-awaited freedom: "Paris applauds them. Paris appalauds the Spaniards who have weathered a nine-year battle, and who today smile upon the liberated nation. Paris applauds the heroic Spain of yesterday, the strong, free, and democratic Spain of tomorrow. It's like a dream. . . . It's like a dream" (189).[23]

Manuel Benavides's *Los Nuevos Profetas* (1942)

The surrealist painter Dorothea Tanning has recorded her impressions of prewar Paris in a 1979 reminiscence: "July 1939, Paris, France. Gay Paris? A city paralyzed by anxiety, almost empty, breathing painfully before the imminence of war."[24] Victoria Kent noted that "secrecy, isolation, and camouflage" (*Cuatro años*, 109) were the order of the day, especially if one were so unfortunate as to be a refugee fleeing fascism's advance through Europe. For a cowed government motivated either by the dread of provoking Hitler's ire, the search for an easy political scapegoat, or by a pathological suspicion of all members of the Left following the Soviet Union's August 1939 pact with Germany, such foreigners seeking haven in Paris were preferably kept under police surveillance or forced into prisons. Therefore, as Kent's narrator counsels in *Cuatro años en París*, in this paranoid, xenophobic environment, the émigré had best disguise his or her otherness, and try, however futilely, to blend in with the natives: "If you don't want to raise suspicions, don't dare offer your opinion about the most trivial matters, because the person in front of you, who's checking you out, isn't like you, he's on the other side, and your difference, if it's noticeable, is suspicious. It's an asphyxiating atmosphere for you, but for 'them' it's perfect. You should take a deep breath, fight off nausea and ... put a good face on it. Try to look like them: you have no legal rights, no country, no home" (72–73). Other foreigners residing in Paris on the eve of war and immediately following France's September declaration against Germany have documented the underworld of persecuted refugees who inevitably ended up together in police custody. The Hungarian journalist Arthur Koestler as well as the German writer Gustav Regler (who had each spent extended periods of time in Spain during the civil war, and likewise coincided in the notorious concentration camp of Vernet crammed with Spanish refugees) report strikingly similar experiences. Each remembers with precise detail the exact moment when the police came for them. In his 1941 work *Scum of the Earth*, Koestler writes of the "tide of Xenophobia [that] swept over France with morbid rapidity" in 1939, and that branded each foreigner in its path with the searing epithet *sale meteque*. Expecting every night to hear "the police ringing at the door of my flat," Koestler recalls when the fateful moment finally arrived: "I was sitting in the bathtub when they rang at my door on October 2nd, 1939." Initially held at the Salle Lépine police station, Koestler shortly joins the ranks of what France now deems the dregs of society: "But the majority, like Poddach and the Polish woman and myself, had been through prisons and concentration camps in Germany, Italy, Eastern Europe, or Spain. We had been defeated partly by our own fault, partly because the Powers who should have been our natural allies had abandoned and betrayed us. A few years ago we had been called the martyrs of Fascist barbarism, pioneers in the fight for civilization, defenders of liberty, and what not; the Press and statesmen of the West had made rather a fuss about us, probably to drown the voice of their bad conscience. Now we had become the scum of the earth."[25] The company Koestler keeps in the Vernet camp represents a kind of

League of Nations of the Persecuted: "Each of us carried a weight in his memory to put in the Past scale of the balance and lift the Present scale. Yankel carried the weight of his two pogroms and the prison in Lubliana, where people were made to talk by introducing rubber tubes into their nostrils and pouring water through them; Mario had the weight of his nine years of prison in Italy, including torture by electric shocks during the preliminary investigation; Tamás, the Hungarian poet, had his three years of hard labour in Szeged—to quote only my three immediate neighbours in Hutment No. 34 in Le Vernet. The fourth one, myself, had his 100 days under sentence of death in Seville."[26] Gustav Regler traces a similar trajectory in his autobiography *The Owl of Minerva*, remarking in fact of his encounter with Koestler at the Roland Garros sports stadium where hundreds of detainees were corralled. His saga of arrest in Paris and internment in Vernet is chronicled in the chapter aptly titled "The Undesirables," and follows the events of early September 1939 that ensue after his arrest, one day after he volunteered for the French army: "Fourteen hours later, at exactly six o'clock in the morning, six *agents de police* burst open the door of my flat. The night had been hot, and I confronted their pistols stark naked."[27] Soon he counts himself among the masses of international émigrés who have been swept into the concentration camp of Vernet on the wave of hysteria and paranoia that passed through France: "The first (and, as the event was to prove, the only) prisoners-of-war of the French Republic were now safely behind barbed wire. They amounted to 560 fugitives from every country in Europe. For years they had found asylum in Paris; their shelter now was a collection of ramshackle wood huts at the foot of the Pyrenees, without beds, without light and without heating. There were possibly a few dozen profiteers among the prisoners, as well as the full strength of the central Committee of the German Communist Party; but the great majority was composed of opponents of the Third Reich. Not a single National Socialist [Nazi Party] had been arrested, or any Italian Fascist. Many carried papers showing that they had reported for service with the French Army. We lay on planks and were forgotten."[28] According to a March 1940 notice entitled "The Plight of Some Intellectuals" published in the exile journal *Romance* in Mexico City, Regler was fortunately not forgotten among the Spanish Republican exiles; the journal's editors publicized the plight of Regler for their readership, and even included a mailing address: "The Germans, without exception, are in the French concentration camps. Among the prisoners are some famous émigrés of Hitler's Germany, writers and professors, including: GUSTAVO REGLER, in the camp of Vernet, Section C, Barrack 33, Work Company (Ariège). He is sick and still suffers from injuries sustained in the Spanish war."[29]

The world of the war-weary refugee in Paris at one remove from the concentration camp, as described by writers like Max Aub, Regler, and Koestler, is also evoked in the 1942 novel published in Mexico by Spanish exile Manuel Benavides (1895–1947), *Los nuevos profetas* (The New Prophets). The novel's central characters belong to a self-proclaimed group, "The enemies of the Empire," comprised largely of antifascist activists who have fled to Paris to escape their home countries ravaged by war or oppression. The eight members include among others Napoleón Jaroslaw, a Polish veteran of Spain's International Brigades, the Spanish Republican refugee Carlos Játiva, German and Czech antifascists, a Chinese nationalist; a liberal Belgian priest. Luis Alfonso Richard, the French protagonist with family ties to Spain, remarks wryly: "We all formed part of the scum of the universe. My best friends!"[30] The novel's tripartite structure places Luis Alfonso, the initially abulic Frenchman whose political apathy mirrors Mother France's, at the center of the key historical events that precede the outbreak of World War II in September 1939. Part 1, "Madame Europa," introduces the eponymous allegorical character to Richard, who both anemically watch the evolution of Spain's Civil War, largely from behind the safety of the Pyrenees. In part 2, "The Enemies of the Empire," Richard meets the band of international refugees whose frequent and spirited *tertulias* serve to educate the Frenchman about his mother's native land, Spain. Their discussions of Republican politics and war within the context of a wider European arena make clear just how tightly France's and England's own destinies are joined to Republican Spain's. But as the empires' enemies observe, those two countries' failure to intervene with military aid as the moribund Republic's civilians and troops flee across the border, seals the fate of that nation; one of the refugees explains, beginning by sarcastically mimicking the tone of the reactionary French press, "'And the red thieves, the red murderers, the red cowards disappeared in the concentration camps'.... At that precise moment, France and England landed on the German bayonets. They were doomed.... They needed to understand. And they did not" (202). Part 3, "The Great Experience," includes the events from the outbreak of war in France until the fall of Paris in June 1940 and describes the now-familiar police *razzias* and the atmosphere of betrayal, repression, and fear that they engender. In fact, in the opening pages of the first chapter of this section, the Polish expatriate Jaroslaw is arrested in September 1939 and dies shortly afterward in police custody; the narrator refers to the tragedy as a senseless death in a city gone mad: "The police never explained why they arrested Jaroslaw nor why they beat the life out of him instead of getting the information they wanted out of him" (254).

The notion suggested earlier by writers like Herrera Petere, Kent,

Regler, and Koestler—that for the foreigner, all roads out of Paris in 1939 lead directly to the concentration camp—is expressed as well by Benavides. In the second chapter of part 3, the Spaniard Carlos Játiva is forced into the camp of Argelès-sur-Mer following a formal complaint that he lodged against the police for the death of his friend Jaroslaw. The author precedes the narration of Játiva's Calvary in the camp at the beginning of chapter 2 with the text of a damning letter brimming with black humor written by Jaroslaw just before his death, an unsent missive that Játiva reads at the conclusion of chapter 1. Jaroslaw had written to the director of the La Haya Zoo, which apparently had agreed to provide safe haven for animals from zoos threatened by war's violence or privation. In the letter, Jaroslaw (who already has friends who did not survive police custody) begs for himself and his Spanish wife Emilia to be admitted: "Your hospitality is of great personal interest to me. These days, a cage is nothing to turn your nose up at" (267).[31] He goes on to say that he realizes that such a deal with the zoo would require that he and his wife provide the same spectacle of exoticism and fiery savagery expected of the zoo's animal residents. The civil war veteran assures the director that given the widespread notoriety in France of the *rojo*'s monstrous and primitive ferocity ("the Spanish Red is still a rare specimen of ferocity" [267]), that their public exhibition behind bars would be sure to be a crowd pleaser, "a sensational attraction" (268). He promises that both he and his wife are prepared to earn their keep, to literally sing for their supper: "For my part, I can imitate pretty accurately the sounds of certain animals. As for my wife, I'm sure she'll be a big hit. Ever since a fascist bomb decapitated the child she was carrying in her arms, she erupts into superhuman shrieks every day at sunset, like clockwork" (268). The only stipulation that Jaroslaw makes is that he and his wife be placed in the same cage, or at least in contiguous cages; such a request perhaps would have been granted in the zoo of La Haya, though it was certainly denied in concentration camps like Argelès-sur-Mer.

In the concentration camp, Carlos Játiva finds that the French authorities themselves have provided a caged space where new arrivals and visitors alike can witness the spectacle made of the Spanish *rojos*; the chapter's opening sentence introduces the inhabitants of Argelès as nervously pacing zoo animals that have come to life: "Guys on the loose paced back and forth; these were no stuffed animals" (269). Inside one of the smelly *barracas* strewn with straw like a lion's cage, Játiva makes out the shapes of the human inhabitants, half hidden in the shadows, "they were on the straw, dark and hard to make out" (269). One of the men crouches in a corner, mumbling to himself as he contemplates the fleas on his body like a curious chimpanzee: "'They bite you. . . . They don't bite. . . . It doesn't matter if you scratch or you don't" (270). Outside, a band of four or five inmates scuffle on the sand, snarling at one another like a pack of wolves, providing instant entertainment for their desperately bored fellow creatures. When the inmates learn of the circumstances of Játiva's arrest, they jokingly refer to his capture as if occasioned by foolishly falling in a trap laid by big-game hunters: "'My friends,' said one of them, 'it's my pleasure to introduce you to a fool.' Játiva stepped out. 'You fell in the trap,' they shouted. 'They got you' (270). Later, befriended by a fellow academic-inmate, Professor Ortiz, Játiva makes the rounds with his self-appointed *cicerone*, observing the strange world of this particular concentration camp where in September 1939 thirty thousand Spanish Republicans still live like animals. He is introduced to a father-and-son team, the Olots, who furtively gulp down food while buried under their blankets like mangy dogs with a bone, to avoid sharing their stash with others. Játiva begins his miserable first night with a flea infestation and ends it with a dogfight when his sleepless stumbling through the camp wakes another inmate; the two men viciously fall upon one another: "They hit each other over and over. With fists flailing . . . Játiva fell beneath his adversary. He covered his face. His enemy's fingers relaxed their grip around his throat" (276). His tour of the beach the next morning includes the sight of an inmate sprawled out in the sun, naked as a jaybird, methodically picking fleas. The guide Ortiz takes care to point out this man ("Notice the calm demeanor with which our fellow man down on his luck cleans his private parts" [279]), explaining that such exhibitions are particular favorites with visiting locals: "You just can't imagine how the girls around here love to come down to the barbed wire on Sunday mornings and how fond they are of seeing the Reds naked!" (280).

Játiva is overwhelmed by the enormity of the process of dehumanization to which his fellow Republicans have been subjected by the French authorities: "Thousands and thousands of refugees suffered under the whip of the French authorities. The enemy was all over the Red in order to steal his valuables; they stuck *spahis* on horseback in front of him and trained their machine-guns on him; spy planes flew overhead. . . . Little by little, they took away his few material possessions, things that man has fought for since prehistoric times: clothing and food" (278–79). In a delirium of insomnia that first evening, as the winds of world war swept through France, Játiva had heard in the fierce roar of the gale-force *mistral* the outside world's merciless message sent in to the inmates, "You could hear the sounds of a hundred machine-guns, then cannonfire, and the ghosts of Europe, with insinuating sarcasm, attacked the vanquished: 'Die, Reds! . . . Go to hell, Reds! . . . You are screwed, Reds! . . . Fuck you, Reds!'" (274–75). It is left to his sagacious escort Ortiz to show him that the first impression of the refugees' passivity, impotence, and defeat is deceiving; in fact, the same fighting spirit that brought the Spaniards to exile in the first place is still discernible in the sandpit of the concentration camp. Ortiz regales Játiva with a tale plucked from Argelès's book of fables, a story of action and revenge of mythical proportions that the professor retells as God's own truth. Word spreads that *franquistas*, suspected spies and camp informants, were preparing to leave the camp when they were overcome by a powerful, punishing force: "Somebody said: 'Some Francoists are going to come by here.' And the people got moving. Hundreds gathered. Thousands joined them. . . . One man on horseback and four on foot were headed toward the barbed wire. Slowly, the crowd came towards them. No one ran away. No one struck the first blow. The great multitude of thousands mowed them down, crushed them, scattering their body parts, their clothing . . . and in their wake didn't leave a drop of blood. There were no screams, or if there were, no one heard them" (272). Later, Játiva watches as Ortiz transforms the sand of the camp into the sacred soil of commemoration and memory. He conducts a memorial for a deceased comrade, his disciple Antonio Hernández, who saved the professor's life during the war and then died in his arms of typhoid in Argelès. Calling his friend's name out over the breaking waves from the shores of exile, Ortiz performs a nightly ritual in which he fulfills a promise to his fellow refugee Hernández not to forget him, to inscribe his individual life within the larger history of his nation: "Antonio Hernández, from Burguillo del Cerro—I told him—, you can't die. On your eighteen-year-old shoulders you've carried the burden of the whole history of Spain and you've earned fame and eternal life. . . . You can't die, Antonio Hernández, de Burguillo del Cerro!" (273). Játiva asks if he may join his new friend in memory's simple ceremony, and their two voices unite in a shared elegiac cry for one of the Republic's own ("¡Antonio Hernández! . . . ¡Antonio Hernández! . . ." [274]), who fought on the battlegrounds of Spain and fell in the campgrounds of France.[32]

The ongoing guided tour includes overhearing heated political debates ("'He's a cocksucker.' 'And Largo Caballero?' 'Another cocksucker.' 'And Prieto?' 'He's as bad as Largo.' 'So, what were you fighting for for three years?' 'I'll be damned. Why do you think? . . . Because I'm a cocksucker too,'" [278]) and concludes in front of a veritable museum piece, which Ortiz wryly deems the most perfectly subversive exhibit that the concentration camp internees have produced so far, *la muralla de la mierda*. Here along the beach, in lieu of latrines, the inmates use fourteen kilometers of open sand for evacuation purposes, which the civil war veterans have carefully baptized in honor of the

European "non-intervention" politicians who have helped get them where they are today: "The wall of shit! . . . That is, my friend, the Red's eloquent response to the Pharisees who betrayed him. Here begins the dividing line that separates us from the West's infamy. Behind it, we preserve our honor and our purity. . . . Close to 300,000 rearends have given their all to erect this hygienic cordon, that has become the kingdom and the glory of shit. The first kilometer is named 'Daladier Avenue,' the second is 'Chamberlain Avenue,' and then there's 'Blum Avenue,' 'Imperial Avenue,' 'Pétain Avenue' . . ." (280). Deprived of political power but not of political expression, the Spanish Republicans have left an eloquent manifesto written without words: "It was built with enormous patience and methodical efforts, and it doesn't need linguistic crutches to tell us the story of its meaning and majesty" (280). Before Játiva is released from this barbed-wire hellhole and returned to Paris, Ortiz has demonstrated to him that the passions of Republicans, vital life forces spoken through the debased body as well as through ragged emotions, continue in spite of the French government's best efforts to control their strength like caged zoo animals: "The republicans were still fighting. They hadn't lost heart; they kept going. It would be worse if they didn't scuffle, if they weren't full of rage, if they didn't insult one another, if they acted like some obscure group of defeated emigrants, locked in their own silence, resting their heads on the bars of the cage like bears in the zoo" (279).

In a pattern reminiscent of both Luis Rodríguez's *Ballet de sangre* and Max Aub's *Morir por cerrar los ojos*, Benavides uses his extended reference to the concentration camps in order to lay the groundwork for his contrastive representation of the Spanish Republicans' passionate, committed fight for freedom on the one hand, and of the anemic response to fascism's advance exhibited by official France on the other. In the chapter that preceded Játiva's illuminating five-day internment in Argelès-sur-Mer, the city of Paris, whose native sons had just declared war, was described as a soulless space bereft of courage and spirit: "There were no songs. No one sang. What can become of men, how can you ask them to fight, if they are sent into battle with no songs? Without song, there is no hope. And without hope, man becomes a ghost. And that's how the war in France began, as a war of ghosts" (253). In the chapter that returns Játiva to Paris, the narrator indicates that nothing has changed in the empty heart of the capital except for perhaps the government's stepped-up efforts to chase down members of the Left, both foreign and domestic: "The only living things in France were the guards and the Reds. The guard chased the Red, he shut down his meeting places, he got rid of his local leaders, he put a stop to his newspapers and continued to sow seeds of conflict among the French people. That's how he treated the local Reds. The foreign Red was simply a hunted animal who had to protect himself by wearing a gas mask disguise" (284). In view of France's apparent lack both of conviction of political ideals and of faith in the French people, states Benavides's narrator, the Spanish refugees of the concentration camps feel a moral confidence that lifts them above the authorities who may imprison them, but who certainly seem incapable of facing down the real enemy: "In spite of their gloomy prospects, the refugees in the camps had little regard for anyone who hadn't fought for the Republic, and even overwhelmed as they were by a sense of their own helplessness, their confidence in their cause comforted them, and lent them a feeling of moral superiority over those who had failed to recognize the Republican truths of Spain's war. The specter of the Spanish war confused these people, they didn't trust the refugees, who despite their despair, never lost their heads. They had found in their war . . . more political sustenance than they had in all of the leaders of the democratic nations" (304–5). An almost unanimously shared feature in the literature written by civil war refugees, who watch as world war entangles the European "Non-Interventionist" nations like France, is the irrepressible urge to shout "We told you so!" as the German army moves forward. Even before his own incarceration, Carlos Játiva had shared with his fellow *enemies of the Empire* what the "new prophets" of our times, the Spanish Republicans in exile, were thinking behind the barbed wire in August 1939: "The Spaniards in the concentration camps rubbed their hands in glee. . . . 'Now the democracies will get what's coming to them' they say" (247). In a satisfyingly ironic instance of role reversal, the narrator describes the same scene of mass exodus out of Paris that both Max Aub and Luis Rodríguez referenced in their respective works. Benavides's narrator explains that a certain militarized fortification contingent comprised largely of foreign conscripts, especially Spaniards pulled from concentration camps, was charged with containing deserters from the French army who cowardly fled with civilians from Paris along the evacuation routes southward: "The Spaniards got down to business, they let the soldiers go by but they came to blows with the commanders and the officers. They had learned to say *Allez!* and they were quick to use that word and to pummel the faces of these men eaten up with dishonor, who had betrayed their own people" (338). Certain witnesses interned in concentration camps, not so very far from where French tourists used to watch the spectacle of Spain's war ("Hendaye thrived with the new tourism. . . . The taxi-drivers shouted: 'Twenty francs round-trip to Biriatou! . . . Come see the savage battles of Irún! . . . Twenty-five francs includes binoculars'" [338]), vicariously experience the frightened retreat as déjà vu: "From the other side of the barbed-wire fence in the concentration camps, the prophets saw their prophecy come true. The Spanish-speakers had announced, as the Furies let loose, what the Furies would do, and they had predicted for other nations the same exodus that they themselves had initiated" (338).

The novel ends as Paris falls to Nazi Germany. In a symbolically laden twist of plot, the French protagonist Luis Alfonso Richard has married the International Brigades veteran Jaroslaw's widow, the Spanish Republican Emilia, and waits for the imminent birth of their child. The family will welcome the new life that will join them from the grounds of their French country home. They will not flee the advancing army, but stay and resist. The closing image is of sniper shots that fell Nazi soldiers, one by one. Luis Alfonso asks his visitor Madame Europa, "And in Spain, when do we start?" And Manuel Benavides, concluding his novel in Mexico in May 1942 as world war continues to rage, puts hopeful words in Madame Europa's mouth: "In Spain . . . In Spain we don't need to start the fight. . . . We need to finish it!" (344).[33]

6

Luis Suárez's *España comienza en los Pirineos* (1944): World War without Borders

> Se maldice en todos los tonos de la exageración a los franceses. "Ahora que les aplasten los boches van a saber lo que es bueno." Un regordete, de voz aflamencada, comenta en otro grupo: "Me gustaría estar en la mejor cervecería de México y emborracharme a placer cuando lea en los periódicos que la tierra de Francia les quedó pequeña a sus soldados para correr en retirada."
>
> [Everyone curses the French, saying everything imaginable. "Once the *boches* crush them, they'll see how it is." A chubby guy with an Andalusian accent, says: "I can't wait to be drinking to my heart's content in Mexico's finest bar when I read the news that there wasn't enough room in France for all the soldiers who ran away in retreat"].
>
> —Eulalio Ferrer, May 1, 1939, Argelès-sur-Mer

IN A LETTER WRITTEN FROM THE CAMP OF SEPTFONDS IN NOVEMBER 1939, two months after France's September entry into the European war, the Spanish Republican internee Alfonso González recalled a pithy phrase that summed up a popular stereotype among certain European nations about Spain's backwardness and remoteness: "The French who said 'Africa begins in the Pyrenees' were right."[1] Having spent many months in French concentration camps, González goes on to explain that he now fully understands where the demarcation lines separating so-called civilized and uncivilized societies are located: "I've been in Africa, and I can assure you that yes, our Pyrenees separate the world of hospitality from the rest of inhospitable Europe. . . . I tell you, I hate France. . . . I will never forgive them for what they are doing to us in these damned Concentration Camps."[2] In the title of his 1944 concentration camp memoir *España comienza en los Pirineos* (Spain Begins in the Pyrenees), fellow civil war veteran Luis Suárez López (1918–2003) — who achieved a successful career as an award-winning journalist in Mexico City after living in the camps of St. Cyprien, Barcarès, and Agde — similarly plays with the long-held cultural concept that Europe ends where Spain begins, on the other side of the Pyrenees.[3] Suárez suggests that this antiquated, skewed geopolitical view of Spain has most recently manifested itself in the misguided policy of nonintervention so deeply despised and fiercely resented by the Spanish Republicans now forced into exile: "Europe doesn't end in the Pyrenees; Spain was still there on the other side of the mountains, and the continent of the old world couldn't go on much longer with its eyes closed. Among other reasons, because the same aggressors' cannons that they had once ignored, would force them to open their eyes."[4] Suárez, like so many other refugees writing from Mexico during World War II, assigns blame to Spain's shortsighted neighbors for failing to recognize that the Iberian Republic's war against totalitarianism was a fellow European democracy's struggle on a European battlefield, ultimately in the name of a free Europe against the fascist forces of Hitler, Mussolini, and Franco. Suárez's message is reiterated more than four decades later by Cuauhtémoc Cárdenas, son of the Mexican president Lázaro Cárdenas, whose administration received the first wave of refugees; the younger Cárdenas paraphrases the Spanish author's position in the preface that he writes for the 1987 edition of the work: "Spain begins in the Pyrenees. There lay the struggle, the ideal, the hope, memories of the past and a vision for the future. Upon crossing over the mountains, they found a very different reality: incomprehension, betrayal and disappointments, aggression, scorn, and suspicion. The Spanish tragedy would soon be commonplace in the rest of Europe and in the rest of the world."[5] This point of view, which fully informs Suárez's representation of the Republican army's border crossing and internment in concentration camps, as I will show below, is not limited to the displaced Spaniards nor to their Mexican supporters. Shortly after the capitulation of France to Hitler's invading army, French journalists would begin to echo an identical sentiment in their eyewitness testimonies likewise published from America. Before analyzing Suárez's memory of the camps, I first briefly review selected French texts in order to demonstrate that the exiled Republicans' insistently reiterated and indefatigably disseminated argument (that their long struggle dating from 1936 unites them now with the Allied democracies' fight) is a political position increasingly acknowledged in the 1940s beyond the émigré community of Mexico City. It is ironically not the fall of Madrid in March 1939, but rather the fall of Paris in June 1940 that finally lends credence to the exiled Spanish point of view.

In perhaps the earliest and best-known of the French accounts, *"J'Accuse!": The Men Who Betrayed France* (1940), the French author (who uses the pen name André Simone) remembers the day on July 18, 1936, when he was on assignment in Spain: "Francisco Franco, supported by

Nazi Germany and fascist Italy, launched his uprising. It shook not only Spain but all Europe to the foundations."[6] While the progressive sectors of the French people identified with the Republic's fight against the forces of reaction and injustice, the representatives of official France responded with the now infamous nonintervention agreement: "Without this nonintervention pact—which in reality sanctioned intervention in Spain—Hitler's triumph in Czechoslovakia would have been inconceivable. The road from Spain led straight to Munich."[7] A comparable position is defended in Jacques Maritain's 1941 book *France My Country: Through the Disaster*. In his search for the "real causes of the French disaster," the author (who in 1937 had published a defense of the Spanish Republic against the military insurgents, *Los rebeldes españoles no hacen una guerra santa* [The Spanish Rebels Are Not Fighting a Holy War]) identifies at the outset of his project the influential role of the conflict in Spain as well as the anemic joint response to it from Great Britain and France: "There was also the fact that the European war in reality had its prelude in the Spanish civil war—a period during which the policy of the Chamberlain government assumed heavy responsibilities."[8] Spain's fratricide is but a precursor to the larger European bloodbath that Maritain deems by extension "an international civil war."[9] The author reminds his reader that Hitler's feeble puppet head of state in Vichy France—the eighty-six-year-old Marshal Pétain, France's first official emissary to Franco's Spain—was a longtime friend of the Spanish military dictator, "an admirer of his brand of crusade; he came to think that the only way of saving France was through a Catholico-dictatorial regime on the Spanish line."[10] The French author Francis Martel elaborates more fully the ideological bonds that Pétain shared with Franco in his damning 1943 indictment of the former World War I "hero of Verdun," *Pétain: Verdun to Vichy*. Like Simone and Maritain, Martel's task is to elucidate the causes of France's capitulation to Hitler; he divides his study into two parts, "The Why" and "The How." Martel traces the origins of the current war to a now familiar source, the enemy invasion of the Spanish peninsula by Franco's rebels, airlifted from Tetuan by German Junkers, accompanied by North African mercenaries: "[It] began when a handful of rebel generals landed in Cádiz with a few thousand professional Moorish warriors. . . . These were the people whom the idle, reactionary, parasitic mass of Spaniards hailed as 'saviors' and upon whom they fastened the distinction of being holy warriors." And France, Martel notes, did nothing, not in the early, "fateful weeks of 1936," nor ever: "France spared little time for the Spanish upheaval. . . ."[11] France's most meaningful contact with Spain before the fall of 1940, says Martel, is that established by Marshal Pétain as the first French ambassador to Nationalist Spain; he describes Pétain's respect for Franco as a harbinger of things to come in Vichy France: "Franco demonstrated to the Marshal—who desired nothing so much as to be convinced—the advantages of a strong hand over a nation which had seceded from the severer virtues of order and the quasi-military religion revered by the clerico-fascists. Here Pétain found emphatic support for his conviction that the decadent Third Republic deserved to disappear."[12] Martel subsequently widens the bonds that encircle Pétain and Franco to include Hitler as well: "But as Pétain plotted and debated with the Spanish friends to whom he so confidently predicted an uprising in France, Hitler acted. The attack began upon May 9 [1940] and the Marshal knew that the hour had come."[13] Another Frenchman, Henry Torres, reminds readers in his 1942 *Campaign of Treachery* that Italy's declaration of war against France had been writ large in the soil of Spain years before: "How naive were the democracies and their allies! . . . As though Italy, since the moment when her first 'volunteers' trampled Spanish soil, at Málaga, Santander, Bilbao and Tortosa, had not considered herself at war with us!"[14] A Republican sympathizer, the author was arrested by Franco's forces during a stopover in Las Palmas in July 1940 as he attempted to flee Nazi-occupied France. Here he had occasion to see additional tracks of "the barbarians of the Twentieth Century" inscribed within the borders of Spanish territory: "Wherever the swastika flies over buildings or is worn on armbands, or, as in the police station of Las Palmas, is traced on the walls."[15]

These French authors who do make the same connections as the Spanish writers between the war in Spain and the war in France generally fail to accord significance to the place of the French internment camps. In their critiques of "official France's" moral bankruptcy, corrupt bureaucracy, and political sympathies with Franco, the story of the government's treatment of the refugees in the camps does not appear. One exception is André Simone's brief reference to the plight of the hundreds of thousands of war refugees who fled to France: "There they were placed in camps. They suffered neglect, inclement weather and undernourishment. Henri de Kérillis wrote at the time that the disorganization in the refugee camps showed the shocking incompetence of the French civil and military authorities."[16] An unusually impassioned denouncement of Vichy France's policies toward the camp refugees is made in a letter written by the French political activist and intellectual Simone Weil. In the winter of 1940–41, this onetime militia volunteer in Spain's early months of civil war begged Admiral Leahy (the U.S. ambassador to Vichy) to withhold U.S. financial support to the French government in the name of France's camp victims: "You know, of course, all the facts about the bad treatment of aliens in France, the concentration camps, etc.—facts which I, as a Frenchwoman, can scarcely bear to think upon for very shame. In spite of all official promises, these shameful things are still going on. I even happen to know that in the Camp du Vernet there has been lately an aggravation. For the sake of these unhappy people, for the sake, also, of the French men and women to whom honour is dearer than food, I think America should refuse to give any help until these cruel treatments have really ceased."[17] One may contrast these remarks to those of another 1940 account by Pétain apologist René de Chambrun, who cursorily refers to the Spanish refugees in the Department of Perpignan in terms of numbers of mouths to be fed, though he does not reveal that these hungry mouths are in fact behind barbed wire.[18] Certainly Elie Bois, former editor of the *Petit Parisien* that on February 14, 1939, had published an ingenious solution to the problem of the Spanish war refugees ("Instead of keeping them in our prisons, why don't we deport them to the place where they accuse of us locking them up, to Guayana? With an ocean between us and them, wouldn't that make us feel more confident about our security?"), omits any mention of the Spanish exiles from his hand-wringing analysis of the debacle in France, *Truth on the Tragedy of France*, written during his own exile in 1940 at a more modest distance, from the shores of Great Britain.[19]

Like the French authors who draw direct connections between the fall of free France in 1940 and the fall of free Spain in 1939, the Spanish refugee Luis Suárez publishes his 1944 story of the events between February 1939 (his exodus through the Pyrenees in the company of his military unit and his immediate internment in the camp of St. Cyprien) and May 1939 (his transfer to the camps of Agde and Barcarès; his departure for Mexico) during the years of the Second World War following the Nazi invasion of France and the creation of Vichy France in 1940. In his memoir the author makes many of the same points argued by his French counterparts: the Spanish Republic's pleas for help against fascist aggression fell on the criminally deaf ears of nonintervention; democratic France was betrayed by a fifth column headed by her own wily leaders; the Spanish war was the first stage of the current world war. And like his compatriots writing alongside him in Mexico, Suárez will appropriate as a key discursive construct the place of the concentration camps in France in order to lay a firm foundation to ground his accusations against the enemies of the Spanish Republic, a nation that in 1944 is still fighting for its life in exile. Suárez dedicates his book to his comrades left behind in the camps: "To those left behind in France."

I read Suárez's autobiographical text first and foremost as a two-hundred-page treatise on the folly of the French government's policy of nonintervention during Spain's recent civil war; this blindered political position of "neutrality" in essence is responsible for bringing France to its knees in short order at the feet of Nazi Germany. In her 1940 prologue to the collection of concentration camp testimony, *Los de Collioure (Relatos de un crimen)* (The Men of Collioure [Stories of a Crime]), Margarita Nelken had attempted to unmask the empty rhetoric of a two-faced policy "disguised beneath the social-democratic rhetoric of 'Order' and 'Pacifism.'"[20] In order to more fully exploit the central tension obtaining between France's smug illusion of civil order and peace (i.e., an armed conflict held at bay behind the Pyrenees) and the ugly reality of a war that respects no borders, Suárez employs a series of "doubling" techniques in both temporal and spatial terms. As a principle organizing strategy throughout his narrative, the author juxtaposes the historical time of the events chronicled (winter/spring 1939) with the insights garnered by the time of writing (period of German occupation of France). The spatial juxtapositions and layerings that Suárez lays down in his text are an even more effective means for revealing the truth of recent history "beyond the Pyrenees" for an unbelieving France: the place of raging war in Spain will mirror the place of impending war in France, as both are joined on the European soil of a common destiny.

Suárez's central trope of the Pyrenees as a porous, not impenetrable, topographical marker of a shared European landscape is the focal point of the introductory chapter of the book, "Memories on a Bridge." The international bridge that unites the borders of Spain and France through the Pyrenees is the very first space presented in the book's opening sentences: "I sit down but I'm not tired. I wish I had in front of me immense tracts of fertile plains, surrounded by mountains from where you could see the whole world. And I wish I could scream; I want to scream to a world that refuses to hear. I want to drown out the shouts of the gendarmes and the French authorities on the international bridge who are trying to cover up their own fear with their loud voices" (7). The bridge, by definition an instrument of connection and continuity, is the site on which the narrator begins to fashion together in his mind a chain of life events in which memories of his Andalusian childhood in Aznalcóllar merge with those of war-torn Spain. The protagonist, standing on the edge of exile, begins his postwar narrative by pulling together a series of stories that have the potential for sustaining his imperiled sense of self. The unifying thread among the disparate images that flood his thoughts as he prepares to cross the border into France is the experience of injury, illness, or danger; in short, he recalls moments of intense fear and trauma (and concomitant bravery and survival) as a way to order and link earlier stages of life to subsequent ones. A boyhood slingshot attack from a local group of bullies is inextricably tied to a near-death scene experienced one month ago during the bombing of Barcelona. The tendency to describe one phase of life events in terms of their function as presage and prelude for later episodes is in fact a common narrative pattern that Suárez employs to communicate the primary message of his work. In general terms he preaches that the past is prologue; more specifically, he insists throughout his book, "The defeat of Spain was a harbinger of things to come in France" (117).[21]

The metaphor of the mirror, a magical looking glass in which France might see its future reflected in the surface of Spain's past, is deployed in a series of symmetrical figures that arise out of the landscape that Suárez describes at the foot of the Pyrenees. The two nations that initially face one another at the border are presented as perfect mirror opposites, flip sides of a single frontier. The Republican soldiers in retreat lay down the well-used firearms recently wielded in "an almost three-year struggle against a much stronger enemy and against their 'Non-Intervention' Committee" (7), leaving their weapons behind on the international bridge "in order to save ourselves in France" (15). Their "saviors"—civil guards, soldiers, and colonial troops—receive the new arrivals with shoves and blows, repeating over and over "with a stupid look on their faces: ... 'Pistols? Ammunition? ¡Alé!'" (18). All the while they brandish their own weapons, "small, still sheathed, untested, never before fired" (40), like so many toy guns in all their virgin newness. The still-new shine of the French firearms gleams as a garish beacon of nonintervention: "A ring of guards and soldiers, elbow to elbow, were pushing forward the shiny points of their bayonets. They were so clean and shiny, polished with the sheen of a false peace that could never be maintained, that wasn't maintained, after what had happened in Spain" (55).

The defeated Republican military units who lay down their arms at the border are represented in terms of noble martyrdom.[22] A civilian face that Suárez spots in the crowd of Spanish emigrants belongs to "Isabel," wife of Etelvino Vega, a lieutenant colonel who will die fighting in the war's final hours of Alicante. Suárez devotes almost one half of his chapter of crossing the border-bridge to documenting Vega's inspiring exploits of bravery and selflessness during the war. This section is counterposed to the second chapter "War Materials," which in turn chronicles the French guards' brazen, and illegal, confiscation of the Republican soldiers' personal possessions—watches, fountain pens, flashlights, cameras, lanterns, binoculars, and other personal effects—justified with the excuse of collecting "war materials." Suárez's juxtaposition of Spaniards and Frenchmen at the border as an encounter between heroic warriors and cowardly, thieving thugs is inscribed within the author's familiar pattern of foreshadowing with hindsight; he narrates the French officials' actions in 1939 in light of historical events to come in 1940: "As we think about the future, we ponder this burning question: Is it possible that this country, with this government, and with representatives like these guards, can successfully confront Hitler? People like this who abuse their authority as easily as professional thieves could never raise the level of Western morality to that of Hitler's savagery. It was also possible that they were simply bitter enemies of the first army that fought against fascism; in other words, that they themselves were fascists" (38). The locus of defeat that the Republican soldiers are forced to inhabit as they cross to the other side of the bridge will soon be shared, warns the narrator knowingly, with their French jailers: "You had to cross over to the other side of the bridge. . . . Gendarmes and soldiers wouldn't allow anyone to escape that arch of humiliation. They had their Arch of Triumph in Paris, where later with the shame of their own defeat they would slip through" (18).

Of course the central space of defeat that the Republican exiles are forced to occupy, the site at the heart of Suárez's book, are the concentration camps themselves. The title of the third chapter, "The Cage," refers to Suárez's depiction of the camp of St. Cyprien in terms of a space of both containment and erasure. The camp is an enclosed area in which the French government has attempted at least to cordon off, at best to make disappear, as it holds at bay behind the new border of a mountain range of barbed wire, the specter of war that the thousands of sick, wounded, and bedraggled refugees present to the French people. Tramping along the road toward the rumored destination of the camps ("Not very far from the border are concentration camps where everyone—soldiers and civilians, men and women, children and the elderly—are interned. They say that everyone's treated badly. We thought it was a lie, since although it's true we had no idea what would happen to us in France, we certainly couldn't imagine a situation like that. They must be exaggerating. . . ." [29]), toward Perpignan, the refugees pass through the tranquil town of Elne, offering themselves up to the town's onlookers as a scary, albeit mesmerizing, spectacle of war: "The trucks, the cars, the carts, the people—those 'strange' people—, on foot, looked like something straight out of one of their fairs" (38). Here, muses Suárez as they march by, the "peaceful neighbors," supposedly shielded by the "pacificist" pacts of nonintervention and of Munich, watch the freakish parade go by with something akin to horror: "Those frightened people were seeing the flesh-and-blood characters out of the legendary tale of terror that the best newspapers in the country had created. They were scared that they would catch their diseases and be robbed by them" (39). The fearful faces peering through the windows needn't have worried, as Suárez makes clear in his description of the "barbed-wire cages" (53) where tens of thousands of the refugees are immediately corralled. Here, Suárez states wryly, is the optimum location for the dirty "plague" of Republican Spain that has spilled over the border "into the peaceful and sleepy official France" (104). Taking every precaution that the Spaniards should not come into contact with the French people, the kilometers of barbed wire are extended even out into the open ocean itself: "At the end of the row of barbed wire, where dry land ends and the ocean begins, the pickets that held up the wire went all the way out into the water. It was necessary to even take over a bit of the sea. To make sure no one escaped, it wasn't enough just to have the wire fence come to the water's edge, so they've nailed the wire down out in the waves themselves. To be able to get out of either end, you'd have to really risk it. Two men, two shadowy Senegalese, stand guard with a machine-gun in place" (72). The machine-guns that the unarmed refugees find trained over them ironically mark the French effort to seal off the bloody battlegrounds of Spain within the bleak concentration campgrounds of France.

Suárez describes the camp of St. Cyprien drawn within a metallic spiked boundary, a peripheral place literally dug into the sand, as essentially a spatialization of the French nation's deepest dread of war and chaos. The crippling fear that Suárez attributes to the French is a prevailing leitmotiv of his book, one that he introduces in the opening sentences cited earlier of the first chapter; he characterizes the French border guards' harsh treatment of the Spanish army in retreat as a manifestation of abject fear. This fundamental fact of fear echoes throughout the pages of the book like an insistent refrain and materializes in front of the refugees' eyes wherever they look. Initially it confronts them in the border guards' blustery bullying ("They were either trying to act important or else hide their fear" [46]), or stares back at them from their jailers' faces at St. Cyprien ("An expression of total fear flickered on the faces of those who, armed like we were just a short time ago, were guarding us" [92]). The half-starved internees who sink in the sand present a skeletal phantasm of war "to the frightened gaze of the whole world" (98). Nowhere is the fear and loathing that they inspire more pronounced than on the visage of official France, which has acted to preserve "a false peace" (55) at all costs. The mayor of the town of Agde, site of yet another concentration camp, where Suárez's group will later be transferred, is described sardonically as "that peaceful and terrified Mayor" (201), part of an administration paralyzed by fear. Suárez continues to portray the "terror that our presence inspired in the municipal authorities in Agde" in terms of a sublimated topography of confinement, "In that new concentration camp we would continue to be locked up, isolated, under guard, as hated as ever..." (201). Perhaps only the useless French Maginot Line—another ill-fated boundary-construction founded on the denial of war's inevitability—is a comparable concretization of national fear.

Characteristic of Suárez's tendency to present emigrant Spain and official France in reverse mirror-image terms, he likewise develops the motif of fear experienced by the Spaniards within the camps. Unlike their untested captors, from the moment the Spanish war veterans cross the international bridge they are always connected to memories of their courageous fight on the other side of the Pyrenees: "At least we had done everything in our power to stop the enemies from the outside, aided by the enemies from within" (35). Following his numerous descriptions of the look and smell of death experienced during the civil war of Spain, confronted with rising casualties and demoralizing conditions within the camps as well, Suárez once again affirms that the present struggle, "the battle of exile" (67), is but a continuation of the previous one. The author measures the "depressing fear" he feels in the camp as so much less than the terror he felt fighting for his country's survival in Spain (53); the ground of that battle, he assures his reader, was "so much harder than the sand that France offered us" (81). Unlike Pétain's France, which will meekly sign an armistice with Hitler, Suárez like his fellow Spanish exiles has openly confronted his worst nightmare ("I have looked death in the face" [58]), and will face down fear again: "In the concentration camp I felt fear and fought against it. I refused to give in to it" (58). As Suárez and other groups of interned Republicans overcome their fear of the camps and of their uncertain future in exile, they exhort one another to resist the temptation to accept repatriation back to Franco's Spain. In a powerful act of emplacement, these refugees claim the shifting sands of St. Cyprien for "the real Republicans, for the true patriots," bolstered and strengthened as always by the experience of their fight against fascism. These memories have channeled their own fear into a potent, transformative weapon much greater than the pile of firearms left behind on the bridge: "And little by little, relying on the strength of their own resources, reserves that they had stored in Spain during the struggle against death and the unexpected, these men began to stand firm, defying the incomprehension and the close-minded attitude of these French who yesterday touted 'Nonintervention.'" (99). The geopolitical lesson of Suárez's book is not only to remind his 1944 audience that the currently disputed map of Europe also extends through the Pyrenees into Spain. Conversely, the brave contingents of exiled refugees in camps at the foot of the mountain border actively assume their collective identity as the true representatives of "Spain": "Because we weren't just anybody; we were Spain. If we stood naked now, then so was Spain; if we were enraged, desperate, then so too was our country, our Republic" (107). Spain begins on this side of the Pyrenees.

The renewed sense of moral integrity and political cohesion that Suárez traces in his concentration camp testimony informs his depiction of one of the primary spaces of the St. Cyprien camp, the *Bulevar de la Libertad*. In the central chapter of his memoir, "A Stroll Down the Avenue," Suárez describes the changing topography of the rapidly growing camp that eventually includes this primitive "main street" that the inmates jokingly baptize the "Avenue of Freedom": "The barbed wire closed in on us. But about 60 meters further down, another fence ran parallel to the first one. Behind this there were the tents and the guard posts that they kept separate from the lake and the fields of freedom that led to cities with homes, with movie theaters, with restaurants, all full of life! And they built an avenue in the concentration camp. It was dangerous to keep the men shut up in their huts, always forced to walk in sinking, shifting sand. So we were then able to walk along a strip of land that stretched between two strong barbed-wire fences. It was about 70 meters wide and a kilometer long, more or less. It ran the whole length of the camps. It's true that it too had a sand floor, but in certain places it was packed down harder than the sand where we made our beds" (116–17). In this passage, Suárez draws attention to the radically bifurcated space that French citizens and Spanish refugees inhabit. On one side of the barbed-wire border, life in 1939 France seems to go on as pleasantly as ever, apparently untouched by violence or strife; on the other, men are sleeping on pillows of sand.[23] Elsewhere the author had compared the two "St. Cypriens": the sleepy French village, and the incongruous beach–concentration camp of the same name: "Saint Cyprien—the camp, the beach, not the town that, like hope, was as white and blue as ever—was still a center of misery and death" (187). The contrasting landscapes set side by side of lovely tranquility and unbearable suffering allow Suárez to denounce the French efforts to carry on the illusion of peace and order despite the evidence of the ravage of war that languishes now on their very own shores. He describes the almost otherworldly beauty of the town of St. Cyprien as simply a mirage: "Saint-Cyprien peeped through the trees from a distance. Its white and greyish houses were the color of rain. The smell of bricks, of wet stone, wafted over to the camp. It was like the mirage of an oasis for a dying man who, totally defeated, lies motionless in the desert sand" (106). Equally deceiving is the sense of security that the French cling to during these days as Hitler marches through Europe. In the introduction to the chapter "A Stroll Down the Avenue," Suárez describes France as a nation with its head in the sand: "Abyssinia was far away. What had happened in Austria was forgotten. The invasion of Czechoslovakia was a done deal. Spain had become the enemy. Little Albania was falling. . . . And still France was untouched. Her borders seen from the other side formed a strong circle of steel . . . France was unscathed, with her colonies, her empire, her ancient victories and a dream of freedom" (115–16). In other words, Suárez concluded, "The French were scared of war" (116). At this culminating moment of the book, situated along the concentration camp's laughably designated "Avenue of Freedom," the lesson that their war has taught the Spaniards is held up to the French nation: "Let your sense of duty be greater than your fear. The brave are courageous because they know they have to be. Maybe that is the meaning we find in the Spanish people's amazing ability to resist; that is the example we have in the considerable numbers of Spanish young people who fought and died, or who survived, with courage" (121). Years before Suárez published his memoir, Juan Negrín had addressed the last session of the Spanish Republican parliament in Figueras, referring to the powerful legacy of the Republican struggle: "Nations do not only survive because of their victories, but they also live on through their example in moments of adversity and misfortune. The lessons that may be derived from such historical times are fruitful for the life of the nation."[24] Even in defeat, the refugees at St. Cyprien claim a moral victory from a skinny tract of sandy earth that only appears to be a parodic inversion of truly free space: "We didn't take Llerena and we weren't able to take Spain, because at that time France, England and the United States refused to risk their own Avenues of Freedom, many of which today lie beneath the invaders' feet or have been destroyed by their tanks. But a tiny path of freedom was saved for us, like a reward for our premier efforts in the fight for democracy: the Avenue of Freedom. Here, as we stroll along, we can again ponder how to fight, because maybe one day we'll need to fight again" (132). Suárez concludes his book at the moment that he and a selected group are released from the camp and prepare to join the historic *Sinaia* voyage to Veracruz, Mexico. As he faces exile to America, France teeters on the brink of war with Germany. His last view of the border towns that France and Spain share ("Those were the little towns of the Pyrenees, at the shady foothills of the mountains shared by Spain and France" [194]) encompasses finally a common landscape and hopefully a shared future of freedom.

The possibility that other nations that at last have joined the Spanish Republic's struggle against totalitarianism and fascism will support that exiled nation's efforts to reestablish her rightful place on the Iberian Peninsula is one of the strongest sentiments expressed in the early exile literature published in Mexico. This dream of reclaiming Spain from Franco's dictatorship following the Allied victory over the Axis powers of course was not to come true. But in the early 1940s, when the Spaniards in Mexico wait and watch, the belief in the righteousness of their cause, the integrity of their ideals, and the legitimacy of their political position informed every word they wrote. And hope sprang eternal. In the 1966 prologue to the second edition of *Morir por cerrar los ojos*, Max Aub remembered his difficult days of the concentration camp as the world war raged, when ironically everything about the future seemed possible: "The sad thing is that when I wrote those scenes—in circumstances much worse than those of today—hope was so much stronger."[25]

Part III
Creative Transformations: The Camps as Construction Sites of Cultural Resistance and Continuity

7

Manuel Andújar's *St. Cyprien, plage . . . campo de concentración* (1942): A Survey of History

>Allí estaban todos, formando los gremios, en grupos, todos vestidos de soldados de la libertad de España y del mundo. Ibamos a asistir a la fundación de un pueblo, el pueblo de España.
>
>[There they all were, grouped together in unions, all dressed as soldiers of the freedom of Spain and the world. We were getting ready to witness the foundation of a nation, the nation of Spain.]
>—Jaime Espinar, Argelès-sur-Mer

Allez! Allez!: Going Nowhere

In the introduction to their edited 1998 volume of *Borders, Exiles, Diasporas*, the authors point out the fundamental paradox of the exilic experience; founded on "anguish, dispossession," the destabilizing space of displacement may ironically provide a firm surface for recovery and renewal: "Exile carries a potential for salvation as the hope of a possible future instills the urge to speak and reappropriate history."[1] But for all the promise of historical and personal reconstruction, the editors remind us that the starting point on the way through exile is initially situated in a vast space devoid of meaning, "We begin in the abyss."[2] As I have indicated earlier, the physical locations of places like Saint Cyprien or Argelès-sur-Mer are literally represented, whether in photographs or in writing, as just such empty sites precariously predicated on their radical disconnection to prior systems of signification. Referring to survivors of the Holocaust, Ulrich Baer has indicated that the sense of "geographic placelessness" is a commonality shared by the witnesses and frequently recorded in their remembrances: "Survivor accounts often recount the deportation to a *non-place* and the destruction of the symbolic notion of a 'place' that could hold experience together."[3] So too does the feeling of going nowhere, and ending up "no place," define the experience of the Spaniards herded toward the French camps like so much livestock: "Walking and walking; with your eyes on the ground. . . . Walking on and on. Walking on relentlessly, herded like livestock," writes Jaime Espinar in his 1940 memoir; "We are a pitiful, exhausted flock that just wants to rest," recalls Lluís Ferran de Pol.[4] Almost without exception, the masses of refugees—civilian as well as military alike—trudge onward with no idea whatsoever of where they are headed; the only response that those who dare to inquire receive from their armed guards is the incessant refrain to just keep going, *Allez! Allez!* Solano Palacio's 1939 account records the blind march ("They lead us in an unknown direction") as an aimless odyssey punctuated by the relentless command, the "the brutal, emphatic *Allez*."[5] Jaime Espinar reports the Republicans' initial journey into the land of exile in similar terms; he opens his third chapter, "The Brigade," with an exchange between a bewildered Spaniard and an impassive gendarme: "And where are you taking us, guard? '*Allez, allez!*' "[6] The juxtaposition of the traveler who has lost all bearings, all sense of direction, with the senseless imperative to keep going toward an unknown destination underscores the inextricable relationship between movement and meaning stressed by cultural geographers like Vincent Berdoulay: "The French word *sens* stands for meaning, but it may also designate direction, way. . . . We are concerned with meaning as well as with direction, movement, or change when we think of place." If one accepts Berdoulay's premise of "meaning as a geographic process," then the Spanish refugees' entry into exile can only be understood as a passage into an inexplicable, incomprehensible environment.[7]

The jarring disjunction between meaning and movement, between orientation and place, is even more exacerbated in the testimonials as the writer-witnesses describe the long-awaited end point of the exhausting sojourn essentially as one that occupies a surreal nonplace. Juan Carrasco perfectly captures the incongruity of the moment of arrival both pictorially and linguistically in his *album-souvenir*. Alongside a photograph of an endless stream of hunch-shouldered men stumbling through the sand under the vigilant eye of uniformed gendarmes, the caption reads: "Here the long trek ends, this is the endpoint that each of us was wondering about. It's a harsh reality: a deserted beach! '*Allez! Allez!*' the gendarmes insistently repeat; as we see in the photograph, they are armed with clubs to make the stragglers catch up."[8] Carrasco's definition of "Here" as a deictic marker that has absolutely no capacity for naming place ("a deserted beach!") is found as well in Jaime Espinar's description of the arrival at Saint-Cyprien: "Since everything must come to an end, the column crested a hill. From there you could see the ocean. Some of the soldiers didn't know what to make of it and were bewildered. . . . *'Ici, ici!,'* said a guard with a friendly smile. *'Ici?* And what is *'ici?'* 'Here, idiot! Down there, next to the sea. Don't you see the group that's already in that clearing?' And sure enough, on the brown stretch of beach, some tiny black dots were moving. There were the founders of the 'camp' of San Cipryent [*sic*]."⁹ Espinar's exile experiences confusion not only because he doesn't know the French word for *here*. As is made abundantly evident in every ensuing account after Espinar's early 1940 document, the disorientation originates in the fact that the *campo*, as Espinar's use of inverted commas suggests, is apprehended by the refugees less as a meaningful place in time than as a literally unfinished, still unformed location that also is simply inconceivable as a destination point. In his autobiography, Juan Renau recalls his incredulous exchange with a gendarme upon arrival: "But, where's the *camp?*, I warily ask a gendarme. *'La bas!,'* he curtly replies. 'What? . . . . But there's nothing but sand!' 'Well . . . , that's the camp!'"¹⁰ Artís-Gener describes his own first view of the camp at Prats-de-Molló: "We arrived at the concentration camp marching four abreast, watched over by guards who flanked our stumbling columns. It was, simply put, the embryo, the outline of a concentration camp, where there was a surplus of evil and a shortage of all goodness. The only thing they had set up was the barbed-wire fence."¹¹ The only physical marker that denotes the place of a camp, the internee-authors all agree, is the ubiquitous barbed-wire fencing. Lluís Ferran de Pol records in particularly poignant terms his horrified realization that the empty expanse of sand stretching before him and his comrades, broken only by the jagged barbed wire, is actually their final stop:

> Our only welcome was the distant sight of an immense beach, darkened by the crowd of first arrivals. Suddenly, we are in front of a barbed-wire fence that encloses the beach. We pass through a vast entryway where, with bayonets fixed, black soldiers stand sentry nearby. We can't believe our eyes. Astonished, we walk inside the fencing. We feel something akin to panic, as we are forced to accept the reality of our situation. We look at these dunes, these waves of desert against the backdrop of an impassable sea, and, incredulous, our eyes search in vain for some change in the scenery. In this place that apparently has been assigned to us, there is a kind of reed and a few blades of grass. Nothing else. Not a single tree, no canebrake, no barracks, nor any type of refuge from the cold and the wind. Absolutely nothing. Sand and solitude . . . But now everything is clear. We are just prisoners and we will have to get used to the idea. A barbed-wire fence is not just a holding area but, in fact, a prison.¹²

Place accords identity; Jaime Espinar sums up the transformative trajectory, "from the trenches to the confines of the beach," that takes members of the "heroic Spanish army" out of Spain and replaces them in France as prison inmates. Being "here" in this nowhere, the new inhabitant of such phantasmagoric camps quickly senses that he is no longer who he was, "now he was a nobody."[13]

In earlier chapters I have examined the place of the camps as a symbolic terrain in the exiled national imaginary, either in terms of its constitutive function as a commemorative "place of memory" or as a locus that grounds the exiled Republicans' claims of political legitimacy and moral authority during the uncertain years of the Second World War. In what follows, I argue that the concentration camps are also frequently configured as a kind of construction site for the nation in exile, a place where the survivors of civil war begin to inscribe a new national history as well as reassemble their political identity as fighters united in solidarity for social justice. The camp refugees who have just emerged from the rubble of recent defeat, housed now in the sandy squalor of makeshift huts of sticks and blankets, often remark on the persistent ringing of hammers that resonates through the camps during the early months of their internment. Ever so slowly more permanent shelters, the infamous *barracas*, are being raised as thousands upon thousands of Spanish Republicans stream over the border into France. A parallel building project, the early-stage construction of the Spanish exile identity and consciousness, similarly takes hold in the sandy soil of the camps. In his remarks about the Jewish diaspora, Simon Schama has referred to the image of drifting, blowing sand as the quintessential trope of the space of exile: "The diaspora was sand."[14] Remarkably, the Spanish writers I discuss here manage to ground themselves on this barren, sinking terrain, shoring up a foundation capable of at least figuratively weathering the storms of exile. In this section I examine a series of texts written primarily during or shortly after the authors' confinement: Manuel Andújar's 1942 camp memoir *St. Cyprien, plage . . . Campo de concentración*; Celso Amieva's 1960 volume of poetry *La almohada de arena*, which Amieva began to write during the almost four years that he spent in camps throughout France; and the Catalan author Agustí Bartra's novelized memoir *Cristo de 200.000 brazos (Campo de Argelès)*, first published in Catalan as *Xabola* in 1943. These three works document the authors' (and more generally their fellow interned Spaniards') efforts to make sense out of this early phase of the Spanish exile experience that plays itself out within the barbed-wire perimeter of the concentration camps. In the following three chapters I explore how the unfamiliar physical space of the beaches of France is ultimately encoded by the camp inmates who inhabit and represent them, as a place of subversion, resistance, and agency. This process unwittingly exploits the double meaning of the word that most fully defines the Spanish internees' "landscape" of exile; the bleak topography of sand (*arena*, in Spanish) is successfully transformed into a site of struggle (political arena/

arena, in Spanish). In chapter 1 of this study, I traced the trajectory that the emigrants follow into the land of exile, figured in their testimonies as both a hostile physical locale and an indecipherable land lacking meaning. Their ability to crudely transform the very material limitations of this world into a more habitable environment in turn prepares the terrain for symbolic representations that skillfully inscribe the concentration camps as an emergent place capable of sustaining of the Spaniards' being-in-exile.

Place Taking Shape: Activating Agency

Even as the memoirists recall the radical ground zero from which they were forced to lay the foundations of exile, they acknowledge an ability among the camp inmates to change the space of the inhospitable French landscape into the place of an emerging exilic experience. The authors Tellado and Sánchez-Bravo have described the sprawling Argelès-sur-Mer complex as a generative matrix, albeit a terrifyingly savage one; they refer to this "alma mater" of the French concentration camps as a vast womb that spawns other, similar exiled places where the Spanish people will struggle for survival: "Something like a mother-camp that produces more and more camps. A wounded, bloodied she-wolf that was going to subject her injured offspring to even more hardship and humiliation."[15] The refugees are expelled into a hostile world, always physically delimited by the barbed wire where they are truly left to their own devices with which to fashion a new life. Sánchez-Bravo and Tellado explain: "We were abandoned for the time being, left to our own imagination and determination."[16] The creative "make-do" capacity for reworking the raw reality of exile into a sustaining space of survival is expressed as a response to a moral imperative, a notion that is widely disseminated throughout the exile community generally; an August 31, 1939, issue of the Mexico-based journal *Boletín al servicio de la emigración española* is printed under the large-print banner slogan: "The moral health of both men and nations is measured by their capacity for creation, which in difficult circumstances is improvisation, pure and simple."[17] One of the most oft-told tales that takes shape specifically in the concentration camp literature is the story of how the refugees take the raw materials of the new environment (the sand and shells, pebbles, and driftwood) and craft inventive tools for living. Particularly instructive in this instance is the ingenious appropriation of the barbed wire itself as an improbable instrument of utility and even power. In their hands the barbed wire, the earliest and most recognizable marker of imprisonment, is transformed into a series of quotidian aids that help to ease the harsh conditions of the camp. In his 1941 memoir aptly named *Alambradas* (Barbed Wire), Manuel García Gerpe explains that the inmates' defensive tool used against the ever-encroaching dirt and trash was a special kind of broom, "the wire broom."[18] Cesáreo de la Cruz y Gómez, crediting his own talent for making something out of nothing to his cultural heritage ("Spain is a country of clever rascals"), describes a fine little grill he was able to make out of the wiring.[19] In another instance, he was able to further enlist the wire as a weapon in the fight against hunger in the camp; he shapes a handy hook that he pokes through a hole in a supply hut and fishes out stolen turnips and carrots. Celso Amieva finds an unlikely ally against the invasive sand in the pieces of the barbed-wire fencing; following a transfer from Argelès to Barcarès, the inmates find a new way to keep off the damp ground at night: "We used the wooden pikes to construct beds."[20] Adela Carreras (aka "Adelita del Campo"), one of the contributors to the weekly *Boletín de Estudiantes* improbably published in Argelès-sur-Mer in the spring and summer of 1939, describes in a May 25 issue the careful production of a refugee newspaper that is fastened together with pieces of wire: "Orts puts the pages in order. Almiñana glues the covers, Monzó sews. Very interesting: a humble little needle pokes holes in the pages, facilitating the entry of a tiny, fine thread of wire, wrapped around a bobbin that Torralbo unwinds and cuts to size. And I, with these notes, reveal the intricacies of their journalistic confection."[21] A couple of weeks earlier, the editors of the *Boletín* had even promised, tongue-in-cheek, to cleverly harness the brute force of their seaside environs in order to more perfectly publish their work: "We have set up some magnificent workshops that will be powered by the waves of the ocean. We will compete with *The Times* of London."[22] But certainly the master of invention must be Manolo Valiente, who gained some renown in the camp of Argelès for his workshop where he made toys for the refugee children. Later his *taller* successfully produced small nails, used in a first instance to repair roofs and secure shelter against the elements, "sharp tips that were hard to find in those days, used to secure the metal sheets that had blown off of the huts."[23] Valiente describes the process that garnered the attention and interest of the French officials, who rewarded the resourceful industrialist and his workers with additional rations of food: "We made mould out of two pieces of scrap iron, used it to press the wire pieces from the barbed-wire fence and then worked the tips into nail ends." Valiente dreams wistfully of annihilating the entire camp's wire walling by transforming it all into sturdy pieces of construction: "I said to myself: if only we could get rid of the barbed wire by making nails out of all of it, what joy!"[24]

The refugees' strategies for converting the topographical markers of the camps, most notably the barbed fencing, into innovative tools for improved living conditions are not limited to a purely material craftsmanship. Part of the process of changing the unfathomable space of exile into a familiar, lived place, Amy Kaminsky reminds us, is achieved through discourse, through "naming reality and one's place in it"; laying down this grid of language over the as-yet undifferentiated space is a "means of taking action, a way to stamp a difference on what has been the same."[25] The internees prove themselves to be as able wordsmiths as they are artisans, adept at subversively rearranging the physical landscape of the camp through newly minted systems of toponymy. In a display of ironic humor, the inmates give grandiose "hotel" names to their ratty little huts such as the Hotel mil y una noches (A Thousand and One Nights), the Bristol, the Royal, or the Gran Hotel de Cataluña.[26] In Argelès, a group of homesick *montañeses* from the region of Santander gathered for meals in La Tierruca, a cane-and-blanket hovel playfully described as a kind of "little chalet, with mountains of sand artistically arranged all around it."[27] Later, as an inmate of the St. Cyprien camp, Ferrer recalls the frequency with which the numerous *barracas* on the desolate French soil were named for the beloved places of home: "They've made an inventory of all the names used to baptize the huts. The order of frequency is: Barcelona, Gerona, Asturias, Madrid, Málaga, Santander. . . ."[28] In Luis Suárez's memoir of the St. Cyprien camp, *España comienza en los Pirineos*, as I have shown, the inmates baptize the strip of sand where they kill the interminable hours by strolling together, talking, exchanging information, and planning for the future, *la Avenida de la Libertad*. Another stretch of beach in St. Cyprien, recalls Antonio Vilanova, was also appropriated linguistically by the inmates, this time for scatological purposes. Vilanova describes how the inmates' daily activities carve out a new place in the French shoreline: "Throughout the camps were areas that served as streets leading to the beach or to the Avenue of Freedom, that is, either towards the sea or towards the outside. We named the former 'hurry-up streets.' . . . The reason was because, since there weren't any latrines in the camps for several months, we had to relieve ourselves on the beach. And since the water that we drank was pumped in from the sea, the salt water, combined with the cold, the damp, and the lack of decent food, caused us to have permanent dysentery that in turn obliged us to race through these 'streets' on our way to the beach."[29] The campers' ingeniously retaliate by naming this filthy piece of earth in honor of the French government administration that has subjected them to such a vile place of suffering: "And that beach, populated by one hundred thousand crouching men, was immediately baptized 'Daladier Avenue,' in honor of the French Prime Minister who had provided us with such a 'brotherly' reception."³⁰ Vilanova also reports that in the camp used as a kind of holding area for refugees selected for emigration to Mexico, the latrine there had been similarly baptized: "In the middle of the camp was a kind of platform that we called 'Kroll Opera' in memory of the theater of the same name in Berlin, where around that same time, on the fourth of May, Hitler had given a pompous speech."³¹

Other speech acts, disassociated with physical locales, allow the inmates to assume a space of agency where they can twist the rules and mandates spouted by their oppressors, just as they had remolded the barbed wiring into useful tools. Even (or perhaps, especially) the hated, obsessively shouted *Allez! Allez!* loses its power and punch as it is transformed into a silly song; Jaime Espinar describes how the Cuban soldiers of the International Brigades raise the spirits of the other camp internees with their playful lyrics: "But the Cubans made a joke out of it and composed a little ditty: '*Allez! Allez!, Allez! Allez! Ay, mamá Inés, Allez! Allez!*' These Cubans who had fought in Spain for the cause of freedom . . . '*Ay, mamá Inés, Allez! Allez!*'"³² Other inmates describe a particularly despised part of the daily ritual of the camps, the raising and lowering of the French flag. García Gerpe has described the ceremony in the Septfonds camp in which all inmates were forced to participate: "At the entry of the camp next to the central office, there was a big loudspeaker on one side, and on the other was a flagpole where the French flag was raised and lowered daily, and 17,000 inmates were required to observe the 'ceremony of the flag.'"³³ But such rites in front of France's national symbol of Liberty, Equality, and Fraternity also provide the occasion for subversive self-expression on the part of the Spaniards. Marie Rafaneau-Boj describes in her 1993 study of the camps that a group of Catalán anarchists in the Vernet camp took special devious pleasure in saluting the *drapeau*: French for flag, and so close to the Catalán "*drap*" for rag. French authority is similarly challenged and undercut by the Spanish announcers who speak through the large loudspeakers, installed throughout the camps after the first several weeks. They broadcast the material they are given by the French authorities: music, news, announcements, camp rules, and roll call for those inmates who have visitors or are being transferred or released. Sometimes the inmate is being sought by the authorities under suspicion of "dangerous" political affiliations or "criminal" acts. Antonio Vilanova describes the methods used by the broadcaster to tip off his listener: "The word in the camp was that the fellow campers who worked as announcers were very loyal and that, whenever somebody was called in over the loudspeaker for something bad, they tried to warn him, with an ingenious ruse, acting like they couldn't make out the name and adding pointedly, 'It's not clear.'"³⁴ Even in one of the most repressive spaces of all the camps, the fortress of Collioure that served as a brutal labor camp, the inmates managed to secretly and creatively subvert the command of their French tormentors. Collioure camp survivor Angel Sánchez Ramírez recalls a special painting project that the violent commander Rollet ordered two units of the prisoners to carry out in the medieval fortress. One job was to paint simulated bricks on the terrace. Using the crisscross line design as a camouflage, the workers crafted an expressive record, the informant says, "yet another trace of our passage through Collioure." If you were to look closely, says the Spanish witness, you would be able to make out the marks of their identity and emblems of their history that the prisoner-painters signed into the primitive walls of their cavelike jail: "There were drawings left behind of enormous five-pointed stars, symbols of the Italians' hunger strike, ox heads in honor of Captain Rollet, various renderings of the figures of women, and a huge sign that said: 'Long live the Spanish Republic!'" Upon inspecting the work, continues Sánchez Ramírez, Captain Rollet noticed nothing: "And there those drawings are, waiting for somebody to fill in the outline of the silhouette, bringing them to life one day when the French nation has achieved justice, done away with the Mobile Guard, and abolished the Collioure Fort as a Prison."[35] The images of rebellion and political ideology, the visions of love and dreams of freedom—memories of this hell and hopes for the future—will tell the story of this place long after its inhabitants are gone.

In his illuminating reading of Jorge Semprún's autobiographical account of his internment in Buchenwald, Angel Loureiro has stressed that the inmates who emerge from the netherworldly space of the concentration camp face the difficult task of "restoring solidity to reality and reconstructing themselves"; elsewhere he notes that "Reality as a discursive construction has to be undergirded by a Real that offers a space of resistance and agency for the subject."[36] The writers included in this section fashion a strong position of both "resistance and agency" out of the harsh landscape of the camps. Like their fellow camp inmates who twist barbed metal into tools for survival, these authors shape and mold the razor-edged reality of the camps into a enduring place of history and memory: a building site for reconstructing identity, a foundational place to support the continued struggle of exile.

Manuel Andujar at the Beach

In the 1942 preface to his account of the four months he spent in the St. Cyprien concentration camp in 1939, Manuel Andújar (1913–94) joined fellow exiles in Mexico City like Margarita Nelken, Antonio Mije, Juan Rejano, and Luis Zapirain in calling on the international community to act on behalf of the Spanish refugees interned in France.[37] A future prolific novelist, essayist, and literary editor in Mexico City, Andújar publishes the pages of his testimony "exactly as they were written 'there'" in order to provoke a political response from his readers in America.[38] He explains the events of May 1942 that account for his sense of urgency: "The plight of the Spanish refugees in France and Africa has reached the maximum degree of desperation and destitution. . . . Today only the pressure of international opinion can stop the treacherous hands of Laval, who wants to turn over thousands of our fellow countrymen . . . to the man and the regime that all legitimate Spaniards hate, Franco and the *Falange*" (13). The express purpose of the book to evince both outrage and empathy for the thousands of refugees still living behind barbed wire is stated unequivocally. The confidence about why Andújar shares his work with an audience in 1942 ("*St. Cyprien, playa* will have served its purpose if it foments—or revives—the feeling of anguish and hope that was its motivation and impetus" [14]) belies, however, the author's central dilemma in 1939 about how to tell this story. A fundamental question he faces is how to name the experience in the camp when referential language seems powerless to adequately designate the dimensions of this new "concentrationary universe," a term Ulrich Baer has used to refer to "this unbridgeable distance between the notions of a 'place' or 'world,' and the occurrences in these non-places."[39] In one of the most incisive studies published about *St. Cyprien, plage . . . Campo de concentración*, José Naharro-Calderón has carefully examined the problem of language confronting Andújar and all concentration camp witnesses who attempt to chronicle their unreal reality: "The jarring contradictions obtaining in the language of the camp, slice through linguistic signs as if they were rag dolls . . . ."[40] Andújar's efforts to make meaning out of a senseless environment ultimately encode this bleak landscape as a kind of blank slate on which the exile-inmates will begin to inscribe their collective history and record their voices of protest.

The pervasive disconnection obtaining between signifier and signified that runs through this text is patent in both Andújar's linguistic references to the world of the camp as well as in Julián Oliva's photographic documents of the place that are interspersed among the short (one- to two-page) vignettes. Neither in words nor in images are the respective witnesses able to close the gap between what is represented and what it means, between the "thing" and its name. In one picture the "camp" is recorded by Oliva as a sprawling expanse of confusing figures; throngs of men are standing or sitting all along the beach as far as the eye can see amidst a mess of blankets, backpacks, and suitcases. Fully a third of the photo of the "camp" is simply blank sky. Using a shorthand style with its own plasticity, Andújar jots down his sketch, equally devoid of the recognizable markers of a "camp": "Alambradas, senegaleses, un rincón—que debió ser vertedero de basura—y la playa" [Barbed wire, Senegalese soldiers, a corner that's used as a garbage dump, and the beach] (19). Oliva's photograph of a "bed" shows a sleeping man curled up in a tomblike excavation in the sand, which perfectly captures Andújar's reference to the place where he and his friends sleep, "el hoyo en la arena" [the hole in the sand] (22). The concept of "meal" is rendered by Oliva as a bizarre event where dozens of men reach through a barrier of barbed wire, begging for food from two beleaguered servers. Andújar's definition of a "meal" is equally at odds with the conventional meaning of the word, "una ración de pan para veinticinco en toda la jornada" [a ration of bread for twenty-five inmates for the entire day] (21); elsewhere he describes the moment of the "dessert": "un remedo grotesco de café, fumando colillas" [(drinking) a poor excuse for coffee, smoking cigarette butts] (103). In this bizarre universe, nothing is what it's supposed to be; words are useless for naming this reality. The infirmary is a place of death ("Desorden en su mayor apogeo. No se efectúan curas, falta por completo la visita médica . . ." [Disorder to the greatest degree. No one is healed, total lack of medical attention . . .] [20]); the latrine is an open shoreline ("el anillo irregular de la playa" [the irregular line of the beach] [29]); and a shower is a squalid episode of suffering ("En calzoncillos, viejo y joven se propinan, a la intemperie, algo así como una ducha. Aúlla el viento, las nubes entoldan el espacio, la arena despide la aviesa humedad de la noche reciente. . . . Un cubo hace funciones de regadera, y moja espalda y busto. Como gatos escaldados se refugian, al terminar, en la chabola" [Under inclement skies, dressed in their underwear, the old man and the young man give one another something like a shower. The wind howls, the clouds hover above, the sand is still terribly damp from the night before. . . . A bucket serves as a spigot, and soaks back and chest. Like scalded cats they take refuge in the hut when they finish] [48]).[41]

Certainly the clearest and most readily available example of the ironic disjunction between signifier and signified is captured in the book's title, a header that Naharro-Calderón has aptly called "the incongruous title with the bizarre flavor of a beach holiday": *St. Cyprien, plage . . . Campo de concentración*.[42] The titular revelation that this beachside location, so evocative says Andújar of "un sol claro, un cielo terso, una campiña de redonda fecundidad suave" [a bright sun, a cloudless sky, lush and fertile countryside] (47), is in fact a filthy prison for eighty thousand "walking cadavers" (21) foregrounds the unstable relationship between place and meaning so characteristic of the world of the camps. The juxtaposed terms joined by the ellipsis (*"plage*/campo de concentración"*) are not the only spatial fields suggested in the title. Frequently when referring to the place of St. Cyprien, inmate-authors will make a distinction between "St. Cyprien, town" and "St. Cyprien, beach" to clarify references made to the concentration camp as opposed to the little French town. Luis Suárez, for example, begins the final chapter of his book *España comienza en los Pirineos* by placing side by side the contrastive spaces of the two "St. Cypriens." When finally leaving the reviled camp, Suárez again makes the double topographical reference that now inheres within the very name "St. Cyprien": "We crossed the little town of Saint Cyprien, the same Saint Cyprien as always, the one that had been there since before we arrived and not the later one that had been created for us, and its streets were quiet."[43] Similarly, Eulalio Ferrer and his fellow inmates note comparable reverse realities when, transferred from the Argelès camp to another, they pass through the "the picturesque town of Argelès." The two flip sides of a place called "Argelès" are underscored by Ferrer's juxtaposition of his memories of the strange world just left behind ("The damp that went to the bone. The lice, traveling from one body to another. The diarrhea, like a common birthright"), with the sights and sounds of this "normal" Argelès that he marches through: "We are amazed to see homes where people live; people at work; stores with tempting, although unattainable, merchandise."[44] Manuel García Gerpe makes the point in his memoir *Alambradas* that the name of his camp, "Septfonds," referred to two very different places: "Two kilometers away was Septfonds, the *petit village*. This, though, was *Septfonds the Concentration Camp*."[45] The first part of Andújar's title then, *St. Cyprien, plage*, evokes the place of the camp as an "other space" counterposed to the central, normal St. Cyprien town. Such a space brings to mind Foucault's concept of heterotopia, a site, he says, that has "the curious property of being in relation with all the other sites, but in such a way as to suspect, neutralize, or invert the set of relations that they happen to designate, mirror, or reflect."[46] The concentration camps, typically designated with the same name as the neighboring village (Argelès, Agde, Septfonds, etc), reflect a perverted mirror-image of daily life in their homologous French communities. Jaime Espinar describes a savage bread-distribution system forced on the starving inmates of Argelès-sur-Mer ("And the people trampled one another on the sand. The weakest fell. The maimed and injured gave up"); he concludes that chapter with a contrastive view of Argelès, *la villa*: "And the contented neighbors of the Town continue to lead their civilized lives. Another twenty-four hours have gone by. On his bicycle the boy from the bakery makes deliveries of the warm, delicious 'croisants' for the family breakfast."[47] Andújar describes the multipurpose usage accorded to the single stretch of sand that actually shares its border with the outside world, the camp's infamous "Avenida de Libertad" ("It serves as a place to stroll, as a watering hole, as a soccer field—or rather 'fields'—, as a market" [39]), in terms of its deformed refraction of a town's activities, "giving the illusion of a city—replicating it—along the arid path" (40).

This strange new space, according to Andújar, defines itself by constantly subverting categories of meaning: "The incongruity, the arbitrariness. The name rarely denotes the meaning of the object" (39). Such is the central feature of Foucault's heterotopia, a locus where systems of signification utterly break down: "*Heterotopias* are disturbing, probably because they secretly undermine language, because they make it impossible to name this *and* that, because they shatter or tangle common names, because they destroy 'syntax' in advance, and not only the syntax with which we construct sentences but also that less apparent syntax which causes words and things (next to and also opposite one another) to 'hold together.' . . . Heterotopias . . . desiccate speech, stop words in their tracks, contest the very possibility of grammar at its source; they dissolve our myths and sterilize the lyricism of our sentences."[48] Andújar's self-conscious realization that the reality he attempts to transcribe defies the "lyricism of our sentences" is expressed very early in his work. In the second introductory piece entitled "El agrio" (The Bitter Wind), Andújar rejects as inadequate any textual version penned by "eventuales líricos imaginistas, violadores soeces— en su almibaramiento—de la neta realidad" [future pretentious lyric poets, obscene violators—for their honeyed embellishment—of reality] that purports to portray the brutal wind that relentlessly hammers the camp as a "pretexto plausible de blandas efusiones redondas, motivo de expansión para las metáforas sacadas de quicio" [plausible pretext for mild, comfy effusions, an expansive excuse to use irritatingly ridiculous metaphors] (17). Such depictions may apply to the tranquil topoi of the neighboring world ("Enfrente, articulado, el escorzo montañoso de los Pirineos, las pelladas lisas de la arena, el lejano verdor de las campiñas civiles" [Facing us, in clear silhouette, the mountainous slopes of the Pyrenees, the smooth mounds of sand, the distant green of farmland] [17]), but are powerless to connote the sheer magnitude of human suffering within the camp's perimeters. The only way to convey the meaning of the elements of this place is to express them directly in terms of the material reality of this epic human drama, specifically through the medium of the human body. In the case of the wind, for example, it begins to take shape and make sense only when referred to in relation to the camp inmates' most visceral experience of it: "It slaps your face till you want to die, it pierces your flesh and rattles your bones" (17–18). But the wind that reveals itself through the bodies it buffets and batters is still not easily transformed into language. In a metatextual moment, Andújar tries to imagine how veterans of the camps would translate this "unforgettable phase" (18) into a text of testimony. Ideally, he declares, all survivor speech would culminate in a Genesis-like, primordial act of naming that would call into being the entire world of the camp in the annals of posterity: "Con léxico multiforme, en párrafo estilizado o mediante una interjección enérgica, que identifica paisaje, vigilantes, humor, esperanza y desilusiones de cada hora, os contestarán en la posible encuesta: ¡El viento!" [Using a vast and diverse lexicon, in a stylized paragraph or by means of an energetic interjection that identifies landscape, guards, humor, hope, and disappointments at every turn, (the witnesses) would answer a hypothetical survey like this: *The wind!*] (18).

In these early pages of Andújar's work, the author suggests two key points about the place of the camp and how he will represent it. First, he aims to record a collective memory and chronicle a group's history rather than engender a purely personal, autobiographical narrative; second, he suggests the primacy of the body as a vehicle for this expression. The "posible encuesta" [hypothetical survey] that he imagines in the future, a format that would allow all the inmates to be surveyed so as to give voice to their multitudinous experiences, would be an optimum instrument for recording a shared historical moment. However, the disjunction between the signifier and the signified in this heterotopia, as previously discussed, as well as the internees' varying abilities to put their experiences and feelings "into words," hampers a project that rests solely on a grammar of linguistic speech acts. Ask, for example, the illiterate camp inmate nicknamed "the peasant" (33) why he refuses to return to Franco's Spain, and he will not be able to articulate his response: "He can't give you a 'political' explanation for his stubborn refusal to return to fascist Spain, for his decision to make do with the crumbs that are tossed his way at the foot of the Pyrenees . . ." (33). But *el campesino*'s refusal to go back, his stubborn though miserable occupation of the camp instead, defines him and others like him. Their resistance to repatriation (the very issue that Andújar so fiercely condemns when he publishes his book) is a powerful act of emplacement that both accords agency and identity to the displaced refugees and engenders the first chapter of their collective history in exile. In his discussion of Andújar's descriptions of the inmates' physical degradation—plagued as they are by lice, dysentery, and scabies—Naharro-Calderón has observed how the story of suffering is inscribed on the body: "The disjointed and fragmented history is rewritten on the only available paper that is minimally controlled by the prisoner: the skin of his bodily instincts"; indeed, Andújar and his fellow inmates' story is "spoken" through the body, but the tale of misery is not the only one told. Andújar uses the signs of a physical corporality as well as the language of the body-in-place to establish the position of the Spanish inmates as agents of resistance and subjects of solidarity.[49]

Andújar begins his story of St. Cyprien, told in thirty-two brief vignettes, with the only chapter that takes place outside the camp, in the border town of Boulou. Serving as a kind of prefatory note to the barbed-wire world on the beach, these opening paragraphs to the book introduce the recently arrived refugees in terms of a jumbled, anonymous mass of confused humanity: "Thousands of women, children, soldiers, civilian men of all types, temperament, and ages" (15) . The first night of exile is spent in a crowded shelter amidst a crush of human bodies. The initial voices that are recorded are the strangled sounds of moans, cries, and wails; the first movements simply revolve around bodily functions and broken body parts: "Whenever someone got up to go relieve himself, jumping over bodies, . . . bales of straw, he provoked a string of moans, he crushed noses, he stepped on arms in casts" (15). These are the future protagonists of Andújar's camp who will be further brutalized by the ravages of hunger, chronic diarrhea, skin diseases, and illness. In subsequent chapters the author will draw stark sketches of the physical toil that is taken on the inmates. But if he represents the body as a site of suffering, he also reveals its concomitant function as an active site of signifying practices and even creative resistance. In one of the chapters most fully given over to chronicling the physical hardships of the camp, "Lice and Other Niceties," Andújar observes that the massive infestations of lice generate a significant series of speech acts, a common language, and a shared, however unwelcome, "page of daily life" in the story of St. Cyprien: "It's strange to point out that [these lice attacks] provide the most well-worn twists of conversations, inspire the coarse muse of jokes, are the source of aggressiveness, dampen spirits, ruin one's mood" (27). The author offers a kind of body-based semiotics of the lice-infested, suggesting a psychological typology based on the individual inmate's reaction to the vermin invasion: "They characterize the owner, who either resigns himself with a passive gesture, or desperately fights them, or sinks into a state of revulsion that tears away at his mental epidermis" (27). As the self-appointed camp chronicler, Andújar goes on to record a bevy of voices that inventively damn their minuscule tormentors: "'Two fewer today.'. . . 'Every new arrival replenishes the wildlife.' 'Look how much blood the little critter drank, just like the fascists!'. . . 'What a fatty! By the looks of it I've had it on me since the retreat!' 'For all the nits it's left, they should send this one to a stud farm'" (28). The jokes and spirited exchanges, the blasphemies and witty invectives ("Amusing contests, reverse flattery, statistics, genealogy") that are elicited by the invasion of the body are, says Andújar, staunch responses to an irritating distraction, expressive reactions to a misery inducing stimulus, "Positive suffering. It lays siege to the man, awakening—by the sight and feel of it—his depressed state of mind" (28).

In his ongoing efforts to decipher and document the signs of the surreal surroundings, Andújar finds other unlikely figures in the landscape that similarly codify the story of St. Cyprien. In "The Lines," the author describes the scene of the enervating wait for the revolting chow ("The kitchen chimneys belch out a thick, black smoke, giving off a smell of dirty grease") and discovers another flesh-and-blood tableau that speaks like a text: "The chow line, especially at midday, is a poem. An indictment. A living, breathing document" (95). Again, Andújar gives shorter shrift to the offending material reality (the disgusting slop) than to the inmates' stinging, sardonic responses to it: "'Lentils again!' 'I found more sand here than on the beach.' 'You wouldn't feed this to a dog!' 'Well, at least this way we'll keep our figures!'. . . 'You need a good imagination to call this coffee'" (96). Yet another gathering of refugees that has assembled to listen to a fellow inmate-reader's oral translation of selected articles from a French newspaper provide Andújar with an opportunity to register the role of this audience as provocative participants in their own right.[50] This scene inverts another from the opening chapter of the book, *"Paris-Soir,"* named for the right-wing French newspaper that derisively reports the Republican retreat and exodus across the border with "defeatist remarks and a disgusting sensationalism as they stick their noses into our affairs" (16). The solitary, silent newspaper reader in that first instance simply responds by muttering in disgust, "Sons of bitches!" (16). But now in the camps, the scorned "other" of that earlier negative journalistic portrayal enacts its own collective subjectivity in an energetic performance of opinion. When the group's reader intones a headline, "The Rearmament of England," an outraged voice yells out: "Oh, so now they realize that the Munich Pact was a stupid mistake!"(35). Another listener clamors for a reading of the bulletin published by their Republican neighbors in the camp of Argelès-sur-Mer; the suggestion unleashes the enthusiastic hum characteristic of a shared space of fellowship, "An emotional release is expressed as a collective sigh, a satisfied murmur, so similar to what you hear coming out of a class . . ." (36). But the wishes of the audience are most vigorously expressed when the shout goes up to "first, read about Spain." The wave of patriotic emotion and nostalgia triggered among the listeners by the received news of beloved *España* momentarily obliterates everything else: "Nothing else matters, not the weather conditions, the salty taste in one's mouth, the bitter ignominy of the newspaper accounts, the news agencies' pat reports and half-truths. Longing, hatred, passion, all revive. Their brows are furrowed with expectations, hope, anger" (36). The faces of the inmates are an open book.[51]

It is the love and memory of a free Spain that engenders an early episode in which Andújar most pointedly records the speech of resistance and a shared political agenda on the part of the inmates. The title of the fourth vignette, "Plebiscite," indicating the democratic expression of the will of the people, refers to a unified response to a familiar phenomenon during the very early days of the camp. Gathered to watch as groups of inmates opt to return to Spain rather than endure the misery and uncertainty of exile in the camps, a motley crew joins their voices together to protest the repatriation; the most marginalized among the Spaniards in exile, among whom the narrator includes himself, stake out a position in the sands of St. Cyprien: "The most vocal spectators were, for the most part, the war-injured, the infirm, and women. Rude words and curses began to rain down. And along the rows of deserters who hesitated, we shouted words of encouragement, of faith in the cause, of ardent patriotism, cries that broke through their ranks, and created two moral categories of campers" (24). The confrontation between those who turn back, defeated, and those who literally "hold their ground" and struggle on is a fundamental episode in the story of exile as narrated by the memoirists of the concentration camps. The refusal to leave the camps is generally inscribed as a moment of maximum defiance of French and/or Francoist authority and as an occasion for a display of loyalty to the ideals of the Spanish Republic. In his 1945 novelized account of life in Argelès-sur-Mer, Angel Samblancat paints a humorous picture of the official exhortations that all Spaniards "who do not have blood on your hands" should return to Franco's Spain. The representative implores a huge group of inmates that has been assembled before him: "All of you who haven't committed a robbery or murder, please step forward." The narrator reports with irony, "Not a soul moved a muscle to make a mark in the sand. Apparently, every single person there was a self-confessed murderer or thief." The increasingly impatient and frustrated official finally gives up, shouting to the group, "You're all a bunch of sons-of-bitches." "We knew that already!" one of the inmates murmurs sardonically.[52] The collective refusal to move an inch is described as a moment of maximum group solidarity by another memoirist, Miguel Giménez Igualada. In a letter from the camp dated November 18, 1939, he describes the outcome of the stepped-up pressure exerted by the French government to persuade a group of the inmates to go back to Spain: "The fact that not a single person, not one!, volunteered to go back to Franco's domain, has united all of us even more."[53] Eulalio Ferrer explains in a diary entry from Barcarès dated August 14, 1939, that the Spaniards took the occasion of resisting repatriation as an opportunity for colorfully and creatively expressing political subversiveness and intransigence: "The French command has ordered us to answer a questionnaire. Isidoro, always the joker, in answer to the question about whether he wants to go back to Spain, responds: 'Yes, to cut off Franco's head.' For the one that asks, 'Why don't you want to go back to Spain?,' he says: 'Because I don't goddamned want to.' There are a lot of guys who reply with these kinds of answers on the questionnaire."[54] Perhaps the most concerted effort to respond to the question of repatriation with an act of political resistance is reported by Manuel García Gerpe, inmate of Septfonds. He describes the summertime dissemination in the camp of Franco's "Law of Political Responsibility" enacted in February 1939 against supporters of the Republic. This law, described by Franco's biographer Paul Preston as "the first step in the full-scale institutionalization of a repression . . . a massive wave of political arrests, trials, executions and imprisonment," became the text of a kind of minicourse on political science that García Gerpe gave to fellow inmates.[55] Reading out loud to them the full text of the "Ley," which García Gerpe also reprints in his 1941 concentration camp memoir, the author argues for a united response to the document; not only should it incur their outrage, but should be received as a catalyst to mobilize themselves in the continued struggle against Franco, "[a call] to all democrats, all humanists, all those who love peace, to protest, to stop the assassins, to come to the aid of the heroic Spanish nation."[56] García Gerpe adds as an afterthought that he received five days of punishment for his political preachings against repatriation.

In his "Plebiscite," where the refugees like all exiles vote with their feet, Manuel Andújar summarizes the pivotal instance of political protest as an inaugural episode in the history of exile politics, still in its infancy: "Facing the Pyrenees, the Spanish antifascists demonstrated for the first time since beginning their emigration" (24). He continues to trace a timeline of noteworthy political anniversaries as the months of internment drag by. In the piece entitled "April 14," the author describes how the signs of Republican identity are rebelliously displayed in the camp in order to commemorate the founding of the Spanish Republic in 1931; the flags of the Republic mysteriously materialize, "From what truck's cadaver?" (51), and are brazenly raised before flying in the face of official control. Confronted with a similar repressive order against political expression on May 1, the International Day of the Worker, the inmates surreptitiously share their subversive response to the "Official prohibition" (57) through covert communions and silent pantomimes of a fraternal conspiracy: "On today's date, jubilation and anger run through the veins of the workers and laborers. Some commemorate the day by decorating a cake—obtained through scrimping and sacrifice—that leads to toasts in the main barrack, others march by two's along the main walkway as if they are just innocently strolling, winking knowingly at one another" (57–58). Through furtive gestures and encoded body language, the Republicans publicly perform a private parade to celebrate the first May Day of the Spanish exile of 1939. Andújar devotes fully half of his very brief account of this day to the citation of the "snatches of conversations" that are later overheard as night falls in the camp; the text, which reads like a single, cohesive, motivational call to action, begins like this: "May 1st demands that we Spanish antifascists affirm our unity and our fighting spirit. The struggle is not over. We are living in a new phase" (58). The author connects the spirited commemoration of May Day to a new position of solidarity that gives the inmates a firmer footing in exile: "It seems now, as you wrap up in an overcoat trying to get to sleep, that the sand isn't so hard on your hips, that the 'bedroom' is less squalid. There's something . . ."(58).

The Spanish refugees' fervent desire to believe that they are in fact purposefully embarking on a "new phase," and not aimlessly biding time in a sandy purgatory, is evident in Andújar's depiction of the camp as a first-stage location in the campaign of national reconstruction. If the most committed fighters for a free Spain decisively take their place on the soil of exile, then it follows, argue Andújar and other camp memoirists, that the spirit and shape of Spain will be embodied there. In a chapter entitled with powerful biblical allusions to the book of Genesis, "Cataclysm, Flood, Fire," the author documents a key moment in the young history of the concentration camps; more than two months after the refugees' arrival, a massive construction project finally begins to erect wooden barracks, the *barracas*, replacing the primitive stick-and-blanket *chabolas* as shelter for the inmates. Andújar surveys the changing landscape, observing the pieces of the torn-down huts; the camp's chronicler takes stock of this place amidst the ruins of history before it disappears into oblivion. He commits to memory the primitive building supplies that first housed civil war Spain's most violently uprooted exiles: "The boards have torn loose, strips of metal as well. The blankets lie about, neatly folded" (44). He reads in the abandoned personal possessions scattered on the beach the first installment of an exiled people's biography: "The chessboard made out of cardboard, the handwritten calendar pulled off the ex-wall, an evicted shirt that soaks up rain in its folds, twisted pieces of iron, a guitar pick, a torn hat. Bizarre objects, the equivalent of words from a special, suggestive language, lifted from the most banal biographical episodes, are charged with symbolic significance. This dense chapter—rich in details about the first ten weeks of a prison constructed not with walls of stone, but rather with those made out of the beach, of mountains, of hunger, of nostalgia, of an epileptic chaos that time and instinct have vanquished—this chapter is coming to an end" (44). A similar scene of the dramatically changing landscape of the evolving camps is detailed in one of the newsletter articles printed in the neighboring camp of Argelès-sur-Mer in July 1939, "The Camp." This author, like Andújar, registers the quickly disappearing *chabolas*—engulfed in flames to make way for the wooden *barracas*—as highly expressive architectural landmarks, however physically impermanent, that mark the end of the emotional first chapter of the refugees' saga:

> The Argelès camp is changing its physiognomy. That motley group of huts made up of so many styles and shades, that gave us shelter during the early months of our stay, those pieces of canvas, blankets, and cane, that protected us from the night dew and the cold North wind, have been transformed into dense columns of smoke. And while the flames of fire destroyed these remains, we watched with gratitude. All those nights of rain and cold. That early morning frost. Everything disappears in the purifying fire, the wind-blown smoke is lost out to sea. . . . Gone now is the unique stamp that the personality of each of the huts' inmates left on its construction. Gone too the competitive spirit that was evident in the way we decorated our dwellings. We salute our vanished huts, some of which are still smoldering, and may the mark of our energetic spiritualism be similarly left on the new ones.[57]

Throughout his own manuscript, Manuel Andújar carefully records other transformative, though equally transitory, topographical markers or human figures that tell the story of a Spain that resourcefully carries on in exile. Artful signs and slogans, textual memories of the fight at home, have been crafted by inspired inmates: "In certain places, the place names and emblems of our fight have been constructed by using multi-colored pebbles and shells, giving it the look of a city park" (60). The specially designated *barracón* houses a hodgepodge of cultural activities: "Poetry recitals, or choir performances, or a filmmaker's lecture, are included in the general curriculum and French language courses that the railroad workers, helped by the FETE [Spanish teacher's union], have devised" (78). A jolly band of ragged musicians plays tunes that transcend the limits of the camp. Committed to laying the foundations for a new national history, Andújar chronicles the signs of the collective will to maintain cultural continuity that he observes all around him: "If similarly courageous initiatives don't die out here, they will one day be accorded a permanent place in history!" (61).[58]

Manuel Andújar had begun writing his story of the concentration camp of St. Cyprien by imagining how camp veterans would respond to a future survey questionnaire about their experiences. In one of the closing chapters, called "Aquella encuesta" (That Survey), the author explains that he himself had proposed to conduct and publish just such a survey during his time at St. Cyprien, "A survey asking about one's most profound personal and political feelings" (99). He still regrets that the project did not materialize, lamenting particularly what may have been forever lost to history: "Walking from one camp to another, conducting a . . . survey of fellow companions of oppression—thousands of them—it pained me that no one ever pieced together the spirit of their answers, in an eloquent and intimate account, nor captured their ineffable, enduring, transcendent expression. . . . Because the void is on record. And tomorrow we will regret the omission" (102). But of course the pages of the text that Andújar composes in the camp, "in all different colors and sizes, using my knees for a desktop" (8), replete with the voices of his fellow inmates—illiterate, maimed, diseased, or weakened though they be—serves a similar purpose, consigning the life of this exile community to the annals of history. The promise of this enduring record is alluded to in the final image of the book. In the very brief, two-paragraph concluding chapter, Andújar describes the moment that he and others selected for emigration to Mexico pass through the arched gate out of the camp; he looks back over his shoulder like a modern-day Lot's companion: "Now we can read the letters, tied heart and soul to our experience: 'SAINT-CYPRIEN, PLAGE.' We hoist ourselves up into the trucks. The arch . . . of triumph blurs into a blotch of color, but we know that the pain and outrage of the camp experience will be fruitful" (107–8).[59] Moments after the truck loaded with refugees rumbles away from the sign at the gate, the despised location left behind has already begun its metamorphosis into a "place of memory," fertile terrain for establishing the basis of a national history in exile. For his part, Manuel Andújar will become one of the most articulate voices of his generation of post–civil war émigrés. He fulfills his objectives as a champion of cultural continuity as cofounder of the long-lived journal *Las Españas* and as publicist for Fondo de Cultura Económica in Mexico City; following a 1967 return to Spain, he works for another major publishing house, Alianza Editorial, and is cofounder of the journal *El Urogallo*. In 1989, fifty years after pulling away from the so-called "arco

. . . triunfal" of the prison gates, Manuel Andújar defines his generation's arduous path of exile as an ultimately transformative journey that originated in the ashes of defeat: "We did our best to transform the iniquitous physical defeat that was inflicted upon us into a legitimate and productive course of action" (9–10).

8
Celso Amieva's *La almohada de arena* (1960): Exile Identity as Buried Treasure

. . . cobraremos todos en arena.

[. . . we will stake our claim in sand]

—León Felipe, 1939

OF ALL THE SPANIARDS WHO EVENTUALLY MADE THEIR WAY TO Mexico, none spent more interminable days and nights behind the barbed wire of the concentration camps of France than did Celso Amieva (1911–88), who holds the unenviable distinction among the exiled writers in Mexico of having lived the longest time as an inmate in a variety of locations including Argelès-sur-Mer, Barcarès, and Bram.[1] According to his own painstakingly precise count, the early weeks of initial imprisonment stretched into endless months and years: "My imprisonment lasted exactly three years, nine months, one week, and one day. As exact a sentence as if it'd been conferred in a court of law."[2] Amieva is the keeper of his own calendar of confinement, routinely signing the individual poems that he composes during these years with careful "anniversary" dates—"Year III of Exile, Month XXXII of Internment" *(Poeta)*—that ironically echo the exultant Nationalist commemorative calculations of time since the victorious takeover of Republican Spain, "Year I of Victory."[3] Living as long as he does in an empty vacuum of sand, a "sandy limbo," it is not surprising that a frequent poetic image in Amieva's verses is the hourglass, an ancient timepiece that uses grains of sand to measure time at a maddening snail's pace; in one of his last poems of the collection *La almohada de arena*, entitled "Noviembre 1942," he begins: "Grano a grano, el reloj de arena / en la playa del Mediterráneo / rodeada de alambre espinoso / azotada por viento inhumano, / a fuerza a marcar las horas, /años, más años fue marcando: / un año, dos años, / tres años, casi cuatro años" [Grain by grain, the hourglass / on the Mediterranean beach / surrounded by the barbed wire / whipped by a merciless wind, / was obliged to record the hours, / years, and even more years were recorded: / one year, two years, / three years, almost four years].⁴ The despair and anguish occasioned not only by the recent trauma of war but also by the desperate waiting in the sandy prisons, combined with the intolerable living conditions, resulted in episodes of emotional breakdowns and mental collapses that were referred to by the inmates as *arenosis* (sand-neurosis). In his 1977 memoir of life in the camps, *Asturianos en el destierro (Francia)*, Celso Amieva has described this psychological phenomenon that took its name from the source itself of the disorder: "We were already feeling the effects of a peculiar nervous disorder, a neurosis of the concentration camp, a neurosis of the sand: *arenosis*" (23).⁵ The seemingly permanent camp resident Amieva reports that he was particularly susceptible to *arenosis*, experienced as bouts of anxiety and depression, so much so that his companions kidded him that his very being was slowly being turned into hardened sand like a petrified man made of concrete: "Barral, a medical student, used to say that I had sand running through my veins. Méndez added that everyone would get out of the camp, some would go to Mexico, others to Russia and still others to Chile, except for me. I would become one with the sand" (*Asturianos*, 34).

The well-known exilic pattern of loss of self (i.e., sand-induced fits of *arenosis*) concomitantly experienced with a loss of place (the nowhere of the camps) is extant in Amieva's descriptions of his early environment in the camp of Barcarès; this isolated geographical site was literally located somewhere between sand and water, like an eerie archipelago of deserted islands: "It was built on a tiny peninsula of sand: the sea on one side, a lagoon on the other. The setting, well, it was perfect: the whole thing was an internment camp for 'undesirables,' according to the description in *L'Indépendant*, a newspaper in Perpignan. A huge rectangular section of sand, divided lengthwise by a road built—like everything else there—by the first soldiers who had arrived, remnants of the 'defeated army,' as the French soldiers took cruel delight in calling us. Additionally, the two halves of the rectangle were divided into a series of smaller 'isles,' as numerous as the letters of Victor Hugo's alphabet. When you'd seen one, you'd seen them all," (*Poeta*). Amieva and his comrades are assigned to the isle aptly designated "O," where they debate whether the cipher is a letter or a numeral, "For the pessimist Sarmentero, our sign and our destiny was the zero; for the carefree Noloma, the song we should be singing there was 'María de la O'"(*Asturianos*, 32). Either way, says Amieva, the place that the sign represents is equally devoid of signification for the internees. But following the familiar path of the camp exiles' eventual transference of empty space into meaningful place, this piece of ground zero on foreign soil slowly begins to take shape: it is a site of reunion between Amieva and his long-lost friend Méndez from the civil war; as part of the unlikely "University of the Sand" (*Asturianos*, . . . 33), it engenders a kind of cultural center and school; it becomes the place where Amieva translates his experiences into words. The conversion of this encircled strip of beach, the round hollow "O" carved into the sand like a barbed-wire tomb, into a foundational topos in the story of Spanish Republican exile, is in fact the project that Celso Amieva undertakes in his important book of concentration camp poetry, *La almohada de arena*, published in Mexico City in 1960. Proving that the empty signs of the concentration camps can be productive (the publisher for the book is coincidentally listed as Suplemento de Ecuador O O O), Amieva chronicles the history of the camps in France, whether in the isle of "O" of Barcarès or in Argelès-sur-Mer, as a new national myth of cultural continuity. Ultimately the same sands that threatened physical health and psychic unity function in *La almohada de arena* as a gritty repository of subversive strategies and as a rich reservoir of hidden strength into which the roots of exilic survival and identity are deeply embedded.

I read Amieva's collection of concentration camp verse—thirty-two poems, almost half of which bear the dates of their composition during the author's confinement—within the wider context of the ongoing efforts on the part of the inmates to carry on the Republican campaign of cultural values, most notably from within the auspices of the *barracones de cultura* (cultural barracks). An early newsletter circulated in the camp of Gurs dated August 10, 1939, defined these barracks as a busy center of multifaceted cultural enrichment: "The Cultural Barrack is a graduate school where a hundred of our fellow campers receive daily instruction; it's an academy where other companions learn languages; it's a cultural center situated in the middle of the sand that has brought together the most authoritative voices of our comrades in exile; it's a stage where authentic regional folkloric groups perform from all over Spain, including Santander, Galicia, and Catalonia. A real standout are the chorus members of the Teaching Professionals *[Profesionales de la Enseñanza]* that perform folk tunes in four-part harmony."[6] Another camp bulletin, this one printed in Amieva's Barcarès on July 27, 1939, summarizes the massive conversion of the watery isles into a stronghold of educational initiatives organized and conducted by the inmates themselves: "On 25 isles there are French classes with a total of 1,300 students. On 23 isles there are basic culture classes with 740 students. On 21 isles there are classes to teach internees to read, with 125 students. On 10 isles there are general culture classes with 470 students. On 4 isles there are English language classes with 97 students. On 4 isles there are typing and accounting classes with 65 students."⁷ The idea that the zero-value of *islotes* like Amieva's "O" has been transformed into circles of cultural edification is proclaimed from the pages of the *Boletín de Profesionales de la Enseñanza* of Barcarès. The ambitious pedagogical programs of the *barracones de cultura*, says the author, were conceived in order to help make something out of nothing, transcending the limits of imprisonment: "What we wanted, and what we still want, is for the concentration camp not to be a concentration camp for us."⁸ In the same issue, another impassioned teacher-internee proudly touts the instructional work in progress behind the lines of barbed-wire fencing: "A Pedagogy Seminar in the Concentration Camp! A laboratory of teacher-training that emerges from behind barbed wire! Our spirit is what forges such magnificent ideas; our will is what makes them reality."⁹

Celso Amieva has described the early stages of the "University of Barcarès": "Barral, one of Méndez's young deputies, founded along with some others the University of Barcarès, that held classes in a designated hut on each isle. Barral was to be a philosophy professor; as for me, I'd teach literature. 'Each isle, its own school!' he'd say. 'Twenty-five schools?' 'Sure, man, don't be stingy.' Classes, lectures, exhibitions, concerts, the University of the Sand was pure pandemonium" (*Asturianos*, 33). Not only did these classes carry on the same educational mission sponsored in the Spanish Republic by organizations such as the Misiones pedagógicas, but as the critic José Cruz emphasizes in his study of the *barracones de cultura*, they also represent an important link between the struggle in Spain and the struggle in Exile, "they helped dignify the plight of the internees, creating continuity between their stay in the concentration camp and their struggle during the War."¹⁰ This fervent desire for the continuity and survival of Spanish Republican culture in exile informs the very first issue of the *Profesionales de la Enseñanza* published on July 1, 1939, in the camp of Argelès-sur-Mer:

> With today's premiere issue of this Bulletin, the tangible reality of so many dreams, we invite our enthusiastic readership to join us on the arduous road between the past and the future. We offer our journal as an incentive and optimistic promise of good things to come, all the sweeter since they will be achieved through our own determination.
> The Teaching Professionals of the Argelès Camp, those of us who in Spain had placed our hopes in raising the country to a new level of culture, who even far from Spain feel that it is our duty to continue that task, salute all Spaniards in exile. . . . And along with this greeting we entreat our readers to join us in our work, so that despite the difficult circumstances and meager means, we may achieve positive results through our redoubled efforts.

The faith that guided our work in Spain, our unyielding resolve that was simply a reflection of the cultural aspirations of our people, have not abandoned us. We want to continue the task that we set before us in our homeland, more beloved now than ever. We want to stay the course that, like knights errant in pursuit of culture, we undertook some time ago. . . . KEEP WORKING! KEEP FIGHTING FOR OUR CULTURE! THIS IS OUR GREAT DUTY![11]

The image of an exiled nation's quixotic efforts to keep its cultural identity intact, alive, and well ("like knights errant in pursuit of culture") brings to mind the most emblematic representation of "wandering Spain," Antonio Rodríguez Luna's *Don Quijote en el Exilio*, now part of the permanent collection of former Barcarès inmate Eulalio Ferrer's Museo iconográfico del Quijote in Guanajuato, Mexico; Ferrer has described the painter's portrayal of a culture in exile: "Rocinante advances wearing a blindfold; riding him is Don Quijote, in shades of dark blue and gray. Behind them, the great diaspora. At the head of the group, León Felipe, Antonio Machado, Juan Ramón Jiménez . . ."[12] Like so many of his displaced compatriots, particularly those in the camps, Celso Amieva also picks up this central motif of Don Quijote as the symbol of exiled Spain; in his poem "Epístola a Miguel de Cervantes," after drawing a parallel between two historical moments of imprisonment (Cervantes in Argel; the Republicans in Argelès), he concludes by addressing his Republican comrades wherever they are: "Luche vuestro Quijote en suelo hispano, / otros Quijotes en solar francés / luchemos sin reposo mano a mano" [May your Quijote fight on Hispanic soil, / may other Quijotes in French lands / tirelessly fight hand to hand] (*La almohada*). Just as Rodríguez Luna had located the Spanish Republicans' exodus firmly behind the tripartite leadership of the nation's cultural icons, Amieva also inscribes the incipient struggle for cultural continuity that he chronicles in *La almohada de arena* under the aegis of three poets who are eternally tied to the story of civil war, cultural memory, and exile: Federico García Lorca, Antonio Machado, and León Felipe. These celebrated names function as a trilogy of supportive intertexts in the three introductory poems of Amieva's collection of concentration camp verse. By inaugurating his book with intertextual references to the work of these three canonical figures—the war's martyr, exile's casualty, the diaspora's clearest voice—Amieva begins to connect the tenuous threads of his emerging story of the camps with the tightly woven cultural history that accompanies, and deeply sustains, the Spaniards in exile.

In his 1944 account of the physical and emotional hardships that overwhelmed thousands of refugees in Argelès-sur-Mer, memoirist

Angel Samblancat begins his description of the world of the camp with a chapter entitled "The Crown of Artificial Thorns."[13] This barbed-wire symbol of the internees' tortured existence is likewise invoked in the first poem of Celso Amieva's work, "Corona de espinas" (Crown of Thorns), the homage-poem composed on the occasion of Machado's death in Collioure. As I have indicated in my analysis of this poem in chapter 2, the commemoration of Machado's death is one of the most significant expressive acts that marks the birth of a collective consciousness in exile. The protagonist of the poem who artfully crafts an enduring tribute to the beloved poet of the Spanish Republic is one of the camp's *locos*, just another victim of the pervasive *arenosis* that also plagued the author Amieva. But here in the very initial verses of *La almohada de arena*, this humble hero, a mere shadow now of his former "normal" self, is championed because of his enviable, exemplary talent. El Loco, using nothing more than scraps and remnants he finds scattered on the soil of exile, is able to transform the barren place of suffering into a fertile place of memory: "Sangre brota de sus dedos / y la viene a restañar / la ruda caricia helada / del huracán" [Blood spurts from his fingertips / the flow of blood is frozen / kissed by the coarse caress / of the winter wind's icy touch]. The bloody marks resulting from the arduous act of commemoration stain the frozen sand as the refugees' history begins to be painfully composed on the grounds of the camps: "La corona goteante / ya ensangrienta el arenal" [The dripping crown / now bloodies the sandy ground]. In this metatextual moment, Amieva/*El Loco* creates the first page of the story of the camps as a piecemeal artifact that will be ingeniously tacked together with guiding voices from the past, subversive scraps from the present, and tenaciously held hopes for the future.[14]

If the evocation of Antonio Machado engenders the first signs of exilic identity spilled onto the sands of the first poem, the poetic cosmology of García Lorca provides the intertextual scaffolding for a new camp mythology in the second poem, "Romance de la Guardia Móvil francesa" (Romance of the French Mobile Guard). As the title and subtitle, "Parodia del 'Romance de la Guardia Civil Española,' de García Lorca," make clear, Amieva superimposes the universe of the French concentration camp onto the mythicized world of Lorca's Andalucía in order to record a new chapter of oppression and violence against a marginalized community of Spaniards. Amieva's predilection for the *romance* form of the Spanish traditional lyric may have been particularly stimulated by his readings in the camps. He has explained that he read whatever he could get his hands on, and that a stolen copy of the "magnificent" *Romancero español* (Spanish Ballads) was a special favorite (*Asturianos*, 40). The critic Monique Alonso has stated that in the camp of

Barcarès a group of poetry enthusiasts printed up "who knows how many copies of *Gypsy Ballads* by García Lorca and handed them out among the internees in the camp."[15] Amieva pens several *romances* with direct allusions to Lorca's *Romancero* poems, such as "Romance de la tramontana" (Ballad of the North Wind) and "La luna de Barcarès" (The Moon of Barcarès) (which chronicles the notorious *razzia* of Gypsies and their internment in Barcarès on orders of Hitler, who by 1942 was taking control of the French camps); but at more than two hundred verses, "Ballad of the French Mobile Guard" is clearly the most important Lorca-inspired composition of the book. The poem's placement as an introductory text further underscores its significance in the overall scheme of the work. By interpolating the imagery and events of Lorca's best-known "gypsy poem," Amieva is able to inscribe specific historical incidents in the camps within the parameters of a generative Ur-text of the Spanish cultural canon. Layering his poetic story onto the dramatic background of Lorca's galloping black horsemen and their apocalyptic destruction of a defenseless people, Amieva endeavors to transform the transitory history of the camps into the immutable material of legend and lore.

Amieva begins his poem with prefatory verses in which he identifies Lorca's lyrical depiction of the black-hearted Civil Guards and the City of Gypsies that they decimate as a stunningly prophetic evocation of the brutal French Mobile Guards and the City of Refugees that they torment. From his prisoner's pillow of sand, the author discerns the echoes of Lorca's voice like the sounds of an oracle: "Tú la viste, tú la viste, / la Guardia Móvil francesa. / . . . / Y yo voy desentrañando / la voz de tu adormidera / que me canta, arena arriba, / hasta llegar a mi oreja. / . . . / iay, playa la de Argelès / dentro de tu calavera!" [You did see them, you did see them, / the French Mobile guard. / . . . / And I try now to make out / the hypnotic sound of your voice / that sings to me, above the sand, / it reaches my ear. / . . . / oh, the beach of Argelès / burned into your skull!]. Like visions of a dream, the physical locale of the camps is translated into an imaginative landscape with strong parallels to Lorca's poetic universe: "La Luna sobre la mar. / La Mar bordando en la arena. / Ciudad de dolor y lona, / de cañas y de madera. / Con avenidas de sueños / y torreones de ideas / está, castillo de naipes, / gravitando en las tinieblas" [The Moon over the sea. / The Sea makes stitches in the sand. / In a canvas city of suffering / of cane and wood. / With avenues of dreams / and sandcastle turrets of ideas / a house of cards / floats through the shadows]. This City of Sand reverberates with the same sense of foreboding elicited in the original poem; the impending danger that the guards introduce in Lorca's verses ("Con el alma de charol / vienen por la carretera. / Jorobados y nocturnos, / por donde animan ordenan / silencios de goma oscura / y miedos de fina arena" [With patent-leather souls / they come down the highway. / Hunchbacked creatures of the night, / commanding wherever they go / black rubber silences / and a finely ground fear]) is replicated in Amieva's version: "¡Ciudad de los Refugiados! / En las esquinas, sorpresas: / nidos de ametralladora / con sus huevos de culebra. / Levántate ya, que viene / la Guardia Móvil francesa." [City of Refugees! / Surprises hiding around every corner: / machine-gun nests / with their serpent's eggs. / Get up now, they're coming / the French Mobile Guard]. Using Lorca's structural framework to prepare the terrain for the inevitable confrontation between the guard-antagonists and the refugee-protagonists, the author reveals the surprising cause for the real-life armed raid on the *chabolas* that he chronicles in the poem. Filling the space of his poem with references to representative figures of French authority and leadership (the "Prefect" of Argelès; the despised triumvirate of "Herriot, Daladier y Blum / —carroña, estiércol y mierda—" [Herriot, Daladier, and Blum / —carcass, manure, and shit—]; even the patron saint of Paris, Santa Genoveva), Amieva explains at last the motive for the violent attack on the huts sanctioned by the French officials: "quieren oro de Figueras" [they want the Figueras gold]. The guards are feverishly looking for buried treasure, gold bullions of the Spanish national depository that the interned soldiers from Lister's division carried from the castle of Figueras across the French border and allegedly into the camps.[16] This frantic search for gold results in complete devastation for the internees and furious disappointment for the treasure hunters: "La Guardia Móvil arrasa / chavolas, pieza por pieza. / Van destripando macutos, /entran a saco en maletas. / . . . / Ya vuelan picos y palas / desde el cielo hasta la arena / y de la arena hasta el cielo . . . / pero el oro no se encuentra / . . . / Por el confín de la playa / —fusil, revólver, linterna— / los guardias móviles tiran, / ciegan, funden, apalean" [The Mobile Guard demolishes / huts, piece by piece. / They gut knapsacks, / they lay siege to suitcases. / . . . / A flurry of picks and shovels / swoop down from the heavens / and soar up from the sand . . . / but there's no gold / . . . / Along the edges of the beach / —rifle, revolver, lantern— / the mobile guards knock down, / cover up, lay ruin, throw blows].

This surreal myth of a new El Dorado improbably buried in the filthy sand of a concentration camp was certainly one of the most popularly held notions about the Spanish refugees that circulated not only as gossip among the French camp authorities and local citizenry, but was reported in the press as well. Luis Suárez devotes an entire chapter, "Gold," of his 1944 memoir to this legend of the stolen Spanish gold reserves hidden beneath the huts of the camps. An obsessive collector of French newspaper clippings published about the Spanish refugees and the camps—dozens and dozens of translated newspaper excerpts run along the bottom of the pages of his memoir like wire-service teletype—the career journalist Suárez refers to the widespread dissemination of the story of the gold: "The French newspapers published daily news of fantastic caches of gold found beneath the sand. They spread the word of miracles: that a guard, with his horses's hooves, or with the butt of his rifle, or with his own feet, however it was, struck gold, he discovered the gold ingots or buried silver. . . . [French] eyes shone just thinking about it, like the gold diggers of yesterday. They saw valuable property in that arid, sandy ground, thinking that beneath the sands lay an amazing fortune."[17] In a way, the myth of the gold serves quite literally as a "foundational fiction" for Amieva's camp of Barcarès. According to Suárez, in order to conduct a thorough search of the section of the St. Cyprien camp most likely to harbor the treasure, those soldier-inmates were the first to be transferred from overcrowded St. Cyprien to the new site of Barcarès. But like Amieva's poetic antagonists of Argelès, these guards also came away empty-handed. "Crazed soldiers and gendarmes, armed with tools, feverishly dug in the sand. You had to laugh at their frenzy of activity. Searching for gold where there was nothing but lice and squalor!"[18] Silvia Mistral, a short-time resident herself of the women's camp of Argelès, similarly recalls in her 1940 testimony the concentration camp gold rush that she witnessed: "Some gendarmes make holes in the sand. I thought they were going to bury a body. I was amazed to find out that they were looking for gold. GOLD. 'They struck a motherlode,' says somebody sarcastically."[19]

In Amieva's 1977 memoir *Asturianos en el destierro (Francia)*—a prose text that can be usefully read as a companion volume to his collection of verse—the author describes the struggle between the men in the camps and the gold-crazed guards who ransack their meager belongings: "There were severe beatings. Lister's men fought back and more than a few ended up thrown in the prison of Collioure" (27). In the final section of the poem itself, the author imaginatively infuses myth and history as he expands the parameters of the inmates' rebellion against the destructive, senseless pillage to include angry women refugees as well: "Ya en el campo de mujeres / las mujeres se sublevan: / arrancan de la alambrada / piquetes de hierro. Llevan / en alto palos, ladrillos, / puñados de arena y piedras" [By now in the women's camp / the women themselves rise up: / they tear from the barbed wire / stakes of iron. They brandish / sticks, bricks, / handfuls of sand and stones]. Drawing on the facts of a historic riot in the women's camp of Argelès (protesting the forced transfer of disabled and sick inmate-veterans of the International Brigades to a labor camp in Algiers), Amieva rewrites Lorca's *saqueo* of the "city of the gypsies" to include the compelling myth of resistance that is such a pervasive thread generally in the story of the "city of the Refugees."[20] In the earlier poem, Amieva's Loco had learned to twist pieces of wire into an artful tribute fit for a king; here, the resourceful women transform the raw materials of the camp—metallic barbs, sand, and pebbles—into expressive weapons of power. The *ladrillos* with which they arm themselves bring to mind an earlier reference in the poem to the blackened bricks that are uncovered by the guards in the frantic dig for gold ingots, "Ladrillos de un fogaril / disfrazados de realza / como tres lingotes pasan / por evidentes sospechas" [Bricks from the fire / their gloss disguised / as if three gold bars they / raise suspicions]; the author sarcastically refers to them again in his memoir, "So much for the famous 'Figueras ingots'" (*Asturianos*, 27). These burnt bricks apparently without value have, however, covertly cooked the inmates' stolen scraps of food; now other bricks like them are hurled in defiance at the French tormentors. The inmates half buried in the sand likewise discover valuable reservoirs of strength and an impulse for survival hidden within themselves that will have far greater currency than the mythical bars of gold.

The twin motifs of suffering and resistance are carried over into the third and final poem of the introductory trilogy, "Arenosis." In this text, Amieva develops his most complex and suggestive intertextual dialogue of all with the work of León Felipe (1884–1968), the poet whose powerful lyric voice has been universally acclaimed as the finest exponent in Mexico of the Spanish exile experience. The connection with Felipe's poetry is marked by the opening epigraph, ". . . cobraremos todos en arena" [. . . we'll stake our claim in sand], a line of verse lifted from the older writer's 1939 book published in Mexico City, *El hacha (Elegía española)* (The Hatchet [A Spanish Elegy]). In this early work of exile, Felipe had used the eponymous trope of the hatchet as the embodiment of an age-old force of divisiveness and destruction that has left Spain in ruins. He describes postwar Spain as an absolutely decimated wasteland, its signs of life stripped down to the barest, most atavistic level of existence: "La consigna es el corte, / el corte, / el corte, / el corte hasta llegar al polvo, / hasta llegar al átomo. / . . . / Y desierto es también un calabozo; / el desierto amarillo / donde el átomo roto / no se pone de pie. / De aquí nadie se escapa. Nadie. / Porque dime tú, amigo cordelero, / ¿hay quien trence una escala / con la arena y el polvo?" [Our watchword is the cut, / the cut, / the cut, / the cut down to the dust, / down to the atom. / . . . / And the desert is also a prison; / the yellow desert / where the splintered atom / cannot become whole again. / Nobody gets out of here. Nobody. / Because tell me, my rope maker friend, / Is there anybody who can weave a ladder / out of sand and dust?].[21] The parallels between Felipe's apocalyptic landscape

("Tierra arenosa sin riego, / carne estrujada sin llanto, / polvo rebelde de rocas rencorosas y lavas enemigas, / átomos amarillos y estériles / del yermo" [Sandy soil without water, / torn flesh bereft of grief, / rebel dust made from spiteful rocks and hostile lava, / yellow, sterile atoms / of parched earth], *Obras*, 145) and Amieva's beach prison in "Arenosis" where he himself is reduced to nothing, are noteworthy: "De cualquier lado que me dé el sol / se encarniza en una nueva llaga / En mis células cerebrales / arena / A las hormonas de la alegría / que daban su tónica a mi sangre / sucedió un arrastre de moléculas de arena / Me tendí al pie de la alambrada" [On whichever side the sun hits me / an angry new wound takes shape / In my brain cells / sand / Hormones of happiness / that once fortified my blood / succumb to the pull of molecules of sand / I lay down, huddled against the fence]. In fact, in his 1964 concentration camp collection of prose and poetry, *Poet in the Sand*, Amieva cites Felipe's spatial descriptions in *The Hatchet* as an intuitive, albeit unintentional, evocation of the stark world of exile within the camps. But most inspiring for Amieva is the message that Felipe suggests in the conclusion of *El hacha*: even out of the cataclysmic dusts of death and devastation ("polvo con el que nadie . . . / ¡nadie! / construirá jamás / ni un ladrillo / ni una ilusión" [dust with which no one . . . / no one! / will ever be able to make / a brick / nor build a dream]," *Obras*, 150), new forms of cultural life and a new history to replace "La Historia [que] se deshace" [The History [that] falls apart], *Obras*, 148, can emerge.[22] In the concluding section of Felipe's book "Estamos en el llanto" (We Are Grieving), the author explains that the pain and grief of the vanquished Spanish people will in fact provide the raw materials needed to mold their experiences of war and exile into a potent means of expression. Appropriating the language of the Gospel, Felipe intimates the moment when the tears of exile will transform "the dust" into pliant clay: "El Verbo vino y dijo: Aquí está el barro; / que el barro se haga llanto / . . . / Y el Verbo se hizo llanto / para levantar la vida. / El Verbo está en la carne / dolorida del mundo . . ." [The Word came and said: Here is the clay; / let the clay become grief / . . . / And the Word became grief / in order to sustain life. / The Word is in the suffering / flesh of the world . . .] (*Obras*, 156). In a second book of poetry also published in Mexico in 1939, *Español del éxodo y del llanto* (Spaniard of Exodus and Grief), Felipe picks up the thread of his thoughts on exile and cultural renewal exactly where he left off in *El hacha*. In the section entitled "Dust and Tears," he writes: "Vivimos en un mundo que se deshace y donde todo empeño por construir es vano. . . . Nadie tiene hoy en sus manos más que polvo. Polvo y lágrimas. Nuestro gran tesoro. Y tesoro serían si el hombre pudiese mandarlos. . . . Y tal vez la gracia del poeta no sea otra que la de hacer dócil el polvo y fecundas las lágrimas. Y ésta es mi angustia ahora: ¿Dónde coloco yo mis sueños y mi llanto para que aparezcan con sentido, sean los signos de un lenguaje y formen un poema inteligible y armonioso?" [We live in a world that is falling apart and all efforts to build it back up are useless. . . . Nobody holds in his hands anything but dust. Dust and tears. Our great treasure. And it would be treasure if man knew what to do with it. . . . And maybe the gift of the poet is exactly his ability to make the dust pliant and use his tears to make things grow. This then is my dilemma: Where do I place my dreams and my tears so that they make sense, so that they become the letters of a language and take shape as a meaningful, harmonious poem?] (*Obras*, 116–17). Felipe's most provocative concept for Amieva, the inmate-poet of the concentration camp who is surrounded by sands supposedly covering up buried treasure, is that the very soil of suffering, "dust and tears," is in fact the valuable asset, "our great treasure." In his 1943 *Ganarás la luz* (You Will Reach the Light), Felipe will make his point ever more clearly. In the poem "Todos tendremos para pagar la entrada"(We'll All Be Able to Afford the Cost of Admission), he writes, "Se acuñará la lágrima / como se acuña el oro" [Tears will be minted / like gold] (*Obras*, 214); the text "La Esclava" (The Slave) includes the verses "Lágrimas, / lágrimas, / lágrimas . . . / el dinero del pacto, / el tesoro del arca, / el precio de la luz . . ." [Tears, / tears, / tears . . . / the money of the pact, / the treasure of the coffer, / the price of the light . . .] (*Obras*, 215). In "Los muertos vuelven" (The Return of the Dead) the poet states, "Nuestras lágrimas son / monedas cotizables. / Guardadlas todas . . . todas, / para las grandes transacciones" [Our tears are / valuable currency. / Save them all . . . every one, / for the big transactions] (*Obras*, 219). Felipe's image of the civil war emigrant in 1939, "profiled in the wind," portrayed that individual as a solitary figure who goes forth into exile with a coffer filled with potentially useful treasure, even though right now the contents only resemble the ashes of defeat, "Con su Arca; con el arca sagrada. Cada uno con su Arca. Y dentro de esta Arca, su llanto y la Justicia derribada" [With his Ark; with the sacred ark. Each person with his Ark. And inside this Ark, his grief and his battered Justice] (*Obras*, 124). In his book *La almohada de arena*, Amieva, like an exiled Cid, shows how even reserves of sand can produce a cultural currency worth its weight in gold; with his concentration camp poem's epigraph, ". . . cobraremos todos en arena" [. . . we will stake our claim in sand], he gives a new twist to León Felipe's lyrical meditations on exile.[23]

The poem "Arenosis" is primarily a portrait of the stultifying, absurd existence of the Spanish refugees who languish in the French concentration camps; it begins with an enumeration of the inescapable quotidian routines that drive the inmates to despair: "Las órdenes absurdas /

las reacciones idiotas / los mandamás estólidos / las sarcásticas fauces del buzón de correos / son granos de arena / en el desesperante reloj de arena del exilio" [The absurd rules / the idiotic attitudes / the stupid big shots / the empty jaws of the mailbox mocking us / all are grains of sand / in the anguished hourglass of exile] *(La almohada de arena)*. The poem's narrator goes on to denounce the empty rhetoric of international organizations whose ineffectual response to the crisis in Spain has created the ugly truth of concentration camps and prisons: "Venid a buscar la verdad a la playa / aquí aquí / a la playa / O mejor aún / a las mazmorras de Collioure" [Come search for your truth here on the beach / here here / on the beach / Or better yet / come look in the dungeons of Collioure]. The concluding section of "Arenosis" introduces the earlier cited description of the protagonist's psychological breakdowns and his physical anguish as he is battered by the incessant winds "crucificado en las aspas de un molino de tramontanas" [crucified on the blades of the north wind's mill], suffering like the "Cristo ibérico" [Iberian Christ] invoked in a later poem ("Al escultor Manuel Pérez Valiente, autor de una cabeza de don Quijote" (To the Sculptor Manuel Pérez Valiente, Creator of a Bust of Don Quijote). The poem ends as the narrator's thoughts drift home to Spain, remembering his love who remains there ("Qué es de ti la que me amabas" [Whatever became of you who once loved me]).[24] He is haunted by the echoes of the memory of those left behind the Pyrenees, both the dead and the living: "Oigo un llanto detrás de los Pirineos / detrás de esa tapia de cementerio" [I hear a mournful cry beyond the Pyrenees / beyond that cemetery wall]. As he is overcome with grief, the dual geography of the Spanish graveyards and the phantasmal concentration camp becomes conflated; the speaker recognizes that he himself belongs to the ranks of the walking dead: "sólo pienso estúpidamente / obstinadamente / recalcitrantemente / en cómo puede ser que lloren los cadáveres." [I can only dully / stubbornly / recalcitrantly ponder / how it is that dead men cry].

Unexpectedly sandwiched between these despairing verses, toward the very heart of the 104-line composition, Amieva describes a powerful scene of imagined collective rebellion, reminiscent of the women's protest of the previous poem. In the boisterous liberation that he foresees, a ragtag army of inmates ("Saldremos con los pantalones cortos / saldremos con los camisones largos /saldremos con las alpargatas del 46 / con el uniforme grotesco de Argelès / de Saint Cyprien / del Barcarès / de Bram / de Septfonds / de Agde / del Vernet / de Collioure" [We'll come out dressed in short pants / we'll come out dressed in long nightshirts / we'll come out with our sandals from the 46th / with our grotesque uniform of Argelès / of Saint Cyprien / of Barcarès / of Bram / of Septfonds / of Agde / of Vernet / of Collioure]) will confront the outside world that has tried to forget them, making themselves known by the very instruments of their oppression. They will fight "con puñados de esta arena" [armed with fistfuls of sand]; their battle standard will fly the colors of their suffering, "Enarbolando los piquetes arrancados de las alambradas / En ellos habrá aún jirones rojos" [Lifting up into the air stakes torn from the barbed wire / where bloody tatters still cling]. Although by the previously cited conclusion of this early poem in the book a sense of desperation and defeat will prevail, these centrally positioned verses do point toward the enactment of a reconstructed identity. Amieva refers to "todos los carnets soterrados / en la arena de los campos de concentración" [all those buried I.D. cards / in the sand of the concentration camps]; emergence into exile when the sands of the hourglass at last register the post–concentration camp era will necessarily be accompanied by new signs of identity.

Amieva's lyrical imagery of the sand as a weapon, the sand as subterfuge, is not just another metaphor, though it certainly is one of this writer's most significant tropes. Inmate-memoirists have described their internment as being buried alive; so Amieva explains the fate of one of his protagonists, "la tramontana / le enterró vivo en Argelès" [the north wind / buried him alive in Argelès] *(La almohada de arena)*, while another laments coming to France "para enterrarme vivo en el destierro" [to bury myself alive in exile] *(Poeta en la arena)*. The historian Marie Rafaneau-Boj has even documented a brutal method of punishment used in the camps: "Sometimes, to make an example of them, the prisoners were buried in the sand up to their necks, in full view of everyone."[25] But as I have indicated in earlier discussions, the refugees use this same sand to transgress the limitations of their captivity. Amieva has described its use as a creative tool during the campers' first exuberant commemoration in exile of the anniversary of the Spanish Republic: "April 14th arrived and Republican patriotism flourished in the camp despite all the odds. Tons of painstakingly crafted works of art popped up everywhere, that used sand as a raw material, and that were decorated with seashells and colored pebbles. Huge maps of Spain, the Republican shield, mural newspapers. In one hut there was an exhibition of paintings, sketches, and sculptures made out of the most unlikely materials. And poetry, cartoons, whimsical creations made of barbed wire, string, vines, tin. The French were flabbergasted. . . . The next day, *L'Indépendant* published reviews and photographs of our Republican commemoration. Come and see world, our nation still stands!" *(Asturianos*, 28–29). Agustí Cabruja-Auguet describes watching another inmate as he fashions carefully sculptured images of mother and child: "at this moment, using sand and mud, he's creating on the beach what he couldn't make out of wood, marble or bronze in his studio. 'Mother and child' . . . This is what he made."[26] The sculptor Manolo Valiente has recalled much more subversive statues of sand that were constructed in Amieva's Barcarès in observance of Bastille Day: "One group made a life-size bust of Franco that was covered in a kind of sugar syrup. An hour later, Franco was covered in flies."[27] Perhaps even more significant than the sand's capacity to externalize forms of artistic expression is its power to aid and abet the inmates' efforts to cover up forms of political or cultural resistance. In his description of the border crossing, Jaime Espinar had imagined the French soil some day sprouting surreal vegetation out of the kilometers of the refugees' abandoned possessions: "The south of France seems to be sown with Spanish suitcases. When the sprouts germinate, extraordinary plants will grow out of the seeds. They will bear strange fruit: shirts, undershirts, suits, toothbrushes, all kinds of knick-knacks, love letters, letters, lots of letters, 'photos' for an inspired exhibition of romantic love, and the most diverse objects made of gold, silver, copper and steel."[28] So, too, might one envision the beaches of the concentration camps as a potentially rich archaeological site, according to the pervasive references to the inmates' own versions of buried treasure.

In 1951, Teresa Juvé, a former internee of the women's camp of Argelès, returned to the place of her confinement and found a rusty lantern stuck in the sand; she is flooded by memories of knitting children's clothing by lamplight to sell for a few francs.[29] Other inmates remember purposefully using the sand to hide signs of subversive activity from the ever watchful eye of the guards. In Luis Suárez's description of the insufficient supply of building materials for the St. Cyprien camp, he explains that stolen planks of wood were prized possessions for the inmates attempting to construct shelter. When word spreads through the camp that the guards will confiscate all pieces of lumber, the Spaniards quickly react, "And the scarce wood scraps were buried in the sand. When the gendarmes went by, without finding what they were looking for, they must have wondered in their dull-witted way if the refugees got so hungry that they ate the missing wood."[30] Intense hunger is in fact responsible for another sabotage of French-issue supplies; this time the buried loot is bread. The Collioure prison survivor Angel Sánchez Ramírez recalls an incident from the Argelès camp: "an act of sabotage was discovered in the Administration which was huge quantities of bread buried in the sand."[31] Unfortunately in this instance, the French authorities get the ultimate revenge by forcing Sánchez Ramírez's comrades in Collioure to either eat the horribly moldy bread brought in from Argelès or have nothing. Other memoirists report—perhaps apocryphally, as part of the camp mythology—that occasionally the sandy shores swallow up the evidence of crimes committed against the hated guards. In a June 12, 1939, diary entry, Ferrer writes of desperate acts: "This conflict with the Senegalese is a secret page from the story of our camp. Guys seeking justice or vengeance tricked these soldiers of color with cunning schemes, especially under the cover of darkness. Several of their bodies were buried on the beaches or thrown out to sea in Argelès."[32] Amieva's version of the same kind of episode records another attack on a *spahi*; following an incident in which the mounted guard savagely beat an elderly refugee, the author explains: "minutes later, both the whip and the *spahi* disappeared beneath the sand and the appetizing smell of grilled horsemeat wafted through the camp from several makeshift rotisseries" (*Asturianos*, 17).

Certainly the most numerous examples of buried contraband are textual in nature. The most common pieces of paper that are secreted away are those that display the owner's political affiliation, an increasingly dangerous revelation in the ideologically charged atmosphere of France in 1939 and 1940. Amieva has described the inmates' response to the heightened pressure on the part of French officials to ferret out Communist Party members and suspected left-wing revolutionaries: "In Barcarès, some men, either fearful or cautious, began to bury in the sand their political party or trade union membership cards, as well as any other document that could incriminate them" (*Asturianos*, 41). Ironically, a celebrated text by Amieva's beloved poet León Felipe ends up beneath the earth during this time of tension. The interned writer explains that he retrieved a copy of Felipe's 1937 *La insignia* (The Insignia), a poem that Guillermo de Torre has called "his first great war poem" (*Obras*, 17), from among the mounds of fellow refugees' abandoned belongings at the border of Port-Bou *(Poeta en la arena)*. The fiery verses, composed after the fall of Málaga and first recited by León Felipe from a dais shared with Antonio Machado in Valencia before a teeming crowd of Republican soldiers, exhort the combatants to unite together. Felipe urges his audience to rally around one single political identity and rise above divisive party politics: "Ya no hay cédulas de identificación. / Ya no hay más cartas legalizadas / ni por los Comités / ni por los Sindicatos. / ¡Qué les quiten a todos los carnets!" [The time for identification cards has passed. / The time has passed for letters authorized / by Committees / or by Trade Unions. / Give up all your cards!] *(Obras*, 935). The polemical 450-plus lines of text are read out loud in the *barracón de cultura* of the isle "O," provoking heated debate that goes on for weeks among the listeners about the meaning of the poem: "the awesome message of the great prophet of war and exile made the rounds through the islet and the camp, stirring things up from one end to the other. For weeks *The Insignia* controversy raged. The situation became dangerous" (*Asturianos*, 34). Due to the French au-

8: CELSO AMIEVA'S *LA ALMOHADA DE ARENA* (1960)   183

thorities' growing concerns about "the 'suspicious meetings' on Isle 'O'" *(Poeta en la arena)*, a decision was made to bury the booklet, which Amieva deeply regrets, even as he recognizes that the entombed words will always be burned in his mind and memory: "A sad symbol, that burial. . . . But it doesn't alter the continuing relevance of *The Insignia*. Once you've got it under your skin, it could never be erased even if the pages it's written on are buried fourteen leagues under the earth" *(Poeta en la arena)*. Fittingly, these verses that were literally (and given the message of the poem, coincidentally) buried alongside the political party membership cards ("I already buried it, my brother. Next to my I.D. card it will rot away beneath the sand") are resurrected in a fifty-year commemorative volume about the French concentration camps, the 1989 *Plages d'exil: Les camps de réfugiés espagnols en France, 1939*. In a concluding section entitled, "La mémoire fertile," a facsimile of León Felipe's signed, handwritten copy of *La Insignia*'s most famous verses is reproduced: "La Justicia vale más que un imperio, aunque este imperio abarque toda la curva del Sol. Y cuando la Justicia, herida de muerte, nos llama en agonía desesperada nadie puede decir: 'yo aún no estoy preparado.' La Justicia se defiende con una lanza rota y con una visera de papel" [Justice is worth more than an empire, even if it's one where the sun never sets. And when Justice, mortally wounded, calls out to us with its last desperate breath, nobody can say: 'I'm still not ready.' Justice can be defended with a broken spear and a helmet's visor made of paper].[33] These words once interred in a concentration camp continued to resonate for those Spaniards whose quixotic efforts during the civil war were sorely put to the test in exile.

Promises of similar future resurrections of dormant texts abound in the camp literature. The myth of the beaches littered with buried testimonies reached an almost legendary status. Agustí Cabruja-Auguet introduces his 1947 memoir *La ciudad de madera* with a prefatory note worthy of Cide Hamete Benengeli's editor: "I am not the author of this book. The author, the real author, is unknown. . . . All I've done is to make corrections and modifications, the way a gardener prunes his rose bushes, organizing these pages that I discovered one day wrapped in an old folder half-buried in the sands of the Argelès-sur-Mer beach. On a loose sheet of paper, written in pencil, the young author had explained the reason why he left his work behind. . . . The poor boy was going to end his life!"[34] (n. pag.) Miguel Giménez Igualada, fearing deportation out of the camp back to Spain, carefully prepares the paper trail he will leave behind him, "I carefully wrapped up my papers in a shirt, all tied together, and buried them in the same place where I always lay my head."[35] Seven years later when he published most of this manuscript package in Mexico as his *Más allá del dolor*, he refers to the formerly buried pages as incipient signs of life capable of sustaining the nascent narrative of Spaniards in exile. According to Giménez Igualada's description, "These tender shoots, that were scattered about in the plot of land where I sowed the seed—old notebooks that I covered with furrows and watered with my tears during the long days spent in the Concentration Camps— . . . ," are the sprigs of new life that miraculously emerge out of the sandy ground of the French camps, producing "mature grains . . . [that] still bear nutritious fruit."[36] So prevalent is the motif of the buried manuscript that some critics like Monique Alonso have even gone so far as to refer to hidden volumes of a camp bibliography forever lost to history: "There were many books that were written or conceived in the concentration camps: some saw the light of day as soon as their authors left the camp or else years later; others, unfortunately, were never made public because they remained buried beneath the sand and the storms."[37]

If I have allowed myself such a lengthy digression about the camps' "buried treasure" in order to more fully contextualize Celso Amieva's book *La almohada de arena*, it is because no other writer-inmate so completely appropriates this trope as a means of expressing the exile's campaign of cultural continuity. His former companions of the camp write him letters long after their own liberation, and refer to him himself as a forgotten piece of history left behind in the sand; in *Poeta en la arena*, Amieva cites one letter: "Oh you, champion of the camps, eternal internee. . . . [Y]ou are something that somebody forgot on the sandy ground, something that was left behind among the papers that were burned because they were too dangerous and the letters that were buried because they were too sad. . . . That sand, grain by grain, will one day turn you into gold!" The alchemical process of converting the experiences lived on the barren expanse of exile into the precious stuff of spiritual and cultural renewal is a central concern of Amieva's book. In an early composition, "Abrid mi carne con el hierro" (Cut My Flesh with a Knife), the narrator conveys a scene of intense, painful longing for his *amada* back in Spain. The hated sand-jail that he inhabits almost annihilates him; he chokes and flails as he tries to escape the torment of exile's hell on this earth: "Ahora / que son uñas y dientes lo que hinco / en la tierra extranjera / dura fría y amarga" [Now / it's fingernails and teeth that I sink / into the foreign soil / hard cold and bitter]. Gradually, the poems begin to chronicle a movement toward autonomous emplacement, a sense of being-in-place as the refugee slowly constructs a new identity in exile. The centrally placed poem of the collection of thirty-two texts, "Era la misma . . ." (She Was the Same . . .) begins with the oft-imagined dream of reunion with the loved one left behind during the war: "Atravesaba por el bosque / como un rayo del amanecer. / Yo la conocí desde lejos. / Con toda mi vida la llamé." [She crossed the wood / like a ray of dawn's light. / I recognized her from afar. / My whole life called out to her]. But the émigré-protagonist's voice doesn't carry over and his feet won't obey; he is other now, rooted in a foreign soil, surely unrecognizable to the woman he calls out to: "¿Ella tal vez / llegaría mañana a mi sombra / sin saberme reconocer?" [Would she perhaps / stand in my shadow tomorrow / without being able to recognize me?]. Upon awakening, the speaker is released from his unsettling dream, and the poem concludes with an oddly clear-eyed view of where he is: "Desperté sin ramas ni sombra. / En el destierro. En Argelès-sur-Mer" [I woke up with neither branches nor shadow. / In exile. In Argelès-sur-Mer]. Almost juxtaposed with this work is another poem that describes the two phases of the refugees' life, Before Exile and After Exile, in terms of the familiar image of the buried text, "El manuscrito" (The Manuscript). On the occasion of the Nazi invasion of France, the poet decides to inter his potentially compromising autobiographical journals that he kept throughout the war and that he brought with him across the border into France. Like the buried roots of the tree of exile in the previously cited poem, the pages of his life story will provide the foundation for a new chapter that will be written outside of Spain: "Aquí te quedas enterrada / en el Arenal de Argelès / Leve te sea la arena. / En verso habrás de renacer" [Buried here you remain / in the Sands of Argelès / May the sand be no burden. / In poetry you will be reborn].[38] Grains of sand, the gold dust of Argelès.

As I have argued earlier in my discussion of Amieva's strong use of intertext in the first three poems of this collection, by creating a dialogue with the work of the giants of Spanish poetry (Antonio Machado, Federico García Lorca, and León Felipe), the younger poet so untethered in exile essentially strengthens the ties that bind him to a stabilizing cultural tradition. Certainly, as we have seen, no cultural legacy is more potent for the Spanish refugees than the figure of Don Quijote. Not surprisingly, the two poems of *La almohada de arena* that most forcefully express confidence in the Spaniards' capacity to survive and carry on in the land of exile are written around the *Caballero de la Triste Figura*. The poem "Aquí está el español...," (Here Is the Spaniard...)—with its insistent repetition of the locative verb "está," the deictic marker "aquí," and prepositional objects of place ("en playas extranjeras," "en Argelès," "en la arena," "en la playa" [on foreign beaches; in Argelès; in the sand; on the beach]—rhythmically fills the space of the poem with the emplaced body of the refugee: "Aquí está el Español aún, / a solas con su verdad. / Lejos de España, mas no importa. / Está España donde él está. / Aquí está el Español aún, / hiel en el pecho y en la boca sal, / acorralado en playas extranjeras" [Here still the Spaniard, / alone with his truth. / Far from Spain, but it doesn't matter. / Spain is wherever he is. / Here still the Spaniard, / bile in his throat and salt on his tongue, / penned up on foreign beaches]. His story of suffering and imprisonment on foreign soil is inscribed alongside the history of the great Cervantes; the majestic opus that followed Cervantes's years in prison in Argel is an illuminating model and fertile promise for the refugee who waits and waits in Argelès. Amieva describes the civil war veteran-inmate as the newest incarnation of a quixotic fighter for justice who purposefully digs in for the long battle ahead, undefeated and undeterred:

> Si ya Argel vio a Cervantes cinco años cautivo,
> hoy Don Quijote en Argelès lo está.
> Con los pies fuertemente hincados en la arena
> removida por el vendaval,
> Don Quijote en la playa—la de su vencimiento—
> aún por vencido no se da.
> Aquí está, pues, el Español. Aún.
> Puro, químicamente puro en su hispanidad.
> [If Argel held Cervantes captive for five years,
> today it's Don Quijote held in Argelès.
> With his feet firmly planted in the sand
> whipped by the wind,
> Don Quijote on the beach—the place of his defeat—
> hasn't given up yet
> So here, then, is the Spaniard. Still.
> Pure, chemically pure in his Spanishness].

In a kind of gritty, alchemical transubstantiation enacted by the winds and the sands of exile, the refugee is distilled down to the bare-boned essence of his existence; Amieva represents his Republican warrior, who has followed León Felipe's exhortation to defend Justice *"con una lanza rota y con una visera de papel"* even into exile, as the embodiment of authentic cultural integrity.

"El macuto" (The Knapsack) one of the final poems of the book, reads like a companion piece to "Aquí está el español..." (Here Is the Spaniard...): both poems celebrate the concentration camp internee as the living incarnation of the quixotic spirit; both poems establish the notion of "Spain" as a portable patrimony that resides wherever the Republican, the true Spaniard, may be: "Está España donde él está" [Spain is wherever he is], states the first poem; "¡España va en tu macuto!" [Spain is in your knapsack!], says the second. "El macuto" is structured like a dialogue between the narrator (who asks "—Español y refugiado, / ¿qué llevas en tu macuto?" [Refugee Spaniard, / what's that you've got in your knapsack?] and his interlocutor, the roaming refugee whose only possession is the knapsack on his back. The magical *macuto* encloses a rich temporal conflation of present, past, and future; the Spaniard proudly assumes ownership of all the phases of the peripatetic journey that his life has become: "—Llevo toda la alegría / de mi pasado difunto, / llevo todos los dolores / de mi presente infortunio / y llevo las esperanzas / de un justiciero futuro" [I carry all the joy / of my dead past, / all the sorrows / of my present misfortune / and all the hopes / of a more just future]. He explains that he carries within the folds of the pack a national treasure that will guide him in the future renewed struggle against tyranny that awaits him upon liberation from the camp: "—Don Quijote va conmigo. / Armado y, por hoy, oculto. / . . . / Hambre de justicia siento / y sed de justicia sufro" [Don Quijote's going with me. / Armed, and for now, hidden. / . . . / I hunger for justice / I thirst for justice]. Most notably, this poem reconnects with the earlier notion introduced by León Felipe that the Spanish émigrés' *tesoro del arca*, their original currency of exchange, will be their tears: "Y dentro de esta Arca, su llanto y la Justicia derribada" [And inside this Ark, the remains of their grief, their Justice] (*Obras*, 124). The capital that the Spaniards take with them out of the camps into the world of exile is not the stolen gold of Figueras. In the second poem of this book, "Ballad of the Mobile Guard," the frenzied gendarmes had left the backpacks in shreds as they desperately searched for gold, "Van destripando macutos, / entran a saco en maletas" [They gut the knapsacks, / they lay siege to the suitcases]. The *macuto* praised in the later poem has been filled up with valuables; the earlier victims of guard violence are now armed with the wealth of their shared experiences and seeds of a collective memory, priceless material for rebuilding cultural identity: "—Español y refugiado / cargado con tu macuto: / que los dioses te conserven / la hispanidad y el orgullo. / —Así sea. No trocara / las hambres, miseria y luto / que este macuto acarrea / de los campos a los grupos, / Por la escarcela dorada / de negreros y verdugos" ["Refugee Spaniard / loaded down with your knapsack: / may the gods preserve / your Spanish pride and identity." / "Amen. I wouldn't trade / the hunger, the misery, and the sorrow / that this knapsack carries / from the camps to the work crews, / For all the bags of gold / of the slavemasters and assassins"].

In April 1948, Celso Amieva was living and working in postwar France (before eventually moving to Mexico in 1953), when a newspaper article caught his eye: "According to the French press, they've undertaken excavations on the beach of Argelès, in search of the 'treasures buried in 1939 by the Spanish refugees'"(*Poeta en la arena*, n. pag.). The myth of El Dorado in the concentration camp of *los vencidos*, the myth of ragged refugees' buried treasure, still captured the imagination of gold diggers decades after the first camp inmates burrowed in the sand seeking shelter. Editors of a 1981 compilation of archival and testimonial documents about the French camps report that gold fever persisted into the 1980s: "The 'treasure' hunters still haven't given up; one of them in 1980 spent several hundreds of thousands of francs to purchase detection and drilling equipment to be used on the former site of the Argelès camp."[39] Years earlier, on the twenty-fifth anniversary of the Spanish Republicans' massive border crossing into the concentration camps of France, Celso Amieva writing from Mexico City had explained the paradox of the Spanish exiles' hidden deposits of wealth; one man's trash is another man's treasure: "COBRAREMOS TODOS EN ARENA, había dicho con frase de fuego el Profeta español. Y, en efecto, ¿otra cosa que arena es el exilio? ¡Exilio alquimista, que trueca en arena el oro mal habido por algunos y que en oro transmuta la arena no merecida por otros!" [WE WILL STAKE OUR CLAIM IN SAND, the Spanish Prophet once said with words of fire. And, in fact, what else is exile but sand? Alchemical exile, that turns into sand the gold so badly coveted by some, and that turns into gold the sand so little deserved by others!], "Mexico City, February of 1964, Year XXV of Exile" *(Poeta en la arena)*.

9

Agustí Bartra's *Cristo de 200.000 brazos (Campo de Argelès)* (1943): Resurrection, or the Redemptive Beauty of Fraternity

> Entonces, todos los hombres de la tierra
> le rodearon; les vio el cadáver triste, emocionado;
> incorporóse lentamente,
> abrazó al primer hombre; echóse a andar . . .
>
> [Then, all the inhabitants of the earth
> surrounded him; the corpse looked at them sadly, moved;
> he sat up slowly,
> embraced the first man; started to walk . . .]
>
> —César Vallejo

IN A LECTURE PRESENTED AT THE ATENEO ESPAÑOL DE MÉXICO IN ITS inaugural year of 1949, Manuel Andújar referred to fellow Catalonian writer Agustí Bartra (1908–82) as "the most representative writer of Catalonian literature in exile."[1] Not surprisingly, part of such a "representative" view of the exile experience necessarily extends to life in the camps, and is chronicled in Bartra's deeply personalized 1943 novel that Andújar describes as "one individual's depiction—or at best a small group's view—of the concentration camps."[2] The title of this novelized version of the six months in 1939 that Agustí Bartra spent as an inmate of Argelès-sur-Mer and Agde, *Cristo de 200.000 brazos (Campo de Argelès)* [(*Christ with 200,000 Arms [The Camp of Argelès]*), portrays the massive internment camp as a colossal body of Christ, an anthropomorphic symbol of collective pain and suffering. The use of Christ imagery lifted from the pages of the Gospel is one of the most pervasive features of the forms of representation that depict the Spanish exile community's experience of the border crossing and the camps. In perhaps the earliest published memoir of both the exodus and of life in the early months in France, Solano Palacio recalls seeing a man standing up in the back of a truck teeming with refugees as it lumbered toward France and the camps; the solitary bearded figure, with arms outstretched toward the world around him, is the vision incarnate of a tormented messiah: "In the back of the truck, a tall and muscular bearded man was standing up, arms outstretched, as if to say, 'Shoot once and for all, and put us all out of our misery.' The sight of that figure rising up out of that little world of misery and moral despair, of pain and suffering, reminded me of a scene from the Bible reenacted by a crowd that kept pushing forward out of a sense of self-preservation."[3] Manuel Benavides, sarcastically describing in 1942 the French government's ill-conceived internment camps as the product of political cowardice, presents the camp inmates as long-suffering figures of redemption whose dangerous message carried over from war-torn Spain is simply locked away: "What kind of monsters were these that carried their crosses on their backs and showed the whole world the way to salvation? They would have to be kept behind fences of barbed wire and under the vigil of threatening bayonets."[4] Such brutal vigilance and such physical misery inspire Miguel Giménez Igualada's description penned in 1939 of the refugees and their guardians: "And so, carrying the burden of our paltry possessions, thirty thousand Christs, guarded by ten thousand centurions, crept along centimeter by centimeter, without stopping to rest. The winter wind's icy touch tore shivers from our flesh and the stubborn rain made it impossible for us to keep our luggage on our shoulders."[5] The German antifascist activist Gustav Regler, a combatant of the International Brigades during the siege of Madrid, has reported the scene he witnessed at the border as "a medieval picture of the Crucifixion."[6] In Federica Montseny's 1950 collection of testimonials, she includes her deeply felt lament inspired by the "calvary of the Spaniards in France" of which she herself was a part: "Onward! Onward! Onward! Until you can't take another step. Until you fall exhausted upon the rocks along the way. Until the cross crushes you. Until you can no longer see for the blood. Until the open wounds have bled dry the last drop of blood from your veins. . . . Your suffering, greater than Christ's. Your death, more wretched, more absurd, more sorrowful."[7] One of Montseny's informants, identified simply as "J. Plazas," bitterly describes his arduous months laboring in the work companies of Barcarès and Saint-Cyprien in the familiar language of Christ's martyrdom and sacrifice: "We were nothing more than a pitiful band of pariahs, with no rights, no home, no country. And all this for the crime of having dreamed of a better world and for having fought to make it come true. How cruelly all the dark forces of the world had made us pay for that crime! Every one of us bore the sign of *inri* on our forehead."[8]

Certainly the stark beach landscape that Agustí Bartra lyrically and deliberately pieces together in the opening pages of his novel's first chapter, "Ciudad de derrota" (City of Defeat), evokes a backdrop that seems to serve no other purpose than that of supporting an unbearably bleak environment of physical suffering and silent hopelessness: "City of defeat. Every day the trees are farther away. You could say that every night the green plain is more distant. The clouds trample one another like frightened flocks. The sea hides its foam. No children's laughter nor girlish shouts. Hunger and squalor . . . Lice, scabies, dysentery . . . Not the sound of an organ nor the song of bells. No one is born here. . . . Who can speak now? Suffering babbles; shame hides its face. Between light and shadows, hope bows its head."[9] In fact, so monstrously outsized and ill-contained is the form of human anguish locked up here ("a vast isolation ward for an enormous reclining torso with two hundred thousand arms" [*Cristo*, 124]) that it would seem to mock the power of salvation that is ultimately encoded in the body of Christ, alluded to in the novel's metaphorical title. But at the very limits of this truncated world devoid of the sights and sounds of a redeeming life force, the narrator immediately juxtaposes his introduction of the novel's four protagonists. He presents the quartet of civil war veterans first and foremost as a brotherhood of men whose bonds of fraternity and friendship will provide the source of spiritual strength and renewal that is the central message of Bartra's novel:

> There were four of them.
> Four who knew defeat, hunger, and death. Much bound them together yet there was much that separated them. Their profound solidarity sometimes resounded in the strangely opaque voice of Roldós, sometimes it would shine through in Vives's smile and in his hazel eyes. At other times it could be seen in a swift movement of Puig's long hands, or in Tarrés's elementary words of wisdom when he spoke of his oxen, of flowers. Four men among one hundred thousand or maybe against one hundred thousand. When they said *we* it implied a special meaning that only touched the four of them. None of them was unaware of the burden of carrying around a past that included the memory of the horror and tragedy of these past years. All four knew that it would be necessary to free themselves of the burden of the past in order to embrace the future with full consciousness. They knew as well that their ideal vision of tomorrow was fraught with danger, the danger of the group's dispersal or obliteration, which was to be avoided at all costs. (*Cristo*, 13)

The poet Bartra has stated elsewhere that the fundamental mission of his writings is to "get closer to the gospel truth of man"; clearly this ambitious project of transcribing the story of humanity's transformative journey toward spiritual transcendence ("Being, existence, consists of taking spiritual possession of reality . . .") assumes particular urgency in the war-torn early 1940s, the period of Bartra's exile in the Dominican Republic, Cuba, and Mexico, where he began to write the novel.[10] In fact, in a 1946 letter to the sister of his closest comrade in the Agde camp, Pere Vives, the model and inspiration for the fictionalized writer Vives of the novel, Bartra tells her that Vives's death in the German camp of Mauthausen would have occurred as he was writing parts of the novel itself in Mexico City: "You tell me that he died on October 30, 1941. During those days I was writing the *Bardo* chapter, with Pere's letter in front of me."[11] In the preface that he wrote for an edited volume of Vives's concentration camp correspondence, Bartra recalls Vives's faith, a belief that he himself affirms in other writings, in the power of poetic language as an instrument of salvation: "He believed in poetry as if it were a magical essential being, and he considered it potentially as a vehicle of individual and collective salvation."[12] In the opening pages of the novel, Bartra's narrator identifies a primary goal of this work that attempts to immortalize a community's experience on such unstoried ground of loss, death, and despair. The narrator dreams of shaping an epic song (he hears plaintive "songs of nostalgia next to small bonfires" [*Cristo*, 28]; "on the shores of Homer's sea" [*Cristo*, 27] capable of wresting history and memory from these shifting sands of time: "City of defeat. Where there's not even a stone to record its history. Maybe someday in the triumphant resurrection of souls this history will be heard as a powerful cry, intoned in the epic and sorrowful rhythms of the poet who has the greatest depth of feeling" (*Cristo*, 12). *Cristo de 200.000 brazos* (*Campo de Argelès*), the tale of four refugees fresh from the trenches of civil war, a narrative in which the words "Spain," "Spaniard," "Republic," or "homeland" do not ever appear, is not the story of a national rebirth and cultural continuity per se. It stands rather as an exilic hymn to fraternity and humanity, to the ties of compassionate friendship and brotherly love through which the survivors of apocalyptic war and mass destruction now seek spiritual and moral redemption, paradoxically from within a concentration camp.

In his *Facing the Extreme: Moral Life in the Concentration Camps*, Tzvetan Todorov quotes a passage from the Spaniard Jorge Semprún's 1963 novel *Le grand voyage*, a story inspired by Semprún's internment in the concentration camp of Buchenwald: "In the camps, man becomes that animal capable of stealing a mate's bread, of propelling him toward death. But in the camps, man also becomes that invincible being capable of sharing his last cigarette butt, his last piece of bread, his last breath, to sustain his fellowman."[13] Contemporary scholars of the literature and history of the German concentration camps as well as survivors themselves have long discussed the question of fraternity among the inmates within the broader debate about the limits and possibilities for ethical life behind the barriers of barbed wire.[14] Of course the circumstances of existence in the German death camps built for purposes of mass annihilation are by definition more extreme than those obtaining in the French refugee camps like Agde and Argelès. However, the strategies for mental and emotional survival as well as the expression of one's responsibility for the other are common points of departure in the literature and testimony of both groups of inmates. For the purposes of my analysis of the sustaining solidarity that runs through the world of Bartra's novel, I find particularly suggestive Todorov's observations about the function of "ordinary virtues" (that he distinguishes from "heroic" virtues) performed in private, daily acts of dignity, caring, or creativity among the camp inmates. These gestures of fraternity and empathy, the impulse toward beauty and self-expression, are affirmative forms of humanity that those internees who can, cling to like the last proof of human identity and spiritual integrity that they have left. In his reading of Jorge Semprún's autobiographical *L'écriture ou la vie* as a reinscription of Primo Levi's canonical work on the Holocaust, Angel Loureiro has stated: "[T]o Levi's insistence on shame and selfishness, Semprún responds with his thematic emphasis on the inevitability of Evil and the equally unavoidable but corrective counterpart of brotherhood. Where Levi sees degradation inflicted by useless cruelty and shame provoked by one's own ignoble behavior, Semprún shows the grandeur of fraternity, the unremitting responsibility for the predicament of the other. . . ."[15] Certainly in Bartra's novel, which his wife Anna Murià has called "a poem to friendship," the concept of fraternity is configured as a constitutive force that is ultimately responsible for the four protagonists' spiritual survival.[16] The fraternal bonds of camaraderie and compassion that fill the unsturdy *chabola* prepare the ground as well for the future "powerful cry in the triumphant resurrection of souls" (*Cristo*, 12) capable of telling the postwar story of exile.

The primitive little hut where the four friends live together following their internment in the inchoate Argelès-sur-Mer camp is the unlikely space par excellence of restorative refuge and shared sanctuary; in his prologue to the original 1943 edition of the novel, the poet Josep Carner refers to the shelter as "a symbol of the friends' close-knit brotherhood."[17] Its very genesis serves as a material incarnation of the themes of transformation, renewal, and creative metamorphosis that run through the pages of the book. The first "event" that is related in the novel, documented in detail in a chapter fittingly titled "The Hut," is the laborious construction of a humble home. Scraps of apparent refuse (a sack riddled with holes, empty cans, pieces of wire, pages from a newspaper) and stolen pieces of wood are gathered by the resourceful team of scavengers and given new life in the form of a makeshift house.

Roldós trades cigarette butts for cane, offering precious bits of recycled tobacco to the hoarders of the reeds necessary for building. Endowed with the gift of gab, Roldós walks up and down the beach for hours, seducing the greedy owners of the coveted raw materials. His successful speech acts ("using clever little tricks . . . wheedling what he needed out of those who let him do so" [*Cristo*, 37], literally lay the foundation for the place of refuge, gaining for the group the most basic construction supplies for their first fragile dwelling in exile. The final touch that completes the hut is the symbolic transference of individual pieces of protective covering from the past—each of the ex-combatants' old blankets, including those of army-issue—into a single, collective fabric enclosing the shelter where the four men will together prepare themselves for the future.[18]

No sooner do the refugees finish their ramshackle domicile, before they even have a chance to go inside, than the camp loudspeakers blare the inevitable news that all Republican exiles have dreaded: "'Attention!,' bellows the loudspeaker. 'Important news! Attention! . . . We are going to announce the latest communiqué from the General Headquarters of Salamanca. It reads: The war is over . . .'"(*Cristo*, 46). The war is over, the Republic is lost, and exile has a place: the four men quietly go inside the flimsy hut they have just built in the concentration camp. In the penultimate chapter of the first section of the tripartite novel, the narrator describes this very first evening of the official "postwar period" spent in the *chabola* as a night of insomnia for the writer Vives and the tubercular Roldós. To pass the interminable wakeful hours and to calm their restless thoughts, Vives reads aloud a traditional prose poem/folk tale called "Bardo."[19] The story is simple: The tyrant Silvio Scaurus, "one of those arrogant Romans who has divided up Germany and her people" (*Cristo*, 51), celebrates the day of his marriage by allowing the tribe of Germanic people that he has enslaved to have a day of rest to celebrate the momentous occasion. One of their poets, Herik el Bardo, is urged to recite his verses; to his audience's surprise, he sings a mournful song of loss and nostalgia that profoundly moves the listeners: "He sang of days gone by and the feats of their heroic ancestors; he sang of the freedom of the forests and the happiness of the caves. And the flash of joy in our eyes was suddenly extinguished, our breasts collapsed like empty wineskins" (*Cristo*, 52). A brutish guard nearby overhears Herik's wistful song of beloved dead heroes and elusive freedom, and punishes the man who dares to speak such memories and such longing, "he cut out his tongue with his dagger" (*Cristo*, 52). Undeterred, Herik opens his mouth to speak again, and the stupefied group stares as a red vapor rises from his lips, forming a misty screen on the horizon upon which the events and places of a community's war-torn past are projected: "Then, as if on a huge canvas, we saw the battles waged by our fathers, our forests in flames, our women raped by the Roman armies" (*Cristo*, 53). Before this awe-inspiring magic show is over, other images fill the air, the faces of the poet's own loved ones among them. Meanwhile, the poem's narrator explains, the grand wedding festivities continue in Silvio Scaurus's palace, though they inexplicably end badly for the newlywed tyrant: "And that night, the bride received more lovers than any Roman before her, while nearby Silvio Scaurus vomited up his wedding feast with the force of a hundred bloody mouths" (*Cristo*, 54). After the reading of this interpolated story, the first of many that fill the novel's pages, neither Roldós nor Vives says a word about it, nor is it ever mentioned again. But the poem's message—the unifying power of collective memory, the function of the remembered past as a fortifying source of truth and energy for a group's future action, the beauty and transcendence of poetic language—is deployed in subsequent intertextual iterations of this foundational piece. Throughout the novel, the four characters will entertain one another hour after hour with stories that predate life in the camps, obviously drawing on memories of the war and memories of home; these snatches of the past, poignant remembrances that swirl around inside the hut like scenes on Herik's aerial canvas, slowly merge together into the new shared history of Argelès-sur-Mer that eventually will become the men's first story of exile.

The central section of the novel, placed exactly at the midpoint of the narrative, are three such stories (juxtaposed in the two chapters "A Story," "Two More Stories") that three of the characters (Puig, Vives, Tarrés) tell one another and Roldós from within the walls of their blanketed hovel. Though the individual memories invoked in each narrative are quite dissimilar in terms of content, place of origin, and informing life circumstances, the trilogy of tales do share a significant common feature: each relates a moment of self-revelation, a discovery of personal truth and transcendence that originates through an intensely intimate interaction with the Other. Puig's contribution is the story of how he as an oddly solitary child, completely estranged from other children and family members, overcame his sense of alienation and even fear of the other. One day as he strolled along, carving a flute from a reed, he was surrounded by a jeering gang of boys and threatened by them. Taking the group in turn by surprise, the ten-year-old Puig unexpectedly hands his knife to one of his taunters, daring him to use it. When the boy refuses, Puig grabs the blade back and cuts a deep, jagged incision into his own flesh, facing down his fear of injury by inflicting it first on himself. His bizarre act of self-mutilation triggers a transformative moment; the dynamic between self and other is instantly changed: "I continued on my way, followed by the silent gang, that from that moment forward considered me their leader" (*Cristo*, 81). This crucial moment of identity formation can only be enacted with the aid of the other; it is the latter's gaze that reflects back to the protagonist the constitutive meaning of his own actions: "I looked up, ready to humiliate my enemies, but I stopped in my tracks when I saw the rigid circle of silence that surrounded me. It was my first victory: they offered up their silence like a tribute, born of fear and admiration. . . . But the experience went beyond me; it was too much. I was armed against them, but not against their silence, so free of hatred. It was a response that I could neither accept nor reject, since their silence returned my own actions to me as if sent from a deserted country. I did not experience this incident with a serene sense of accomplishment, but rather was overwhelmed by it, feeling its effects every subsequent moment of my life" (*Cristo*, 82). The still unformed reed flute that the young Puig had handed over to his onetime childhood antagonist prefigures the perfect instrument that Puig finishes carving in the *chabola* as he winds up his story to Vives. The message of his memory, like the melody for Vives that he coaxes from the handmade flute, are personal creations that resonate only when shared with another: "Sticking that knife in my arm was a culminating act, the ultimate action, and over the years it became a memory with a hidden truth. A living, profound truth that was no longer just mine, it was as if I had nothing to do with it. . . ." (81).

The second story belongs to the writer Vives; like Puig's reminiscence, it fills the hut with imagery from the distant days of childhood. The central motif of Vives's memory, his father's hands, is tightly connected to the theme of creativity, the capacity of the human mind and spirit for transformation, that unifies much of the novel's narrative. Vives relates his discovery, literally at his father's knee, of the plenitude and promise of reality's latent forms that are waiting to be activated by the forces of the imagination. The young boy Vives is enchanted by his father's large, expressive hands that nimbly make a coin disappear from sight and then mysteriously pull it back into the realm of being, magically drawn out of the wide-eyed boy's own ear, from his forehead, out of his nose: "And I never tired of the touch of those hands, enlivened by my father's wonderful wisdom that made everything seem possible. These hands showed me that the world was a place with inexhaustible stores of riches and mystery. They could even draw from me both the known and the unknown. . . ." (*Cristo*, 89). The father makes the boy aware of the endless possibilities that he holds within himself that likewise await release into creative forms of expression. Later, his father masterfully maneuvers a multicolored kite, filling the sky with the agile movements of a high-flying bird whose heavenly flight is directed from earthbound controls: "Suddenly, his hands moved to give a few tugs on the kite's string, and then the movement became rhythmic and measured, like when you pull on the rope to raise a bucket out of a well. At the same moment, I saw with amazement how the mountains wavered on the horizon, how the white cloud fled swiftly towards the South, how the cornfields swayed, how the trees marched along and the bird took wing. . . ." (*Cristo*, 90–91). Finally, the adult Vives, who spends hours in the hut writing feverish pages in his notebook, recalls his father's conversion of "a sheet of white paper" (*Cristo*, 92) into an animated world of newly minted people and places; he would deftly draw the figure of a girl sewing nearby, a bearded gnome, a house, even his son's own face. The father's lesson to the boy Vives, that the potential for creation by human hands is limitless, is shared with the adult Vives's fellow refugees during these early days of postwar exile when the forces of destruction and defeat would seem to be insurmountable.

Tarrés relates the last tale of the trilogy that Bartra positions at the heart of his novel. Like so many of the stories that are told and retold in the huts and barracks of the concentration camps, this memory resurrects the events of the recent civil war. Tarrés begins his narration in medias res, immediately drawing his three listeners back into the world of bloody fratricide from which they had only just emerged: "By the middle of the afternoon we had attacked enemy positions; we sustained many casualties and were forced to retreat in a disorderly fashion" (93). Left for dead, Tarrés painfully crawls along the rough terrain after nightfall, feeling increasingly overcome by loneliness and despair: "It wasn't fear, but rather a sharp sense of despair and loneliness. . . . a terrifying awareness of the void filled my soul, as if all of a sudden the line between being and nothingness had disappeared. . . ." (95). Groping blindly in the darkness, he bumps into one fellow soldier's cadaver, then another, then still another. At this juncture he hears a pitiable moan, and discovers a mortally wounded soldier delirious with pain who weakly repeats over and over, "Don't leave me, comrade . . ." (96). Knowing he can do nothing for the nearly unconscious dying man, who remains unaware of Tarrés's presence, he prepares to continue on his way back to his encampment when he spots a starving dog that emerges from the shadows. Horrified, Tarrés crawls back to the wounded soldier, now dead, and stays with the body through the night, keeping the wild dog at bay with rocks. Bartra uses Tarrés's story to connect the place of civil war (construed by some Republican exile writers, as Angel Loureiro has indicated, as "a utopian space of fraternity") with the place of the *chabola* in the camp, which the author similarly represents in this novel as an arena of camaraderie.[20] Bartra's inscription of Tarrés's powerful memory evokes as well the best-known paean to fraternity written during the Spanish war, "Masa" (Mass) (whose verses begin, "Al fin de la batalla, / y muerto el combatiente, vino hacia él un hombre/ y le dijo: 'No mueras, te amo tanto!' / Pero el cadáver ¡ay! siguió muriendo" [At the end of the battle, / and the combatant dead, a man came toward him / and said: "Don't die, I love you so much!" / But the corpse, alas! kept on dying]) by the Peruvian poet César Vallejo.[21] Vallejo, who died in Paris in 1938, wrote his last book of poetry as a hymn to the Spanish Republic besieged by war, *España, aparta de mí este cáliz (Spain, Take This Cup from Me)*. Bartra uses verses from Vallejo's earlier *Poemas humanos* as an epigraph for his final section of the novel and seems to write Tarrés's story alongside the text of Vallejo's "Masa." In those poignant verses, a dead soldier is finally resurrected by the sheer vitality of will that emanates from the kindred spirits who surround him and beg him to live: "Entonces, todos los hombres de la tierra / le rodearon; les vio el cadáver triste, emocionado; / incorporóse lentamente, / abrazó al primer hombre; echóse a andar . . ." [Then, all the inhabitants of the earth / surrounded him; the corpse looked at them sadly, moved; / he sat up slowly, / embraced the first man; started to walk . . .].[22] The dead soldier that Tarrés watches over throughout the night did not "start to walk"; however, Tarrés's response to him in death paradoxically revives his own earlier waning spirit, helping himself to keep his own demons, like snarling dogs, at a distance. Constant stories are not the only creative forms that positively shape the raw experiences of Roldós, Vives, Tarrés, and Puig within the *chabola*. The cramped, dirty, malodorous interior will be transformed by quasi-totemic objects that in themselves embody the conversion of one material into a more beautiful, more useful form of another. Each of these objects that serves to illuminate and enhance the physical space of the hut is in turn created or discovered by each of the four residents. Tarrés, the peasant of the group, has made an oil lamp out of two empty milk cans. With its greasy exterior and constantly dripping hot oil, the rustic lantern is a constant source of irritation for its creator, but it provides a flickering light every evening for the men who huddle around its flame, talking and remembering. Tarrés also takes an old shirt of Vives and fashions a "magnificent pennant" that flutters above the hut, a sign marking the group's identity that distinguishes their *chabola* from hundreds of others that crowd the beach landscape. Puig selects one of the reeds from the hut and carves a simple flute; the first night he plays it, the notes mix with the sound of the falling rain, and Vives experiences beauty for the first time in the camp: "Rain drizzled on the sand, on the huts and on the sea, and the fine threads of water fell silently, hanging like shiny strands from a sky of luminous ash. Vives could still hear the soft strains of the flute from inside of the hut, and his spirit felt indescribably captivated by the cool sweetness that fell from the sky, by the childish tune of the flute, by the light of his friend's face . . ." (*Cristo*, 85). For his part, the sickly Roldós furnishes the group's mascot, a tiny butterfly that he finds perched precariously on the barbed wire.[23] He keeps the fragile creature on his blanket where he sleeps; even long after it dies, it is preserved as a rare specimen of delicate color and beauty. Finally, Vives creates a notebook, the *carnet* in which he constantly writes the observations that form four of the fifteen chapters of the book, each entitled "(From Vives's Notebook)." The bits and pieces of fleeting thoughts, lyrical musings, and slowly receding memories of the past that he writes down will one day be the document that also will immortalize the transient events, the passing conversations that take place within the walls of the *chabola*. In a metatextual moment in the last entry in the *carnet*, for example, Vives reflects, "I doubt that I'll ever have the opportunity to use what I've written here in a work that would be the poignant, living testimony of someone whose whole reason for living is to not forget" (*Cristo*, 185); of course, the book the reader holds in her hands belies Vives's doubt-filled declarations.

The aspiration toward beauty and the urge for creative transformation, registered in the unremarkable objects that each friend presents like a redemptive offering to the others, wondrously emerge from a physical world of unremitting harshness. Each of the novel's three major sections, comprised of four or five chapters apiece, begins with the description of the same unforgiving, inhospitable environment; the painfully slow passage of time in each is marked throughout the book by the introduction of a new season—winter, spring, and summer, respectively—apparently none of which provide a space of comfort or respite. The initial winter weather is merciless: "No more rain! The sand doesn't need any water. The sand doesn't give anything back. The sand isn't like the earth that drinks water slowly and later returns it as spring showers. No more rain! The roofs made of blankets quickly let the water in and as long as the rain doesn't let up you'll be shivering and your teeth will be chattering. Each man's bed is the mark left by his body lying in the sand" (*Cristo*, 11). The advent of spring brings no harbingers of hope nor of relief: "But in the camp, spring appeared only as a distant promise of reinforcements that would never get close enough to liberate the place. Sudden showers rained down and then the wind prolonged their absence. One morning the first swallows appeared . . . but they disappeared towards the North never to return" (*Cristo*, 67). Summer advances onto a landscape deprived of fresh vitality: "It was understood that the sun's spring-like fire would soon bow to a summer that appeared in name only. The ever-present seagulls showed up every day, while the sea's horizon remained bereft of ships. The barren hours made scratches in the sand, listening for the chimes and looking for the memories of yesterday. With all course of action in shackles, mere words and silences reigned supreme. Chaos was accepted with a discouraged passivity that created a widespread sense throughout the camp that here was a defenseless people with no future" (*Cristo*, 123). Despite the existence of such an impossibly resistant reality, fledgling signs of incipient creativity creep into the text even from the very beginning. Whipped by winter winds, inmates still craft ingenious chess game pieces. In a place seemingly skipped over by nature's spring renaissance, new forms of man-made creation dot earth and sky. The refugees have shaped their own versions of a fertile Mother Earth, sculpting outsized female nudes out of wet sand; hastily made kites soar in the sky like paper promises of freedom: "And as the morning progressed, in the skies of the camp through the dusty haze, you could see countless kites swaying in the breeze" (*Cristo*, 68). On a summer's evening, Vives meets up with *el loco del caballo invisible* [the crazy man with an invisible horse], a filthy, half-naked crazy man who, eyes closed, gallops around the camp with a magnificent steed that only he can see through the eyes of the imagination and the dreamworld of insanity. Vives returns again and again to this stranger's hut, to sit as a silent witness to the *loco*'s daily baptism of his "exclusive dream" (*Cristo*,147). The old man inventively calls his fantasy vision into being each day with a different, marvelous name: *Zodiaco* (136), *Almas muertas* (137), *Hiperión, Fénix, Tao, Hipnos, Picarol, Halalí, Vala, Duino* (146); this limping seer, eyes tightly shut, with a body and mind deeply scarred by war ("He surely was in the war, because he's got a shrapnel wound on his back" [138]) is capable of making his fellow men look beyond the black-and-white lines of their hard material reality: "With his heart pounding, Vives notices that no one, including himself, is looking at the man any longer, but rather looking behind him, there where the horse *is*. . . ." (139).

Certainly the most direct expressions of human creativity figured in the novel are Vives's own journal-notebooks. Each of the four notebook entries (comprising one chapter per section, plus the epilogue) reads like a rich textual tapestry: of memories (of family, of the beloved, of war), of favorite verses and text fragments (of Rimbaud, of Villon, of folktales, of his own precamp poems), of observations of the camp world (about his sleeping comrades, the stray dog (Niebla) they have adopted, camp characters he meets). The very first entry (juxtaposed with the events of the evening following the announcement of the war's end and the completion of the *chabola*) is the most disjointed and uncertain. Vives stumbles from one subject to another, disconcerted by the task before him: How to create poetic language in these times and in this place? Following the prosaic statement, "This morning I found ten lice in my shirt" (*Cristo*, 56), he muses, "Where have all the maidens gone, the virgins who sang beneath the apple trees? Where are all the girls of white, the girls of green who laughed beside the nodding sunflowers drenched by the rain?" (*Cristo*, 57). Contemplating one "writing exercise" (*Cristo*, 59) after another, he begins to jot down fleeting snatches of remembered aesthetic beauty or glimpses of potential creation: "In praise of white . . . Seagulls, Moby Dick. The albatross. Annabel Lee. In the house of snow, words of fire . . . Yesterday's joy . . . Images! Images! The pain of creation. Oh, burning pain of the fires of creation! Images of the spirit's world! How these images scream in fear when the air whistles above their heads and they run to look over the balconies into the future! Oh, my walking staff of metaphysical support!" (*Cristo*, 59). The trajectory that subsequent notebook pages trace is the writer's ongoing efforts to establish a point of view from which to apprehend the raw forms of reality that meet his eye, in order to transcribe them into a literary language capable of capturing the truth and meaning of this world. In a statement of poetics published a decade after the novel, Bartra stated, "Being, existence, is realized by taking spiritual possession of reality, a reality susceptible of being transformed into lived experience. This means that nothingness, despair, loneliness, the other, the absurd, even death itself, are ideas and concepts that may be transcended by a consciousness that is imbued with this reality, that is confident that the world lies open and available to it."[24] Converting the ugly, harsh space of the camp into a remembered place of shared beauty and fraternity is the writer's project. In a pivotal moment in the second notebook entry (replete now with images of fulsome plenitude: Eskimo creation myths about the origin of light and the origin of mankind; a memory of making love), Vives confesses he has made a peephole in the *chabola*'s blanket-door: "I want to see *outside* from *within*" (*Cristo*, 101). This journal entry culminates with Vives's detailed description of what he sees from his vantage point, a new position of subjectivity that allows him to reestablish himself in poetic language:

> [I]'ve seen a small portion of my *Hell* through the little hole in the blanket that covers one side of the hut. And it was *beautiful*. Here it is. In the foreground, the sand slopes gently, smooth and shiny in the sun, with a few shallow holes left by the wind in the night. At the base of the sandy knoll, a hut in the shape of a half-sphere stands alone, like a dirty igloo. Behind it, in a small clearing, are three more huts; above them, on the horizontal line of the platform at the top, a row of twenty different huts, of various sizes, but all dark and all with a cane mast atop each roof. That is where the eye comes to rest. The twenty golden reeds, all long and some with little flags,

bow slightly to the east, surrounded from behind and from above by blue sky. Two different skies. The blue sky behind is like a backdrop painted to give the illusion of distance. The sky up above not only appears to weigh the reeds down, bending them over, but it seems that if it weren't for these fragile columns of support, the sky itself would cave in. . . . My gaze has taken such pleasure in the beauty of the reeds and the sky. It looked like a Chinese engraving. (105)

Miraculously, Vives has transformed the concentration camp landscape into an aesthetic object, which he compares to an Oriental piece of art. Previously hidden lines of beauty emerge unexpectedly from within the folds of reality like signs of the sacred that reconnect the human spirit to its own powers of transcendence. Such is the achievement of true poetry, says Bartra elsewhere, "The poet, in capturing the details of his time, always gives back more than he takes in: the illuminated depth of his own interior measurements."[25]

Tentative signals of an aesthetic dimension of the world are perceived as well by Vives's companions in two incidents that open and close the central trio of interpolated memory-narratives discussed above. In the scene that immediately precedes Puig's childhood story of the knife, Roldós and Tarrés walk together around the perimeter of the camp; the latter stops short, asking his friend if he hears that sound: "'What?' Tarrés listened now with his eyes shut, smiling at what he heard. Pointing towards the trees, he said: 'Over there . . . far away.' 'I don't hear a thing! What do you hear?' Tarrés opened his eyes, fixed a vacant gaze on his friend's face, and murmured, 'A nightingale . . .'" (75–76). Later, at the conclusion of the chapter "Dos historias más" (Two More Stories) in which Vives and Tarrés had related their respective tales of creativity and fraternity, the four men share an intense moment of communion engendered by the breathtaking natural beauty they witness from within the *chabola*: "'Look!' cries Tarrés, stretching his arm towards the door. 'After the rain, the moon . . .' It was a full moon, huge and miraculous, that seemed to hang like a nest of pure white from the left corner of the hut's door; it flooded the interior with light. Unspeakably amazed, they watched the slow ascent of the lunar disk until it disappeared completely from the opening in the door. Suddenly, they noticed with delicious surprise, that Puig's small flute released its sweet music . . ." (*Cristo*, 99). Such scenes recall others recounted by witnesses of the German version of the "concentrationary universe"; Todorov cites Victor Frankl's remembrance in Dachau, "One evening when we were already resting on the floor of our hut, dead tired, soup bowls in hand, a fellow prisoner rushed in and asked us to hurry outside to the assembly grounds and see the wonderful sunset!"[26] Primo Levi has described a similar aesthetic experience in Auschwitz, emerging even from the unsightly man-made surfaces of the death camp itself: "But today the eternal puddles, on which a rainbow veil of petroleum trembles, reflect the serene sun. Pipes, rails, boilers, still cold from the freezing of the night, are dripping with dew. The earth dug up from the pits, the piles of coal, the blocks of concrete, exhale in light vapours the humidity of the winter. Today is a good day. We look around like blind people who have recovered their sight, and we look at each other. We have never seen each other in sunlight: someone smiles."[27] Todorov has referred to such episodes as "morally uplifting," arguing that "there is inherent moral virtue in either the production or the reception of aesthetic pleasure or in the intellectual effort to understand. . . ."[28] To experience art and/or aesthetics, he says, "is to be in some way elevated and enriched. The accounts born of the experience of life in the camps, . . . have value as moral acts, not just because they bear witness or because they advance political struggle but because they help unveil before us, their readers, the truth of the world. The search for truth nourishes the moral life."[29]

Todorov's interrogation into the relationship between beauty and ethics is the subject of Elaine Scarry's illuminating meditation on the aesthetic experience as a dimension of justice. Although Scarry does not directly discuss the concentration camps—she mentions the German camps only in passing in her references to the French intellectual Simone Weil ("whose mystical writings and life practices—working side by side with laborers in the Spanish Civil War; carrying out a hunger strike [in London in 1943], from which she died, in camaraderie with those who were starving in German concentration camps—were inspired by her commitment to justice")—she does state, "[I]n periods when justice has been taken away, beautiful things (which do not rely on us to create them but come on their own and have never been absent from a human community) hold steadily visible the manifest good of equality and balance."[30] Arguing that beauty is available to anyone's sensory perception and is therefore readily accessible in ways that abstractions like "justice" may not be, Scarry champions beauty as an inherently equitable instrument serving spiritual renewal. Illustrating her argument with the image of "the wild rose that, with the sweet pea, uses even prison walls to climb on" (*On Beauty*, 100), Scarry describes beauty as a source of the sacred that is capaciously and democratically open to all: "By now we can begin to see that the equality of beauty, its pressure toward distribution, resides not just in its interior feature of symmetry but in its generously being present, widely present, to almost all people at almost all times . . . a distributional availability that comes from its being external, present ("prae-sens"), standing before the senses" (*On Beauty*, 108–9). Echoing observations by camp witnesses like Levi, who describes his group's aforementioned glimpse of beauty and fleeting flash of joy as "providential and is our means of surviving in the camp," Scarry posits the experience of beauty as "lifesaving": "Beauty quickens. It adrenalizes. It makes the heart beat faster. It makes life more vivid, animated, living, worth living" (*On Beauty*, 24–25); she clarifies that "What has been raised is not the level of aliveness, which is already absolute, but one's own access to the already existing level of aliveness . . ." (*On Beauty*, 90).[31] Citing Weil, Scarry explains that becoming attentive to forms of beauty is responsible for a radical decentering of the perceiving subject, forcing the beholder "'to give up our imaginary position at the center' . . . We willingly cede our ground to the thing that stands before us" (*On Beauty*, 110, 111). Scarry describes this new decenteredness ("an opiated adjacency" [*On Beauty*, 114]) vis-à-vis other perceiving subjects as a position of equal footing par excellence with respect to the Other: "[W]hen we feel ourselves to be merely adjacent, or lateral (or even subordinate), we are probably more closely approaching a state of equality" (*On Beauty*, 113). The "ethical alchemy of beauty" (113) also transforms single moments of individual perception into the raw materials of communion and fraternity; the optimum experience of beauty, says Scarry, is attained by sharing it with others: "This impulse toward a distribution [of beauty] across perceivers is, as both museums and postcards verify, the most common response to beauty: 'Addis is full of blossoms. Wish you were here.' 'The nightingale sang again last night. Come here as soon as you can'" (*On Beauty*, 6).

Scarry's reflections in *On Beauty and Being Just* provide a useful lens for reading Bartra's novelistic ruminations on the redemptive function of beauty and fraternity in the concentration camp. In a climactic scene of the novel, Tarrés steals away from the *chabola* and attempts to escape the camp by swimming past the barbed wire and the guards toward freedom. Confiding his plans only to Roldós, Tarrés is dogged by the nagging feeling that "his individual action went against the united front of solidarity within the group" (109). Later, washed ashore like a shipwrecked Odysseus—the mythical wanderer who captured Bartra's imagination his whole adult life ("Ulysses and Holderlin have accompanied me throughout my whole life")[32]—Tarrés emerges from the waves onto firm ground where an object of incredible beauty welcomes him to a new life outside the camp:

Before seeing the tree he smelled its perfume, a delicate and intense fragrance of almond in bloom that made him stop on the edge of a small wood. In a moment he saw it, in the middle of a field, a blur of white blossoms and moonlight, wondrously solitary, open branches and thick trunk. He didn't run towards the whiteness and the aroma; agile and deliberate in his pure joy, he approached the tree little by little, as if the tree upon sensing his proximity, had flowered just for him in order to welcome him ashore. . . . He touched the trunk with the palms of his hands and looked up to see the stars through the branches, he drank in the fragrance that rather than intoxicating him, calmed his roaring blood. . . . And then, serene and blind to all else, enraptured like a young lover and grateful for the marvelous stroke of luck that had provided this chance encounter with the almond tree, he danced around its trunk. . . . (*Cristo*, 114–15)

This scene of the novel—a narrative that elsewhere compares the camp to Odysseus's world—essentially redeploys Odysseus's memory of an epic encounter with Beauty in the form of another awe-inspiring tree: "I saw the stalk of a young palm shooting up. I had gone there / once, and with a following of a great many people, / . . . /And as, when I looked upon that tree, my heart admired it / long, since such a tree had never yet sprung from the earth. . . ."[33] Coincidentally, in her first detailed discussion of the defining features of beauty, Elaine Scarry has referred to this scene from *The Odyssey* ("Odysseus, washed up on shore, covered with brine, having nearly drowned, comes upon a human community and one person in particular, Nausicaa, whose beauty simply astonishes him" [*On Beauty*, 21]) in which the hero recalls the palm tree. For Scarry, the scene illustrates the characteristics of beauty that she will elaborate in the rest of her treatise: beauty "conveys a sense of the 'newness' or 'newbornness' of the entire world" (*On Beauty*, 22); "beauty is sacred" (23); "beauty is lifesaving" (24); "beauty [is] a 'greeting'" (25). For Bartra's "Adam of the waters" (*Cristo*, 114), the aromatic almond tree that allows him to glimpse the heavens through its branches, that seems to want to "welcome him ashore," will fulfill the promise of its beauty only when he is able to share it with the three friends he has left behind. Even after being apprehended by a gendarme ("completely indifferent to the beauty of the night" [115]), Tarrés is allowed to continue on his way toward freedom. But the ex-combatant, who once had turned back to keep vigil over the body of a fallen fellow soldier, realizes that his place is with the others: "Yes, freedom, like love, could only exist as a shared treasure" (*Cristo*, 119). He breaks a fragrant branch from the tree and begins the long swim back. Upon his return to the *chabola*, Tarrés presents his gift of beauty and fraternity to his hut-mates; eventually it too is transformed into a treasured possession that will never be forgotten: "The almond branch was stuck in the sand, in the corner with the lamp, and stayed there for several days. When all the flowers had fallen off, Vives made a little walking cane out of it that he was never without. 'Somewhere down the road,' Roldós told him one day, smiling, 'you'll tell somebody the story of the almond branch, huh?'" (*Cristo*, 125).

Throughout each introductory section of the three parts of the novel, the narrator had insisted not only on the concentration camp's radical sense of placelessness, but also its status as a no-man's-land outside the vital flow of time and history: "The cities of the world are a triumph of plowed furrows and harvests, of sheer will and the dream of generations, it's a name that rises up from the spirit of those who have longed for this place. . . . But this was a city of defeat, a city of violent, sudden birth" (*Cristo*, 10). In this stillborn non-place, time is inert like a lifeless thing: "Time did not exist in the camp" (*Cristo*, 65); only the past tense seems to still exist; the present and the future are dead: "In the camp, the habitual images of life belonged to a past that swallowed up every man engaged in the search for his own lost time, in an irascible coupling between the imagination and the ghosts of his dreams" (123–24).[34] The victory that the four refugees of Bartra's Argelès share is not escape from death (Roldós succumbs to tuberculosis at the story's end) nor escape from the camp (Vives, Puig, and Tarrés remain in the camp at the novel's conclusion), but rather the successful conversion of an apparently meaningless temporal vacuum into a portion of history's dynamic narrative. One by one the friends signal their renewed relationship with the present and/or the future by an act of autonomous emplacement in the camp. Tarrés's Odyssean return to the camp is heralded by the almond branch (an emblem of his conscious decision to stay there); it is dug into the sand, provisionally rooted to the same soil that will nourish the wandering refugee's existence in exile with postwar memories of the camp. A visit to the camp by Puig's girlfriend Joana similarly provides him with a nascent point of departure for a life outside of Spain; the night of lovemaking that he spends with her, the first significant "event" for Puig that occurs in the camp, initiates a new phase of personal history: "The wonder of love was, more than anything else, a reconciliation with the world. He didn't need anything else to be able to trust and believe in the future" (*Cristo*, 158). Realizing that the presence of Joana in the camp, however temporary (she must leave at dawn), has eliminated the need to conjure up consoling images of an absent past, Puig breaks his flute in half and buries the pieces in the sand: "The resurrection of the day has already begun" (*Cristo*, 159). For his part, Vives serves as chronicler of the camp history that will immortalize the lives of the *chabola*'s occupants. In the chapter preceding his own death, Roldós awaits a nightly story that Vives always tells him, realizing that one day that he, like all of the camp inmates, will form part of history's narrative: "He himself, Roldós, would be a story.

And even Vives as well. Everything becomes history in this world" (*Cristo*, 170). When Vives's familiar voice breaks the silence in the hut, for the first time ever the story told belongs to the camp: "Once upon a time there was a crazy man and an invisible horse. . . . '" (*Cristo*, 111). Finally, Roldós's death on the sandy floor of the hut is represented not as a senseless effect of exile's hardship, but rather as a fulsome (albeit tragic) moment of destiny: "There are so many places to live in the world: countries, mountains, cities, farms, hometowns, refuges that protect and sustain us, roads that receive us and keep us going; places of roots or places of winds, places of benign stars or adverse moons. But there's only one place to die. Irreplaceable . . . An ascetic in his own death, Roldós, rather than die, had allowed life to leave him, and in his secret simplicity, in his quiet dignity, he understood from the beginning—and hastened to claim it as his choice—that the corner of the hut was his final, definitive place. It was all he needed" (*Cristo*, 178–79).

Shortly after Roldós's death, Vives picks up the dried butterfly from the corner of the *chabola* and lays it to rest on his friend's body. Here in this cocoonlike space, a haven for camaraderie and compassion, the broken lives of four civil war refugees are tied forever together through the bonds of fraternity. In the novel's conclusion, Vives writes his last entry in his journal, imagining the day when the experiences of the concentration camp inmates will be metamorphosed into the language of history and memory. Clutching his pen like a magic wand worthy of Herik el Bardo or a tool of his father's own creative genius, Agustí Bartra's fictional alter ego is confident that the story of Argelès-sur-Mer will one day be told, and so resurrect the lives of those who once shared the space of a blanket-covered hut:[35]

> The cane wand will be waved again, and its magical whistle will set in motion the five figures; one alongside of the other, they will advance toward their new reality. Puig with his little reed flute, Roldós with his dried butterfly, Tarrés with his dripping lantern, Niebla with her long droopy ears . . . and I myself with my staff. Creatures of life and of the imagination for whom chance will determine their paths and their dwellings among men. They will tirelessly tell the story of what happened to them during the sordid period of history in which they were destined to live, a fate that in their hearts they accepted like a demand of the Destiny of their times, so prodigious in hecatombs. (*Cristo*, 187)

Part IV
The Camps as Battlegrounds of Emigration: The Struggle for Liberation

10

Telling Stories of Getting Out: The Politics of Emigration

Me despierto. / París. / ¿Es que vivo, / es que he muerto?
¿Es que definitivamente he muerto? / *Mais non* . . . / *C'est la police* . . .
Pero ahora . . . / Este viento, / esta arena en los ojos, / esta arena . . .
(Argelès! Saint-Cyprien!) . . .
(América del Sur es una gran barrera / para mirar los toros.
Cuesta cara la entrada. / Si el SERE no te ayuda, una cornada.)

[I wake up. / Paris. / Am I alive, / or have I died?
Am I in fact dead? / *Mais non* . . . / *C'est la police* . . .
But now . . . / This wind, / this sand in my eyes, / this sand . . .
(Argelès! Saint-Cyprien!) . . .
(South America is your best seat / from which to watch the bullfight.
It's hard to get a ticket.
If the SERE doesn't help you out, consider yourself gored.)
  —Rafael Alberti, "Vida bilingüe de un refugiado español en Francia"

The Year 2000. An American tourist visits Rosellón and, recalling the old story of the concentration camps for Spaniards, crosses the immense beaches of Argelès, Saint-Cyprien, and Barcarès. They are deserted. Only the occasional dune breaks the sandy monotony. Suddenly the Yankee stops. A dune half covers a hovel made of broken, rotting boards. Spirals of smoke escape through the cracks. Intrigued, the tourist draws nearer. Out of that lair, dragging his feet, emerges an eighty-nine-year-old man, but he looks at least nine hundred years older. His white beard is his only clothing. Moved, the yankee asks: "My man, who are you?" "My name is Braulio Ríos, Spanish refugee." "Spanish refugee? Haven't you heard that Franco died many years ago, that the Second World War ended as well, that there are no longer Spanish refugees? What in the hell are you doing here, old man?" "I'm waiting for a letter from the SERE, *mister*. . . ."

So WENT THE HIGHLY PERSONALIZED JOKE THAT ANGEL MÉNDEZ, former internee of Argelès-sur-Mer, kiddingly wrote in a 1941 letter to his friend still left behind in the camp, Celso Amieva, aka Braulio Ríos.[1]

The amusing anecdote captures the sense of the camp inmates' seemingly eternal wait for the magical missive—the coveted letter from the official Republican refugee aid and evacuation agency established in Paris in March 1939, the Servicio de Evacuación de Republicanos Españoles (SERE)—that informs the lucky recipient of his release from imprisonment and selection for emigration to America. But as Amieva's disheartened reply in verse sent to his correspondent Méndez indicates, only a privileged few would ever receive the cherished notification; his Argelès poem honoring the civil war dead, "Dichosos los que cayeron" (Fortunate Are the Fallen) includes the sardonic lines: "Refugiados irrefugiables / fuera de España recemos, rezad / a esos dioses que habéis aquí inventado / para la redención que no veréis jamás" [Refugees without refuge / so far from Spain let us pray, pray / to those gods you've invented here / for the redemption that you will never see].[2] The obsessive fantasies of liberation and escape engendered by the intolerable conditions of confinement—colored by the news widely disseminated in the camps that Lázaro Cárdenas's Mexico would open its shores to tens of thousands of refugees—shaped themselves around images of the Aztec nation. An affirmative answer from the SERE was the inmate's ticket out of the barbed-wire penitentiary and potentially provided passage to Mexico, described by former Argelès residents Antonio Tellado Vázquez and Antonio Sánchez-Bravo (for whom the letter never did arrive) as "the ticket of golden dreams."[3] In the words of historian Javier Rubio, the chance of such an emigration for those fighting repatriation was "about as likely as finding the real *El dorado*."[4] And such a golden opportunity would prove to be, just like the El Dorado of long ago, an equally elusive treasure; the transatlantic adventure remained completely out of reach for all but a minority of the Spanish refugee population. The emotions of hope and frustration experienced by the majority of the waiting internees are perfectly distilled in a series of camp-inspired cartoon pictures, *aleluyas* with rhymed captions published in 1944 as *Historia del refugiado*. Three drawings from the multipaneled comic book–style camp history ironically refer to the dreams of Mexico and the despair of disappointment. The first frame represents the slumbering inmate who imagines himself, under an improbably wide-brimmed sombrero, galloping freely on horseback along a cactus-lined landscape; the caption reads: "La esperanza y la ilusión / le dan una indigestión" [His hopes and dreams / will give him heartburn]. The next drawing shows a pompous figure in full-dress uniform marching up the gangplank of an ocean liner named *Mexico*; this official is trailed closely by a second man holding tightly onto his coattails: "Embarcan privilegiados / y unos cuantos enchufados" [The privileged get to go / and a few well-connected cronies]. The third panel depicts the ship now on the horizon, separated by a barrier of barbed wire from the weeping dreamer who remains behind, half buried in the sand: "Si no ha podido embarcar / ha alcanzado aterrizar" [He wasn't able to embark / but he's certainly landed].[5] These simple line drawings and the pithy couplets that accompany them succinctly introduce a series of key issues related to the final topic of my study, the emigration out of the camps. The three chapters of part 4 consider how the inmates are chosen by the Paris-based relief agency for liberation, and how this story of struggle for selection—an embattled saga of privilege, disenfranchisement, and sometimes dumb luck—is told in the camp literature. I examine the extent to which the increasingly fractured relationships among the Republican groups in exile (embittered by tensions and divisions extant during the civil war and ever more exacerbated afterward) play a role in the politics of camp emigration. Additionally, I explore how "Mexico"—the object of desire for thousands of Spaniards in the camps of France—is constructed in the exile imaginary. A central question that unifies my readings in these three chapters pertains to how the exiles who successfully escaped the barbed wire—both those who write from the privileged position of Paris as well as from Mexico City—represent and remember those unlucky thousands who remained on the beaches of France and the shores of world war. Their memories of these comrades "left behind" significantly inform the story of exile that begins to take shape in Mexico during the early post–civil war years. Like the fallen soldiers on the battlefields of Spain, the abandoned refugees in the camps of France are idealistically encoded in the pages penned by the "liberated" exile-survivors, as the true martyred heroes and the frontline fighters of a Spanish people who waged a war in the name of justice.

Between Heaven and Hell: Mexico, The SERE, and the Camps

In the letter cited above, Angel Méndez imagines a hypothetical American visitor's walk on the beaches of France and his stunned encounter with the dismal signs of the concentration camp experience: the feeble, disoriented old man, the ramshackle shelter, the desolate sandy surroundings. On February 12, 1939, just days after the first wave of thousands of refugees began to fill up the shoreline, a flesh-and-blood American visitor from Mexico, the diplomat Isidro Fabela, initiated his own eye-opening walk along the beaches of Argelès and St. Cyprien. Fabela sent his abbreviated preliminary assessment to President Lázaro Cárdenas in a February 23 telegram: "SPANISH SITUATION CON-

CENTRATION CAMPS FRIGHTFUL, SO I ADVISE ACTIVATE PLANS AND GRANT AUTHORIZATION TO ENTER MEXICO ACCORDING TO SELECTION DETERMINED BY TEJEDA [Adalberto Tejeda, Mexico's ambassador to Spain]."[6] A lengthy follow-up letter written to Cárdenas the next day, based on the eight days that Fabela had spent among the inmates interned in the Perpignan area camps, gave the Mexican president his first view into the world of the Spanish refugees. Fabela, like so many of the Spanish witnesses, communicates his impressions of the camp in terms of a totally negated space of the void: "When it was created, the concentration camp (such as it was) did not have as much as a tent, a hut, shelter of any kind, a wall, a gully, a hill; there were no trees, bushes, or stones. Here the refugees from Spain have been living, either along the open, sandy beach facing the sea, or else in inland areas of uncultivated fields and bare vineyards. In the beginning, the one hundred thousand men housed (?) in Argelès did not have any kind of shelter, nor was there any source of heat to protect them against the winter cold, nor a roof over their heads to shield them from the north wind. Not even a wall between them and the frigid sea air."[7] Fabela goes on to enumerate the brutal weather conditions; the lack of food and the inadequate system of food distribution; and the cruel practice of separating family members.[8] Fabela reports that he has learned that the former speaker of the house of the Spanish parliament, Diego Martínez Barrio, is part of a committee to coordinate evacuation efforts to America. Fabela, who has obtained copies of the committee's application form for the refugees who will petition for emigration, not only encloses a sample in his letter for Cárdenas but also begins to set in motion a general distribution of the forms among the camp inmates: "I returned to the concentration camps in order to hand out printed application forms to those among the refugees who seemed to have some standing or else were ranking military officers. This way they could pass the forms out among their compatriots, showing the others how to apply for as many slots as we have."[9] Writing on February 24 with a nervous eye to France and England's imminent recognition of the Franco regime (which occurred on February 26, the day before Manuel Azaña resigned as president of the Republic; one month before Madrid fell to Nationalist troops in the last days of March), Fabela emphasizes both the desperation among the panic-stricken petitioners to avoid forced repatriation as well as their conviction that Mexico is their only salvation: "They see our country as their hope of salvation. But everyone knows that the decision regarding their pleas for help will not be quickly made, and this makes them feel deeply worried and even desperate. The prospect of returning to a hostile Spain, where they could lose their lives, is for them a kind of torture."[10]

The Mexican historian José Antonio Matesanz has carefully traced the crucial role that Mexico played in the development of the evacuation effort—including decisions made about selection criteria—that resulted in the eventual emigration of more than twenty-five thousand displaced Spaniards to that American nation by 1948.[11] As Matesanz indicates, just days after Fabela's dispatch of information to Cárdenas, the Mexican ambassador to France, Narciso Bassols, wrote a February 28 letter to Spain's Martínez Barrio in which he explained Mexico's position on the question of emigration: "Due to the essentially political nature of the aid that Mexico wants to offer to the Spanish Republic, I especially would like to draw your attention to two key ideas. First, we prefer to admit those refugees who have been recommended by a selection committee made up of either representatives of the Spanish Republican government or national parties making up the Popular Front. Secondly, instead of giving preference to people with the greatest economic resources or professional training, we believe that it is our duty to grant entry to those refugees in greatest need, either for political or economic reasons."[12] Indeed, the membership of the first executive committee of the new Servicio de Evacuación de Republicanos Españoles (a decision-making body of ten individuals charged with the disbursement of relief funds and the supervision of the selection of refugees slated for emigration) did represent a diverse coalition of Popular Front constituencies: Republicans, Communists, Basque and Catalonian nationalists, socialists, anarchists, and UGT and CNT trade unionists.[13] Overseeing the activities of the executive committee was a seven-member advisory board (Ponencia ministerial), headed by Prime Minister Juan Negrín (in exile since the early days of March) and comprised of former Negrín cabinet members.[14] Just as the constellation of executive Committee membership attempted to equitably represent the diverse political entities comprising the Spanish Republic, so too did the SERE officials endeavor to assign emigration quotas proportionately according to party and trade union affiliations. Rubio describes the following political membership-based quota system as a model devised "with the objective of avoiding favoritism": 55 percent Socialists, Communists, and UGT trade unionists; 22 percent anarchist-libertarians (CNT-FAI); 20 percent Republican parties, including the Catalonian groups; 3 percent no party affiliation.[15] By early April 1939 the SERE offices had been inundated with more than 250,000 petitions for emigration.[16] Faced with the overwhelming disparity between the sheer quantity of requests and the very limited number of spaces for emigration, the best-laid plans for a judicious, carefully crafted, and dispassionate system of selection began to be threatened as cronyism, personal influence, party prejudice, and bureaucratic inefficiency crept into the process.[17]

The miserable plight of the hundreds of thousands of Spanish Republicans in the concentration camps, an early factor as seen above for the sense of urgency surrounding Mexico's mission of emigration, will continue to be a central point of reference for Mexican and Spanish officials who orchestrate the ambitious relief and evacuation programs during the first months following the civil war. The second of Ambassador Bassols's earlier cited guidelines for Mexico's response to Spanish refugees (following his first recommendation that decisions be based on criteria agreed upon by a representative coalition of Republican points of view)—that priority be given to those in most dire need of assistance "for political or economic reasons"—indicates that Cárdenas's envoy was especially concerned about a particular sector of the refugee population. In a March 4, 1939, letter to Léon Jouhaux, a leading figure in the French labor union CGT, Bassols explains: "It is our wish that the Spanish proletariat find on Mexican soil the support and encouragement they need to further their political and social agenda. Therefore, we will allow the Spanish leadership of the Popular Front to be the ones to pick and choose which refugees should be brought to Mexico to keep the struggle alive."[18] Matesanz cites this passage to suggest that Bassols, who as a well-known Communist was accused at the time of partisanship by disgruntled refugees, saw the Spanish emigration to Mexico as an opportunity to strengthen his own party's support. In any event, Bassols's communications written after the first of the large-scale emigrations to Mexico in May (transported by the ships *Sinaia* and the *Flandre*) repeatedly stress his government's commitment to the most beleaguered members of the refugee community: the inmates of the concentration camps. In a June 16 letter, Bassols directs Fernando Gamboa, the Mexican liaison to the SERE, to give final approval to the passenger lists submitted for the upcoming voyage onboard the ship *Mexique* according to a list of four criteria, including one directly related to the camps: "In order to heed the cries and pleas for help that come out of the concentration camp and that the Mexican Government cannot ignore, at least four-fifths of the total number of emigrants should be those individuals who come directly from said camps."[19] Two months later, in a telegram to President Cárdenas, Bassols again reiterates the importance of aiding the camp prisoners first and foremost; as regards future emigration to Mexico, he recommends the following: "At least ninety per cent will be people who have come directly from the concentration camps *stop*.[20] Earlier in a March 28 letter, Gen. Vicente Rojo, military commander of the Republican army, had made a similar plea to Juan Negrín to remember the plight of the thousands of combatants now corralled within the camps. Shortly thereafter, Rojo recalled the purpose of his communication to the Spanish leader charged with the relief program and the evacuation project: "I wrote him a letter, since I couldn't see him, reiterating for the last time the necessity of taking care of our countrymen now crowded into concentration camps like human ant hills."[21] But according to statistics provided by Javier Rubio, in the early days of emigration the greatest financial aid granted by the SERE was directed to those Spaniards in France who had been fortunate enough to avoid concentration camp confinement or had been expeditiously released: "Out of the almost 100 million francs deposited into the SERE by December 1939, the payments directed to the concentration camps, where the greatest number (and the neediest) of the expatriates in France resided, scarcely reached 14 millions francs, in other words, a seventh of the total budget."[22]

Regardless of the slim statistical chances for emigration to Mexico obtaining for the vast majority of concentration camp inmates, for every one of them the very mention of the name of that American nation conjured up images of hope and freedom. Eulalio Ferrer recalls that he and his fellow inmates in Argelès-sur-Mer nicknamed President Lázaro Cárdenas "the Marshal of Hope."[23] Writing in 1940, another former resident of Argelès, Jaime Espinar, stated: "All of us put our faith in the young Mexican nation and in her democratic government."[24] In his analysis of concentration camp literature, Michael Ugarte has referred to the idea of Mexico for the refugees as their own "Zion"; in fact, for Ugarte a key distinction between the camp testimony authored by Spaniards and the writings of Jewish survivors of German concentration camps are the former's repeated allusions to a promised land, "the constant presence of America as a possible salvation; salvation not only in a spiritual sense, but as a real place that meant the end of their sojourn through the concentration camps, and the end of immediate danger of death."[25] In a memorable scene from Roberto Ruiz's poignant fictionalized memoir of life in a women's and children's refugee camp in La Marniere, the starving group huddled around a fire begs the resident *maestra* to tell them stories of America. A fanciful, fantastical place in the deliciously warm tropics emerges from the teacher's uncertain exchange with her eager and imaginative audience: "'Tell us what they eat there, and how they make all that gold. . . .' 'Let's see, since we're talking about the tropics here, they probably eat birds and fruits. As for the gold, which is a metallic element, I guess they must get that from the mines. . . .' 'And is it true that there are so many pineapples and bananas that they just rot in the streets?' 'Oh, I don't know about that. . . .' 'And that nobody works, and that every house has a beautiful garden?' 'Well now, we'll have to see. . . .' "[26] Within the world of the camps, "Mexico" specifically was construed as a place of freedom and refuge in quite literally spatial, topographical terms. Immediately adjacent to the Barcarès camp was a kind of holding area, a way station designated for the lucky inmates who had been tapped for emigration to Mexico; its name: Campo México. This intermediate stage arena built between the camps of France and the freedom of America is described by St. Cyprien internee Antonio Vilanova as "a camp like all the others, but without the barbed-wire fence"; Vilanova goes on to explain why the barbed wire was absolutely unnecessary to keep the men in place: "We had one foot in France and another in Mexico, so no one dreamed that we would escape and remain behind in France when we had already been chosen to go to America."[27] Here the inmates begin the process of physical and legal rehabilitation that prepares the way for a new life in America. The hopeful applicants for selection from the Barcarès camp next door occasionally managed to sneak inside the Campo México for a curious look around this special place filled with men slated for imminent departure. Celso Amieva's friend and future pen pal Angel Méndez, ever the optimist long before he eventually was released, was a habitual visitor who, when he had to slip back through the barbed wire, usually did so with a prized possession from the promised land, "he always came back with Aztec cigarettes in hand."[28] The very presence of the Campo México, says Celso Amieva, was tangible proof for the internees waiting on the other side of the fence that the somewhat mysterious, faraway SERE did exist and actually operated beyond its imprimatur on hundreds of application forms sent in from Paris that the refugees feverishly, and repeatedly, filled out: "The SERE showed signs of life: the 'Camp of Mexico' housed many men who were waiting for a ship."[29] Even one of these ships that transported an exceptionally large group of refugees to Mexico in July 1939 bore the name of that country like an inscription of freedom across its bow: the *Mexique*. But for most of Amieva's fellow companions of Argelès and Barcarès, the ship they boarded was relegated to the confines of the imagination. Amieva recalls Nilo, a frequent visitor to his *chabola* in Argelès, obnoxiously announcing his arrival with a booming foghorn greeting, "From the minute he walked in, he loved to imitate the bellowing ship's whistle: 'Uuuuuuuuu! All aboard for Mexico!'"[30]

Mauricio Fresco, a Mexican diplomatic official deeply involved in the early 1940s with the coordination of rescue, relief, and emigration efforts in France, has described another physical haven of hope and liberty standing just kilometers away from some camps. Outside of Marseilles the Mexican government converted two enormous castles, the Reynarde and the Montgrand, into refugee centers for Spanish men as well as women and children, respectively. Housed within the Montgrand were two schools for children, each baptized for the Mexican leaders who helped create and sustain these spaces of refuge: the Presidente Lázaro Cárdenas and the Presidente Manuel Avila Camacho. Fresco has described each of the ancient edifices as a fairy-tale vision for the groups of dispossessed Spaniards who passed through their portals: "At the very top of the castle tower waved a flag in the wind, an unfamiliar one for the men in the area, but a beautiful symbol of a country so far away from the horrors of the European old world: Mexico. Over the doorway of the mansion was this sign: 'Residence of the United States of Mexico.'"[31] In Fresco's version of events, published a decade after the fact, Mexico is cast in the messianic role of savior; the story of the Spanish exiles (including concentration camp internees) who make their way to the refugee oasis is chronicled as a tale of resurrection. Even before the inmates gained release, says Fresco, they had turned their eyes toward the banner of Mexico waving over the castle buildings, "which were like ports of salvation in the great shipwreck of the Spanish Republic" (40). Later, standing on the threshold of the stone structures, the new arrivals from the camps, "emaciated and dressed in rags," lift their gaze to that flag of freedom. Immediately reinstated to a realm of basic decency and human dignity ("Clothes, a clean bed, good food, and moral support were what the Spanish refugees received from the moment of their arrival at the Residence of the United States of Mexico" [42]), the refugees experience a spiritual and moral rebirth, brought back to life through the intervention of a nation committed to "the task of salvation" (40): "Physically, they were transformed into new men, they became again what they had been before; some of them cried tears of gratitude for the asylum that Mexico offered them. Their morale was bolstered as they cast aside their fears of being perceived simply as their enemies' victims. Now they saw the possibility of rebuilding their lives in a free country, maybe even continuing their struggle that had been interrupted by Francisco Franco's betrayal" (42). As news of this incredible sanctuary on French soil travels back to the camps nearby, remembers Fresco, the Mexican consulate is newly flooded with wave after wave of desperate petitions: "At one point the Consulate received up to two thousand letters a day and three hundred telegrams" (43).

Nowhere is Mexico-as-Savior more dramatically expressed than in the memories of those fortunate few who found themselves transported out of the camps and onto the deck of a ship headed for Mexico in the spring or summer of 1939. Typically, the survivor-witness figures his saga out of the clutches of the camp and into the fraternal embrace of a sympathetic democracy as an odyssey that takes him from material squalor and hopelessness toward a clear horizon of renewed possibilities. Manuel Serra, Catalonian labor leader for the Unión General de Trabajadores, was imprisoned for five months in the infamous Collioure punishment camp. Most of his interminable hours and days were consumed by Sysiphean tasks, either moving heavy stones from one place to another or emptying enormous latrine vats of excrement. Serra, like other unlucky memoirists assigned to the latter stinking duty and haunted by its painful evocation, recalls the chore as one of the most humiliating aspects of his concentration camp experience: "We filled up enormous containers, the kind that are used in the grape harvest, and two of us prisoners hauled them down to the sea where we emptied them. I moved an incredible amount of excrement, huge metric tons of it! Believe it or not, after a bit I got over my squeamishness; I got used to it. It didn't make me sick like it did at first. And I even got used to walking around covered in filth the whole day, with this stinking stuff oozing from my clothes. There was no way to change into clean clothes; I couldn't even bathe."[32] The notification that this prisoner has been given permission to emigrate to Mexico—the result of a process initiated by a chance encounter at the border months earlier with a young woman from the Mexican consulate—grants safe passage out of France's filthy hellhole. Traveling handcuffed under armed guard from Collioure to the port of departure outside of Burdeos, Serra finally finds himself miraculously deposited at freedom's door: "They took off my handcuffs next to the boat *Mexique*, named for the country that was offering me sanctuary."[33]

Other campers of course had to wait much longer for their ship to come in, if it ever did. A case in point is that of Miguel Giménez Igualada, who spent more than two and a half years interned in France before emigrating to Mexico. In a letter dated December 3, 1939, from the Bram camp, he replies to a fellow refugee now living in Falaise; his correspondent, Benigno Bejarano, had written bitterly to Igualada on November 6 about the self-serving politics and corruption that in his opinion plagued the Paris-based SERE office: "I am not exaggerating when I say that that damned S.E.R.E. is like a malignant tumor that needs to be removed immediately. The life in Paris that the Spanish bureaucrats lead, living off the millions that they took out of Spain, is simply scandalous, not to say sickening."[34] In Igualada's tongue-in-cheek response from the concentration camp, he gently broke the news that he himself was a SERE employee: "I hadn't told you before out of fear that, knowing you, you'd be disgusted. You'd think I was one of the bureaucrats that you so magisterially portray in your 'In the Fatal Circle.' But now I feel I must make this painful confession: I am an employee of the S.E.R.E."[35] He goes on to explain the nature of his work for the Service for the Evacuation of Spanish Republicans, a job position that requires his daily attention to four large metal receptacles placed strategically below the four openings of a raised platform. Igualada writes sardonically of the morning routine he assiduously performs each day: "At dawn, before the blissful souls still resting their bones on the soft straw have awakened, the battery of men, as we pompously call it, brooms in hand and lances ready for action (the lances are the white poles we use to carry the steel cylinders, sarcastically referred to by some as the diving pools), head toward the office to begin the transport of 'absolutely everything' from the evacuation. Then we wash the platform, we polish the walls, we give the surrounding area a once-over with the brooms, leaving everything sparkling clean and shiny so the morning sunlight will smile upon it (I don't think I could have painted a 'cleaner' picture nor could I have explained more clearly the bureacratic position that I enjoy in the S.E.R.E., the Service of the Evacuation of Spanish Refugees)."[36]

Perhaps not coincidentally, another emigrant to Mexico and future filmmaker, Carlos Velo (who on May 30, 1939, arrived in Veracruz on board the ship *Flandre* with 326 other Spanish refugees) remembers his wait for liberation as taking place in a stench-filled purgatory of the basest kind. In an interview conducted more than four decades after his release, Velo endeavors to explain to his listener "what Cárdenas meant to us."[37] He begins his tale by inviting his interlocutor, the Mexican novelist Ricardo Garibay, into the sordid arena of the refugees' struggle to survive and to surmount the limits of the barbed-wire confinement: "'I'm going to tell you,' Carlos Velo told me, 'the *battle of the shit* in the concentration camps.'" He describes how he and his companions were waiting futilely, helplessly, with growing despair, for news of aid from outside agencies. On one day of gale-force gusts, the camp of open-air latrines was particularly overwhelmed with a suffocatingly foul odor of excrement. The wind whipped the men's faces with soiled pieces of paper unearthed by nature's strength, smelly scraps that flew through the air like sarcastic replies to their pleas for help: "We had been waiting for weeks and weeks for news of assistance, for a response to our desperate situation, and now the replies arrived indeed. They came by way of the heavens, in the form of our own dried-up shit. This was our future, can you imagine? That's how it was for us."[38] Into this world of hopelessness, word of relief from Mexico took shape in the form of the Mexican official Fernando Gamboa and his wife Susana, wielding a loudspeaker as they walked through the sand like two saints of salvation. Velo recalls the gist of Gamboa's amplified message as if spoken in God's own voice: "'Spanish Republicans! Lázaro Cárdenas, the president of Mexico, in the name of his government and on behalf of all the

Mexican people, says to you: Mexico is waiting for you; it is your home, it will be your new country. Mexico opens its arms to the men of the Spanish Republic . . . !' And he spoke of a boat that would come in no time, which it did, he spoke of freedom, of bread, of respect, of the future as a sure thing, something to hold onto."[39] Velo's sense of being brought back to life through Mexico's generous intervention is shared by Antonio Sánchez Barbudo. This émigré to Mexico on board the May voyage of the *Sinaia* remembers the day a well-dressed visitor to his camp seemed to appear out of nowhere; he was searching, with SERE-approved permits in hand, for those inmates who had been selected for emigration. Sánchez Barbudo describes seeing the figure approach as if in a vision, from his own prostrate, defeated position in the sand. Amazingly, impossibly, says the future University of Wisconsin professor, the first name on the list was his own. Shaking off the camp's mind-numbing inertia, Sánchez Barbudo (and others like him) returned to the land of the living by joining the privileged ranks of the liberated.[40] A few weeks later, just as Silvia Mistral prepared to board the Veracruz-bound *Ipanema* (a departure she had for some time dreamily envisioned "on a ship that you imagine to be white, clean, charming"), she receives a despondent letter from a correspondent in the camp: "We feel completely abandoned, especially by our representatives who themselves enjoy excellent stipends and send us pat replies to our petitions. In summary: our current horizon of possibilities is reduced to the same old thing: destitution, egotism, exploitation, and abandonment."[41] Two days later as the ship weighs anchor, Mistral records her final thoughts upon leaving the shores of France as an indelible memory of those who remain behind: "Our thoughts are with those who are still imprisoned in the inhospitable sand of the beaches of the eastern Pyrenees."[42]

The Push of Conscience and the Pull of Privilege

Primo Levi, one of the most articulate witness-survivors of the German concentration camps, has written eloquently in his collection of essays *The Drowned and the Saved* on the subject of survivor guilt: the recriminations of conscience about getting out of the camps when so many others did not; the sense of shame for having access to some privilege—connections, extra food, dumb luck—that gave one an advantage over the others; the nagging self-doubts (or worse, the unsettling certainty) that one did not always act in solidarity with one's fellow sufferers. In his moving essay "The Gray Zone," Levi painfully concludes, "The ascent of the privileged, not only in the *Lager* but in all human coexistence, is an anguishing but unfailing phenomenon: only in utopias is it absent."[43] The question of preferential treatment—rooted in political affiliations, social class, professional connections, and personal spheres of influence—is an important key to understanding the story of the politics of Spanish emigration as told both by the authors of the concentration camp literature as well as by those "privileged" writers living in Paris who managed to stay on the other side of the barbed wire. In the powerfully evocative sketches that accompany the text of Molins i Fábrega's 1944 *Campos de concentración, 1939-194* . . . , Josep Bartolí draws a particularly stark contrast between the camp inmates' world of destitution and the infinitely superior environment of Republican *enchufados* in Paris who have ready access to the exiled government's funds earmarked for SERE-sponsored relief projects, stipends, and safe passage to America. On one page, the artist places an empty plate and spoon at the feet of a starving, faceless internee; on the other, in a rare full-page scene that includes a bright urban landscape beyond the fenced perimeter of the dismal camp, a richly laden table of the finest haute cuisine that Paris has to offer is set before an insatiable Republican "fat cat," his fleshy mouth stuffed to overflowing with food. Molins i Fábrega's text minces no words as it savagely accuses the greedy exile of privilege of criminally devouring the bulk of financial reserves that rightfully belong to the "rank and file" of Spanish refugees, corralled en masse behind kilometers of barbed wire as Bartolí's sketch illustrates: "Swine who call yourself brother. If your ignoble layers of fat allowed it, you could turn your head and see the man you betrayed, hunted down by bloodthirsty beasts, you could see how he suffers in graveyards and cemeteries. You turn a deaf ear to the brother you betrayed. The cities of the world, smiling upon you because of the millions you robbed from the poor, are grim and gloomy places for him."[44] This indignant sentiment that a self-serving minority of exile elite are lining their pockets and paving their way toward safe haven abroad at the expense of a dispossessed majority who themselves courageously filled the front lines of combat during the war is frequently expressed among the earliest authors of exile and concentration camp literature. The bitterest critics of the SERE agency, who denounce it as an institution plagued by corrupt partisanship, infighting, and a pervasive sense of *sálvese quien pueda* [every man for himself], are often, it must be noted, fiercely oppositional *antinegrinista* (and virulently anti-Communist) members of libertarian trade unions like the Confederación Nacional de Trabajadores (CNT) and the Federación Anarquista Ibérica (FAI). Solano Palacio, whose own anarchist-syndicalist connections in France helped keep him out of the camps until he emigrated to Chile on the Winnipeg expedition, is one of SERE's most vocal detractors. In his 1939 chronicle of the saga of the flight out of Spain and

France published shortly after arriving to America, *El éxodo por un refugiado español*, Palacio condemns the factionalism of the Spanish groups in exile that colors the policies and politics of the SERE as a culmination of long-standing divisiveness and opportunism during the civil war among the upper echelons of the Republican ranks: "In Paris things were no better than they had been in Spain: the same irritating preferential treatment, the odiously unfair favoritism was worse than ever. In spite of our tragic circumstances, when common misfortune should have brought us all together, the infighting reached epic proportions and the antagonism that already existed among different sectors, just got worse every day. . . . The actions of the S.E.R.E. were disastrous for the Spanish evacuees. Things had changed very little from the kinds of tactics used in Spain during the war."[45] Later he angrily, and with considerable naïveté, decries the consequences for "the true antifascists, with a proven revolutionary track record" who derive no benefits from the exiled Spanish government's transfer of gold deposits out of Spain into foreign bank accounts: "With honorable policies in place and with the money that was salvaged from Spain, all the exiled Spaniards in France could have gotten out of this country. But precisely the opposite has happened. The people's money is being used so that a few rogues can live like kings, while thousands of worthy Spaniards are rotting in concentration camps."[46]

Similarly, the CNT activist Silvia Mistral, who publishes from Mexico her 1940 memoir *Exodo*, contrasts the privilege of the few with the powerlessness of the interned masses: "The refugees will continue to pay tribute to hunger and death in the inhospitable camps. Meanwhile, the petty tyrants of the Republic, themselves drenched in prodigious amounts of Spanish gold, just keep sending the inmates more blank application forms for emigration."[47] Ricardo Baldó García, former internee of the North African camp of Morand, recalls as well the sense of disenfranchisement that was shared among his fellow prisoners: "The letters that arrive in Morand say that the gold of Spain will only be used to liberate the leaders. It will not be enough to liberate the great majority of ex-combatants. . . . Everyone understands now that the war has been lost and only a few will be saved."[48] Argelès veterans, the *mutilados* Tellado Vázquez and Sánchez-Bravo, who escape from one concentration camp only to be interned again in another, acrimoniously refer to "the privileged Spanish exiles" who live, they imagine, in the lap of luxury: "All of them magnificently housed in splendid mansions of repose and opulence. . . . All of them receive lavish monthly government stipends paid in foreign currency, in French francs."[49] Even some "élite" exiles with former posts in the Negrín government lament the state of affairs that characterized the official Paris-based relief efforts in the early postwar days. Mariano Ansó, whose onetime position of political prominence is highlighted in the title of his 1976 memoir *Yo fui ministro de Negrín* (I Was Negrín's Cabinet Minister), recalls the "every man for himself" atmosphere that reigned among the frightened Spanish refugees vying for the same pot of limited resources: "In Paris, as in the rest of France, the exiles got caught up in internal fights among individuals and groups, completely at odds with the common good. . . . Now, instead of fighting for their ideals, they fought to control the economic means that would secure their place in emigration politics;" elsewhere Ansó remarks, "I made an appearance in the French capital only once, for personal reasons, and I never wanted to go back again. In the case of some very well-known personalities, concerns for personal safety and comfort totally outweighed any concerns for the well-being of the majority."[50] Negrín's last foreign minister, Julio Álvarez del Vayo, concurs with other memoirists in the fall of 1939 that the losers in the political battles among the exiles are the concentration camp internees, ultimate victims of the "rancour and personal animosity of a few emigrants from loyalist Spain who, rather than use their energy in serving the cause of the Spanish people, spend their time in writing dissenting articles and in other contentious activities." Such negative naysayers who, according to del Vayo, threaten the future of a free Spain, cannot measure up to the stature of the heroic "true believers" locked up in the camps: "All of them put together are not worth a single one of the refugees who, after eight months of anguish and privation in the French concentration camp, still long for the day when they can return to Spain in order to carry on the fight for freedom and their country's honour."[51] Interestingly, when the vast majority of exiles, *privilegiados* and *olvidados* alike, all dream of escaping France and Europe's world war, of heading not for Spain but for places of refuge, del Vayo constructs the exhausted campers as patient patriots yearning to cross the Spanish border to continue the "good fight."

In an incongruous coincidence of opinion, even radically reactionary critics of the Republican exodus and their "invasion and occupation" of Paris concur with the exiled Spaniards' own assessment of the plight of the camp inmates vis-à-vis a privileged minority of Republicans. In December 1939, designated on the book's frontispiece as the "Year of Victory," José Esteban Vilaró publishes in Spain a vitriolic account of the Republicans in France, *El ocaso de los dioses rojos. Barcelona, Perthus, Argelès, París, Méjico* . . . , (The Twilight of the Red Gods) in which he demonizes the Republican leadership in exile for disingenuously sacrificing a guileless *pueblo* in the name of personal comfort and security: "In fact, only the masses were left locked up in the camps, people who individually were politically and socially harmless. Meanwhile, the true scoundrels, the real danger and menace to the public, swarmed outside the camps as free men."[52] The great Red felons, spits Vilaró, remain at large: "The big shots, the most guilty of all, were living in Paris protected from discomforts, thanks to the large sums of money and preventive measures that they had set up outside of Spain during the civil war."[53] With their duped minions securely locked behind barbed wire, he says, they are free to pull all the strings needed to live the good life: "Argelès, St. Cyprien, Barcarès . . . For some, three different hells; for others, the threat of hell. For the real criminals these three names refer to a terrifying place that stands between them and the vengeance of their disillusioned and betrayed ex-supporters. These camps provide a kind of personal security system, guaranteeing their own peace and tranquility inside of their sumptuous domiciles. For everyone else, they are a punishment."[54] Oddly enough, the fervent *falangista* Esteban Vilaró's references to the potential threat of disgruntled inmates' attempts to take out their frustrations on their former leaders are improbably echoed in the Republican refugees' own accounts. The disparities obtaining between classes of refugees will one day be avenged, says Molins i Fábrega, alluding to the day when the forgotten Republican stuck in a concentration camp will demand redress from the political leaders who abandoned him there: "One day soon the wretched man will drag his bones out of the cemetery and find the ones who left him there. It will be a terrible day for you. Your gold and all your perks will be useless then. You will return to the mud and he, cleansed through suffering and sacrifice, will continue on the path of light, a light that will shine only for him. You scoundrel who call yourself his brother!"[55] One of Manuel García Gerpe's companions in the Septfonds camp refers to "those gentlemen of Paris": "Today there's nothing we can do to expose them. They know perfectly well that we can do nothing to them as long as we're locked up here . . . their impunity depends on the barbed wire. But the day that the barbed wire disappears, they will have so much to answer for."[56] So, too, warns Silvia Mistral of a Judgment Day when the truth will out; bound now for Mexico, she guiltily leaves behind hordes of fellow refugees teeming in the camps and imagines the inmates' day of reckoning: "The ones left behind will one day claim their right to wave a banner of protest, and speak out against those who, like Cain against Abel, set their sights on the golden prize of emigration, and abandoned them on the beaches of desolation"[57]

A Place at the Table: Antonio Ros's
Diario de un Refugiado Republicano

Certainly one way in which the refugees left behind will raise their voices in protest will be to record their plight in the pages of the history of Spanish exile. I devote the final two chapters of this book to two stories of the conflictive struggle for emigration, penned by longtime camp residents Manuel García Gerpe and Eulalio Ferrer and subsequently published as *Alambradas: Mis nueve meses por los campos de concentración de Francia* (Barbed Wire: My Nine Months in the Concentration Camps of France) and *Entre alambradas* (Inside the Barbed Wire), respectively. Before examining these two accounts by witnesses who watch from within the confines of the camps as the desperate events of emigration unfold, I offer an unusual glimpse into one Republican exile's enviable access to a Parisian world of good living and exquisite fine dining, all available thanks to his professional status, social standing, and impeccable political connections. Antonio Ros documented a year of his life spent in Paris in a series of 1939–40 diary entries originally published in Mexico City in 1968 as *Horas de angustia y esperanza* (Time of Hope and Anguish); the work was reissued in Barcelona in 1976 as *Diario de un refugiado republicano* (Diary of a Republican Refugee). Though revealing himself to be a committed antifascist, an enemy of the totalitarian state that Franco continues to build in Spain at the time of his writing, Ros's example also connects an individual name and a specific experience to the somewhat anonymous collective face of "privileged exile" alluded to by other Republican memoirists. Many of these commentators, as I have indicated in the preceding pages, speak with firsthand knowledge of the underbelly of the space of privilege and comfort, the concentration camp. As an ophthalmologist fleeing Spain who quickly establishes a following among a wealthy clientele in France, Ros maintains from his successful Parisian practice his own ties to the refugees in concentration camps through his responses to their various pleas for monetary aid or help obtaining passage to America. During his yearlong wait in Paris for his infant daughter, his wife, and his sisters' arrival from Franco's Spain (prior to their own subsequent emigration to New York and Mexico on board the *Champlain* as Hitler invades France), Ros rubs elbows with all the right people implicated in the question of Spanish emigration: the Paris-based SERE officials, the embassy delegates of the Dominican Republic involved in the refugee selection process, and the ranking French police inspectors charged both with granting or refusing the coveted identity papers as well as making arrests of undocumented Spanish refugees. The account that Ros documents in the twelve-month portion of the diary recorded in Paris (from May 25, 1939, to May 16, 1940), is a story of currying favor among the powerful and getting exactly what one can pay for. Ros chronicles his tale of privilege quite literally as a movable feast of opportunities; the deals he makes are brokered at sumptuous Parisian tables like the one imagined by Josep Bartolí, groaning under the weight of gourmet delicacies, vintage wines, and sheer political clout that belong to a world completely out of reach for those malnourished Spanish refugees interned in the camps.

Just days after arriving in Paris, Ros describes the city in terms made familiar to the reader by other Spanish refugees like Max Aub, Victoria Kent, and José Herrera Petere, as a pitiless hunting ground for undocumented civil war exiles, who as captured prey all end up in the same sandy prisons; in a May 30, 1939, entry Ros writes:

> Afterwards I go to a café in the Clichy Plaza to meet some friends. They warn me about all the dangers that lie in wait for the Spanish exiles in Paris. With the cleverness of a fox and the nose of a ferret, the zealously cruel police sniff out the plazas and the avenues, the cafés and hotels, the department stores and the parks. If they catch a Spanish refugee without his papers in order, they imprison him without compassion or else they pitilessly take him to one of those sad, desolate, and inclement concentration camps. Here, like in Argelès for example, the poor man is trapped with no other roof than the sky, no other bed than the sand, with no water other than the occasional rain. Completely humiliated, he is forced to descend the rungs of the zoological ladder until he is transformed into a primitive and filthy being.[58]

In the conversations in Paris that the author has with prominent figures in his own political party, the Izquierda Republicana, his well-known interlocutors make no mention of the threat of the concentration camps; they do, however, echo the prevailing notion that France, indeed all of Europe, teeters now on the brink of widespread war and destruction. The mantra murmured among the most well-placed members of his party's pedigreed *plana mayor* is to get out now; he must go to America before it's too late. His good friend Álvaro de Albornoz, "ex-Minister of Justice, ex-President of the Committee of Constitutional Rights [Garantías Constitucionales] and ex-Ambassador to Paris," himself leaves the capital bound for Mexico City on May 29, 1939, urging Ros to follow his example (85, 87). Ros's close companion Luis Jiménez de Asúa ("the illustrious professor, one of the most knowledgeable and erudite jurists in Europe"), on his way to accept a post in the law school of the Universidad de la Plata in Buenos Aires, assures him he can arrange the doctor's easy entry into Latin America: "'Go to Chile or Colombia,' he tells me. 'To get permission to enter Colombia, I'll introduce you to my good friend Dr. Luis Cano, his country's representative in the Society of Nations. He's head of the Colombian liberal party and a presidential candidate" (87–88, 96). Ros meets on more than one occasion with fellow doctor Gregorio Marañón, a Parisian resident since the outbreak of the Spanish war whose accolades have made him a celebrity abroad. Despite his own decision to remain in Paris, Marañón repeatedly encourages Ros to emigrate to Mexico (176, 300); one month before Hitler's troops enter France, Marañón once again counsels his friend: "This, my friend, is a lost cause. If the United States doesn't get into the war soon, as we hope they will, the future of the democracies is decided, with no hope of salvation. Except for Spain and maybe some other country, all of Europe will be embroiled in the encroaching chaos. Go far away. Go to Mexico, *the promised land, home of the proud Aztec emperors and the Mayan forefathers*" (393). Similar advice came months earlier in a letter from Mariano Ruiz-Funes, "the great expert in criminal law . . . until a few months ago the Spanish ambassador to Poland," exhorting Ros to follow his own personal decision, "to go live in Mexico" (157). Ros's record of his conversations with his illustrious fellow exiles makes clear the climate of urgency that surrounded all communities of Spanish exiles; the majority with the means and the connections for doing so would abandon Europe as if fleeing from a sinking ship.

Postponing his own plans for travel to Mexico until his wife and family can join him in Paris from Spain, Ros focuses his energies on maintaining strong ties and good relationships with the key players in the complex game of Spanish emigration. Within days of his arrival in Paris, Ros makes an appearance in the offices of SERE, where he reports being rudely received by the representative for his party, Izquierda Republicana; Emilio Baeza Medina brusquely tells Ros that he is not entitled to a subsidy since he did not serve in a public post—military, political, administrative, or otherwise—during the war. Ros, who insists that he did not come looking for money anyway, "although I need the money" (91), shares Eduardo Ortega y Gasset's disdain for the directors of the relief agency, "whom he calls adventurers, scoundrels and resuscitated parasites" (92). His low opinion is reinforced during a second visit a month later, toward the end of June: "The spectacle that Negrín's relief agency has become, is depressing. The *personalities* in charge, people who have not exactly worshiped at the altar of decorum, treat whomever needs any kind of aid, in the most rude and dishonest manner imaginable" (112). He notes with scorn that his antagonist Baeza Medina is guilty of playing fast and loose with the selection criteria used to grant passage to America: "Some time ago he agreed to find a spot on a boat bound for Mexico for a pretty young thing in need, all fiery eyes and heaving bosom. All she would need to do would be to pass through the hot-blooded customs office of a cozy bedroom" (112). As the months pass, Ros's estimation of the organization is further eroded; in a February 26, 1940, entry, he writes, "This morning I was at the S.E.R.E. offices, and I have to say I didn't like in the least the chaos I found there. I think they are liquidating everything and the hour of 'every man for himself' has come" (363). Unable to effectively get what he wants by operating through the "front office" channels with his party representative to the SERE, Ros has other means of working the system, as he amply demonstrates in numerous diary entries. Apparently believing that the way to a bureaucrat's heart is through his stomach, Ros carefully documents a series of lavish dinners to which he invites selected members of the SERE organization. In the following example dated November 23, 1939, Ros frankly admits the motivation for hosting one particularly memorable meal:

> I invite the top brass of the S.E.R.E. to dine at *Zatoste*: Federico Miñana, my good friend Pepe Ballester Gozalvo, Gascó and Ramoncico García. Andrés Conesa also joins our table. I invite them because I want them to help Salvador Martínez, who was the editor of the newspaper *Justicia* back in my beloved Cartagena, and also his two brothers-in-law. I want them to get them a spot onboard the next boat for Santo Domingo and to get all their expenses covered. Here's the *menú*: Egg soufflés, *tournedós del delfinado*, *Livarot* cheese. All served with the finest wines of Emilionnais, with the *Château Ausone*. Afterwards, Madagascar pineapple, coffee, armagnac and *Romeo y Julieta* cigars. This meal was worth it not only because of the pleasant conversation with good friends but because I got what I wanted (266).[59]

When Salvador Martínez and his brothers-in-law are subsequently unable to get their documentation processed in time to make the boat they are approved for, Ros simply treats everyone in the same special SERE group, the "the trip committee" (325), to another meal at the *Zatoste* in order to assure the Martínez group's passage on a later voyage.

On other occasions, Ros's lucky dinner guests are members of the delegation of the Dominican Republic, embassy representatives who according to preestablished criteria either approve or reject the names of selected refugees submitted by the SERE officials. Obtaining the visas for the Martínez party requires no small effort on the part of Ros, due to the stipulation that Spanish emigrants should be "people with *agricultural training*," and these particular individuals are listed as "*naval mechanics.*" After pulling out all the stops ("I argue, beg, cajole, stubbornly insist" [327]), Ros's persuasive powers are rewarded, "they end up giving me what I want." Ros, who subsequently overhears part of a conversation between the SERE's Félix Templado and the Dominican Porfirio Rubirosa (the latter asks the former "Did you bring along the hundred thousand *franquitos* that we discussed?" [327]), is later informed by Templado about this aspect of the "business" transaction of Spanish emigration: "Ah yes, my friend, yes indeed. And today was nothing. It's the only legation that's doing favors for our refugees, but man, at what a price!" (328). For his part, Ros more informally seals the deal at a Corsican restaurant, the *Carboni*, with the handsome playboy Dominican minister Porfirio Rubirosa (future philandering husband of the Woolworth heiress Barbara Hutton, and later love interest of Hollywood's Hungarian émigré, Zsa Zsa Gabor) and the chief secretary of the Dominican office, Paradas: "We try the famous *garbure* soup, made of pork and vegetables; an omelette *al broccio*, roasted fowl with *pebronata* and a dessert of *castagnacci*. And we drink a first-rate wine from the island, a red *Calenzana*" (330). Often the bountiful banquets offered by Ros include a mix of SERE and Dominican embassy personnel, such as the farewell party for the Dominican Paradas, off to Belgium to accept a post as consul general. In the company of the new Dominican foreign minister Moisés García Mella, Rubirosa, and Paradas as well as SERE stalwarts like Federico Miñana and Pepe Ballester, the host Ros chooses a particularly unforgettable Spanish menu: "A Pedro Domecq cream sherry, boiled lobster, rice, pork with greens, and Manchego cheese. Afterwards, fried egg bread and grapes. A white Ribeiro wine from Avia, a hearty red wine from Villa del Arzobispo and a fine muscatel from Sitges" (345). In between the diary entries that regale the reader with mouthwatering descriptions of fine foods, Ros refers to the petitions that come his way from the concentration camps or individual refugees elsewhere, cries for help with problems that are often paradoxically resolved from within the finest dining rooms of Paris. A telegram arrives from Mexico City from the brother of a SERE official with a plea for a camp internee ("You ought to get together the money needed for Miguel Angel Fernández's trip, he's imprisoned in the special camp of Saint-Cyprien, Hut C" [309–10]) that Ros immediately answers; three months later, Ros makes a visit to the SERE offices, interceding now on behalf of another inmate, "Arreba, the exmayor of San Pedro del Pinatar, imprisoned for thirteen months in the filthy camp of Argelès, who wants to go to America" (389). In the final weeks before his own emigration to Mexico City in May 1940, Ros comes to the aid of a recently liberated camper: "Ramón Morales, Marcial's brother from my hometown of Cartagena, came to see me. He's coming from a concentration camp, with a pass for only two days. He wants to set sail as soon as possible. For wherever. I've taken him around to meet the people he needs to know. I've taken good care of him" (407). Days later Ros is again in the SERE office, smoothing the way for the emigration of yet another fellow refugee from his *patria chica*: "I still have time this afternoon to work out a deal at the S.E.R.E. office on behalf of a dockworker from Cartagena, Sánchez Flores, who came to see me today from Montauban, where after a series of mishaps he now resides" (413). Neither a designated SERE representative nor a member of any organized relief agency charged with reviewing applications for emigration, Ros nevertheless reveals through his activities how refugee selection decisions were also made through the powerful, though unofficial, channels of personal connections and informal recommendations.

Given the French state's vigilance and relentless police *caza* of Spanish refugees that characterized the 1939–40 world of Paris when Ros resided there, perhaps his most strategic dinner invitations were those extended to high-ranking police officers and government officials involved with immigration issues. A favorite dining companion is Monsieur Boulet, "head of the prefecture's Department of Foreign Affairs," who warmly tells the Spaniard that he is one of the few foreigners who flatters him with these pleasant gastronomic "little tributes" (*Diario*, 234). Boulet's gratitude is understandable, given the following *castizo* menu that he enjoys at Ros's expense: "Monseiur Boulet again expresses his preference, after a couple of glasses of dry sherry, for a Spanish wine. And so we have a *Viña Pomal*, from the Bodegas of Bilbao. After some slices of sausage and Catalonian *butifarra*, they bring us a paella that wasn't as delicious as the ones they prepare at La Marcelina in Valencia, but still it wasn't bad. Later, we had pork chops with potatoes fried in olive oil, not butter, the way the Spanish like them. We had coffee and cognac from Jerez, Domecq's Carlos I. And he smoked a Cuban *Corona* cigar" (234). Such obsequious "little tributes"—which include a gift of a box of premier Dominican cigars on a later date (335)—are not offered in vain to the Parisian police commissioner. Months later when a friend of Ros's brother, José Benavente, is arrested in France and threatened with deportation to Spain, Ros is able to arrange the detainee's release through his police connections: "I spoke in the prefecture with Monsieur Boulet. 'Don't worry; that boy's not going back to Spain'" (357). Another French official who makes good dinner company is Monsieur Dubois, "head of the cabinet of Minister Sarraut," who Ros seeks out after receiving a panicked letter from Juan Sánchez Blaya in Algiers, who reports that he and a group of Spanish refugees have been arrested and interned in a concentration camp. Explaining his plans to show this letter to Dubois over dinner, Ros must have certainly made a persuasive case for action, judging from the meal that the two men enjoyed at the restaurant *Périgourdine*: "At my request, we had as an aperitif a couple of glasses of Moriles wine. They served us frog legs, sole, and braised rabbit, *Pont-leveque* cheese, and strawberries. We drank a white *Château Pomarede* and a full-bodied red *Jurancon*. Monsieur Dubois chose a French cognac rather than a Spanish one, and they served our table with glasses of Napoleón, *Roi de Rome*" (235). Seeking permission for another Spanish friend, Pepe Mingarro, to be allowed to reside in Paris, Ros hosts yet another culinary orgy for Dubois, this time in the *Rotisserie de la Reine Pedoque*: "I order *bouilleture d'anguilles* prepared in the Angers style, accompanied by a white Alsatian *Riesling*, and some *côtelettes de porc à la sauce*. With this, as well as the *Valençay* cheese that we had immediately afterwards, we drank a marvelous red *Aloxe-Corton*. With the *crêpes flambées*, we drank icy cold *Roederer* champagne" (298). When at last Ros's brother Paco is able to leave his place of refuge in Oran, it is Dubois's secretary Jean Sée who will facilitate Paco's paperwork. Ros is nothing if not grateful, which he demonstrates with painstakingly chosen gifts for the two Frenchmen's wives: "In La Marquise de Sevigné in Boetie Street, I bought two beautiful Bohemian crystal vases, filled them with candy, and arranged to have them sent to the wives of both Monsieur Dubois and his personal secretary, Jean Sée" (382). Such good relations will pave the way for the positive outcome of one of Ros's most complicated and personally significant cases: the successful arrival on March 22, 1940, of his own wife and two sisters from Spain to Paris. Dubois himself makes the final phone calls that set the last wheels in motion for Ros's family's long-awaited arrival.

When the time comes to petition for an emigration visa to Mexico, Ros's wide sphere of influence again serves him well. Having previously been rebuffed in the Mexican embassy upon applying for an entry visa when Narciso Bassols was in charge (a man that Ros scornfully dismisses as "capricious, rude, and communist" [194]), Ros now six months later gleefully sings the praises of the Spanish politician who has taken his case all the way to the top: "The Mexican Legation has already received permission to grant a visa for me and all my family as well. Indalecio Prieto managed to obtain this authorization directly from President Cárdenas. What would that sectarian Narciso Bassols have to say if he were still here?" (395). In a fitting ending to this gourmand's diary, Ros describes the final meal that brings together some of the powerful players of the Parisian circles that helped make emigration possible for some lucky Spanish refugees; the group includes friends from the SERE bureaucracy (Pepe Ballester Gozalvo), from the Prieto-founded relief agency JARE (Fernando Valera), and from the Dominican Republic's embassy (Moisés García Mella). All convene at the residence of Manolo Muñoz, a former director of the Spanish Republic's Dirección General de Seguridad, who now lives in Paris with a beautiful mistress as a guest in the elegant home of a wealthy Frenchman. Muñoz, one of Ros's closest friends in Paris, is introduced by the author as "one of the individuals most despised by the newspapers of General Franco's regime, because Manolo was the head of the police when the horrible crimes at the Modelo Prison in Madrid took place" (155). Muñoz had decided not to emigrate to Mexico, citing his life of privilege in Paris: "'But I can't go,' he tells me. 'Here I'm living for free in a magnificent house, with all the amenities, besides the six thousand francs that the S.E.R.E pays me monthly. In Mexico I don't have anything. I don't know how to work. I've been a military man my whole life. Except for that, I don't know how to do anything else. How do I make a living there?'" (408). Ros's fears for Muñoz's safety ("If the Germans enter Paris, as I expect they will, Manolo will be in a lot of danger, a lot of danger" [408]) were indeed well founded. Just months later, Muñoz, along with the journalist Cruz Salido, ex-minister of justice Julián Zugazagoitia, and most notoriously the president of Cataluña, Luis Companys, were arrested and deported to Spain, where all four were jailed and executed. On this night of the farewell gathering for Ros, the uncertainty of these days in May 1940, as Hitler's troops advance on France, leaves a bitter taste in everyone's mouth. The celebratory champagne they sip as they wash down their last sumptuous supper together is, for the first time, very hard to swallow: "The champagne sticks in our throats and we can barely make it go down" (421).

11
Manuel García Gerpe's *Alambradas* (1941): Performing the Politics of Identity

—Por si fuera poco el SERE, ahora inventan la JARE: Junta de Ayuda a los Refugiados Españoles. Si el SERE lo maneja Negrín, la JARE la maneja Prieto. Habrá subsidios para algunos. Para la mayoría no habrá SERE ni JARE, sino arena y más arena. Y viva la igualdad. No tardó en enriquecerse el folklore musical de los campos.... Y el vals del SERE y la JARE, música de Don Gil de Alcalá, y que terminaba así: "A los del SERE y la JARE / los tendremos que ahorcar."

[As if the SERE weren't enough, now they've invented the JARE: Relief Agency for Spanish Refugees. Negrín runs the SERE, Prieto runs the JARE. They'll be stipends for a few. For the majority, there'll be no SERE and no JARE, just sand and more sand. So much for equality. Pretty soon the folk music in the camps was playing a new song.... The waltz of the SERE and the JARE, to the tune of Don Gil de Alcalá, went like this at the end: "Whether they're from SERE or JARE / let 'em all hang."]

—Celso Amieva

It is difficult to imagine two exile experiences more radically different than those belonging to the two men who shared membership in the political party Izquierda Republicana (the same party affiliation as Republican president Manuel Azaña): Antonio Ros, author of *Diario de un refugiado republicano*, and Manuel García Gerpe, author of the 1941 account of his days as an inmate in the concentration camps, *Alambradas: Mis nueve meses por los campos de concentración de Francia* (Barbed Wire: My Nine Months in the Concentration Camps of France). Both texts do cover the events of exile in France during the same months of 1939, however, and they address as well many of the same issues and concerns, albeit with widely divergent points of view and points of departure. Both memoirists, for example, record the details of daily life and subsistence, although the circumstances of Ros's life of privilege in Paris and those of García Gerpe's confinement in Septfonds produce very different testimonies. Surely nothing points up the contrastive directions of their exilic paths like the gustatory memories penned by each man. As I have indicated in the preceding chapter, Ros's diet was certainly never better than while living in the culinary capital of France; he boasts in one May 1939 entry that not even Franco himself could be dining more exquisitely than he: "The food was of high quality and in great abundance; in these days of scarcity, the residents of the Pardo Palace [Franco's new palatial residence] could only dream of a Sunday meal like this: appetizers with caviar, *poché* eggs, lobster, duck *à l'orange*, a chocolate and cream dessert, with ice cream; cheeses, grapes, and coffee. All of it washed down with sherry, with a white Chablis and with a red *Château Latour*, and for the dessert course we even had a half a bottle of champagne *Charles Heidsieck*" (*Diario*, 154). García Gerpe's Septfonds menus, of course, were much more modest, though no less memorable: "'Time for dinner . . . time for dinner.' 'What are we having today?' 'Lentils, just to be consistent . . . take 'em or leave 'em.' Like beggars, we formed a line Indian-style in front of our cook. . . . There are five . . . five spoonfuls of a warm semicolored water. A few fistfuls of salt, that with equivalent proportions of the lentils, added whatever aroma and taste there was to our 'grub.' 'Today I had better luck than last night . . . I counted them . . . fourteen lentils . . . yesterday, on the other hand, only twelve.' And that's what we had, day after day . . . always the same . . . for lunch! . . . for dinner! . . ."[1] But even Ros reported receiving bad treatment at the hands of the French once war broke out with Germany; on September 10, 1939, he noted difficulty with service, food, and mail delivery: "The Parisians are getting hard to take, with their jingoism and suspicions of foreigners. In a bar in the Plaza of Chatelet, the owner refused to serve us some beers at midday, because we looked like foreigners to him, and tonight we had a lot of trouble getting them to serve us in a restaurant in Gaité Street. For the same reason, the mailman refuses to deliver our mail" (*Diario*, 184). For his part, García Gerpe includes the text of his wife's letter, dated April 14, 1939, "Campo de Concentración de la Carolue (Côte d'Or)," in which she too registers similar complaints (bad treatment, inadequate food service, and problems with mail delivery) but on a scale of suffering that the well-fed Ros could ill imagine: "They call us reds and say the vilest things you can imagine. The meals: lentils, beans or rice, all cooked with water and salt, no oil or lard, and they give us very little, a ladleful per person. We're dying of hunger. Whatever is left over once they've served everyone, is puréed. Sometimes it's three or four days old, and fermented to the point that it has on more than one occasion made everyone sick. You can send letters if you have the francs for it; two months ago I turned in three letters so that they could put them with the mail, and yesterday they returned them to me for postage" (*Alambradas*, 79–80). Nor do the two Izquierda Republicana exiles in France find themselves coming from the same place in terms of more substantive political positions; they hold opposite views on the feasibility of keeping the Republic alive in exile, with an eye to one day restoring the ousted government to its rightful place in Spain. Ros, frequently surrounded by the top brass of the Republican leadership in Paris, derisively refers to the latter's plans to maintain political institutions abroad to be reinstated in the near future in Madrid as "the make-believe games of children": "They will carry on in exile with their ghost government, they will argue about positions, they will withdraw support, there will be resignations in the cabinet and they will set up office hours" (*Diario*, 147). García Gerpe, on the other hand, pledges to fight for the Republic's integrity and postwar survival even though the campaign he and his fellow inmates promise to wage must necessarily begin from the margins of a barbed-wire periphery. He describes his new "home" in Septfonds as a potential arena for political activism: "Our new mansion will have multiple uses: bedroom, dining room, school, salon for literary gatherings, workshop, office, and, at times, headquarters for a political party or trade union. Because, even there, far from our Spain we continue to be united through the strong ties that bind us to an ideal, for which we are still prepared to die" (*Alambradas*, 49).

Despite the enormous differences that define each man's early experience of exile in 1939 France, the two writers emphatically agree on one key point; they hold the same opinion that the most pressing concern for the Spanish Republican refugee trapped in France as world war spreads is the question of emigration to America. Convinced that there will be no swift restoration of democracy in Spain, Ros expresses his belief that the only course of action to take is the move to America: "For us refugees there is no other option than to forget this problem [Franco's growing power base] and rebuild our lives on the other side of the ocean" (*Diario*, 161). The above-cited letter from García Gerpe's long-suffering wife, Esperanza Panadero Caballero, concluded with a heartfelt exhortation to her husband to somehow get the spouses out of their respective hellholes: "Do whatever it takes to get us out of this hell and on our way to America, where some generous countries have opened their doors to us" (*Alambradas*, 82). The same single-minded, purposeful goal of *getting out* accounts for the activist role that each author assumes in his determination to assure emigration for himself and for others when possible, and provides the focal point for each writer's text. Unlike Ros who was able to work the system from the plush dining rooms of Paris's finest restaurants, concentration camp inmate García Gerpe, imprisoned hundreds of kilometers from the official refugee relief headquarters, will be forced to devise less elegant (though no less ingenious) methods for evacuation out of France.

Object Lessons in Otherness: The Controlling Interests in Immigration

The would-be emigrant to America first arrives with thousands of fellow refugees as an illegal immigrant to France. As I have pointed out in chapter 1, survivor-witnesses remember the border crossing as a traumatic moment when a fractured exilic identity is born; they typically recall these early days on French soil in terms of the unrelenting process of objectification with an attendant loss of individual autonomy to which they are subjected. Similarly, the opening chapters of García Gerpe's *Alambradas* chronicle his first four weeks of confinement in Saint-Laurent de Cerdans as a series of events in which the refugees have been deprived of all traces of either personal or collective agency, control, or humanity. Represented throughout the civil war in the reactionary French press as marauding hordes of savage communists, the Republicans who are now herded through the streets of the French villages are received with fear and suspicion. While conservative newspapers like *Le Roussillon* heralded the arrival of the Republicans as a living incarnation of left-wing politics in retreat with headlines like, "Ouvrez les yeux; c'est tout le marxisme que passe," local bystanders watched transfixed as large groups of refugees were escorted under armed guard toward the camps.[2] García Gerpe recalls overhearing one child shout excitedly to his mother: "Mama! Mama! They don't have tails, they're just like us!" (*Alambradas*, 9). The child's realization that the dreaded *rojos* may not be animals after all is subsequently shared by curious village women who approach the makeshift internment area for a closer look at the sight of the spectacle of thousands of Spaniards ("eight days' growth of beard, clothing covered in mud, feet sticking out of shoes ruined by the damp and by water" [15]) huddled in the snow: "They went back home horrified. They couldn't understand how or why we were being kept there in more than a foot of snow, exposed to the elements. They were so affected by what they had seen, that word of our suffering, our torment, passed from one person to another. The little town decided that the treatment of the Spaniards should be better, and they became quite sympathetic to our plight. 'They're red, but they're still human beings,' they said" (*Alambradas*, 14–15). But an identificatory response is not encouraged by French authorities, and the locals are quickly barred from visiting the camp. The inmates are abandoned to the alienation of their own abject otherness, a dehumanized status that is figured in García Gerpe's text in the form of the impotent, debased body. They are victimized even by their own bodily functions; forced to relieve themselves in the same area where they eat and sleep, the prisoners endure having their own physical misery literally thrown back in their face: "The air was filled with particles of excrement; the discolored liquid from standing pools of urine blew in our faces. Because the truth of the matter was this: in the same area that served as our 'living quarters,' we had to defecate, urinate, and take care of all the other necessities that go along with that. A new and hellish plague made an appearance: little L-shaped pieces, of the most varied and curious types imaginable" (*Alambradas*, 15). The only other references to the human body that García Gerpe offers in these early pages are those that describe in excruciating detail the corporal ravages of death that strike down an alarming number of inmates before each new, icy dawn: "The course of the illness, that spread through the camp at an alarming rate, was the following: the feet froze, then the lower extremities were paralyzed, intense anxiety ensued, then the whole body was immobilized. After a short period of lethargy, the flame of life went out . . . yesterday fifteen died, today it was twenty, tomorrow we don't know how many it will be . . . the specter of death rides through the camp with the greatest of ease" (*Alambradas*, 14).

In addition to the very real material conditions of immobilization and impotence that the internees suffer, García Gerpe points out that they also are the manipulated targets of those who control the official discourse and rhetoric of the French state. Initially prohibited from reading the left-wing press like *L'Humanité* or *L'Oeuvre*, the inmates do have access to conservative papers like *Paris Soir* and *L'Indépendant*. One particular piece published in March 1939 in the latter paper, with its extraordinary title "La bonne organisation des services des réfugiés," catches García Gerpe's eye; he is so flabbergasted by the journalist's rendition of the reality lived by the eleven hundred refugees in the neighboring camp of Le Boulou that he reproduces in its entirety the text of the article in the original French (*Alambradas*, 19–21). His own follow-up commentary reveals the extent to which the representation of the refugee experience in France, restricted to those who hold the reins of power, has been corrupted and falsified by them:

> The text of the transcribed report would be hilarious, if it weren't for the fact that this sad existence, which I endured for nine months, is still a reality for thousands of exiles. Nothing reported could be further from the truth: it was made to seem like a "happy Arcadia" . . . the *"well-organized daily routine and services"* could be deduced from the *"visible satisfaction of the refugees"*;; *"a barbershop was set up outside;"* the *"lack of toilets had been resolved by the authori-*

ties;" the visitors *"had been able to see for themselves that the food was nutritious and plentiful."* Lies, irony, sarcasm. To be truthful, the only thing you could see for yourself was the immense tragedy of our situation, expressions of pain, and grimaces of fear. There's irony in spades with the reference to the barbershop *"de plein air,"* an outdoor shop! And this irony gets worse, bordering on sarcasm, when they talk about how the lack of toilets was resolved by the administration, *"leading the men by the hundreds, along the shores of the Tech River, so that they could do their business in isolated areas, under the watch of the mobile guards,"* although to soften the irony, it was euphemistically reported: *"the aforementioned solution could in no way be unpleasant for the refugees, since it served a dual purpose: besides the hygiene and cleanliness, it gave them a pleasant walk along the edge of the Tech River, in ideal weather"* . . . Ideal weather in the month of March . . . in the middle of winter in the south of France! (*Alambradas*, 21–22)

Juxtaposed with this incredible newspaper report that inscribes life in the camp as a tourist's walk in the woods is García Gerpe's further inclusion of the French press coverage of parliamentary debates about "the refugee problem" (26). According to the blustery politician M. Ibernegaray's simple solution, the refugees could be tidily divided into three groups; their future fate would depend on which group they belonged to. Those worthy of political asylum, argued Ibernegaray, had the right to remain in France, under the strict surveillance of the concentration camps, of course. Other refugees deemed less politically active during the war should be returned to Spain, where "Franco will give them the punishment each one of them deserves" (24).[3] Finally, those broadly defined by French officials to be "criminals" should be set out to sea like a medieval ship of fools: "We'll find them an island in the middle of the Pacific Ocean"(24).

The portrait that García Gerpe paints of the Spanish refugees during the early days of exile depicts a hapless people at the mercy of the French government, squirming under both the thumb of bureaucratic control and the alienating stares of morbid curiosity. Never free of their French jailers and Senegalese guards, when they are transferred to the camp of Septfonds, they are constructed as a terrifying specter of war's losers by the other's gaze: "The people living along the 'route' ran toward us. They watched that gloomy parade with genuine shock. The sight was pitiful. Some of those maimed during the war walked along on their crutches. The weary and unkempt appearance, the faces of suffering and the clothing in rags, all lent to this 'parade' a funereal aspect of tragedy" (*Alambradas*, 45–46). Needless to say, the openly objectifying process of "othering" will only be exacerbated with the refugees' internment in the new "permanent" camp of Septfonds. Each of the seventeen thousand inmates will be registered and cataloged in the camp's

Oficina de la Ficha Antropométrica, a bureacratic clearinghouse whose objectives for the authorities are described by the author as twofold, "to establish a complete archive of the Spaniards, including enough facts, examples, and case studies to carry out an anthropological study. This would allow them to document what they called 'the racial inferiority complex of the Spaniards'" (48). These first fifty pages of García Gerpe's text, roughly one-fourth of his memoir, would seem, then, to set the stage for a sad tale of victimization and vulnerability to be documented from inside the spiked wire walls of Septfonds. But as the author closes this introductory section of his testimony, it is here that he describes his new domicile not as a place of capitulation nor of resignation, but as the site of struggle. The story that García Gerpe proceeds to tell transforms the Spanish concentration camp refugees, France's objects of scorn or pity, into exiled Spain's most energetically determined and active players in the political game of emigration.

"In the First Section of Hut 27 (Tragicomedy)"

Following the prefatory opening chapters that chronicle the events of García Gerpe's trajectory from the border crossing to his admission into Septfonds, the rest of the memoir is written as a loosely structured three-act play, borrowing as its title the designation of the author's own hut. By introducing his fellow inmates as a cast of theatrical characters ("CHARACTERS: The jefe . . . Sr. Bernade. The jefe's son . . . .Antoñito. The Philosopher . . . Don Ramón . . ." [52]) and the camp itself as the stage setting for a play ("The action takes place in the Concentration Camp of Septfonds. The scene unfolds in Section 1 of Hut 27" [52]) García Gerpe essentially foregrounds his story of emigration as a struggle predicated first and foremost on performance, specifically of politics and political identity. This performance, he will show, may be as fiercely fictive, histrionic, and spectacularly staged as the most dramatic theatrical representation that one could find under the theater's own spotlights. On an imagined stage set littered with reminders and remnants of civil war ("Everywhere, hanging from the wire, torn-up suitcases, knapsacks in ruins, military blankets, canteens, things that for us are like warriors' remains" [52]), many of the ensuing scenes will reenact and redeploy the recent conflictive interactions and internal divisions that splintered the Republican war effort up until its final days. These same divisive politics continue to have a profound effect on the emigration efforts that the relief agencies in exile attempt to put in motion. And as usual, according to concentration camp memoirists like García Gerpe, the biggest losers in the political bickering and infighting are the most desperate members of the exile community, the camp inmates themselves.

Typical of other testimonies of the camps, García Gerpe's text strongly construes the events of the concentration campground as a continuation of those that originated in the trenches of civil war. The trappings of the recent military campaign—Republican uniforms now mostly in tatters still worn by the refugees, the threadbare army-issue blankets and dirty knapsacks, dented mess kits that scoop up watery coffee—provide the backdrop of the *espacio vital* lived by the residents of Hut 27. The men themselves, almost all ex-combatants, make constant reference to their exploits during the war; early on, one official entertains the others with a civil war song: "I'm not afraid of cannons / I'm not afraid of mortars" (57). The very earliest accounts published at the end of the civil war about life on the Republican front lines, like the Abraham Lincoln Brigade memoirist Alvah Bessie's 1939 *Men in Battle*, recall conditions that will continue to be experienced by the former soldiers now in exile. Bessie, for example, chronicles the wartime makeshift construction of stick-and-cane *chabolas* in the trenches; the anxious expectations of mail call; the craving for tobacco; the desperate, interminable waiting game ("The men sang: *Wait-ing, wait-ing, wait-ing, / Always fuckin' well wait-ing, / Waiting in the morn-ing / Waiting in the ni-i-i-ght . . .*"); the physical suffering caused by bad food, diarrhea, scabies, and lice; and sleeping on the ground ("I lay in my grave, wrapped in what blankets I could find . . .").[4] Such memories of life in the trenches would be shared as well by Spanish veterans like García Gerpe and are in fact unhappily relived by him and his companions in the camp of Septfonds; the author describes the swift transformation of one recent arrival into a prototype of the camp inmate, a bedraggled figure still marked by the vestiges of the war and its routines: "He decides to buy a 'military overcoat' from an old soldier; he looked and acted just like us . . . one more *milicien*. . . . He washes his clothes, he kills his lice, he talks to himself, and then he takes his little tin can and silently waits in line for chow" (*Alambradas*, 115).

But of all the links that can be made between the war experiences in Spain and the events of its aftermath in France, the role of political connections (formerly in the war effort, currently in the struggle for emigration) is the common ground between both worlds that García Gerpe most fully explores in *Alambradas*. Act 1 serves to introduce the key players of Hut 27, a group of inmates all competing for the same scant resources in the camp and limited opportunities for emigration out of it. One of their number, the plainspoken Frasquito, succinctly sums up the two opposing factions that quickly emerge as soon as the men are assigned to the hut: "What we've got here are two groups. In the back [of the hut] are the same people with influence that you've always got; and they continue to be as well-connected as ever. At the entrance, freezing to death, it's us, 'the ones who went to war'" (*Alambradas*, 59). Belonging to the group of *enchufados* is the pompous, self-important Antonio Bernade, designated as Jefe del Departamento, who rapidly seeks to establish a pecking order and hierarchy within the hut that will of course benefit himself and his hangers-on at the expense of others: "Next to *el Jefe*, agreeing with everything he says, are Don Ramón *el Teósofo* and his two minions—Sánchez and Pérez—, Antoñito, and a group of guys from Málaga. They believe the sincerity of the highfaluting remarks made by our resident big shot, and have faith in his far-fetched promises of help from Paris" (*Alambradas*, 56). This group claims as theirs the "best" spots in the cramped, dirty quarters (i.e., the warmest area farthest from the hut's door); they relegate to others the first round of the stinking latrine detail; they snatch the dry bread out of a near-ruined batch that has been partially soaked in the rain. The men that they take advantage of ("the three Teachers [Manuel García Gerpe, José Barrull, Mariano Hervás], the Andalusians Pepillo and Frasquito [Francisco Gómez], and the Galician [José Ferreiro], who stand behind what the *Comisario* [Juan Cañas] says" [56]) explain the self-centered behavior of their fellows as but a continuation of the dynamics of wartime conduct played out between two opposing poles: the dangerous front lines of combat and the comfort zone of the rear guard. When Frasquito finds himself assigned by the Jefe to the first round of janitor's detail, he remarks ruefully, "Here we go again: the same ones on the front lines" (*Alambradas*, 65). When the Jefe renounces as irrevocably lost the ideals for which the Republic fought and died for, Manuel García Gerpe's mouthpiece, García Maestro 2, tells him that his lack of conviction betrays a waffler's ignoble position located behind the lines: "And if you all don't believe in the sanctity of those universal principles, for which we fought so dearly in Spain, what the hell are you doing here? Or maybe you're the ones who from behind the lines of safety, took advantage of our efforts, our battles, our sacrifices?" (*Alambradas*, 73).

The key distinction between the heroic battle of sacrifice waged *desde los frentes* and the cynical, protected position of self-interest belonging to the *retaguardia* has been made as well by other early post-war memoirists of exile who fault in part the Republic's crippling political divisions during the war for its defeat. Edmundo Domínguez, author of a 1940 eyewitness history of Col. Segismundo Casado's coup d'etat in Madrid against Prime Minister Juan Negrín in the last weeks of the war, fervently defends the rightness of Negrín's controversial position of entrenched *resistencia* in the face of all odds.[5] In his opening "Words to the Reader," Domínguez attributes, as does García Gerpe's spokesperson, a lack of faith in the Republic to the cowardice and insolidarity of the rear guard: "The Republic could have won; the majority of the Spaniards fought against Franco. Whoever denies this fact today are the same ones who were the least likely to be found on the front lines. They were the selfish ones behind the lines who sacrificed nothing like those who were in the trenches."[6] General Vicente Rojo, one of the Republican generals who remained loyal to Negrín, was also an outspoken critic of the inhumane treatment that his troops received in the French concentration camps. In his 1939 memoir of the civil war ¡Alerta a los pueblos!, he makes clear that the bravest frontline fighters during the war are now the very Republicans who occupy the harshest, most exposed lines of exile: the open shores of the brutal camps. In his chapter entitled "The Spanish Combatant," Rojo pays homage to the courage and indomitable spirit of the truest Republican patriots, the frontline soldiers, who were forced to confront adversity from both within and without their ranks: "They fought at the front, selflessly sacrificing themselves in defense of their cause, undaunted by the knowledge of what lay before them: the strength of three nations ready to hunt them down. Nor were they deterred by what they had at their backs, among their own: the dead-weight of a corrupt rearguard. Beyond that, the indifference of the rest of the world that out of selfishness or cowardice, didn't want to understand the justice of their cause nor the reasons for their stubborn defense of it."[7] Rojo goes on to lament that these combatants who have bravely manned the trenches during almost three years are the same who "have ended up in the concentration camps in total destitution." The "example of sacrifice" of the genuine soldier continues in exile: "He still feels a Spaniard's pride; he wants to earn his living, and not live off anybody's charity. So from the sands of the concentration camps, with his head held high and a steady gaze, he waits patiently, with dignity, for the guiding hand that will lead him once more as he fulfills his patriotic duty."[8] The Libertarian militiaman-author Solano Palacio will likewise in 1939 contrast the fate of the "genuine Spanish antifascists" at the war's end ("concentration camps or firing squads waited for them") to that of those who managed to stay off the battlefield, "the illustrious great men, the invincible heroes of a hundred battles waged on the tables of the cafés."[9] To add insult to injury, these very same *enchufados* who "earned their stripes in a cooperative or on a Committee" are the ones who try now to rewrite the history of their role in the war: "Their power goes to their heads and they end up believing that they are the heroes, far from the front lines of battle."[10] Through their political machinations, accuses Palacio, these pseudoactivists in the war effort managed to first save their own hide, and now scramble to the front of the line of emigration, leaving behind the war's true heroes: "In this unfortunate situation, men with no record as revolutionaries, who hadn't been members of a political party for longer than maybe three years, got out of the concentration camps; meanwhile, the real antifascists, with long-standing revolutionary track records, were left behind, without hope of being able to get out of those hellholes."[11]

This highly charged drama of connections and dispossession, of conduct informed either by the rules of engagement and solidarity or by the self-interested politics of *every man for himself*, is the story that García Gerpe stages in his *Alambradas*. His Jefe del Departamento Antonio Bernade exemplifies the political animal who will ruthlessly elbow his way to the top of the heap of emigration; the voice of entitlement comes from his lips as the very first words of Act 1 are pronounced: "I understand the importance of carefully fixing up these quarters, since some people will be here for quite a while. But as for me, I'll be out soon. In Paris they're organizing an agency that will be in charge of the emigration of Spanish refugees bound for the Americas, and I'll be called to join it" (*Alambradas*, 53). Described by his boastful son Antoñito as "Commander, Director of the Training School of one of our Army's Divisions, and very well known in the highest circles of politics. We'll soon be leaving for America" (*Alambradas*, 53), Bernade is the quintessential puffed-up protagonist of the rear guard. Insisting that people like himself are "the most involved in the struggle" (53), and therefore those most deserving of emigration, he works up to a fever pitch of activity: boorishly promoting his credentials, secretly conferring with the French gendarmes, cultivating favors among his slavish lackeys. If only such energy had been expended in the cause of war, says the ironic Frasquito, perhaps the Republic would have won: "Yeah, now you're first in line. Like you never were to go to the front. *Enchufados!* Fakers!" (*Alambradas*, 60).

The events of act 2, which occur one month later, begin with García Gerpe's reading out loud to his friend Barrull the text of a lengthy letter from García's wife Esperanza Panadero Caballero, interned at the women's camp of Carolue, Côte d'Or, eight hundred kilometers away. The spontaneous title that García Gerpe invents for the letter ("Twenty francs for a Gypsy jig," 77) refers to the incident that most interests him out of those that his wife reports about her camp experience thus far, the ability of the Spanish concentration camp inmate to represent for another the cultural identity that she astutely perceives is expected of her: "Now I'll tell you how I managed to get the money to write to you. An engineer's wife came with him to visit the Camp. I got dressed up and started dancing a gypsy jig, telling this lady it was for her. She was thrilled; she hugged me, and discreetly gave me one of those big silver coins worth twenty francs. It's the first and the last French money that we've ever had" (80). Panadero Caballero's nimble dance of identity politics presages a series of political performances in act 2 that similarly help the refugees get what they need from those who hold the purse strings as well as the keys for passage to America. The same mail delivery that brought García Gerpe's wife's letter to the camp includes for one lucky recipient a coveted missive postmarked 'Paris': "Antonio Bernade . . . the Jefe . . . has a letter . . . from the S.E.R.E.!, from the S.E.R.E.!" (*Alambradas*, 76). This initial insertion of the magical acronym into the text of García Gerpe's memoir introduces a subplot, complete with a header in caps "THE S.E.R.E. IS FORMED" (*Alambradas*, 83–100), marked by secrecy ("García Teacher 2 [to Bernade]: 'And you knew all that [that they were accepting applications] and you didn't tell us anything'" [83]); selfishness ("Man, in a situation like this there's only one thing I can tell you: every man for himself" [83]); subterfuge ("You know that if it's not by deceit, you're not getting out of the barbed-wire fence, and that's why you're determined to betray and deceive" [84]); and political pull ("it's a question of influence" [87]). But most of all, the saga set in motion by the SERE is one that takes as its point of departure proof of political identity that must be performed to the satisfaction of another, even if this display (like Esperanza's ersatz gypsy dance) is done in disguise. The contents of the letter received by Bernade, and reproduced in García Gerpe's text, explain the terms that must be enacted for successful selection for emigration: "It is hoped that by next month the first expeditions to Mexico will be underway. To verify who will be included, we will use the criteria of each individual's degree of involvement *[grado de responsabilidades]* in the war effort" (*Alambradas*, 84). This invitation to "make a case" validating one's antifascist pedigree and substantiating one's worthiness as a political émigré lets loose in the camp a frenzy of performative activities destined to persuade the powers-that-be of the authenticity of that individual's self-representation.

The first level of performance is purely textual in nature: all candidates for emigration are required to fill out *fichas de emigrabilidad* issued by the Paris SERE office. García Gerpe includes a photostat copy of both sides of Antonio Bernade's original completed application, reproducing the form in his memoir with a dual objective. On the one hand, the facsimile demonstrates the kind of information solicited by emigration officials to be weighed in decisions regarding selection, including political, geographical, and professional factors. The blanks to be filled are as follows: "*Surnames; Name; Age; Marital Status; Native of; Where you lived before the war; Profession or employment before the war; Political affilia-*

tion; Camp, refugee center, or domicile where you currently reside; Places where you have lived for more than 5 years; Countries where you would like to go in the event of not being able to return to Spain; offices held before the war; offices held during the war; Date of entry into France and further information; Members of your family who live with you" (*Alambradas*, 86–87). To supplement this information, García Gerpe adds a fellow inmate's interpretative commentary of the apparently "black-and-white," objective answers penned in by Bernade. The Andalusian Pepillo uncovers the Jefe's tendency to inflate the significance of his military positions ("Militiaman in the Cultural Corps. Commander of the 149th Mixed Brigade. Head of Section 1 of the 149th Brigade; Chief of Staff of the 149th Brigade. Director of the Training School of the 149th Brigade; Major of the Republican Army") by zeroing in on the latter's stylistic strategies for making something out of nothing: "All these military positions that you mention on your application so they'll ship you out on the first boat, are really the same thing . . . several positions that seem different, but it's just one 'real' position. It's as if I said that I am a man, a rational being, an animal at the top of the zoological ladder, a thinking being, an organism endowed with intellect, and a body with a soul. 'See y' all' [*Veis uztedes*] so many different things but all the same, it's still just one Pepillo" (*Alambradas*, 86). Not only could applicants like Bernade masquerade one single *cargo militar* as multiple positions of political responsibility, but they could also resort to the sheer quantity of their textual supplications, if the quality of what they had to sell seemed thin. The Parisian offices on 94, Rue Saint-Lazare, 2e, must have been virtually buried under tons of amended application forms, according to García Gerpe: "Some guys ended up submitting one after another, up to one hundred applications. 'Damn. I forgot to put on the earlier one that I belonged to the S.I.M. . . . I'll fill out a new one.' . . . 'And I forgot to mention my position as *Delegado de Escalera* . . . no big deal, I'll fill out a new one and send it to the S.E.R.E.'" (87).

The information gathered on these written forms was often conveyed by even more expressive means, in face-to-face interviews with party-appointed liaisons chosen from the camp inmates themselves. García Gerpe explains how the SERE functioned generally within the scope of other relief agencies, and specifically from within the camps:

> More specific information comes from Paris. The S.E.R.E. (they tell us) is not a decision-making body; it's simply an administrative organization. It's made up of representatives of each political party and trade union that in Spain formed the Antifascist Popular Front. The big organizations: the Bankers and Stockbrokers Syndicate, F.E.T.E. (Spanish Federation of Teaching Professionals), and people unaffiliated with parties, also have their

representative in the Parisian organization. The British Committee, the Argentinian F.O.A.R.E. (Federation of Relief Agencies for the Spanish Republicans), the Hispanic Societies of North America, work alongside the Parisian organization with great efficiency so that hundreds of refugees can set sail for the countries of America. . . . Each of these groups makes up its own list of "emigrants" for the next ship, based on the information they receive from their members scattered throughout France. In each Camp, a delegate representing each organization is named. Barrull Teacher 1 is the F.E.T.E. delegate; García Teacher 2 is the delegate for the Republican Parties (I.R., U.R. and P.F.). (*Alambradas*, 88–89)

As his party's Septfonds representative to SERE responsible for gathering and organizing applications to be further reviewed in Paris, García Gerpe receives in his quarters a steady stream of hopeful visitors determined to convince him of their *emigrabilidad*; the author describes the interviews he holds as a series of dramatically executed auditions. One inmate barely out of his teens presents himself as a committed fighter for the Republican cause and pleads that his lack of political activity before the war not be held against him: "Before the war I wasn't active in any group. I was only seventeen years old! But when I understood that the cause the Spanish Republic defended was the cause of workers around the whole world, I threw myself, heart and soul, into fighting the noble fight" (*Alambradas*, 91–92). Another internee offers the death sentence hanging over his head in his hometown as corroboration of his political activism: "The thing is to emigrate . . . a few days ago I got a letter from home telling me that they have sentenced me to death. With this record, sir, I'd think I'd be one of the first to be chosen to emigrate, because my life is in danger" (*Alambradas*, 93). A third aspirant urges García to include on his application form the incontrovertible proof of his *engagement* in the Republican war effort: "What do you think if I reveal that I was a member of the firing squad that shot three friars in the convent of . . . ? With this piece of information about services rendered, I think they'll send me first" (*Alambradas*, 99). But García, who had earlier expressed his own suspicions about the integrity of some of the SERE officials ("I don't have a lot of faith in those hacks that run things on the Paris Committee, and let the record show that I'm not talking about the leaders or the well-known heads . . . but rather those hangers-on who swarm through the *boulevars* with their *partenaires* in the City of Lights, receiving a healthy monthly allowance as a stipend" [93]), urges the candidate for ship's passage to reconsider submitting this part of his curriculum vitae: "But . . . can you be sure what this file they're compiling in Paris will eventually be used for? Because here in France I'm not so sure. That could be a double-edged sword" (*Alambradas*, 99). The men who reenact their political identities for the purposes of emigration must bear in mind that their performance may be replayed to a different audience in the future.

The plot of emigration and the intricacies of the auditions necessary to secure a spot among its players thickens with the narration of the events included in the subsection of act 2 entitled "A Boat Leaves with Refugees" (101–5). During the ensuing month, the camp inmates receive word from Paris that selection is pending for those passengers to be included on board the *Ipanema* expedition to Mexico. A new wave of anxious expectation overtakes the refugees when Delegado García, as naively hopeful as his interviewees, suddenly experiences a painful epiphany: "When I lay down in the straw after night fell, alone with my thoughts, it hit me . . . the 'gentlemen' of Paris had already made their move!" (*Alambradas*, 102). His fears are confirmed when a camp companion tells him that a member of his *barraca* has been approved for the *Ipanema*, a decision clearly made because of the man's political connections instead of the "degree of involvement" previously specified as the SERE's guiding criteria: "It's a colleague of ours who was unsure about whether or not to return to Spain. He's hardly been involved at all in politics, and was even less active in the war effort. But he's been in constant contact with one of those 'heroes beyond the Pyrenees' in Paris, a friend from his old boyhood days" (*Alambradas*, 102). García Maestro 2, who as a delegate for the SERE has spent countless hours in the role of attentive interlocutor during each inmate's concerted effort to convincingly demonstrate his viability for an exit visa, bitterly questions the part he has played in this complicated drama where all the strings are pulled from behind the scenes of a distant Parisian-based bureaucracy: "What part do I play in this tragedy? It's been said before around here, and it's true: 'They figure they're safe because of the barbed wire' . . . the goddamned barbed wire" (*Alambradas*, 102).

Despite García Gerpe's initial disillusionment with his own manipulated part in the process of emigration, he and his fellow *maestros* Barrull and Hervás will eventually assume a fiercely proactive, autonomous role in the *tragicomedia* that plays itself out in Departamento 1, Barraca 27. The men are shocked to learn from an inmate, sent back to the camp on the eve of boarding the *Ipanema*, that the group of emigrants slated to embark for Mexico must successfully jump through yet another round of political hoops. He explains that the representative from the Mexican embassy, Fernando Gamboa, puts the prospective passengers through their paces with a kind of emigration "entrance exam," with both oral and written portions; he who fails, like this inmate, is denied passage to America in the name of the national unity of the Spanish Republic: "[Gamboa] explained to me that I wouldn't be able to be evacuated to Mexico, that there they want Spaniards who know how to maintain a sense of unity [*un sentido unitario*] and will follow a common line of conduct" (107). The disheartened reject goes on to describe in detail the nature of the demanding test that he has flunked: "The questions on the form were categorical: What do you think about England? How did the F.A.I. [Federation of Iberian Anarchists] behave during the war? What do you think about the resignation of Azaña? Did you think the Communist Party's activities during the war were on target? What do you think about the Socialist Party? What about the Casado-Besteiro coup? The idea of a single command? What do you think about Largo Caballero? And the Republican parties? What did you do to try to win the war? This way of polling the opinion of the Spanish refugees could not be more skillful. Put any of these questions, Barrull my friend, to any companion and you will find out both his ideological position, and his precise point of view about the course that Spain's tragic war took" (*Alambradas*, 107). A comparable experience is later related by another Septfonds inmate who did perform to the satisfaction of his examiners. In a letter dated June 10, 1939, Marcial Rodríguez explains to García Gerpe his encounter with the Mexican inquisitor: "Mr. Gamboa, the embassy's representative, is a young man who seems intelligent. Speaking confidentially, I'll tell you that Gamboa is a communist, but not a Trotskyist. These are the questions he asked me: Do you personally know anyone from the P.O.U.M.? (United Marxist Worker's Party). What do you think about the P.O.U.M.'s actions? Do you consider F.A.I. members to be communists? What group collaborated with the P.O.U.M.? There were a lot of rejects, because Mr. Gamboa didn't like how they answered the questions" (*Alambradas*, 124). According to other exile testimonies like that written by Eligio de Mateo Sousa, refugees who planned to travel to Mexico during the month before the *Ipanema* set sail were also subjected to similar questioning. Mateo Sousa, a passenger on the *Sinaia*, recalls: "Getting on board the *Sinaia*, the 25th of May, was slow; it's true that all the passengers were asked about their political leanings, but everybody said they were for Negrín, since we'd heard that was the right answer."[12] Mateo Sousa's suggestion that the cleverest passengers were those who astutely learned to tailor their answers to what the questioners wanted to hear is an observation made by others as well. In Silvia Mistral's June 9, 1939, diary entry, recorded the day before Marcial Rodríguez wrote his informative letter to García Gerpe, she describes how one Spaniard desirous of making passage on the *Ipanema* has rehearsed his lines for the next day's interview: "A metalworker says to me, 'Get a load of what Mr. Gamboa asks me: 'Which party do you think made the greatest contribution to the war?' 'What do you think about Mr. Negrín?'

'What do you think about the Casado-Besteiro Council?' Well now, how does one respond to all this? I, for instance, don't care for any of the politicians, not Negrín, not Azaña, not Prieto. As for the Council of Defense, I do have an opinion: it should have been created a long time ago. So for this they're going to deny me a passport and the opportunity to rebuild my life in Mexico? Well, they might, so I'll have to lie. I'll say that Negrín is the greatest of men and the ideal politician and that Casado, Miaja, Besteiro, and Mera, along with all the other members of the Council, were simply 'traitors.'"[13] Another examinee, reports Mistral, paid a dear price for his frankness with Gamboa: "They turned me away, just because I told the truth: that I wasn't a supporter of Negrín, the same as the majority of Spanish workers. Considering the fact that I wasn't going to their country to be involved in politics, but rather to work, it was absurd that they even asked me such a question. . . . Nobody asked me if I was good at my job, nor did they find out if I had a wife and children that I needed to save from poverty." A third informant confesses that he opted for a shameless act of country bumpkin ignorance and feigned political amnesia in order to secure his passage on the *Ipanema*: "I played crazy like a fox. At the moment of the interrogation, let's call it a 'confession,' I forgot that I was a Libertarian and that I supported the Council of Aragón. I didn't remember that I'd fought against the communists in the May barricades. I stuck to my guns and for every question, I answered the same: 'I'm a peasant, I don't know anything about politics.' In the end, they gave me the piece of paper."[14] Mistral helps other prospective emigrants prepare for their performance ("For many who don't know about the irresponsible passport process, I tell them what I saw in Burdeos"), so that when it's their turn to make an appearance, they will be prepared: "Almost all of them have an answer ready for the imagined questions."[15]

The three *maestros* of Septfonds, who already had set up classes to instruct camp inmates in Spanish and French grammar, math, and accounting, make their own decision to assist fellow refugees in learning the parts they will play for the "entrance exams" of emigration. Following their initial debriefing of the inmate rejected by Gamboa, Barrull exclaims: "A new discipline, a secret science, another Alchemy. But . . . it's really easy. The crux of the matter is knowing how that Mr. Gamboa thinks, and then you've won the battle . . . and formed a new field of inquiry: *Emigration Lessons for Mexico*" (*Alambradas*, 108). García Gerpe plans his own course, "*Ideas about emigration to England, Venezuela, Santo Domingo, and Democratic Countries*" (*Alambradas*, 109). Not to be outdone, Hervás describes the seminar he will teach for those refugees who plan a trip not to England or Mexico, but home to Spain, "*General Principles about the Return to Spain;*" he explains to Pepillo who expresses interest in signing up: "But my course, dear Pepillo, is the most complicated of the three offered for the degree of 'Spanish refugee.' Mine consists of four theoretical parts: Examination of conscience, Heartfelt contrition, Commitment to reformation, and the Philosophy of resignation; and there's a practicum: Training course in how to salute the swastika, stretching out your arm Roman-style" (*Alambradas*, 109–10).

Though Hervás's how-to course in repatriation and reintegration into Franco's Spain is proposed tongue-in-cheek, the events that García Gerpe chronicles in act 3 show that the matter of the refugees' return to 1939 Nationalist Spain is no joke. Throughout the summer months of 1939, as world war looms ever larger on the European horizon, France steps up efforts to send back to Spain as many refugees as possible. Act 3 opens with the author's transcription of two propaganda texts directed to the Septfonds inmates. The first is the July message from the camp's French commander, Lieutenant Colonel Iturburo, who addresses his captive audience through the loudspeakers. He explains to them that France cannot maintain at the current level the burden of "care" for the refugees; the Spaniards must accept the fact that their war is over, and now the French have their own battles to fight: "You've got to get used to the idea that your 'civil' war is over, that it's time to forget this chapter of history. . . . Spain's tragedy has come to an end; now there's a similar tragedy hanging over France" (*Alambradas*, 129). The officer assures them that they have nothing to fear from Franco: "France graciously took you in to save you from the hate and rancor of the early days; but today there is nothing to fear. Go back to Spain; Franco's 'justice' is 'just.' . . . you can't expect anything bad from Franco, a 'just man'" (*Alambradas*, 129). The contents of a second official document immediately follow, a text entitled "To the Spaniards Living in France" issued to the French headquarters of all camps by the Spanish embassy; it begins thus: "At this critical time for Europe, Spain sends this message to her sons and daughters who live in French territory, either in freedom or in concentration camps, inviting them to return to the land of their birth" (*Alambradas*, 130). The next six paragraphs explain that "Spain, United, Great, and Free" (131) generously opens her arms to all her children who wander on foreign soil: "Our Nation ruled by the glorious *Caudillo* Franco, is open to all Spaniards whose conscience is clear of any crime. The great masses, millions of men and women who for years did not live under his authority, have returned to resume their lives; they have been received with clemency and Christian fraternity. . . . Nobody believes any longer in the legend of Spanish repression. Everybody has heard, sometimes through direct communication with their own loved ones, how Franco's justice is administered. They know the degree to which the enforcers of Franco's justice proceed with benevolence, and with what scrupulous care they consider the complex motives of past behaviors" (*Alambradas*, 130–31). Following the initial broadcast over the loudspeaker system, the transcript is posted on a communal bulletin board for all the inmates to read. Immediately, the *maestros* of the "emigration lessons" and their camp disciples begin to counter the official version of Franco's "justice" and "clemency" with unofficial stories gathered through their informal information networks. Frasquito cites a letter from his mother in Spain in which she intimates the fate of one of her son's wartime companions: "'Rafael de la Esquina still lives in the place facing ours, hoping to get a chance to visit your father.' Now mind you: in front of my house is the jail, and my father died ten years ago . . ." (*Alambradas*, 132). Barrull adds the testimony of the sister of a Saint-Cyprien inmate, who as a recent arrival from Spain warned her brother not to go back home under any circumstances:

> The young woman from Catalonia explained how they planned to "capture" the Republican refugees in France. When someone returned who was known to have supported the Republic, they purposefully left him in peace for a while. Then the mothers who had sons in the Camps in France would write them, saying: "Your friend X was much more involved than you were, he came back from the French Camps some time ago, and even so, he moves about freely and nobody bothers him." Sometimes the "Falange" makes the recent arrival himself write a letter in his own handwriting to his former companions in exile, advising them to come home. . . . More fish would get caught, and when everything is ready, they pull in the nets and put the "gullible new guys" on "trial" for their past mistakes. That explains the letter received yesterday at camp headquarters asking for information about my friend and countryman who returned to Spain in the month of April, and at this point his own parents still don't know his whereabouts. Of course not, since he would've been shot at the border. (*Alambradas*, 135)

But García Gerpe is not satisfied to leave to anecdotal evidence the categorical proof of the cynicism and cruelty of the Franco regime's "invitation" to come home ("When the war leaves you orphaned in foreign lands, your Fatherland calls to you" [*Alambradas*, 131]). This "professor of emigration" who has coached his students how to cram for the exit exam of political ideology refuses to sit idly by and watch his companions in the camp (all desperate to be reunited with family members back in Spain) be duped by manipulative messages from Franco's propaganda machine. The new "course" he offers is his most ambitious to date; he has in his possession in the camp the complete text of La Ley de Responsabilidades Políticas (the Political Responsibilities Act), the February 13, 1939, document crafted by the Nationalist government that sanctioned punitive political and economic measures against vast numbers of the supporters of the fallen Spanish Republic. García reprints the text in its entirety in his memoir (*Alambradas*, 136–44), offering this written version of the oral reading of it that he first provided for a few companions in his *barraca*. The private performance is then opened up to a more general public in the camp: "And we were not satisfied with a reading 'in private.' So we got an idea, and managed to implement it. That very afternoon we held an improvised rally in which Frasquito, Barrull and García participated. Using the *comptoir* of one of the makeshift Cafés, we addressed the refugees with a reading and commentary of the 'Political Responsibilities Act' of Francoism" (*Alambradas*, 144). The reading of the lengthy document is followed up by the three instructors' explanatory diegesis, whose bottom line is summarized thusly: "The man who goes with Franco is turning himself in to his executioners" (*Alambradas*, 144). But no good deed goes unpunished, as the refugees' political tutors quickly learn; the three men are arrested the next day by French gendarmes for "spreading propaganda against the national interests of France" and condemned to five days' confinement in the dreaded *fil de fer*: "The *carré* or *fil de fer* is an area measuring six square meters, surrounded by strong barbed wire, next to the camp headquarters. With no other barriers than the sky above, the sand below, and in four cardinal directions, barbed wire, always barbed wire!; in the center, a small wooden box for a seat. Behind the seat, the executioner that shears off our hair until we are left as smooth as a baby's behind; in the back of the *fil de fer*, the cold stares of our custodians . . . and the smiling faces of our comrades" (*Alambradas*, 149). But the gist of their lesson floats freely through the camp now; it cannot be rescinded or controlled by the gendarmes: *The man who goes with Franco is turning himself in to his executioners.*

Previous "emigration lessons" have been similarly effective, as the camp dons soon discover through contact from the outside with their most successful pupils. The irascible Pepillo writes to García on July 13, 1939, from on board the *Mexique*, bound in short order for Veracruz, Mexico, explaining to his mentors that he has put to good use his concentration camp training for the political litmus test administered at the ship's door: "On board the *Mexique* are between fifteen hundred and two thousand refugees. More than five hundred who were ready to leave had to stay behind, not including those that Mr. Gamboa turned away. I was one of the top pupils; I did a great exam, and it wasn't easy. But thanks to your lessons, I avoided any pitfalls. I surely did put one over on him. I think that in the future the following addendum should be attached to Barrull's course title 'Emigration lessons to Mexico,' 'Or the gullibility of Mr. Gamboa'" (*Alambradas*, 151–52). Pepillo also shares his impressions that not all fellow passengers would seem to be those fitting the emigration criteria of "those who most compromised themselves for the cause will leave first": "They send every 'package' imaginable . . . it's incredible that some of these people are getting out, when in the Camps there are people who played a significant role and did so much. I'm not sure who's to blame. You can see there's enormous favoritism at work in Paris, and a lot of vested interests" (*Alambradas*, 152). In these days when the passenger lists for both the *Mexique* and the Chile-bound *Winnipeg* were being compiled, García Gerpe reports that he as his party representative to SERE is the object of disappointed inmates' anger and disillusionment: "In such dire circumstances of helplessness, isolation, and abandonment, which is the plight of the interned exile in a Concentration Camp, one puts all hope in a solution forthcoming from his organization, his party or his representative. Everything depends on 'including me on the next expedition,' and you can imagine the kind of insults, sarcasms, and diatribes that he lets fly in a rage, as the time goes by and still no news about emigration or his situation. Or it's clear that he hasn't been picked for the next departure; so his well-honed anger is directed toward the easy target of his Camp Delegate. So there you have me, getting out of the *carré* after my five-day punishment of 'solitary confinement,' only to be practically lynched by my own fellow men" (*Alambradas*, 151). These frustrated, less fortunate candidates for emigration find that three equally unsavory avenues of liberation from the camps remain open to them: to enlist in a unit of the French Foreign Legion bound for Indochina; contract their labor under exploitative conditions with private employers; or to resign oneself to the ranks of the recently formed work companies. The blaring propaganda emitted over the loudspeakers from the French command post attempts to cast these options in a favorable light. Of the first, a bulletin dated August 4, 1939, promises fabulous benefits, including even moral redemption: "The terms are incredibly advantageous. The commitment with the French government is for three years; your pay includes seven francs a day, room, board, and wine. . . . In the Foreign Legion, removed for a period of several years from your past mistakes, you can find the restorative tonic that your spirits need" (*Alambradas*, 154). Regarding the second path out of the barbed wire, García Gerpe relates a companion's experience upon leaving the camp in a bakery owner's employ: "They agreed on the terms of employment: seventeen francs a day, room, board, and wine. And he set off full of hope. In less than three weeks he was back at the Camp: . . . they reduced his salary to twelve francs, according to the laws established by the locality, they gave him half rations, and on Sunday, when at *après midi* the owner and his wife went for a stroll, they left him locked up in the woodshed, as if he were a dog. If he was going to be a slave, he preferred to come back to the Camp; he was there in the first place precisely because he'd fought to abolish slavery, leaving behind in La Caleta a comfortable life in his neighborhood" (*Alambrada*, 157). Finally, the teams of work groups, deceptively billed through the loudspeakers as "companies of voluntary work crews," represent a cheap and badly needed labor force during the 1939 autumn months of French mobilization. Barull "Maestro 1" has a copy of an official decree issued to the head of each concentration camp by "the vice president of the Council of Ministers (Camile Chautemps), authorizing the creation of 'Companies of Military Work Crews,' not of 'voluntary work crews' as maliciously announced on the loudspeaker" (*Alambradas*, 179). Barrull, ever the instructor, explains how the camp inmates may be further exploited through their conscription in the *compañías* as France's future cannon fodder: "These Companies will be made up of the interned refugees in the Concentration Camps, whose ages range anywhere between 18 and 50 years; but, the worst of it, gentlemen, is that 'in the case of war, they can be transformed into the real rank-and-file enlisted units of the French Army.' It seems incredible that they can control our destiny with such ease" (*Alambradas*, 179).

At the height of the general frenzy to be selected for emigration to America and liberated as well from the myriad alternate routes out of the camps (via forced repatriation, the Foreign Legion, conscripted labor), García Gerpe and his companions find that they are pawns once again in the fractious drama of emigration politics. The climax of act 3 unfolds through a series of letters dated August and September 1939 that the author receives from two different Republican relief agencies, the by now familiar SERE and the newly established (July 31, 1939) Junta de Auxilio a los Republicanos Españoles (JARE), the Relief Committee for Spanish Republicans. The formation of the latter group, as María Alonso has explained, had its roots in civil war dissensions between two prominent Republican leaders that carried over into exile: "There was a certain amount of divisiveness among the Spanish emigrants; in fact this rivalry was nothing more than a continuation in exile of the different political points of view represented by Negrín and Prieto."[16] Years earlier, Salvador Madariaga had similarly referred to the JARE and the SERE as "political instruments" wielded by the supporters of the leader of each group, "[Indalecio] Prieto and [Juan] Negrín respectively."[17] In her excellent summary discussion of the contentious history of these two rival relief organizations, the Spanish historian Alicia Alted Vigil explains the dramatic genesis of the second major Republican emigration agency, the JARE:

The existence of the JARE is bound up with the history of the *Vita*, the yacht purchased by the Republican government toward the end of the war in an effort to "save" the greatest assets possible, with a view to fund the needs of the exiles in the future. The boat left France for Veracruz, but due to a series of circumstances, the *Vita* arrived in port before José Puche, the representative sent by Negrín to receive the boat's cargo. Indalecio Prieto was in Mexico at this point, and he was contacted by Enrique Puente, head of the crew that escorted the shipment, who asked him how to proceed.

As soon as Prieto was apprised of the significance of the events that were unfolding, he quickly spoke with President Cárdenas, who placed him in charge of the *Vita*'s cargo. As a first step, Prieto informed the Diputación Permanente de las Cortes as well as the Executive Board of the Socialist Party about what had happened; both groups ratified their conclusion that Prieto had acted appropriately. Meanwhile, Negrín's attempts to meet with Prieto to reach an agreement, as well as his efforts aimed at the Mexican authorities to regain control of the shipment, were unsuccessful. The definitive break between the two leaders, and between the Negrinist group and the Diputación Permanente de las Cortes, came on the heels of the latter's proposal that was passed at its July 26, 1939 meeting in Paris . . . creating a Committee charged with administrating the patrimony that would act in accordance with its mandate. . . . As a result, two days later the statutes of the JARE's constitution were introduced, and approved on July 31 by the Diputación.[18]

Delegate García and his *correligionarios* waiting for liberation from the embattled frontline position of their Septfonds purgatory were not privy to these details of the behind-the-scenes squabbles that were splitting apart the Republican emigration efforts and resources. But the repercussions of the SERE-JARE schism quickly moved to center stage in the concentration camp in a series of events spotlighted in García Gerpe's conclusion to act 3. The author includes the texts of a flurry of letters sent to him from emigration representatives: Emilio Baeza Medina, writing first in his capacity as the Izquierda Republicana representative to SERE (August 12, 1939), and ten days later as a newly minted representative for the JARE (August 23, 1939); and Federico Miñana, Baeza Medina's successor as the IR representative for the SERE. This tangled snarl of correspondence reveals the extent to which the concentration camp inmates are the ultimate victims of the political bickering among the Republican leaders charged with overseeing the complex emigration enterprise. Baeza Medina's first SERE letter, for example, informs García of the good news that he, his wife, and mother-in-law have been selected for emigration to Chile in September; Baeza Medina's second letter announces that due to his own fresh alliance with the new Prieto organization, the JARE, the previous passenger lists that he compiled for SERE (that included García Gerpe) have been invalidated; yet another letter from Miñana requests urgent resubmission from the camp delegate of recommended names for emigration. Caught up in this bureaucratic nightmare that increasingly threatens the supposedly imminent release of impatient inmates, García Gerpe bitterly criticizes the "posturing of the great magnates who, carried away by their disputes and ill will, forgot that their first duty was to take care of the basic problems of emigration" (*Alambradas*, 167); his sentiment echoes the concerns of Juan Negrín himself, expressed in a June 16, 1939, letter from his aforementioned, ill-fated correspondence with Prieto on the eve of the founding of the JARE: "But I'm not interested in getting into polemical discussions and arguments about the past. What concerns me is rebuilding a friendship that you are unilaterally determined to destroy once and for all. I know that it's my duty to put aside any hurt feelings in the interest of the unity and the solidarity of the emigration efforts that the well-being of both our compatriots and Spain demand."[19] García Gerpe, like every other camp inmate, finds himself in a bizarrely schizophrenic political position, inasmuch as his own membership in the Izquierda Republicana party certainly does not serve as an unambiguous compass of political orientation in the saga of emigration. In his second letter, Baeza Medina explains that IR members now loyal to the JARE are responsible for representing their interned members' interests in matters of emigration: "A Relief Committee for I.R. has been created, charged with overseeing the emigration of our members, raising funds and taking care of basic needs. . . . All correspondence should be directed to me as Secretary at the following address" (*Alambradas*, 164). On the other hand, Federico Miñana, the new SERE representative, assures García Gerpe that all IR members should direct their petitions to his attention (*Alambradas*, 165). Though García Gerpe continues to defend the legitimacy of the SERE versus the JARE (he writes to the disaffected Baeza Medina of his support of the original relief organization, [*Alambradas*, 171]), it is clear that he has lost any faith he ever had in an inmate's ability to effectively play an autonomous role in the confused drama of emigration politics. Act 3 concludes on a bitterly ironic note; his comrade Frasquito is indeed finally taken out of the camp, but what waits for him outside the barbed wire is not a ship bound for America, but rather a truck crammed with forced labor conscripts. The scene closes as Frasquito and his shouts of protest ("No, I'm not a volunteer, not a volunteer" [181]) are overwhelmed by the French guard's brute strength and sarcastic taunts: "*The gendarme*. (Dragging him on the ground). 'Oui, oui, tu volontaire . . . volontaire, volontaire'" (*Alambradas*, 181).

García Gerpe's short epilogue to his memoir refers to the stroke of dumb luck—receipt of a money order from two friends in Buenos

Aires—that sets in motion the events leading up to his eventual emigration to America: his escape through bribery from the Septfonds camp; his reunion with his wife and her mother in Paris; his arrest and brief incarceration in the French capital; his long-awaited receipt of aid in Paris from the SERE in the form of documentation and passage on board the ship *Cuba*. Concluding his memoir on April 14, 1941 from Buenos Aires, on the date of the third anniversary of the Spanish Republic commemorated in exile, Manuel García Gerpe is unable and unwilling to free himself from the bonds of memory that tie him to his fellow players in the story of exile, the concentration campers who still wait behind barbed wire to see how their tragedy will end: "I can't get rid of the image of the Dantesque panorama of the Concentration Camps. It's a nightmare that I'll always carry around that cannot be erased. I myself have witnessed and endured months of tragedy, days of suffering, episodes of terror, wrenching events, sinister scenes, that only the brushes of Velázquez [*sic*] could have painted . . . a people's misery . . . Spain's calvary" (*Alambradas*, 190). This lucky emigrant to America, a privileged minority among the thousands of refugees seeking haven, will not soon forget that living tableau thousands of miles away whose reluctant players continue to enact the most dramatic scenes of Spanish Republican exilic history.

12
Eulalio Ferrer's *Entre alambradas* (1987): A 1939 Diary of the Quixotic Spectacle of Exile

> Padre Don Quijote / Líbranos Señor / De pecar de cuerdo / O de desamor.
> Padre Don Quijote / Que estás en los cielos / Líbranos del odio / Y de los libelos.
> Padre Don Quijote / Líbranos Señor / De la cobardía. / Y del deshonor.
> Padre Don Quijote / Excelso y cabal / Líbranos de vida / Sin un ideal.
> Padre Don Quijote / Todo luz y fuego / Desde tus alturas / Escucha mi ruego,
> El ruego encendido / De mi voluntad, / Soberano Padre, / Padre universal.
> —Manolo Valiente, "Padre Nuestro," *Arena y viento: Romance del refugiado, 1939–1940*[1]

IN A CELEBRITY SURVEY PUBLISHED IN 1990 IN A POPULAR WOMEN'S fashion magazine, the Mexican edition of *Vogue*, the participants were asked what they would want with them if they were trapped on a deserted island. The well-known advertising and public relations magnate Eulalio Ferrer (b. 1921, Santander), founder of the hugely successful Publicidad Ferrer of Mexico City, gamefully responded with a playful wish list: "Beluga caviar; Jabugo ham and all the fish of the sea, preferably lobster and *percebes*; Dom Perignon champagne, a Vega Sicilia-Unico red, and Río Viejo sherry; Beethoven's *Ninth*; Velázquez's *Las Meninas*, and *Don Quijote de la Mancha*."[1] Ferrer did not share with *Vogue*'s readership that a half century before he had indeed found himself abandoned on the sandy shores of France's concentration camps for Spanish refugees; in the camp diary he kept from April 14 until December 7, 1939, he had recorded a fellow inhabitant's appraisal of these bleak beaches as a desolate home for the exhausted survivors of a shipwreck: "The hut is in the shadows, like the keel of a ship, run aground in the sand.... A coffin full of tired souls."[2] Obviously, for Ferrer and his companions isolated in the three different camps where he lived during a ten-month period, gourmet delicacies and vintage wines were only the stuff of malnourished dreams. However, the teenaged inmate (who turned eighteen years old in Argelès in February 1939 just as President Manuel Azaña resigned his post) did proudly count among his meager possessions a 1902 Calleja edition of Cervantes's masterpiece, *Don Quijote de la Mancha*, a copy that he obtained at the border town of Port-Vendres after trading another soldier a pack of cigarettes for it. Fifty years before Ferrer lightheartedly invoked the *Quijote* as part of his hypothetical survival kit in the *Vogue* interview, he had clung to this book like a drowning man grasping a life preserver. From the first frigid night that he and his father spent in the camp of Argelès-sur-Mer, the young refugee literally slept with the novel under his head, "It's my bedside book in the most literal sense of the word. I keep this little book in the knapsack that I use as my pillow" (*Páginas*, 32). He carefully packs it up when he is transferred to the Barcarès camp in June 1939 and moved again to St. Cyprien in September (*Entre*, 83). The book accompanies its peripatetic owner during a brutal five-month work detail when he forms part of a 250-member division of the 168th Company of Forced Labor who perform manual labor in freezing conditions under armed French military guard in Cerdon du Loiret. *Don Quijote* is by Ferrer's side on April 27, 1940, when he says an emotional farewell to his closest comrades from the camps in the work crew, the "Musketeers of Santander," Tino, Abel, Angel, Núñez, and Araguas: "We hugged each other in a circle around the cardboard suitcase where I've got my things: some pants, two changes of underwear, a jacket, three shirts, three pairs of socks, the Calleja *Don Quijote*, the diary notebooks and papers, a lot of paper: my favorite poems, copied in the purple ink from the concentration camps, drawings, letters, souvenirs . . ." (*Páginas*, 75). At last, on June 19, 1940, Ferrer, along with his parents and two sisters, sets sail on board the *Cuba* bound for Santo Domingo, rescued from the "desert isle" of the camps that he ironically remembers as a sandy "Sahara of civilized Europe" (*Páginas*, 42). As always, the self-professed "walking file cabinet" (*Entre*, 76) keeps his dog-eared copy of the *Quijote* close by (*Páginas*, 79); fifty years later in 1990, Ferrer reports that the well-traveled copy of his beloved, inspirational book found a permanent resting place in his home library in Mexico City (*Páginas*, 312). Back in 1940, in a June 15 diary entry from on board the ship docked in Burdeos, Ferrer had looked toward an uncertain future in America with the unwavering idealism of Cervantes's protagonist: "We conclude this chapter of harsh vicissitudes and we prepare to begin another, with the same spirit of hope. It doesn't matter what's out there waiting for us. We continue to believe that to survive is to win the battle" (*Páginas*, 80). This quixotic expression of hope and courage in the face of overwhelming odds, the faith that triumph lies not in the victory but in the righteousness of the fight itself, is not only a leitmotiv of Ferrer's memoir of the concentration camp; it is as well one of the most enduring themes of the exilic Spanish literature written in Mexico after the civil war during the period of the Second World War, as I will discuss in this chapter.[3] A couple of months after the Ferrer family's July 1940 arrival in Mexico, the Mexican writer and great supporter of the Republican emigration, Alfonso Reyes, had referred to the waves of Spanish refugees who sought sanctuary in his country as *náufragos* [shipwreck survivors] from war-torn Europe who, like their freedom-loving brothers and sisters in America, must continue to find strength to carry on against the forces of tyranny: "Evil has not won out, as long as there's still one fist raised in the air. All the religions and philosophies combined are on our side. 'The sun still shines upon the walls' *[Aún hay sol en las bardas]*, says Don Quixote. You must use your conscience to light the fire, and use truth as your catapult."[4] Certainly no cultural icon looms larger in the expression of the Spanish exile of 1939 than that of Don Quijote, and no memoirist will more fully tell his story through the intertextualized language and lessons of this canonical work than Eulalio Ferrer.

Ferrer, a self-described "ex-dead man" brought back to life after the overwhelming hardships of civil war and forced exile, will represent his experience in the three camps (Argelès-sur-Mer, Barcarès, and St. Cyprien) in terms of a quixotic struggle for spiritual survival, both for himself individually and especially for his larger Republican community displaced behind barbed wire.[5] Early on in his 1939 diary, edited for publication in 1987 as *Entre alambradas, diario de los campos de concentración*, the author confesses that he reads and rereads Cervantes's novel with impassioned abandon, jumping backward and forward from one section to another, alternately entertained, enlightened, or inspired: "In this environment of defeated dreams waiting to triumph again one day, maybe I am obsessed with this character, but that's the way I feel" (*Entre*, 53). Additionally, throughout the pages of his daily journal entries, this enthusiastic student of the *Quijote* refers to the world of the concentration camps as a kind of *Maese Pedro* outdoor theater, in which Cervantes's literary landscapes and fictional figures have come to life against the dramatic backdrop of the makeshift prisons; the true protagonist that Cervantes celebrates in his novel, says Ferrer, is one and the same from his own moment of exilic history that he will also admiringly document in the diary, the Spanish *pueblo* itself:[6]

> It's a character that lives with me; he seems real. Over and above its old-fashioned style, beyond the picturesque types, are the ideas that are still applicable to the events that we are living, and to the people that surround

us. I don't just read about Don Quijote, I see him in the flesh. In every face I see, in every gesture, I find parts of him. The book's descriptive power penetrates the atmosphere here and makes it quixotic. We aren't in the seventeenth century; we are in the twentieth century. It's a book that adjusts to the times, that fits with the times. *Don Quijote* may portray a certain epoch, but it transcends it and comes alive with each new generation. . . . Cervantes is the people's writer. And his work is a hymn to freedom, a condemnation of social injustice. There is no mine or yours, only ours. To be a gentleman, you don't need to be rich. Don Quijote's causes are noble and altruistic. The cradle of nobility is found in the souls of the common people. There are times when the sands of this beach are transformed into the plains of La Mancha and I see Don Quijote and Sancho riding along, as if they were real people. I touch them, I hear them, they are among us. . . . Cervantes created them to be immortal. Oh, what a comfort it is to read the *Quijote*! To read it in a concentration camp, as a reminder in this hour of our humanity, to rediscover the ideals that justify the insanity of genius in order to reconvene the reign of reason. (*Entre*, 110–11)

In the first and only copy of *El Descamisao*, a May 1939 newspaper that Ferrer had hoped to launch in Argelès-sur-Mer, the young editor concluded his series of journalistic notices (jokes, announcements of local sports competitions and chess matches, general events of interest in the camp) with a short homage to the indomitable spirit of the Spanish people that he sees embodied everywhere around him in this miserable prison: in the ingenious resourcefulness of the comrade who out of almost nothing crafts a little raft for fishing, in the energetic tenacity of the inmate who builds and rebuilds a cot that the gendarmes tear up each day, in the picaresque cleverness of the prisoner who tricks the guard for his own gain. This spirit of the *pícaro*, says Ferrer, captures the very essence of the national character: "You see it in the admirable ingenuity of our people. You see it in Spain's energy of improvisation, the very same that throughout the centuries, crowned with glory, has spread throughout every nook and cranny of the world. . . . It's what makes our people who they are. Full of vim and vigor. Whose spirit cannot be broken by anyone, even in tragedy. Who stay proud even in the camps of our misfortune, nurtured by a quixotic faith. We are ourselves the very image of the *Caballero de la Mancha*, and like him, the world may believe that we live out our lives as crazy men . . . but when we die, reason will be ours" (*Páginas*, 51, 52).[7] If the universe of the camps seems to be populated with the flesh-and-blood incarnations of *Maese* Miguel Cervantes's fictional imaginings, then Ferrer assumes the role of rapt spectator in this historic reenactment of an iconic mastertext: "I sit on the sand and watch the parade of nomadic types file by" (*Entre*, 111). Remembering his schoolboy involvement with Federico

García Lorca's famed itinerant theater, *La Barraca* (the troupe had performed at the Universidad Internacional Menéndez Pelayo with students from Ferrer's alma mater, the Escuela Laica), Ferrer muses now that the camp scenes that he observes and records in his journal are poignant dramatizations of a nation's real-life *tragedia*; one day the history he chronicles may in turn be reintegrated into an enduring cultural narrative, feeding the imagination of future fablers and storytellers: "Isn't it possible that this *Diary* could one day be a factual sourcebook for a theatrical magnus opus? What I'm trying to do is convey the most accurate testimony possible of a most decisive period of our lives" (*Entre*, 90). Elsewhere, Ferrer admits that the stage on which he hopes these events are one day re-presented is none other than the vast *retablo* of Spanish history: "[The short-lived *El Descamisao* newsletter] is a daily record borne of personal experience. Its purpose is not just to relive the events of today, but rather to project them onto the screen of history tomorrow" (*Páginas*, 41).

Even before Ferrer decided at his father's urging to begin keeping a camp diary—a decision not coincidentally made on April 14, 1939, as he and thousands of fellow inmates in Argelès-sur-Mer commemorated the first anniversary of the Spanish Republic on foreign soil—he had penned his first piece of exilic writing, the poem "¡Silencio!" (dated March 28, 1939). Taking as his interlocutor the crowds of French bystanders who watched with fascinated horror as large groups of ragged Spanish ex-combatants were herded over the border toward the camps, Ferrer introduces the refugees in terms of a powerful spectacle of insanely stubborn resistance to the forces of oppression and intolerance: "¡Silencio! / No, no temáis nada / no asustaros al verlos / porque traigan las barbas hirsutas / y vengan sucios de sangre y de hierro / . . . / Son los nuevos e ilustres Quijotes / del siglo presente y los venideros. / Son los que lucharon / por toda una era de paz y progreso. / Son los visionarios, / los locos modernos / que a los nuevos Atlas y Martes / pusiéronles freno / de ríos generosos de sangre española / donada y vertida por todos los pueblos. / Son los refugiados. / ¡Silencio! ¡Silencio!" [Silence! / Fear nothing, no / Don't be afraid when you see them / just because their beards are long / and they wear the filth of blood and guns / . . . / They are the new, illustrious Quijotes / of the present and the future. / They are the ones who fought / for an era of peace and progress. / They are visionaries, / modern *locos* / who stood in the way / of the new gods of war / by spilling rivers of Spanish blood / a generous gift for the good of all nations] (*Entre*, 21–22). Evoking in their dirty, bedraggled appearance the sorry sight of the legendary *Triste Figura* (outfitted in his case with a ridiculous barber's basin, a rusty suit of armor, and a broken-down nag), these idealistic warriors for "peace and progress" are likewise deserving nonetheless of the tittering public's compassion and respect; the poetic speaker entreats his audience to accord the sad and shabby parade of weary knights errant a silent salute worthy of all soldiers of honor committed to the struggle for justice. This poem's construction of the Republican fight against the Nationalists and the Nazis as a quintessentially quixotic enterprise is a view widely shared by other commentators of the Spanish civil war. Mexican ambassador Luis Rodríguez's 1942 memoir of the fall of France, *Ballet de sangre: la caída de Francia*, includes among its accounts of the Republicans' valiant stand against fascism an illustrated drawing of Don Quijote, tilting at three windmills whose blades form swirling swastikas.[8] In a novel written shortly after the end of the civil war (though not published until 1952), the Spanish exile to Mexico José Gomís Soler describes both Spain's doomed fight and the world of spectators who complacently watches it, in the familiar terms of the *Quijote;* the author's mouthpiece is a fervent Republican military officer: "Onward, Don Quijote! Break the chains of the roguish galley slaves! Run your spear through the prejudice transformed into windmills! Face the lions with your dented sword. And without ever leaving the ground, soar away on your Clavileño toward the ethereal regions of your crazy imagination. Ha, ha! We are the Quijote, and we're Sancho as well. They can beat us, they can throw us about, they can pelt us with stones. We'll tend our broken bones, and between one illness and another, we'll ride our little donkey home, sane again after seeming so crazy. But the day will come when the spectators who have been watching us, onlookers who could never be a Sancho and could only dream of being a Quijote, are going to shed our same tears, and there'll be no relief for their broken bones, no cotton swabs, no ointments, no herbal remedies...."[9] Earlier in the novel *Cruces sin Cristo*, the protagonist Ceferino had remarked that "There's no man alive who doesn't dream or who hasn't dreamed of being a legendary hero of right and justice, of compassion and love," as a group of Republican prisoners of war shuffled out of their jail cell to appear before a merciless *Consejo de Guerra*: "Elbows tied together, skeletons in rags, a halting step, but proud in bravery."[10] Gomís Soler's soon-to-be-condemned Republican soldiers, just like Ferrer's concentration camp compatriots who have survived them, present the same scruffy, unheroic appearance as the Unamunian *Caballero de la Fe* who had preceded both groups; Ferrer, and other exiles in Mexico, would argue that in these marginalized Spanish citizens one finds the same fundamental quality that eternalized Cervantes's most famous son: "Don Quijote represents the man who is guided by a superior ideal" (*Páginas*, 308–9). In his book about the concentration camp inmates, Ferrer especially spotlights the most disenfranchised, the most powerless members among this demonized Spanish community in exile, the *locos*, as the living, breathing legacy of the *Don Quijote* myth: the pursuit of liberty, even to the outer limits of sanity, fuels the ultimate hope that sustains the will to live.

Similar to Manuel García Gerpe's *Alambradas*, the key narrative nucleus of Ferrer's *Entre alambradas* emerges from the ongoing drama among the inmates to achieve liberation from the miserable captivity of the camps. The obsession of *getting out*, either through emigration to America or through the equally unlikely means of a return to Spain under a general amnesty, consumes Ferrer, his father, their friends, and almost every other refugee with whom the author comes into contact. Clearly, the individuals who most overtly exhibit their deep-seated desire for release like a glowing badge of intense anxiety are the numerous sufferers of *arenitis*, war victims and veterans too scarred by the vicissitudes of violence and displacement to maintain any longer their precarious hold on mental stability. In these poignant, fragile figures, Ferrer most completely discerns the presence of his Cervantine hero: "Never has the great *loco* of our history been in better company. And I'm not speaking for myself, since I don't know the extent to which I may be crazy, but I refer to all these admirable crazy men who share my confinement. In every one of them, I believe I see a gesture, a look, a dream of Don Quijote" (*Entre*, 54). Day after day in almost every journal entry, Ferrer trots out the countless inhabitants of the CLI (Center for Incurable *Locos*) (*Entre*, 69), whom the constantly moving camp chronicler encounters as he crisscrosses the stretches of sand with a journalist's zeal. He observes, intrigued, as each of his subjects compulsively rehearses the dreamed-of day of liberation. In Argelès-sur-Mer he comes upon Valentín Cordero, who performs a daily ritual of flagging down a rescue plane that only his eyes can see (*Entre*, 49). A former mathematics instructor throws one pebble after another into the endless expanse of ocean that separates him from Spain, painstakingly recording the number in a little notebook he wears around his neck (*Entre*, 69). A bridge to salvation of a different kind is planned by a Basque engineer in another camp who meticulously works out the details of an underground tunnel linking Barcarès to Barcelona (*Entre*, 165). A still-distinguished-looking professor, don Matías, is engrossed in his own research project, putting to music the complete works of Antonio Machado: "He identifies himself as a *literal liberal* and thinks that one day a giant wave will come that will carry us far away . . . very far away . . . to America!" (*Entre*, 177). Other candidates for passage to America await more conventional means of transportation, and carefully dress for the part of world traveler. In the May entry of his *El Descamisao*, Ferrer describes one hopeful emigrant: "In Camp 3 they've documented the obsession of an inmate who every day, at first light, takes his best suit out of his suitcase, carefully puts it on, neatly shaves, and leaves the hut in great secrecy. He returns at mealtime. He sits on the sand, pulls furiously at his tie, puts his head in his hands, and with a pained expression of utter despair, exclaims, 'It still hasn't come!' 'What hasn't come?' 'What do you think! The plane that's bringing me passports for Mexico'" (*Páginas*, 46). And like almost every other camp memoirist, Ferrer includes in his litany of men made crazy by the trauma of exile and the interminable wait to be free of it, those who decide to walk their way home, or wade across the waves toward freedom. He describes a navy officer's routine trips to the water's edge: "Sometimes, suitcase in hand, he comes close to the edge of the sea, waiting for the ship that will take him to America. He returns to the hut inconsolable, and admits: 'They've left me stranded, but I'm sure that tomorrow the boat won't let me down'" (*Entre*, 69). Weeks later, Ferrer reports on the man's stubborn insistence that he is seaworthy and that these waters will carry him to America: "As has happened in other cases and in other camps, this voluntary sailor of shipwreck went into the water, suitcase and all, heading out to sea. He wore his navy dress uniform. 'Let me on board,' he shouted at his saviors. He believed that a ship with his wife and children was waiting to take him to America" (*Entre*, 94).

Not unlike these desperate internees, neither Ferrer himself nor the sanest of his camp companions are free of the all-controlling dream of escaping their infernal confinement for the shores of America; Mexico, as always, is construed in this camp text as the premier object of desire. Not surprisingly, a prostitute from the *Barrio Chino* of Argelès who appears in Ferrer's *barracón* one day is nicknamed "América" (*Entre*, 65). Ferrer, who has no interest in what this young, bedraggled *Mari Tormes* has to offer, dreamily writes of his Aztec *Dulcinea* like a man in love: "All of us are burning with the desire to set sail for Mexico. It's a magical name that fans the flame of our desire and dazzles us with all the vivid shades of hope. Those of us who dream every day about this trip — Mexican divine, I hope you'll be mine —, whose prolonged flights of fantasy make us known as the 'illusionists of Mexico'" (*Entre*, 64). Letters from lucky friends who have made the magical trip to the promised land increase Ferrer's passion for Mexico: "Julián Falagán writes from Veracruz. . . . The country is splendid and the Mexicans are well-mannered and kind. Under the current circumstances, the letter describing all the good things about Mexico creates a sense of anguished urgency about the trip. Mexico . . . When will I be able to see you, to caress you, to make you mine, to become yours . . . ?" (*Entre*, 145). Another wistful exiled correspondent hoping to make the trip, Mariano Meléndez, encloses a newspaper clipping that says that in *la Nueva Es-*

paña a newly constructed Spanish city will await the new arrivals, "In order to accommodate us, Mexico will construct a city of wood that will be called Madrid" (*Entre*, 96). Extending his own message of encouragement and hope in a letter to his mother and two sisters interned in Belle-Ile-en-Mer, Ferrer writes optimistically of their imagined future home across the Atlantic Ocean as a port of salvation: "I cheer them up by talking about our trip to America. Mexico is waiting for us so we can rebuild our lives, far from the bitter hardships that we've had to endure since 1936" (*Entre*, 137). With an epistolary fervor inspired by his devotion to his "México divino," surpassing even that directed by his fictional Cervantine hero to his own love object, Ferrer begins a months-long letter-writing campaign to SERE officials. The single-minded intensity of this course of correspondence easily rivals that of the compulsive acts geared toward liberation performed by the members of the Centro de Locos Incurables who so intrigue him. In his very first diary entry, Ferrer confesses that he and his companions obsessively dispatch missives to the outside world, like blinking SOS signals begging for help, proof of identity that the senders survived the storms of war and exile: "We've become accustomed to life in the concentration camp, but in the first weeks, lying in the sun or curled up at night, all we thought about was writing letters. Every kind of letter. Letters looking for family members; letters asking for help from all of the agencies in the world; letters on the trail of some rich relative in America . . . Letters [*cartas*], as if we were betting our future on them. Getting a reply was a sign, above all else, that we existed, that our name and surnames had not yet been canceled from life's official registry" (*Entre*, 24). Blessed with a battered typewriter which "miraculously" (*Entre*, 30) appears in his hut, Ferrer pounds out letter after letter, the majority of which are addressed to his PSOE (Socialist Party of Spanish Workers) party affiliates with the SERE: Ramón Lamoneda in Paris (*Entre*, 37; also 55, 103, 114, 210); Manuel Cordero, "an old Socialist from Madrid, member of the executive committee of the party in Paris" (*Entre*, 51; also 89, 123, 210); or Ramón Solar, "who's in Perpignan, we're asking him for speedy assistance" (*Entre*, 51, and also 55, 97; in an ironic twist of fate, Solar ends up himself a prisoner of the camps, 167).[11] Hanging on to every hopeful reply that they receive (a May 1939 letter includes news too good to be true, "Ramón Solar sends us a list of the Socialists from Cantabria that he's proposing for the trip to America. My father's ranked as number 5, and I'm number 47" [55]), Ferrer and his father initially believe that their intermediaries will eventually unite them with the light of their lives, Mexico: "It's a beacon of hope that shines over our destiny" (*Entre*, 37).

But if Ferrer and others imagine "Mexico" as a fair-faced savior, the same coarse realities of the political infighting that clouded the horizon of liberation for Manuel García Gerpe's companions transform the lovely prospect of emigration into an ugly subject of dissension. The camp inmates follow the trajectory of events that grow out of the Negrín-Prieto rivalry and their disputed control over the substantial financial reserves transported by the Mexico-bound *Vita* (resources earmarked for refugee relief and emigration) with rapt attention. It becomes increasingly difficult for the *ilusionistas de México* to stay true to the ideal of rapid rescue as more and more details of the SERE-JARE polemic are disseminated throughout the camps. In an August 7, 1939, entry, one week after the Prieto-led JARE was formed, Ferrer writes of a general mood of depressed uncertainty (regarding the viability of previous passenger lists compiled for the SERE administrators) that hangs over the heads of the men of Barcarès: "It's news that confuses us, and that prolongs in exile the conflicts that undermined the resistance movement during the civil war. It will end up possibly jeopardizing the slow-moving steps that have been made so that we can emigrate to America. The uncertainty is widespread and the disappointment, instead of fanning the flames of hope, snuffs them out" (*Entre*, 119–20). The campers quickly coin a phrase that refers to the new anxiety that the establishment of a second, competing relief agency (the JARE) has occasioned, *el jaretismo* (*Entre*, 129). Throughout the August 1939 entries, the diarist repeats the increased disillusionment felt by the long-suffering inhabitants of the camps: "This is a night of pessimism. The threat of war casts a shadow over our mood and the blow dealt by the former Republican leaders eliminates for many the hope of a liberating trip to America" (*Entre*, 125); a few days later, on August 15, he adds: "Inside and outside of the huts there are arguments and fights between the supporters of either SERE or of JARE. What we do know is that because of the differences between the two agencies, the trips to America have been suspended, which increases the sense of desperation. War in Europe is getting closer and no one wants to be here for that. It's a sad night of a prolonged silence . . ." (*Entre*, 134). The political tensions among the refugees are exacerbated further still following the August 24, 1939, Soviet-German pact. Writing on that very day, Ferrer notes that deeply disillusioned Communists in the camps tear up their party credentials in a fit of rage. Other camp Communists caution restraint, and the political polemicists come to blows; and on this eve of world war, the SERE-JARE controversy continues to fan the flames of bitter internal debates in the Republican camp: "The camp is still buzzing. The struggle of the SERE against the JARE, and vice versa, contributes even more to the feeling of distress you can see on every face. Isidoro tells me we'll be hostages of war. We'll be cannon fodder all over again" (*Entre*, 144–45). The debate rages on throughout the fall; a November 24 entry refers to the inmates' access to the notoriously acrimonious summer correspondence between Negrín and Prieto in Mexico that was published and circulated in the camps of France, "it's the talk of the camp" (*Entre*, 217). Hope flickers and wanes during these days to the point that the excited chatter in St. Cyprien about emigration to Mexico has been essentially silenced: "Nobody talks about America . . ." (*Entre*, 210).

In a familiar pattern throughout Ferrer's diary, at these moments of greatest despair and disappointment, the author resorts to rereading his copy of *Don Quijote* as an antidote to the depressing reality of continued confinement. On October 27, one of the coldest days of the year so far, when the inmates seem to have reached their breaking point ("Hardly any people. Those there are greet one another with such fine phrases as these: 'How are you, goddamn your mother.' And the other one replies, 'Not as well as you, goddamn your father'" [197]), Ferrer spends most of the freezing day in his hut reading his novel, seeking solace and strength in the one ideal figure who never lets him down: "Nothing humiliates him, nothing defeats him. . . . Evidently his highest ideal is freedom. And the whole book is the search for freedom. . . . We have that saying engraved in our minds, 'there's no greater joy on Earth than regaining lost liberty.' That is the happiness that's waiting for us. If we hadn't lost it, we would never fully understand what it means to regain that freedom. To suffer defeats in victory's battles is a kind of treasure when hope overcomes defeat. The pages of the *Quijote* are the crumbs that feed hope" (198–99).[12] Ferrer's model of faith Don Quijote not only inspires him, but as the young memoirist repeatedly remarks, the crazy dreamer seems to be traversing the very sands with him, day after day. One of the outlets through which the inmates exhibit their own insane devotion to *la libertad* (freedom from the camps) as well as a stubborn grip on wishful thinking (the return home to Spain) are the fanciful rumors that race through the camps like wildfire; Ferrer and others refer to this always open line of communication of outside political events as the *Radio Chabola* [radio shack]. The desperate internees feed one another's hopes with bits of *bulos* hot off the wires of the gossip circuits. A May 30 notice spreads the word that France and England have agreed to force Franco to grant a general amnesty: "In a few more days, we'll all be back in Spain" (*Entre*, 65). Sounds of thunder during a June rainstorm are said to be fire exchanged between French and Francoist troops on the Pyrenees border: "The imagination never stops working. Better to have an active imagination than not to. Otherwise, we'd just be animals enslaved by the barbed wire that surrounds us" (*Entre*, 75). Residing in St. Cyprien as the months continue to drag by without relief for the majority of the refugees, Ferrer finds that this camp's creative rumor mill, and the inmates' wishful thinking, work overtime: "They say that the Spanish army has revolted in Catalonia, giving Franco an ultimatum. That Miaja, Asensio and Casado have signed a letter that states that the Franco regime is on its last legs. That Hitler's been wounded and is on his deathbed . . ." (*Entre*, 172). On the eve of the *Día de la Raza*, the word is out that the much-awaited homecoming is imminent, "Franco will announce a general amnesty" (*Entre*, 187); two long months later, the relentlessly optimistic news that circulates among the campers is that they'll all be home for Christmas: "The latest news from the radio shack is that we'll celebrate Christmas in Spain" (*Entre*, 220). The crazy rumors are indiscriminately spread, and to a greater or lesser extent believed, by refugee *locos* as well as exiled *cuerdos*. On the one hand, the flamboyant figure of Colonel Serrano strides through the camp on November 8 making confident predictions: "He's out in his bathrobe on the Avenue of Freedom, with his military cap. Today he's an astrologer. He announces that in the next few days Venus will exert influence over the part of the earth where we are, which will change our luck. This change means a victorious return to Spain. Competing with the Emperor of Optimism's prediction is a knowledgeable informant—the radio shack, of course—that says that everything's been arranged so that starting on the 11th we can return to Spain" (*Entre*, 203). On the other hand, a respected Republican politician like ex-minister Julio Just visits the Barcarès camp in September with a strikingly similar message of a certain return to Spain by the year's end: "We need to be thinking more about Spain than America, since the Franco regime is falling apart so quickly that by December, at the latest, all of us will be home again" (*Entre*, 125).[13]

Though for the most part Ferrer and his young camp comrades dismiss as fantasies most of the rumors that emanate largely from the older internees (A September 15 entry mocks the latest news, "The radio shack just never stops spewing out rumors; there's something for everyone. That the Germans have bombed Paris with laughing gas and the majority of the residents have died laughing. That with England's help, there's going to be a government created in Spain, made up in part by Alcalá Zamora, Azaña, Prieto and Portela Valladares. That the English have a secret weapon they'll use to beat the Germans" [158]), they too become willing broadcasters of even the most unfounded news when it becomes evident that camp morale is in crisis. On the heels of the SERE-JARE tensions, the Soviet-German pact, the Nazi invasion of Poland, and England and France's declaration of war, the dominant mood in Barcarès in late September is one of enervating pessimism; the resident devotee of *Don Quijote de la Mancha* recognizes that the strategy for mental and emotional survival depends on keeping hope alive against all odds: "We've got to keep our spirits up, especially among the older men, who are the most depressed. Now we're the ones who spread the rumors. Without knowing why exactly, we've joined the others who say that by the end of the year we'll be in Spain and that a coalition government is going to succeed Franco. We scurry here and there, moving from one task to another, as if to escape from a terrifying siege. Hope isn't an illusion, but rather a necessity" (*Entre*, 163). The campaign to shore up the refugees' failing spirits was not limited to the idiosyncratic efforts of Ferrer's small band of companions, but fully informed the more widely disseminated inmate-organized cultural programs and in-camp literature. A May 25, 1939, issue of the Argelès-sur-Mer *Boletín de estudiantes*, circulated during Ferrer's tenure there, announces the establishment of an intramural sports program; the article concludes with a cheerleader's rallying cry to the interned readers to keep active, to keep going: "COME ON GUYS! PLAY SPORTS. STUDY. TEACH OUR FELLOW REFUGEES. IN THE FIELD OF CULTURE AND SPORTS ARGELÈS WILL SCORE THE HIGHEST AMONG ALL THE CONCENTRATION CAMPS IN FRANCE."[14] Six months later in Ferrer's St. Cyprien, with emotions among the inmates at an absolute nadir, the *Altavoz* messages that were broadcast each morning through the loudspeakers reflected the program's primary mission to keep hope alive. One grateful listener, Elenterio Lillo Pérez, expresses his appreciation for the daily diet of words of wisdom and spiritual support: "Every day the *Altavoz* broadcasts help soothe our troubled souls, they entertain us, they strengthen our hope that we will see that as yet invisible day we dream about so often: the day of our liberation. So for us *Altavoz*, with its voices carried by the wind, is like a magical tonic that restores the spirit of the individuals who lie here in this painful exile. These broadcasts faithfully portray how an entire exiled nation thinks, what it believes, how it's getting along. *Altavoz* gives us an injection of culture, it creates culture, and when you create a culture, you create a nation, as Valle-Inclán has said."[15] The November 27 installment of *Altavoz*, whose prefatory "Thought for the Day" was "There is no beauty or ugliness, although it may surprise you, it all depends on your point of view," includes an exchange between two internees entitled "Dialogue."[16] One notes the other's morose demeanor ("the tired step of the vanquished and disillusioned"), listens to his depressed words ("I think it's impossible to ever again be what I once was. A feeling of inferiority drags me down; I don't believe in myself anymore, and I expect everyone else to take care of things. I'm a nobody now"), and concludes by urging this interlocutor as well as all the campers at large to stay the course, to draw on their innermost reserves of strength and self-reliance: "Courage, the will to act, can't come from the outside, but comes from within. When you don't feel strong, you can draw on infinite reserves from inside of yourself, because your interior life can conquer the obstacles and difficulties on the outside. Don't ever think that you are inferior to anyone else; you're just as capable as the next person of willing yourself to make the effort, to act. And failure can be just as motivating as success in changing one's lot in life. Keep the long view always, let your thoughts envision a future that your senses can't yet believe. And when your mind has coolly calculated the idea of it, sift these abstract thoughts through your heart, sheltering your dreams in the human warmth of your emotions."[17] The next day's *Altavoz*, introduced by the *lema del día* "No cold, no wind, why so mad? . . . A day without either, it can't be so bad," opens with a piece entitled "Advice from a Youthful Old Man." The sixty-year-old speaker advises his listeners to turn their weary eyes away from their war-torn past ("After all, isn't the past simply a fleeting shadow?") and work toward a future by first daring to dream it: "Now then: if you all want to set in motion the machinery of your future lives, without too many painful creaks and moans, I advise you to start by daydreaming. Imagine a better, more humane existence, a saner, more rational life than the one that fate has given you up to this point. . . . This is the virtue of having faith in yourself, of accepting some things, and dreaming of others; it allows you to transform into tangible reality what frivolous naysayers dismiss as ephemeral and unattainable thoughts, as bubbly imaginings of the heart."[18]

This quixotic sentiment is signed by a "Mariano Potó," interviewed in St. Cyprien's infirmary by an *Altavoz* contributor José Rial, himself an important camp mentor for Eulalio Ferrer: "I pay a visit to my teacher José Rial. On the days that he can, he teaches me whatever I want, because he is knowledgeable about everything" (*Entre*, 130). It is Rial who composes a poem dedicated to the scourge of the camp, the *arenitis*, whose victims are a living testament to the refugee's painful truth: "It doesn't matter if you're finished off or if you endure and keep going, since here it's harder to be than not to be" (*Entre*, 130).[19] The exile's struggle for psychic survival is magnified tenfold in the *loco*'s slipping grasp on his own sense of self; the confused, embattled drama against losing one's place in the world looms large in the crazy camp inmate's vacant stare, in the gaze of this creature caught in a liminal territory between the living and the dead. Ferrer concurs with a companion waiting in the food line: "I have a lot of friends who have just about lost their minds due to this awful situation. It's worse to see the shadow of a man than it is to see him dead" (*Entre*, 177). The hard task of the concentration camp refugee is to survive with body and soul intact, a feat too difficult for the sufferers of *arenitis*. Likewise, Ferrer is moved by the fate of the camps' other most traumatized, vulnerable residents, the maimed and crippled who waste away in the infirmary. These men with broken bodies, like their insanely muttering brothers with broken minds, seem to be caught at the threshold of death's door. When Ferrer stops by to visit a friend's friend, he discovers that this former war hero, who lost a hand and a leg in the war, has committed suicide and was buried the day before. Ferrer is overwhelmed by the specter of death that meets him inside the camp hospital: "The shadow of death stretches from one end of the room to the other. There are some who pass the time by playing cards. But most lie in their beds and talk about death as if it were the most normal thing in the world. Some, particularly those maimed by war, beg for death, they call out for it. In their eyes you see contempt for everything, including life" (*Entre*, 183). Shaken by this "spectacle that causes even the ink in my pen to shudder" (183), Ferrer returns to his hut and once again fights off the black despair that threatens to destroy the whole camp; surrounded by physical and spiritual death, he reads his *Don Quijote* that evening as if his life depended on it: "There can be no better example than the epitaph that the Bachiller dedicates to Don Quijote: *'que la muerte no triunfó / de su vida con la muerte'* [death did not defeat / his life upon dying]. This life lesson is the same one that makes us travel by our own windmills, like Criptana and Montiel; through the plains of La Mancha and the peaks of the Sierra Morena. We too would like to turn the barbed wire into oak trees and the oak trees into spears" (*Entre*, 183).[20] As he completes his diary entry, he notes that he is serenaded by a group in his hut who sing the Catalonian hymn *El Emigrante*: "It's our hymn too, and it moves us. Hymn of longing, hymn of hope" (*Entre*, 184).

Time and time again, Ferrer comments on the fact that he walks through the camp as if walking through the pages of *Don Quijote* itself; all around him he witnesses scenes of life as if reenacted by the novel's own famous players. He feels himself drawn to the example of Don Quijote like a devoted disciple: "I dream about him and in turn he makes me dream. He's such a familiar character that I feel like I say hello to him all the time, in one camp and another, behind this barbed-wire fence and that. He descends from his myth and becomes a person who lives at our side; he joins us in this drama of whether we're just keeping alive or keeping the faith. Like Don Quijote, you can't be a man of dreams unless you have an invincible spirit" (*Entre*, 213). He is reminded of the *Caballero de la Triste Figura* not only by the *locos*, the pathetic, shadowy figures of the insane dreamers of freedom; Ferrer especially detects his hero's presence in the equally quixotic personages of his sometimes frail elders who are capable still of instructing him in life's lessons and inspiring him with their indomitable spirit. These admirable men parade through the pages of Ferrer's diary, evoking in their expressive incarnation of ragged dignity the emblematic silhouette of a battered Don Quijote advancing undaunted on his swayback mare. There is the crippled Liqui Sánchez, who lost a leg in the miners' 1934 uprising in Asturias, and yet energetically and optimistically insists on doing everything for himself (*Entre*, 47, 76). There is Joaquín Toyos, like Ferrer's father a lifelong Socialist, who resolutely reminds the young diarist that "our destiny has not yet been decided" (*Entre*, 104); the aged activist embodies the Cervantine idol completely: "A quixotic figure, who rides on his Rocinante of goodness, who sees through eyes overflowing with dreams" (*Entre*, 93). There is Isidoro, yet another dyed-in-the-wool Socialist from the old school, who rivals Toyos as the premier *filósofo* in the circle of seniors. A victim like so many others of camp robberies, having the clothes practically stolen off his back doesn't defeat the old man: "He complains that he was robbed blind a few days ago. Then he preaches a sermon proclaiming the immutability of ideas. Men will come and go, ideas are for keeps" (*Entre*, 103). And of course the most revered member of the society of elders in whose features Ferrer recognizes Don Quijote's legacy is his own father, "forged in idealism" (*Entre*, 26). Despite his tattered appearance, and even despite his frequent bouts with depression, the older Ferrer's commitment to his ideals shines through: "His suit in rags doesn't matter. What matters is his freedom" (*Entre*, 99). Following his father's transfer to another camp, the two men maintain a correspondence full of words of wise counsel to one another reminiscent of Cervantes's two famous protagonists' shared lessons and advice. One of the most memorable letters the younger Ferrer receives from his father provides direction like a moral compass: "He advises me to do good deeds, to think lofty thoughts, to avoid selfishness by being tolerant and even indulgent of others. For him, all moral values spring from one's will and intelligence" (*Entre*, 182). Ferrer in turn offers messages of encouragement to lift his father's sagging spirits: "And I cheer him up. I overcome my own doubts. I tell him I'm proud that he's my teacher and I ask him to continue to instruct me. His example is my model. Manhood is an empty concept until the time comes when it must prove itself. Soon we will get out and I'll be able to help him" (*Entre*, 194–95).

One of the most distinctive features of Cervantes's narrative is the use of interpolated stories throughout the novel, a device that repeatedly brings together dynamic, fluid communities of storytellers and listeners sharing circles of fellowship and hours of entertainment. Although Ferrer in no way structures his diary around entire segments of others' tales, he does make repeated reference to the frequent sessions of camp inmates' stories of past adventures, former lives, and previous episodes of joys and sorrows. These moments of narrated personal histories in the concentration camps similarly provide individual instances of a collective body of *cautivos'* tales that alternately inspire, instruct, and amuse the fellow members of the captive audience. Obviously, all the narrators are prisoners themselves, as was one of *Don Quijote*'s most famous narrator-characters from Algiers, but often the recounted events themselves revolve around the topic of imprisonment and liberation. The most purely entertaining story of this type that Ferrer records (and the one most replete with echoes of Cervantes's *historia del cautivo*) is the amazing adventure of the Spanish concentration camp inmate who says he escaped all the way to Hong Kong:

> A bunch of people have gathered around a middle-aged man, a Valencian from Gandía, who's telling an incredible story. He escaped from the Argelés camp and with the help of some friends in Perpignan, he made it to Marseilles. There he was a stowaway on board a cargo ship. After a month he arrived in Hong Kong, where he went ashore. He started working with a Chinaman selling crafts from a small boat that went back and forth between the dock and the ships that came into port. A tourist accused them of cheating him. When the police came, they discovered his illegal status. Another French boat returned him to Marseilles, and from there, straight here to the Barcarès camp. Four months of adventure. He never stops talking about it, describing the good life he had and his love affair with a rich Chinese man's daughter, a girl he got pregnant. He's convinced she'll send for him and he'll be able to permanently stay in Hong Kong. Everybody's left with their mouths hanging open, swallowing big gulps of envy. (*Entre*, 98)[21]

More common than the fabled exploits of seafaring camp Casanovas who have returned to tell the story are tales of captives who have been liberated from Spanish prisons. "Jacinto," condemned to die in one of Franco's jails, was able to be released through family connections; he tells Ferrer's group in St. Cyprien hair-raising accounts of watching night after night as the prisoners were taken out to be executed. His truths are stranger than fiction: "Jacinto tells us that he was with a miner from Reocín, also condemned to death. The miner recognized a close friend from his hometown on one of the firing squads. So he asked the director of the jail if his friend could be included on the squad that would shoot him, since his friend was an excellent shot. He wanted to ask him to hit his heart so that he wouldn't suffer" (*Entre*, 175). Earlier in July, news of the homeland had come from other daring voyagers miraculously escaping from the shores of Spain: "Close to Barcarès a Spanish boat came in to shore with 27 escapees. They're all Galicians and they describe the terror that is reigning in Spain. Almost a million prisoners of war, with thousands of executions every week, the brutal persecution of anything and anybody that smells 'red'" (*Entre*, 117). Occasionally the storytellers are former inmates who purposely return to the camps, as is the case of Abel Herce, a fighter pilot veteran of the Ebro offensive: "His escapades were amazing. He was one of the first to sign up for the Foreign Legion, but he couldn't stomach the incredibly severe military regimen of this unit, where he had to live with some of the most dangerous criminals in the world. He deserted and hid for 12 days in Marseilles. He entered the camp as a fugitive, without being documented" (*Entre*, 120). The internees are similarly regaled with the entertaining details of another loquacious prodigal son of Argelès, "Lino," whom Ferrer describes as a *resucitado*: "We hadn't seen him since the Argelès days. He signed up with the Legion, and was wounded in a fight. He ran away and spent more than two months in the prison camp for *undesirables*. . . . He describes a thousand ways that smooth-talkers can get by. He's entertaining and funny; he's what you'd call a man of the world. . . . Colorful characters in our camp" (*Entre*, 210–11).

While tales of successful liberations, regardless of their brief duration, capture the imagination of the inmate listeners, the most significant storytelling sessions are those in which each member of the circle shares a memory that recreates a prior experience of personal courage, self-reliance, or danger overcome. These informal communal gatherings to swap stories are frequently counterposed to intensely threatening moments of emotional or physical hardship. After more than five months of internment, Ferrer records the third anniversary of the Nationalist uprising against the Republic as a particularly bleak day: "It's no holiday. It's a rather gloomy day. The faces of the veterans show signs of sadness. Surely today everyone's much more aware of our defeat—and its consequences—than when we began our exodus into France" (*Entre*, 114). Seeking comfort and support from former comrades-in-arms, the men keep especially close company together on this evening, and the sound of their voices fills the July night: "Everybody tells his story. Sometimes the details and the dates don't match, but it's not easy to correct an emotional, heart-stopping tale. Curiously, most stories tend to evoke key moments when the narrator's life was saved. In the end, it's the story of the battle that was won" (*Entre*, 114–15). More than two long months later, in his third camp in as many months, Ferrer refers to the damaging torrential rains that have inundated part of the St. Cyprien camp. One of the consequences of the raging floodwaters is the destruction of over half of the latrines. The resulting stench and filth are unbearable. In the face of such miserable conditions, the inmates again find refuge in one another's words. One by one, Ferrer registers each of his five companions' war memories, every single one of which recounts a story of survival (*Entre*, 179). Mired in the despair of the present, the raconteurs fashion hope for the future out of fortifying memories of the past.

From the inaugural diary entry on April 14, 1939, Ferrer frequently indicates that as a beleaguered camp inmate, his sense of survival and hold on hope are substantially strengthened by collective acts of commemoration and solidarity. The struggle that brought the Republican combatants to the camps in exile in the first place is a nation's shared struggle that transcends the individual's private battle and personal trajectory. Ferrer takes great care to document the details of the camp community's observances in exile of national and international holidays, when the celebration of a unifying political consciousness creates a sense of optimism and purpose. Choosing to initiate his record of a Republican's first year in exile on the eighth birthday of the young democratic nation, Ferrer weaves the threads of his own story into the larger fabric of national history. The inmates' public performance of patriotism and shared ideals on this overcast day, notes the young diarist, helps shake off the doldrums felt by so many: "From early on, your ears tell you there's a party going on in the camp. Guitars and mandolins accompany voices that sing off-key and shout out the significance of today's date. The infectious, boisterous uproar spreads through the camp. The 'streets'—the walkways between the huts—are swarming with people. Nobody is complaining like they were a few days before; there are shouts of *long live!* whoever and whatever you want, and everybody's talking to everybody else. Just when hope seemed to have disappeared from shared individual confessions, in a rush it is revived again in these collective demonstrations. It's as if these festivities weren't only about today, but also about all the days of the past and those to come in the future. This cry of 'long live the Republic!' is also a cry of 'long live life!'" (*Entre*, 27). For a few hours, they even forget where they are. "It almost seems like we are free" (*Entre*, 27). The day of poetry recitals, boxing matches, sack races, and theatrical performances ends with the *tertulia* among the elder Ferrer's friends, who sit and reminisce together about the events of April 14, 1931. Ferrer the younger, ever the idealist, ends his first diary entry with a tribute to the sustaining bonds of fraternity that tie him to his Republican brothers who from the sands of the concentration camp remember "the good fight": "Today I've been acutely aware of how much our confinement has tightened the bonds of brotherhood around us. It's a brotherhood bound by the love of liberty, by the love for social justice. It's a love that will overcome defeat and is worth more than life itself" (*Entre*, 28). In a camp where public displays of the Republican flag are strictly forbidden, the tricolored banner makes only fleeting appearances (one stubborn inmate in the hut next door raises it religiously every Sunday, "I'd rather die than take it down!" [40]), but the emblem of the nation is always present in the mind's eye.

Other holiday celebrations in the camps are chronicled in Ferrer's verbal snapshots as a series of cultural spectacles in exile where the inmates showcase their revered ideals of freedom and social justice. On May 1, Ferrer adopts his father's long-held Labor Day tradition and dons his best clothes; outfitted in a wrinkled gray flannel shirt, he walks from one end of the camp to another, recording the expressive posters that line the way: "'On May 1, 1939 the Spanish refugees greet the French proletariat.' Another says: 'We demand asylum and work permits.' The most common one is: 'We honor the memory of those who died for Spain.' Here's another one: 'Next May Day, we celebrate in Madrid'" (*Entre*, 48). Once again, the festive atmosphere that surrounds a familiar and favorite holiday, celebrated so many times back home, temporarily transports the inmate out of the camp: "You'd forget that we were in a concentration camp if it weren't for seeing men in rags who trudge along in the sands of the beach" (*Entre*, 48). The author draws strength from the day's homage to justice and the acts of spirited solidarity situated behind barbed wire; it is on this date that Ferrer in fact decides to begin to chronicle the story of Spanish life that carries on in the camps. Two months later, Bastille Day is celebrated exactly 150 years after the historic events of 1789; according to Ferrer's account, such a commemoration in a concentration camp gives new meaning to the concept of "paradox." The quintessential Day of Liberation and Justice for All finds a motley crew of campers, veterans of a long war against tyranny, facing their smartly dressed jailers as the notes of the French hymn of freedom, "La Marseillaise," fill the camp: "Whoever were to see those ragamuffins, that's us, would be reminded of the wretched poor people of the French Revolution. Compared to the dress uniforms of our guards, the spectacle of our appearance must be quite shocking. There are occasional shouts of *cabrones*, but the chorus of voices raised in song brings everyone together. The words of the *Marseillaise* resound poignantly, rising above the brass section of the band. Beautiful voices, cracked voices; voices of men who have survived war, who search for a peace that not all of them will find" (*Entre*, 105).[22] The Spanish Republican prisoners stiffly comply with the orders to salute the French flag, but they reserve their shouts of enthusiasm of *Long live freedom!* for the sight of their own flag; it is proudly raised up, fluttering from a maimed man's crutch: "Tied to a crutch, the tricolored flag of our Republic waves in the air" (*Entre*, 106). Just five days later, on the anniversary of the commencement of the Spanish Civil War, miniature homemade Republican flags reappear in the camps, dotting sand sculptures and pebble-and-stone decorations that memorialize the war dead: "Perhaps the most beautiful of all is the one we made; it shows a kind of tomb, with the effigy of a Spanish militiaman made of out of clay, and a wreath of flowers with this inscription: *in memory of the fallen*" (*Entre*, 112). A corps of shabbily dressed buglers travels throughout the camp, sounding the "toque de honor" in front of each commemorative exhibit. A minute of silence at noon—followed by the cry in unison of "¡Viva la República!"—a half dozen speeches, and an improbable orchestral concert of traditional Spanish tunes performed by a group of camp musicians round out the festivities. Ferrer imagines the triumphant military pomp and circumstance that surely must have ushered in this day in Franco's Madrid, and resolutely defends the humble display of patriotic spirit among the concentration camp inmates as the authentic expression of the Spanish people's greatest ideal, freedom: "In Madrid there must be triumphant parades, headed by the Moors— the Senegalese of Spain—, while here we honor our fallen and sing of freedom from captivity, which is preferable to captivity without freedom and with death" (*Entre*, 112).

Ferrer takes great pride in the fact that the camp's *cautivos* still quixotically lift their voices and speak for liberty; these *perdedores'* defiant gesture recalls the vision of a dream that the author recounts after a hot summer evening's fitful bout with insomnia. In his dream, shadowy figures float above the beach: Luis Cillán, the fellow soldier with whom Ferrer had crossed the French border; Antonio Machado and his mother, whom Ferrer had actually encountered soon after arriving in France; and finally the familiar comrade who urges him to keep the faith ("Here he comes, soaring high with his Clavileño, it's Don Quijote. He winks at me and raises up his fist . . ." [*Entre*, 135]). The emblematic reference to Don Quijote as a shorthand signal of the displaced Republicans' continued hope (for liberation from exile's prison, for justice in their country, for a return and reintegration to a free Spain) will appear as well in exile publications in Mexico during the years of World War II. In a May 1941 essay in *Romance*, Benjamín Jarnés refers to the symbolic Spanish fictional character as an "a man of great faith who, dejected and defeated . . . continues to affirm his admirable insanity." Perhaps no one, says Jarnés, can understand the paradoxical position of the famous knight errant better than the Spanish Republican exiles: "We've seen so many cases of men brought down for simply pursuing their dreams. Too many times in Spain we've seen a man's spirit kicked out of him, we've seen how the dreamer can be crushed. But today, here we are cheering for the loser, determined to lift him up forever and preserve him in our memory, in our innermost thoughts, as a model of faith, capable of transforming a common working lass into a fairy."[23] A few months earlier, *Romance* had published a book review of the Espasa-Calpe *Colección Austral* edition of the novel, a short essay devoted exclusively to the topic of *Don Quijote*'s relevance to the current trauma of war in Europe. The reviewer held up the book's hero as a model of moral integrity and unwavering faith in the guiding convictions of righteousness that the rest of the modern world ignores at its own peril. The article closes with a special nod to the *vencido*: "Even the man who has lost his dignity can recover it as well as himself, if he is able to identify with the impulses—always noble, always manly, though not always reasonable—of Don Quijote. And if, in the last analysis, insanity is, as they say, a contagious disease, and we become infected with the sublimely distinguished derangement of the ascetic knight of the Castilian plains, we come out the winners. Because it's better to lose your mind rather than lose your conscience and human diginity."[24] In their commentary of a postwar special issue of *Las Españas* commemorating the fourth centenary of Cervantes's birth, scholars James Valender and Gabriel Rojo Leyva remark: "It's no coincidence that two of the drawings most frequently used to illustrate the pages of *Las Españas* use the Don Quijote motif. The Republicans may have been defeated in battle, but their sense of moral and spiritual superiority, the same as Don Quijote's after being defeated by the sorcerers' 'black magic,' remained intact."[25] In one of the 1947 essays reprinted in Valender and Rojo Leyva's edition of *"Las Españas,"* José Gallegos Rocafull's "Aún hay sol en las bardas," the author recreates the vanquished Don Quijote's moment of death: "On his deathbed, thinking over his past misfortunes, with a body bruised and broken but with a heart still strong, Don Quijote kills off his hopes, or else they just die. These were all the things and people he'd hoped for. But out of the ruins of these hopes surges a new hope, stronger than ever. He has hopes for himself, for what his destiny can or will be."[26] In his concentration camp diary written eight years earlier, Ferrer evokes the quixotic figure of the elderly mentor whom he loved like a father, Joaquín Toyos: "A good man. . . . His admirable conduct, his daily lessons of fraternal generosity, his understanding responses to all questions are but one example of the high caliber of human qualities locked inside these concentration camps, unsullied by the hardships and contradictions of such places" (*Entre*, 117). Two months after the old man's release from the camp, Ferrer receives a letter from his moribund friend, with advice given as if straight from Alonso Quijano 'El Bueno's' own lips: "'It's my fate to soon die the worst kind of death, to die of sadness. Lalio, try not to lose that great curiosity you have in everything around you. You've had to learn to be a man at a very young age, and that will help protect you in the new life that awaits you. You will be an expert navigator in the sea of life. I hope you will always be guided by your moral compass, your honest conscience'" (*Entre*, 177). Toyos urges the astute young observer of the human condition in the camps to remember the lessons he has learned from this world that he has so carefully chronicled with avid curiosity; he must carry this history and this memory with him into the new life that awaits him.

Like the pages of the metatextual account of their own adventures that Don Quijote and Sancho Panza read or hear about themselves, or whose version of events is well known by many other readers with whom they come in contact, Ferrer's diary is similarly commented upon by the flesh-and-blood concentration camp characters that he documents. Among his circle of friends and acquaintances in all three camps, Ferrer is infamous for his obsessive writing practices; he is frequently the target of good-natured kidding about the piles of pages that he accumulates day after day. The first time he moves camp, he is daunted by the prospect of transporting so much paper: "The papers . . . Without them I would have a lesser sense of life. They are like proof of life that I'm still alive, that I still exist" (*Entre*, 81). The diary also translates this personal, individual memory into a collective history, and the fellow campers love to have their recorded lives read back to them. One of the most memorable members of Ferrer's Centro de Locos Incurables, Don Ricardo (who smokes an unlit pipe, who laughs and cries at the same time, who ends up drowned, suitcase in hand, on his way home) insistently asks the amateur camp historian if he has been included in the diary (*Entre*, 147). Two camp inmates of Barcarès implore him to read them excerpts of the early days of camp life from Argelès: "They ask me to read them a few pages from my *Diary* and I read them the first part about Argelès. They ask me if I'm writing it to publish it someday" (*Entre*, 155). Two weeks later, he's reading pages out loud to another inmate Araguas. "He doesn't understand the enthusiastic patience I have to write it all down. 'We're too young to make life more difficult'" (*Entre*, 168). Another curious comrade in the next camp of St. Cyprien impatiently interrupts Ferrer's writing so that he can hear how he fares in the textual record of the previous day's episodes: "He asks me to read him my notes from yesterday and gives me a mischievous smile because I treat him like a hero" (*Entre*, 181). By the time Ferrer envisions making his *tercera salida* out of St. Cyprien, he refers to the heavy manuscript bundles that he will have to transport as pure history: "They are history" (*Entre*, 198). Ferrer, like so many Republicans forced out of their country and deprived of the right to help craft a public record of historical events, is hyperconscious throughout his diary about who will be writing his people's history. This is a concern similarly voiced by one of Clemente Cimorra's characters in his 1940 civil war novel, *El bloqueo del hombre: Novela del drama de España*. In the penultimate chapter, the exiled schoolteacher Adelaida explains the notebook she has painstakingly carried over the border into France, entitled "Chapter Summarizing the History of Spain. Brief Explanation for Children, about the War against the Second Republic": "The chapter of History pertaining to the recent war in Spain mustn't be omitted; it must be written with restraint, with clarity, free of biased commentary, as opposed to the version that the official historians want to write. After their victory, they will have the authority to introduce into the history books the official story *[una interpretación decretada]*; a story told in the language of amateurish military parades and false patriotism." Adelaida concludes her impassioned speech with the assurance that despite the well-oiled machines of state propaganda, one day all the war's victims' stories will be told: "But the people won't be fooled; you can't make the basic facts of history just disappear."[27] So, too, frets Ferrer about the question of national history, and who will tell that story. Reading in the Argelès camp César Falcón's *Madrid*, an account of the Republicans' valiant defense of the besieged capital, Ferrer takes issue with what he sees as a sectarian version of events: "If we don't know how to write our own history, we should be even less surprised by what the victors will write" (*Entre*, 78). Elsewhere, dismayed by the degree of cynicism he detects in the actions and words of political leaders around the world, he remarks, "Never have the cynics been so cynical. It would be awful if they took it upon themselves to write the history that we are now living. With Spain in our hearts. With our hearts set on freedom. Someday we will recover that freedom in order to erase the memory of these gloomy days. To erase them, but not to forget them" (*Entre*, 186).

Eulalio Ferrer's concentration camp diary concludes on December 7, 1939, when he is literally unable to hold a pen in his hand any longer. Writing the last entry from the frozen town of La Ferté-Imbault, as he embarks on a five-month tenure as a member of the forced labor group *168 Compañía*, he explains that his blistered and bleeding hands refuse to write another word: "The shovel has torn the skin off my writing hand. I wet it with my urine, following Abel's advice, so that it'll heal more quickly" (*Entre*, 226). This entry concludes with the irrational expression of hope of a man who has the blood of Cervantes running through his veins and the words of Don Quijote echoing in his head: "I'm going to face this next stage of my journey with an indomitable force of will whose fortitude has overcome anguish, whose resistance has overpowered suffering. My hope is nourished by the hope I have in the days yet to come. Without hope you can't fight and you can't achieve a better world" (*Entre*, 226). In a beautifully incisive 1988 introduction to the second, revised edition of Ferrer's original publication of *Entre alambradas* in Mexico, the famous Mexican historian Fernando Benítez comments on the process of *quijotización* that the concentration camp survivor has undergone in his life: "The chronicler, always encouraged by his reading of *Don Quijote*, ended up turning into a quixotic figure himself. He used a large portion of his fortune to create a museum devoted to showing how Don Quijote and Sancho have been represented by artists and craftsmen from around the world. He donated this unique museum as a gift to Mexico, he's created scholarships, he's created awards like the Menéndez y Pelayo prize."[28] This Museo Iconográfico del Quijote was inaugurated in 1987 in Guanajuato with the Mexican and Spanish heads of state, Miguel de la Madrid and Felipe González, together in attendance. Ever the assiduous memorialist, on the evening of the museum's inauguration, Ferrer writes in his diary, "If I've ever had a good idea in my life, born of the twin influences of my early imagination and my more mature judgment as a professional, it is the idea that has culminated today in Guanajuato. Don Quijote embodies the greatest symbols of solidarity: lover of liberty; the unassailable, ideal incarnation of the Spanish character; the gratitude borne of fellowship" (*Páginas*, 303). At the time of the death of his friend Octavio Paz in 1998, the founder of the exquisite Don Quijote collection donated to Mexico recalled the great poet's reference to him some months earlier as a "cultural bridge between Mexico and Spain" (*Páginas*, 354). Indeed, the bridge that helped a young Spanish Civil War refugee cross over the first stage of exile in France and safely negotiate the passage to a new life on the other side of the Atlantic Ocean was forged with a strength of spirit quixotically cultivated in the sandy shores of the concentration camps.

Epilogue: Haunted History: Replacing the Specter of Exile

Lo mismo que una sombra / que ha perdido su cuerpo,
busca que te rebusca, / a los remansos del tiempo viejo
he de volver un día, / caminando en silencio.
Mas las gentes al verme / se apartarán con miedo.
Y mi sombra, despacio, / en busca de su cuerpo,
por los bosques de otrora / se fundirá en silencio
con las sombras inmóviles / de los árboles viejos.
—Celso Amieva, "La sombra"

On a sunny day in 1975, former concentration camp inmate Avel·li Artís-Gener returned to visit the places of memory that had haunted him for thirty-five years: the southernmost beaches along France's Mediterranean shores. He looks intently for any telltale traces of the past travails that tens of thousands of his fellow compatriots had endured on the sands of exile. But there's no sign of their shared history. Gone is the "Mt. Everest of human excrement"; nothing remains, he notes, of the once ubiquitous barbed-wire fencing nor of the wooden posts used in a punishment holding area. The reclining bodies soaking up the rays now belong to bikini-clad tourists; the road that in February 1939 seemed to lead to nowhere today boasts a cheery signpost (ST.CYPRIEN VOUS SOUHAITE LA BIENVENUE). Noisy sand-sifting machines assiduously work to clear the beach of yesterday's debris, but in spite of regular sweeps, something invisible is still there: "They separate out tin cans, plastic bottles, and all kinds of trash, but they can't sort out ectoplasm."[1] Scouring the sand as if searching for the refugees' fabled buried treasure, he tries to disinter what was left behind here all those years ago: "I've searched tenaciously for that immaterial something that's here on these beaches." He can't see it, but he feels the ghostly presence of past lives: "And still, the sounds of exhausted footfalls echo in the sand. . . ."[2]

Artís-Gener continues his pilgrimage to the infamous fortress of Collioure, now preserved as a French national monument for its medieval architectural heritage. But it's a legacy of the past of a different kind that Artís-Gener is looking for. In the all-too-familiar company of yet another French gendarme, he is told that there is no entrance to the castle, a "surreal" remark, says the author, recalling that "before there was no exit, but an entrance, yes indeed." Although the building is closed to the public, the foreign visitor ignores the posting of *passage interdit*. He discovers that what was once a house of horrors is now a haunted house, a place of ghostly silences, where absent presences and missing pieces are keenly sensed: "The stone staircase built along the wall no longer has its iron railing. The grass has overgrown everything and the deafening silence cuts me like a knife; its incredible quiet replaces yesterday's anguished screams. Here, exactly here, is where they beat Serra, Vilella, Estivill, Puig-Solá, Dr. Jauma, and my friend, Agapito Perujo. The *poteau* where they used to tie them up is no longer here, but it's easy to imagine that it would have been in this hole in the courtyard pavement."[3] Camera in hand, Artís-Gener is determined to make a record for posterity, to capture the spirits and untold stories of this place, to somehow reveal the faces of a past that hide themselves among the shadows of oblivion. Even though his camera flashes a signal that there's not enough light to take a picture, he deliberately snaps thirty-six shots; he'll scrutinize the opaque images later, irrationally hoping for a glimpse of a ghost he knows must be there: "I want to develop whatever comes out of this roll of film; I'm in a hurry to take the thirty-six pictures. I'll examine them later with a kind of infrared light that I'll invent if I have to, in search of the spirits of my friends who died within these walls of madness. I can't see them, but I know they're here. They are wandering around these horrible dungeons that I'm staring at without understanding how and why human beings were ever housed here. I know that their souls can't have forgiven being sacrificed so pointlessly, and they will haunt this place for centuries to come, world without end."[4]

In his book *Ghostly Matters: Haunting and the Sociological Imagination*, Avery Gordon refers to the barely visible traces of a society's repressed, occluded, or forgotten past, as "hauntings," spectral spaces inhabited by ghosts, by a "seething" presence defined by Gordon as "a crucible for political mediation and historical memory": "The ghost is not simply a dead or a missing person, but a social figure, and investigating it can lead to that dense site where history and subjectivity make social life."[5] In his attempt to answer the question, "How do we reckon with what modern history has rendered ghostly?" Gordon recommends following the path undertaken by ghost-hunting memoirists like Artís-Gener himself, that is, to track "case studies of haunting" in order to chronicle "a story about what happens when we admit the ghost—that special instance of the merging of the visible and the invisible, the dead and the living, the past and the present—into the making of worldly relations and into the making of our accounts of the world."⁶ Citing Derrida's *Specters of Marx* ("To exorcise not in order to chase away the ghosts, but this time to grant them the right . . . to . . . a hospitable memory . . . out of a concern for *justice*"), Gordon emphasizes the necessity of recognizing the "lost subjects of history—the missing and lost ones and the blind fields they inhabit—" as a way to finally let these ghosts rest in peace, by making room for them in "our accounts of the world."⁷ Ironically, Artís-Gener's sense of having failed to document signs of life or proof of prior existence during his return to Collioure is belied by the densely detailed history and testimony of an entire refugee population that he produces alongside the reported "ghost story." Just weeks after Francisco Franco drew his last breath, the Catalonian native Artís-Gener's *La diáspora republicana* is published in Barcelona, effectively relocating, returning home, the stories and experiences of countless witnesses to Spain's long ignored history of exile.

As Artís-Gener was preparing to exorcise the specters of exile by giving them their place in history ("to grant them the right to a hospitable memory"), a fellow veteran of France's cruelest camps, the *Campos de concentración* illustrator Josep Bartolí published his *Calibán*, a 1972 illustrated meditation on the catastrophic humanitarian consequences of twentieth-century violence and warfare. Certainly the casualty that most interests Bartolí is the Spanish Republic, some of whose followers in exile refused to believe that it was dead, "that all the Calibans of the world had killed it."⁸ Bartolí describes the displaced government, officially reorganized in 1945 and relocated in exile in Mexico City, as a spectral body that was never given a proper burial by its most stubborn supporters: "They took upon themselves the sacred mission of keeping vigil and parading the illustrious cadaver throughout the world in hopes of one day giving it an honorable burial on the peninsula."⁹ Such an impossible dream was pejoratively referenced by a member of the Socialist Party in exile, Luis Araquistáin, when he wrote to a friend in 1955, "We are an admirable, wandering *Numancia* that prefers to die a slow death rather than acknowledge defeat."¹⁰ Quixotic aspirations seemed crazier than ever in the face of the harsh reality of 1950s Cold War politics; with the Western democracies' embrace of the virulently anticommunist Franco, one would expect such hopes to have been killed off. Indeed, Bartolí illustrates his account of war and postwar history (a time in which the "'red' Spanish exiles" have found themselves submerged in a sea of "almost absolute silence") with a scene depicting the decapitated bodies of Sancho Panza and Don Quijote crumpled at the feet of violent, marauding crusaders; their shrunken heads attached to spears are raised high in the air, outside the medieval walls of a Spanish city.¹¹ But Bartolí's dead bodies also give rise to wandering spirits who, as Gordon reminds us, will demand their day of reckoning in the annals of history: "Because ultimately haunting is about how to transform a shadow of a life into an undiminished life whose shadows touch softly in the spirit of a peaceful reconciliation. In this necessarily collective undertaking, the end, which is not an ending at all, belongs to everyone."[12]

If coming to grips with the ghosts of the past "makes all the difference to any project trying to find the address of the present," then revisiting the place of exile in Spanish history provides a reliable homing device.[13] While Bartolí may have despaired twenty-five years ago that for the Spanish exiles of 1939 "The sacrifice was useless!" the subsequent recovery of the legacy of this political generation reveals threads of continuity that link the phantoms of history with the destiny of the living.[14] Remarking specifically on the *quijotismos* of the Republicans in exile—the oceans of ink spilled in exile journals, bulletins, manifestos, and magazines; the fervent commemorations held every April 14 in banquet halls or barrooms; and the official convocations and meetings of a parliament in exile—former exile José Prat defends such idealistic activities, so at odds with the limits of political reality, as serving an important function: "But the affirmation of ideas, the expression of the strength of one's convictions and faith in the possibility of a renewed liberal tradition in Spain, are in themselves political values."[15] The longtime Harvard scholar Juan Marichal (who himself arrived as a teenager in Veracruz in 1940) concurs that the quixotic spirit that defined the cultural, social, and political projects undertaken by the Spaniards in exile was its most enduring legacy. He cites Araquistáin's somewhat disparaging reference to his own Socialist Party of the diaspora ("Wandering Numancia") as the most accurate definition of the political exiles as a whole, "as much for their determination to not give up, as for their commitment to offer Spain a continuing model of constitutional legality. It is clear today that the very existence of a Socialist political 'apparatus' in Toulouse played a 'strategic' role in the saga of the return of democracy to Spain."[16] The history professor Marichal goes on to echo the sentiment of another Spanish history professor who in 1939 had offered a series of lectures on Spanish history to fellow inmates in the camp of St. Cyprien, urging his listeners to never forget "We too are History!"[17] Marichal explains: "So it is that the history of postwar Spain (1939–1975) cannot be written without taking into account the Spain of exile. Because the political history of Spanish exile isn't just a story of anecdotal interest or a pitiful story about one more community of men and women who were temporarily displaced from their homes. In fact, the political history of Spanish exile *is*, simply stated, the history of Spain."[18]

According to the popular beliefs and customs associated with the Hispanic observance of the "Day of the Dead," it is the duty of the living to honor the life and memory of loved ones who have died by feeding their spirit with offerings of favorite food and drink. On November 1, 2000, the Ateneo Español de México, the Mexico City home of Spanish culture, community, and intellectual inquiry since its founding by a group of Spanish exiles in 1949, featured an art exhibit entitled Sueños de Argelès (Dreams of Argelès). The Mexican artist Jorge Siqueiros constructed an enormous "ofrenda de muerto" [altar to the dead] displaying a series of vignettes of concentration camp inmates engaged in a variety of activities. Just like their real-life counterparts from sixty years before, the grinning cardboard skeleton figures assume the incongruous role of creators of culture: this one paints a picture, another plays a guitar; here someone sings a song, there someone else writes a book. Wooden posts and barbed wire enclose two skeletons who, wrapped in winter scarves, are begging for food next to a prized copy of *Don Quijote*. A bottle of good Rioja wine, another of Spanish brandy, and a decanter of *Anís del mono* are interspersed among the papier-mâché figures along with the tropical fruit of the Americas, all once the fantasies of starving inmates. Sueños de Argelès, the altar erected to the dead and their dreams, now gives sustenance to the souls, keeping memory alive in the place of history.[19]

Notes

Introduction

1. Manuel Vázquez Montalbán, "Perder la historia," in *Los que no volvieron*, by Carlos Sampelayo (Barcelona: Los Libros de la Frontera, 1975), 7.

2. The North American Nancy Macdonald, founder of the relief agency Spanish Refugee Aid established in 1953 to raise money for the neediest of the 120,000 Spanish exiles still living in France, describes the subsequent stages of the newly proposed pension plan to which Vázquez Montalbán refers: "These pensions had been granted on 7 April, 1976 by the Spanish Government, to be paid to disabled Republican veterans of the Civil War. By 1981 five decrees had been passed, the first very discriminatory. A Republican who had lost a leg received $144 a month. A *Caballero*, who had fought for Franco, received $500. The fourth decree almost equalized payments and the fifth stated that arrears would only be completely paid by April 1985. Exiles in France had to go to their birthplaces in Spain, with three witnesses to justify their claim. If they were too old to travel, they had to find someone to go for them, and to whom they had to give a percentage of the pension." *Homage to the Spanish Exiles: Voices from the Spanish Civil War* (New York: Insight Books, 1987), 335.

3. Vázquez Montalbán, "Perder la historia," 7. Unless otherwise indicated, the translations of all Spanish citations in this book are my own. Due to the demands of space limitations, I include the original Spanish only when citing lines of poetry.

4. José Esteban Vilaró, *El ocaso de los dioses rojos: Barcelona, Perthus, Argelès, París, Méjico...* (Barcelona: Ediciones Destino, 1939), 10.

5. Guillermo Cabrera Infante, "The Invisible Exile," in *Literature in Exile*, ed. John Glad (Durham: Duke University Press, 1990), 10. In order to redress the omissions left by the Franco regime's official story of political history, a series entitled Biblioteca de Divulgación Política (Library of Political Dissemination) published in Barcelona in the early post-Franco years by the Gaya Ciencia Press, produced a collection of political primers on a variety of topics largely unfamiliar to the Spanish public; sample entries among the thirty-odd titles include *Qué son las izquierdas*, *Qué es la democracia*, *Qué es el sindicalismo*, *Qué es el anarquismo*, *Qué es la República*, etc. Needless to say, one of the slim volumes seeking to reeducate a nation suffering from collective amnesia and selective versions of twentieth-century political history was the 1977 *Qué son los exiliados* (What Are Exiles?). The author Ramón Gómez Molina laments the "bad press" attributed to the words *exilio*, *exiliar*, and *exiliado* during the previous four decades, noting that the Spanish Royal Academy of Language did not officially recognize the word *exilio* until the 1950s. Similarly, exile scholar José Luis Abellán recalls that in 1967, when he published his *Filosofía española en América (1936–1966)*, he was not allowed to include the word *exilio* in the title: "To talk in a book about philosophical exile when the physical condition of exile was not even officially acknowledged, was an impossible task," *El exilio filosófico en América: Los transterrados de 1939* (Mexico City: Fondo de Cultura Económica, 1998), 7.

6. Avel·lí Artís-Gener, *La diáspora republicana* (Barcelona: Editorial Euros, 1975), 28.

7. Joaquín Zurita Castañer, *Los círculos del exilio español en Europa (1930–1975)* (Zaragoza: INO-Reproducciones, 1985), 51.

8. Important scholarship on the history of the French concentration camps for Spanish refugees has been published in the last fifteen years, building on the research made available in the 1970s by investigators like David Pike, *"Vae Victis!": Los republicanos españoles refugiados en Francia, 1939–1944* (Paris: Ruedo Ibérico, 1969); Louis Stein, *Beyond Death and Exile: The Spanish Republicans in France, 1939–1955* (Cambridge: Harvard University Press, 1979); and most important, the Spanish historian Javier Rubio, *La emigración de la guerra civil de 1936–1939*, 3 vols. (Madrid: Librería Editorial San Martín, 1977). See especially the work of Spanish historian Alicia Alted Vigil, particularly the 1994 and 1997 installments of the documentary series and the accompanying monographs, *Exilios I, II: Refugiados españoles en el mediodía de Francia* (Madrid: UNED), produced by a team of historians including Alted Vigil and her colleagues from Madrid's Universidad Nacional de Educación a Distancia, as well as the Université de Toulouse Le Mirail. See Alted Vigil's and Lucienne Domergue's edited volume, *El exilio republicano español en Toulouse, 1939–1999* (Madrid: UNED; Toulouse: Presses Universitaires du Mirail, 2003). See also the books by two French historians, Geneviève Dreyfus-Armand's *L'exil des républicains espagnols en France: De la Guerre civile à la mort de Franco* (Paris: Albin Michel, 1999; Spanish edition translated by Dolors Poch, Barcelona: Crítica, 2000), and Marie Rafaneau-Boj's *Los campos de concentración de los refugiados españoles en Francia (1939–1945)* (Barcelona: Editorial Omega, 1995). Studies focusing on both the history of the camps and the creative work of the inmates may be found in Jean-Claude Villegas's beautifully illustrated edited volume, *Plages d'exil: Les camps de réfugiés espagnols en France, 1939* (Nanterre: BDIC; Dijon: Hispanística XX, 1989); see also *Vous avez la mémoire courte . . .*, a collaborative work by René Grando, Jacques Queralt, and Xavier Febrés (Perpignan: Edition du Chiendent, 1981). José Naharro-Calderón has written a series of illuminating essays on the literature produced by former concentration camp inmates; his forthcoming book, *Sangrías españolas y terapias de Vichy: de los campos de concentración a las vueltas de exilio* will be published in Barcelona by Anthropos. My project is the first book-length monograph in any language on the representations of the camps in the imaginative literature written by Spanish exiles during the 1940s.

9. Eulalio Ferrer, *Entre alambradas* (Barcelona: Grijalbo, 1988), 106.

10. *Ultramar*, facsimile edition, ed. James Valender (Mexico City: El Colegio de México, 1993), 19.

Chapter 1. Marking Refugee Territory

1. The French internment camp statistics are found in Rubio's *La emigración de la guerra civil*, 305.

2. The image of the "pharmacy" was one of many that the civil war photojournalist Agustí Centelles recorded and developed in a makeshift darkroom he and fellow photographer Salvador Pujol clandestinely set up in the Bram camp. In January 1939, Centelles smuggled five thousand photographic plates across the French border and managed to save this civil war archive from confiscation and destruction during his internment in the Argelès-sur-Mer and Bram camps; see Jerald Green, "Agustí Centelles: La forja d'un periodista grafic," and Albert Balcells, "Agustí Centelles i el seu

temps: Els orígens d'un reporter grafic," in *Agustí Centelles (1909–1985), Fotoperiodista*, Exhibition Catalog (Barcelona: Fundació Caixa de Cataluña, 1988), 17–27; 29–42.

3. *El exilio español en México* (Madrid: Ministerio de Cultura, 1983), 13–17.

4. Jaime Espinar, *Argelès-Sur-Mer (Campo de concentración para españoles)* (Caracas: Elite, 1940), 79.

5. Antonio Sánchez Barbudo, "El Grupo de *Hora de España* en 1939," in *Ensayos y recuerdos* (Barcelona: Laia, 1980), 100.

6. José Naharro-Calderón, "Por los campos de Francia: entre el frío de las alambradas y el calor de la memoria," in *Literatura y cultura del exilio español de 1939 en Francia*, ed. Alicia Alted Vigil and Manuel Aznar Soler (Sant Cugat de Valles: AEMIC-GEXEL, 1998), 313.

7. An English translation of the 1984 essay inaugurated a special issue of the journal *Representations* on the topic of history and memory; see Pierre Nora, "Between Memory and History: *Les Lieux de Mémoire*," trans. Marc Roudebush, *Representations* 26 (1989): 7–25; this quote, 25. Cultural geographers John A. Agnew and James S. Duncan cite Nora's work in the introduction of their edited collection of essays that interrogate memory, place, and national discourse, *The Power of Place: Bringing Together Geographical and Sociological Imaginations* (Cambridge: Unwin Hyman, 1989). More recent studies, particularly those that address the modern Jewish construction of "Israel," similarly build on the conceptual foundation of *"les lieux de mémoire."* See especially the essays in the special issue of *Representations* entitled *Grounding Memory*, 69 (2000) as well as selected articles in Dan Ben-Amos and Liliane Weissberg, eds. *Cultural Memory and the Construction of Identity* (Detroit: Wayne State University Press, 1999).

8. Nora, "Between Memory and History," 7.

9. Benedict Anderson, *Imagined Communities: Reflections on the Origin and Spread of Nationalism* (New York: Verso, 1992), 202.

10. Edward Said, "Invention, Memory, Place," *Critical Inquiry* 26, no. 2 (2000): 185.

11. Amy Kaminsky, *After Exile: Writing the Latin American Diaspora* (Minneapolis: University of Minnesota Press, 1999), 29.

12. Max Aub, *El rapto de Europa o siempre se puede hacer algo* (Mexico City: Ediciones Tezontle, 1946), 121.

13. Giuliana Di Febo, "Un espacio de la memoria: el paso de la frontera francesa de los exiliados españoles. La despedida del Presidente Azaña," in *Literatura y cultura*, eds. Alted Vigil and Aznar Soler, 467. The numerous testimonies of civil war refugees painstakingly documented as part of the oral history project, "Historia Oral Refugiados Españoles en México" (originally coordinated by Eugenia Meyer and published by Mexico City's Instituto Nacional de Antropología e Historia in a five-part series entitled *Palabras del exilio*), offer evidence of the pivotal place of the border crossing in the collective memory of exile; see especially María de la Soledad Alonso, Elena Aub, and Marta Baranda, *Palabras del exilio: de los que volvieron* (Mexico City: INAH/SEP/Instituto Mora, 1988), especially 80–86. See also Dolores Pla Brugat's important study, which includes equally compelling testimony, *"Els exiliats catalans": Un estudio de la emigración republicana española en México* (Mexico City: Instituto Nacional de Antropología e Historia, 1999), especially 58–86.

14. Belén Sánchez, "'Yo fui esclavo de los nazis,'" *El Semanal* 698 (March 11–17, 2001): 30.

15. Artís-Gener, *La diáspora republicana*, 29.

16. Antonio Tellado Vázquez and Antonio Sánchez-Bravo Cenjor (Bravo-Tellado), *El peso de la derrota, 1939–1944: La tragedia de medio millón de españoles en el exilio* (Madrid: Edifrans, 1974), 16.

17. Clemente Cimorra, *El bloqueo del hombre* (Buenos Aires: Claridad, 1940), 168.
18. Solano Palacio, *El éxodo por un refugiado español* (Valparaíso: Editorial Más Allá, 1939), 32.
19. Manuel Altolaguirre, *El caballo griego*, in *Obras completas*, vol. 1, ed. James Valender (Madrid: Istmo, 1986), 115, 118.
20. Manuel Altolaguirre, "De mis recuerdos," *Hora de España* 5 (1937): 70.
21. Silvia Mistral, *Éxodo* (Mexico City: Editorial Minerva, 1940), 22. For a commentary of this text, see Neus Samblancat Miranda, "*Éxodo: Diario de una refugiada española*, de Silvia Mistral," in *II Coloquio Internacional: La literatura y la cultura del exilio republicano español de 1939*, ed. Róger González Martel (La Habana: CHE-GEXEL-AEMIC, 2000), 157–67.
22. Mistral, *Éxodo*, 19.
23. Ibid., 23. Later, from a distance of three thousand miles, Republican exiles in Mexico would follow news of much more comprehensive book burnings, orchestrated now by Franco's cultural watchdogs; a notice in the April 15, 1940, issue of the journal *España Peregrina* announced: "The newspaper *Ya*, of Madrid, on May 2, 1939, reported under the headline '*Auto da fe* at the Central University': 'The enemies of Spain were condemned to flames. On the occasion of the book festival, an *auto da fe* was celebrated in the courtyard of the Central University, where Professor Antonio Luna offered the following words: *in order to build one Spain, great and free, we condemn to the flames all books that are separatist, liberal, Marxist, books about the black legend, anticatholic books, those of a morbid, exaggerated romanticism, awful texts in terrible taste written by cowards and pseudoscientists, as well as the newspapers of the vulgar press. And we included on our list Sabino Arana, J. J. Rousseau, Carlos Marx, Voltaire, Lamartine, Máximo Gorki, Remarque, Freud* y Heraldo de Madrid," *España Peregrina*, facsimile edition (Mexico City: Ed. Alejandro Finisterre, 1977), 136. Pedro Foix reprints this notice in his *España desgarrada* (Mexico City: Ediciones Ibero-Americanas, 1942), 79–80.
24. Mistral, *Éxodo*, 20.
25. Juan Renau, *Pasos y sombras. Autopsia* (Mexico City: Colección Aquelarre, 1953), 410.
26. Enrique Rioja, "Ultimo sol en España," in *"Las Españas": Historia de una revista del exilio (1946–1963)*, ed. James Valender and Gabriel Rojo Leyva (Mexico City: El Colegio de México, 1999), 529.
27. Francisco Giral, *La República en el exilio* (Madrid: Ediciones 99, 1977), 100–101.
28. Antonio Soriano, *Éxodos: Historia oral del exilio republicano en Francia, 1939–1945* (Barcelona: Editorial Crítica, 1989), 123.
29. Bravo-Tellado, *El peso de la derrota*, 32.
30. Concha Méndez, *Memorias habladas, memorias armadas*, ed. Paloma Ulacia Altolaguirre (Madrid: Mondadori, 1990), 106. Another civilian woman, Adelita del Campo, has recalled the merciless bombing of the group of civilians and soldiers with whom she had traveled to the border town of Port-Bou: "We waited there for two nights and one day, enduring bombings and machine-gun fire. . . . Bless that tunnel that gave us shelter!," in "Camino del exilio, camino de la esclavitud," *Canelobre: Revista del Instituto de Estudios Juan Gil-Albert* 20–21 (1991): 62. For excerpts of 1993 and 1995 interviews with del Campo (born Adela Carreras Taurá), see Antonina Rodrigo, *Mujer y exilio, 1939* (Madrid: Compañía Literaria, 1999), 239–58.
31. Pedro Serra, *Memorias de un trashumante: epopeya antinazifascista. Dictadura y exilio* (Mexico City: B. Costa-Amic, 1966), 51.
32. Manuel García Gerpe, *Alambradas: Mis nueve meses por los campos de concentración de Francia* (Buenos Aires: Celta, 1941), 7.
33. Espinar, *Argelès-Sur-Mer*, 9.

34. Artís-Gener, *La diáspora republicana*, 44.
35. Mistral, *Éxodo*, 50.
36. Solano Palacio, *Entre dos fascismos: Memorias de un voluntario de las Brigadas Internacionales en España* (Valparaíso: Editorial Más Allá, 1940), 189.
37. Gustav Regler, *The Owl of Minerva*, trans. Norman Denny (New York: Farrar, Straus & Cuday, 1959), 321.
38. Di Febo, "Un espacio de la memoria," 469.
39. Antonio Miró, *L'exilé: souvenirs d'un républicain espagnol* (Paris: Ed. Galilée, 1976), 132.
40. Foix, *España desgarrada*, 183.
41. Espinar, *Argelès-Sur-Mer*, 32, 54.
42. Rose Duroux and Raquel Thiercelin, "Los niños del exilio: asignatura pendiente," in *Emigración y exilio: españoles en Francia (1936–1946)*, ed. Josefina Cuesta and Benito Bermejo (Madrid: Eudema, 1996), 169. See Alvaro de Albornoz's early exile essay "La supuesta España roja," in his *Páginas del destierro* (Mexico City: Ediciones Quetzal, 1941), for an eloquent refutation of the derogatory *España roja* label constantly used by pro-Nationalist forces both during and after the civil war in order to demonize and dismiss the political and social programs of the Spanish Republic. In his 1939 *¡Alerta a los pueblos! Estudio político-militar del período final de la guerra española* (Buenos Aires: Aniceto López, 1939), Gen. Vicente Rojo, a chief military officer of the Republican army, similarly derided the enemy forces' attempt to "discredit a group of combatants by calling them 'reds,'" 253.
43. Pike, *"Vae Victis!,"* 2; Stein, *Beyond Death and Exile*, 25.
44. Rafaneau-Boj, *Los campos de concentración*, 113.
45. Anderson, *Imagined Communities*, 206.
46. Soriano, *Exodos*, 71.
47. Macdonald, *Homage to the Spanish Exiles*, 103.
48. Miguel Giménez Igualada, *Más allá del dolor* (Mexico City: Tierra y Libertad, 1946), 182.
49. Federica Montseny, *El éxodo: Pasión y muerte de españoles en el exilio* (Barcelona: Galba, 1977), 22.
50. Rojo, *¡Alerta a los pueblos!*, 10.
51. Montseny, *El éxodo*, 28, 31.
52. I use the term "collective memory" according to the now classic definition given by Maurice Halbwachs, who himself died in the German concentration camp of Buchenwald in 1945; for a Spanish exiled writer-survivor's account of Halbwachs in the camp, see Jorge Semprún's *Viviré con su nombre, morirá con el mío*, trans. Carlos Pujol (Barcelona: Tusquets Editores, 2001). Halbwachs, less interested in the working of personal memory than his mentor Henri Bergson and keenly influenced by his colleague Emile Durkheim, argued that though only individuals have the capacity to remember, this memory is socially constructed according to the groups they belong to: "We place ourselves in their perspective and we consider ourselves as being part of the same group or groups as they," *On Collective Memory*, ed. and trans. Lewis A. Coser (Chicago: University of Chicago Press, 1992), 38. Drawing on Halbwachs's early work, Daniel Sherman also offers a useful definition for the purposes of my study: "Collective or social memory, meanwhile, can be defined as the ideas, assumptions, and knowledges that structure the relationship of individuals and groups to the immediate as well as the more distant past," *The Construction of Memory in Interwar France* (Chicago: University of Chicago Press, 1999), 2. For a summary of the theoretical genealogy between Halbwachs's and Nora's work on collective memory, see Jon Cowans, "Visions of the Postwar: The Politics of Memory and Expectation in 1940s France," *History and Memory* 10 (1998): 68–101.

CHAPTER 2. SACRIFICE AND THE NATION

1. Ernest Renan, "What Is a Nation?," trans. Martin Thom, in *Nation and Narration*, ed. Homi K. Bhabha (London: Routledge, 1990), 19.
2. Dominick LaCapra, *History and Memory after Auschwitz* (Ithaca: Cornell University Press, 1998), 10. For a forceful critique of "memory discourse" in Holocaust studies specifically, and in the field of history generally, see Kerwin Klein's article "On the Emergence of *Memory* in Historical Discourse,"*Representations* 69 (2000): 127–50, in which the author overviews significant scholarship in this area of research, and laments this "boom" for the quasi-religious, antihistoricist features that characterize it.
3. Sherman, *The Construction of Memory*, 7.
4. Michael Rowlands, "Memory, Sacrifice and the Nation," *New Formations* 30 (1996): 10.
5. Angel Loureiro, *The Ethics of Autobiography: Replacing the Subject in Modern Spain* (Nashville: Vanderbilt University Press, 2000), 83.
6. For an illuminating study of the exilic discourse on the question of national identity and Spanish cultural values in Mexico, see Sebastiaan Faber's *Exile and Cultural Hegemony: Spanish Intellectuals in Mexico, 1939–1975* (Nashville: Vanderbilt University Press, 2002).
7. Rowlands, "Memory, Sacrifice and the Nation," 10.
8. Valender and Rojo Leyva, eds., *"Las Españas"*; see particularly the section entitled "Dos mentores literarios," 161–81.
9. Teresa Férriz, "Ejemplaridad y tradición inmediata (A. Machado y F. García Lorca en el exilio español de 1939)," *Scriptura* 6–7 (1991): 190.
10. Manuel Andújar, prefacio, *Collioure 1939. Les dernier jours d' Antonio Machado/Ultimos días de Antonio Machado*, ed. Jacques Issorel (Collioure: Fondation Antonio Machado, 1982), 12. For a detailed summary of Machado's life and work during the civil war as well as a careful account of his exodus and last days in exile, see Monique Alonso's *Antonio Machado, poeta en el exilio* (Barcelona: Anthropos, 1985). The author, a daughter of Spanish exiles and former secretary of the Fundación Antonio Machado por el Ayuntamiento de Collioure, has compiled an extensive anthology of essays, correspondence, and poetry written by Machado during the civil war; she includes additional documents dating from 1936–39, including newspaper articles, drawings, photographs, and letters, many of which are directly related to the circumstances of Machado's death and burial in France.
11. José Giral, "Declaración ministerial del Gobierno Giral ante las Cortes de la República reunidas en México el 7 de noviembre de 1945," in Rubio, *La emigración*, vol. 3, 1021.
12. Francisco Giral, "Actividad de los gobiernos y de los partidos republicanos (1939–1976)," in *El exilio español de 1939*, vol. 2, ed. José Luis Abellán (Madrid: Taurus, 1976), 190.
13. Manuel Aznar Soler, "Las literaturas del exilio republicano de 1939: El estado de la cuestión," *Insula* 627 (March 1999): 5.
14. I cite from the 1983 reprint published in *Diálogos* (July–August 1983), 58–64, a Mexican-based journal of the arts whose director in 1983 was Xirau's own son, Ramón Xirau. Subsequent references to this edition will be made parenthetically in the text.
15. Antonio Machado, *Poesías completas*, ed. Oreste Macrì (Madrid: Espasa-Calpe and Fundación Antonio Machado, 1989), 587.
16. Agustí Cabruja-Auguet, *La ciudad de madera* (Mexico City: Vértice, 1947), 26, 107. Further references to this edition will be made parenthetically in the body of the text. For a short biographical profile of the author, see Rosa Castillo Rosas's "Comenta-

rio sobre la obra literaria del escritor catalán Agustí Cabruja i Auguet," in *El exilio literario español de 1939*, vol. 2, ed. Manuel Aznar Soler (Barcelona: GEXEL, 1998), 615–23.

17. Celso Amieva (José Alvarez Posada), *Asturianos en el destierro (Francia)* (Gijón: Ayalga Ediciones, 1977), 20.

18. Celso Amieva, *La almohada de arena* (The Pillow of Sand) (Mexico City: Suplemento de Ecuador O O O, 1960), unnumbered pages; further references to this edition will include parenthetical citations of verse lines for the poem "Corona de espinas."

19. In Isabel de Palencia's 1945 memoir published in English in New York, the former Republican ambassador to Sweden living in exile in Mexico reports: "Dysentery, pneumonia and influenza were great afflictions. But the gravest concern of the Spanish doctors, who were also interned without means of alleviating the suffering all around them, were the mental and neurotic cases. . . . Dr. Joaquín d'Harcourt, medical colonel of the Republican Army, who was trying to bring some help and order into the camp [Argelès-sur-Mer], told me about this," *Smouldering Freedom: The Story of the Spanish Republicans in Exile* (New York: Longmans, Green and Co., 1945), 86–87. Dr. d'Harcourt eventually emigrated to Mexico, and in 1949 became the first president of the long-lived Ateneo Español de México.

20. Machado, *Poesías completas*, 505.

21. In his important book on Spanish exile, published on the fiftieth anniversary of the end of the Spanish Civil War, Michael Ugarte describes as concentric circles of exile the alienated space that the Spanish refugees experience through their imprisonment in France: "Exiled from fascist Spain, as they crossed the border they suffered inner exile from fascist France, this time the ostracism of the internment camp," *Shifting Ground: Spanish Civil War Exile Literature* (Durham: Duke University Press, 1989), 76.

22. Machado, *Poesías completas*, 582.

23. Bravo-Tellado, *El peso de la derrota*, 108.

24. Agustí Bartra, *Cristo de 200.000 brazos (Campo de Argelès)* (Mexico City: Editorial Novaro-México 1958), 12.

25. Soriano, *Éxodos*, 63.

26. Eulalio Ferrer, *Páginas del exilio* (Mexico City: Aguilar, 1999), 27. For the 1998 profiles, see Felipe García-Moreno, "10 Méxicos para 10 españoles," *Viceversa* 61 (June 1998): 8–31.

27. Ferrer, *Páginas del exilio*, 30.

28. Ferrer, *Entre alambradas*, 112.

29. Among other philanthropic projects, the millionaire Ferrer has generously funded two foundations that have established more permanent sites of cultural memory for the Spanish exile community in Mexico. In 1987, in the name of his fellow Spanish war exiles to Mexico, Ferrer donated to the Mexican government his extraordinary collection of artifacts devoted to Don Quijote housed in the Museo Iconográfico del Quijote in Guanajuato. The collection includes the famous painting by fellow exile Antonio Rodríguez Luna, *Don Quijote en el exilio*, which depicts the haggard masses of refugees—headed no less than by Machado, along with León Felipe and Juan Ramón Jiménez—crossing the border behind the imposing figure of Don Quijote. In addition, the Fondo Eulalio Ferrer funds publications through the Colegio de México press that investigate the history and legacy of Spanish exile in Mexico.

30. Mistral, *Éxodo*, 84.

31. Quoted by José Naharro-Calderón, *Entre el exilio y el interior: el "entresiglo" y Juan Ramón Jiménez* (Barcelona: Anthropos, 1994), 292. The author Joaquín Gómez Burón cites, and disputes, a 1966 article published in *Estafeta Literaria* by Juan Aparicio that reports Machado's internment in a camp; see Gómez Burón, *Exilio y muerte de Antonio Machado* (Madrid: Ediciones SEDMAY, 1975), 93. David Pike is perhaps the first his-

torian who apocryphally attributes Machado's death to the camps. Discussing the inhumane living conditions of the camps, he states: "Antonio Machado is just the most famous example of many who in reality died of neglect,""*Vae Victis!,*" 41; Pike goes on to footnote personal correspondence from a war veteran, Juan Sanz y Cardona, who informs him that Machado later died in a hotel in Collioure. The memoirists Tellado Vázquez and Sánchez-Bravo inadvertently perpetuate the legend in a 1974 testimony, in which they honor the death of Machado: "May our great and good universal poet, who ended up in the degrading French concentration camps, serve as an example," *El peso de la derrota*, 50. See also the account by Gustav Regler, a former internee of the Vernet camp who emigrated to Mexico in 1941: "I learned that evening that the Spanish poet, Antonio Machado, was among those lying in the sand of Cerbère . . . I asked [the *New York Times* reporter Herbert] Matthews to drive me there; but at Argelès we were held up by Senegalese soldiers who told us in bad French that we should be arrested if we went any further. . . . And somewhere in the night, sick and tired, ill-used by the murderers of his republic, lay the republic's greatest poet, watched over by the Senegalese, ill-used Africans," *The Owl of Minerva*, 326. For one of the most fantastic accounts by an exiled writer of the events surrounding Machado's death, see the "eye-witness" account by Carlos Sampelayo, *Los que no volvieron*, 40–43.

32. Albert Camus, *(España Libre! (Artículos, discursos y documentos sobre el problema español)*, ed. and trans. Juan M. Molina (Mexico City: Editores Mexicanos Unidos, 1966), 59, 66.

33. Ibid., 74–75.

34. *Plages d'exil*, 89.

35. Ibid.

36. Cesáreo de la Cruz y Gómez, *Mis campos de concentración* (Segovia: CEYDE, 1978), 151.

37. Juan Rejano, "Recuerdo de Antonio Machado a los 20 años de su muerte," *A Don Antonio Machado al cumplirse los 20 años de su muerte* (Mexico City, 1961), 190–91; the text of these remarks was originally read at the Ateneo Español de México on May 14, 1959.

38. *España Peregrina*, 69.

39. Juan Carrasco, *La odisea de los republicanos españoles en Francia (1939–1945)* (Barcelona: Edicions Nova Lletra, 1980), 174.

40. Mistral, *Éxodo*, 138.

41. The civil war veteran Juan Carrasco, who himself survived more than four years at the notorious Vernet d'Ariège (the concentration camp that in fact replaced Collioure as a *campo de castigo*), succinctly summarizes the meaning of Collioure in the history and the memory of the exiles in his fascinating "photo album": "Collioure, for the Spanish refugees, is something else. It brings to mind the two names engraved forever in the history of republican exile: Antonio Machado and the military fortress," *La odisea*,172). For a poetic meditation on the doubly significant place value of the border town, see Melitón Bustamante Ortiz's "Collioure 1962," ibid., 176–77.

42. Gómez Burón, *Exilio y muerte de Antonio Machado*, 137. In his highly critical 1976 review of Gómez Burón's book, Jacques Issorel accuses the author of a series of factual inaccuracies, and maintains that Gómez Burón never was in direct contact with Jacques Baills himself, "Regard critique 'sur un libro en homenaje al gran poeta Antonio Machado,'" *Les langues modernes* 70 (1976): 423. If the concerns Machado voiced about the Collioure prisoners are merely apocryphal tales, it is interesting to note nevertheless that the legend of the shared destiny between Machado and the Republican soldier-prisoners of Collioure persisted for decades after the poet's death in 1939.

43. Soriano, *Exodos*, 120.

44. Amieva, *La almohada de arena*, unnumbered pages.
45. Alonso, *Antonio Machado*, 496; Alonso refers as well to the soldier-pallbearers, "those twelve soldiers—two groups of six—, according to the testimony of one of them," ibid.
46. Jacques Issorel, "Collioure, 1939. Ultimos días de Antonio Machado (a través de los recuerdos de Jacques Baills, Corpus Barga, Juliette Figueres, José Machado y Matea Monedero de Machado)," in *Collioure, 1939. Les derniers jours d'Antonio Machado/ Últimos días de Antonio Machado*, ed. Jacques Issorel (Collioure: Fondation Antonio Machado, 1982), 88–89.
47. Alonso, *Antonio Machado*, 530.
48. *Los de Collioure (Relatos de un crimen)*, prologue by Margarita Nelken (Mexico City: Editorial Morelos, 1940), 185.
49. Angel Samblancat, *Caravana nazarena (Éxodo y odisea de España, 1936–1940 y...)* (Mexico City: Ed. Orbe, 1945), 105.
50. Palacio, *El éxodo*, 110–11.
51. Javier Rubio, "La población española en Francia de 1936 a 1946: flujos y permanencias," in *Emigración y exilio: españoles en Francia (1936–1946)*, ed. Josefina Cuesta and Benito Bermejo (Madrid: Eudema, 1996), 44.
52. García Gerpe, *Alambradas*, 6.
53. Espinar, *Argelès-Sur-Mer*, 119–20.
54. Rowlands, "Memory, Sacrifice and the Nation," 11.
55. Macdonald, *Homage to the Spanish Exiles*, 278.
56. Carrasco, *La odisea*, 109.
57. García Gerpe, *Alambradas*, 94, 11.
58. Ibid., 94.

Chapter 3: A Commemorative Memory Album of Exile

1. Molins i Fábrega and Josep Bartolí, *Campos de concentración, 1939–194...* (Mexico City: Iberia, 1944), 13. All further references in this chapter to this book will be made parenthetically in the body of the text.
2. Edmundo Domínguez has explained that then prime minister and minister of defense Francisco Largo Caballero appropriated the five-pointed star, inspired by the Communist insignia, as a badly needed unifying official emblem for the Republican army during the early days of the civil war: "The emblem became popular, and it also lent uniformity to our Army, that in the early days stood out for the diversity of its emblems and insignias. The five-pointed star later lacked partisan overtones, it was a clear and simple emblem that the Army became fond of," *Los vencedores de Negrín* (Mexico City: Editorial Nuestro Pueblo, 1940), 273–74.
3. Manuel Valldeperes, *Ombres entre tenebres (L'exode de Catalunya)* (Buenos Aires: Edicions de la Revista Catalunya, 1941), 105.
4. Mistral, *Éxodo*, 109.
5. Adolfo Ballano Bueno, prologue, in Giménez Igualada, *Más allá del dolor*, 10–11.
6. Montseny, *El éxodo*, 55.
7. Ibid.
8. The aged World War I hero Marshal Pétain—France's first ambassador to Franco's Spain in 1939 and later the puppet head of the state of Vichy France during the Nazi occupation—is represented in the concentration camp literature generally as the object of scorn and ridicule. Ironically, supporters of the Republic during the civil war had cited stories of Pétain's inspiring leadership in the Battle of Verdun to bolster their

flagging spirits; see for example exile Ramón López Barrantes's recollection in *Mi exilio (1939–1951)* (Madrid: G. Del Toro, 1974), 77. The image of the Venus de Milo included in this drawing recalls a photograph published in the February 1940 issue of *Romance* in Mexico City; the caption describing the Parisian museum workers' efforts to safeguard the Louvre's treasure from war's advancing destruction reads: "The guardians of the eternal clumsily prepare to carry the Venus de Milo to the air raid shelter," *Romance: Revista Popular Hispanoamericana*, facsimile edition, ed. Francisco Caudet (Madrid: Ediciones Turner, 1989), 13.

9. I disagree with Michael Ugarte's curious reading of the concentration camp memoirists' representation of the guards primarily as "victims": "The figure of the prison guard as victim is one of the most pervasive images in the prison camp memoirs of the Spanish Civil War," *Shifting Ground*, 235. While it is true that the inmate authors occasionally remark on the irony that both the *spahis* and the Senegalese soldiers themselves belong to a colonized people exploited by the French, the refugees' stories certainly do not portray the guards as fellow sufferers or fellow victims. Of the *spahis*, for example, one survivor has said: "For the internees, the *spahis* were a reminder of the Moors that Franco had brought to Spain to kill Spaniards; naturally, we despised them," Juan Carrasco, *La odisea*, 98; of the Senegalese, camp veteran Eulalio Ferrer has stated, "Of all of the humiliations that we endured, none was more painful that the ones that those savages forced upon us, taking revenge for their own humiliations. The shame of a colonized existence, of having been treated like inferior beings," *Entre alambradas*, 77.

10. An eerie parallel to this scene of the starving Spanish *vencidos* in concentration camps suffering under the scrutiny of French gendarmes is the predicament of Spanish Republican prisoners living in Franco's jails during this very same time period. Faustina García de Castro, who spent more than twelve years imprisoned in Spain before emigrating to France, describes kitchen detail under the nun-wardens' watchful eye in the women's prison outside of Santander: "When they got potatoes occasionally and ordered the women to peel them, two nuns stood guard so that the women wouldn't eat them raw. If someone lifted a morsel to her lips, she was punished by being deprived of her meal and going without a piece of bread for the day. That day she only had the right to sing El Cara al Sol [*sic*], the Fascist hymn, which we had to sing before each meal," Macdonald, *Homage to the Spanish Exiles*, 231.

11. Artís-Gener, *La diáspora republicana*, 59. This unpleasant reality was improbably put to music in one of the most popular songs that came out of the camp of Argelès-sur-Mer, "Argelès . . . Argelès" (to the tune of "Esta noche me emborracho" (Tonight I'm Getting Drunk); the closing stanza reads, "Y hoy que ni cagar podemos / sin que venga un 'mohamé'/ nos tratan como penados / y nos gritan los soldados / *allez, allez*. . . ." [And today we can't even take a crap / without Mohammed there / they treat us like criminals / the soldiers scream at us / *get going, get going*. . . .]), Eulalio Ferrer, *Entre alambradas*, 240.

12. Serra, *Memorias de un trashumante*, 80.

13. Mistral, *Eaaodo*, 139. The phantasms produced by the unhappy combination of hunger and violence that Mistral describes haunt as well the fitful slumber described by Lluís Ferran de Pol in his memoir about St. Cyprien. The author records a surreal nightmare based on the early system of food distribution actually used by the guards, that of tossing loaves of bread willy-nilly off the back of a truck to a starving mob: "Slices of bread fall, so thin that the wind blows them away. They swirl above our heads and we follow their unpredictable path, determined to catch one. . . . We are no longer men; we are a starving pack of wild dogs, with our snouts raised to the skies. . . . All of a sudden, the black guard's bayonet turns into a cracking whip that comes after us. . . .

I throw myself on the black man and bite his hand. . . . I wake up with my blanket between my teeth," Lluís Ferran de Pol, *De lluny i de prop* (Barcelona: Selecta, 1973), quoted in Artís-Gener, *La diáspora republicana*, 77–78.

14. García Gerpe, *Alambradas*, 40.
15. Cabruja, *La ciudad de madera*, 137.
16. Luis Suárez, *España comienza en los Pirineos* (Mexico City: I. C. D., 1944), 97.
17. Antonio Pérez García ("Mario Zapata"), a Republican veteran who emigrated to Mexico in 1962, spent fourteen years in the Burgos jail; a posthumous memoir was published in 1983 that documented life, and death, in this prison; see Mario Zapata, *Burgos 1940–53: Cárcel de la dictadura franquista* (Mexico City: Publicaciones Mexicanas, 1983). A May 10, 1939, article in the *Diario de Burgos* entitled "How Franco's Justice is Administered" alludes to the massive scale of political retribution swiftly carried out inside jails like the hometown prison: "A fortnight after the Liberation the number of courts martial has already grown from 100 to 200 a day, and it is soon expected to be 300 and possibly 400. . . . There are more than 1,200,000 index cards . . . all of which were checked before we arrived in Madrid, and made out after scrupulously careful work among the thousands of prisoners captured during the course of the war," quoted in Julio Alvarez del Vayo's 1940 memoir *Freedom's Battle*, trans. Eileen E. Brooke (New York: Hill & Wang, 1971), 331. Prison house firing squads were responsible for thousands of executions in Spain, especially during the postwar months of 1939.
18. Machado, *Poesías completas*, 567.
19. Ibid., 568.
20. Cabruja, *La ciudad de madera*, 107, 108.
21. Mistral, *Éxodo*, 97.
22. García Gerpe, *Alambradas*, 79.
23. Nelken, *Los de Collioure*, 29–30.
24. Ibid., 160. Cándido, along with elder brothers Francisco and Julio Souza Fernández, and close friends Pablo and Faustino del Castillo Cubillo (the latter also an inmate of the Collioure prison) would establish Hermanos Mayo in Mexico City. For an excellent history of the life and work of the famed photographers, see the exhibit catalog *Foto Hermanos Mayo* (Valencia: Institut Valencia d'Art Modern, 1992). In the spring and summer of 2002, the work of the Hermanos Mayo was featured in an exhibit at the Museo Nacional del Arte in the Spanish exiles' adopted hometown of Mexico City.
25. Nelken, *Los de Collioure*, 147.
26. Ibid., 169.
27. Amieva, *Asturianos*, 58.
28. *L'Humanité* (26 March 1939), quoted in Suárez, *España comienza*, 165.
29. Antonio Mije, *Los refugiados españoles en Francia y la solidaridad americana* (Mexico City: Editorial Morelos, 1940), 7.
30. Soriano, *Éxodos*, 176–77.
31. Amieva, *Asturianos*, 69. An earlier newpaper article in *L'Humanité* dated February 17, 1939, recounted just such an individual act of desperation, also at a train station: "Yesterday afternoon, at the station in Bayonne, a Spanish soldier named Francisco Moreno, about 40 years old, who was being taken to Irún, asked permission to get off the train for a few minutes. As soon as he was on the ground, he threw himself under the wheels of a convoy that was passing by. The poor man was being transported, against his will, to Francoist territory," quoted in Suárez, *España comienza*, 165.
32. Mistral, *Éxodo*, 100.
33. Giménez Igualada, *Más allá*, 148. This anecdote brings to mind the circumstances surrounding the well-known death of Walter Benjamin less than one year later who, fleeing the German Nazis in 1940 and despairing of being allowed to cross the Spanish border, committed suicide in the French border town of Port-Bou.

34. *L'Humanité* (Marhc 18, 1939), quoted in Suárez, *España comienza*, 164.
35. Ferrer, *Entre alambradas*, 174.
36. Ibid., 175.
37. García Gerpe, *Alambradas*, 134.
38. Cabruja, *La ciudad de madera*, 44.
39. Mistral, *Éxodo*, 102.
40. Amieva, *Asturianos*, 41.
41. Soriano, *Exodos*, 138. Rafaneau-Boj cites additional examples of the encoded contents of the letters mailed to the camp internees from home, including the following: "'You could work in the field not far from the house; they're hiring a lot of people;' now, the only field nearby was the 'Bota field,' where they still executed the people condemned to death by the military tribunals," *Los campos de concentración*, 150. Cruz y Gómez recalls the message his family sent from Segovia to let his father in a camp know that it was safe to come back to Spain: "'The baby is doing better and you shouldn't worry about her health.' My father knew what that meant and he signed up with the next group to be sent home," *Mis campos de concentración*, 166. For one of the most complete collections of letters written by Spanish refugees interned in the camps, see "Des dels camps. Cartes des refugiats i internats al Migdia Francés l'any 1939," ed. Francesc Vilanova i Vila-Abadal, *Quaderns de l'Arxiu Pi i Sunyer* 3 (1998). I am grateful to Oriol Pi-Sunyer for this reference.
42. López Barrantes, *Mi exilio*, 185.
43. Without a doubt, the most unique legacy of one of the concentration camp prisoners' most popular pasttimes—carving pieces of wood, soap, or bone into figurines—must be the massive scale model of Paris's Notre Dame cathedral made entirely out of bones by Argelès-sur-Mer veteran Antonio Gómez Baños. This former Republican civil war aviator, who lost both legs during the war, explained in a 1967 interview where he learned to work with his unusual medium: "I had seen a boy who had made a little model of Notre Dame de Lourdes out of wood and that made me think, because in the concentration camps we had amused ourselves by making things out of bones," Macdonald, *Homage to the Spanish Exiles*, 216. In her book of interviews with Spanish exiles living in France, Macdonald includes a photograph of the stunningly intricate model, detailed with incredible accuracy, completed by Gómez Baños at his home in Perpignan in 1953.
44. Bravo-Tellado, *El peso de la derrota*, 107.
45. Carrasco, *La odisea*, 100. Paco Ibáñez, son of Spanish exiles who spent years in Perpignan listening to his father's friends' memories of civil war and concentration camps, relates that the single most frequently recounted anecdote from the veterans' days in Argelès-sur-Mer was the story of the man who walked out to sea; see his account in Grando, *Vous avez la mémoire courte*, 251.
46. Giménez Igualada, *Más allá*, 10.
47. Bartolí and Fábrega's fellow exile to Mexico, Manuel Benavides, also develops the notion of Spain-as-Prophet as a central trope in his 1942 novel of France on the verge of world war, *Los nuevos profetas*. In Paris, his protagonist Luis Alfonso advises the weak and sickly Madame Europa to draw strength of will and clarity of purpose from the example of the Spanish Republic embroiled in the fight against fascism: "Go to Spain. . . . Spain is full of prophets. . . . All Spanish Republicans are prophets. And all of Spain is a prophecy," Manuel Benavides, *Los nuevos profetas* (Mexico City: Colección Luz Sobre España, 1942), 103.
48. This notion that the Republic's fallen—whether on the battlefields or in the land of exile—will nurture and sustain that nation's rebirth in the future is a recurring motif in civil war literature; see the novel *Cruces sin Cristo* written shortly after the war's end

by another exile in Mexico, José Gomís Soler, in which a Republican soldier condemned to die in a Falange jail exhorts his imprisoned comrades to keep the faith; their deaths today will nourish the political ideals that will come to fruition tomorrow: "'Comrades!' shouted the journalist. 'Salud to all . . . In order for the seed to bear fruit, you have to bury it. We are a ferocious seed that one day will yield a rich harvest,'" (Mexico City: Compañía General de Ediciones, 1952), 163. I am grateful to Roberto Ruiz for bringing Gomís Soler's novel to my attention.

49. In his 1959 memoir, Gustav Regler, former inmate of the brutal Vernet camp, has used strikingly similar language to describe that place: "Vernet was an eerie cemetery. The huts stood like great coffins on the plain. Every morning the dead crept out of their graves to form up in rigid squares, a pathetic soldiery, and then, under the orders of uniformed men, went about the work of clearing paths, digging drains, stopping up rat-holes, burning foul straw and cleaning their coffins. It was a busy scene, as though someone had taken the lid off a churchyard to watch the dead at their squalid employments. But sometimes one of the dead, unable to endure the cemetery, would kill himself a second time. When we cut him down from the beam from which he hung we had a feeling of picking a ripe fruit, and we felt something like envy when we laid him to rest in the real cemetery of the camp," *The Owl of Minerva*, 334.

50. Javier Rubio, "Política francesa de acogida: los campos de internamiento," in Cuesta and Bermejo, *Emigración y exilio*, 112. See, among many other detailed descriptions written by former internees of physical attacks on the hated guards: Amieva, *Asturianos*, 17; Bravo-Tellado, *El peso de la derrota*, 127–28; Ferrer, *Entre alambradas*, 76–77, and *Páginas del exilio*, 50–51; Espinar, *Argelès-Sur-Mer*, 102; Renau, *Pasos y sombras*, 425; and Vicente Fillol, *Los perdedores: memorias de un exiliado español* (Madrid: Ediciones "Gaceta Ilustrada," 1973), 10. Even the *falangista* journalist José Esteban Vilaró includes accounts of the murder of camp guards in his 1939 diatribe against the Republican refugees, *El ocaso de los dioses rojos*, 215–17.

Chapter 4. Max Aub's *Morir por cerrar los ojos*

1. Said, "Invention, Memory, Place," 184.
2. Yossi Shain, *The Frontier of Loyalty: Political Exiles in the Age of the Nation-State* (Middletown, Conn.: Wesleyan University Press, 1989), 71.
3. Elazar Barkan and Marie-Denise Shelton, eds., Introduction, *Borders, Exiles, Diasporas* (Stanford: Stanford University Press, 1998), 4.
4. José-María Naharro-Calderón, "De 'Cadahalso 34' a *Manuscrito Cuervo*: el retorno de las alambradas," in *Manuscrito Cuervo: Historia de Jacobo*, by Max Aub, ed. José Antonio Pérez Bowie (Segorbe: Fundación Max Aub, 1999), 187. For chilling eyewitness accounts of life in Vernet d'Ariège, see the exiled Hungarian national Arthur Koestler's 1941 memoir *Scum of the Earth* (New York: Macmillan Company); Bruno Weil's 1941 *Francia a través de las alambradas: La caída de Francia, la vida en los campos de concentración* (Buenos Aires: Editorial Claridad), as well as Gustav Regler's chapter "The Undesirables" in his autobiography *The Owl of Minerva*, 331–54. Aub's own allegorical depiction based on his confinement in Vernet, *Manuscrito Cuervo*, was first published in Mexico City in four installments of his journal *Sala de espera*, between November 1949 and February 1950.
5. Naharro-Calderón, "De 'Cadahalso 34,'" 187–88.
6. The extraordinary archival documentation related to Luis Rodríguez's campaign to aid thousands of Spanish refugees in their efforts to emigrate to Mexico has been published; see *Misión de Luis I. Rodríguez en Francia: La protección de los refugiados españoles*,

julio a diciembre de 1940 (Mexico City: El Colegio de Mexico/Secretaría de Relaciones Exteriores/Consejo Nacional de Ciencia y Tecnología, 2000) for a fascinating account of the world of Spanish refugees in France during the first months following Hitler's invasion of the country.

    7. Luis I. Rodríguez, in *Ballet de sangre: la caída de Francia*, prologue by Pablo Neruda (Mexico City: Ediciones Nigromante, 1942), 1; Max Aub, *Morir por cerrar los ojos*, 2d. ed. (Barcelona: Aymá, 1967), 72. All subsequent references to these two works are given parenthetically in the text.

    8. Max Aub, "El turbión metafísico," in *Hablo como hombre* (Mexico City: Joaquín Mortiz, 1967), 17.

    9. Donald Shaw, "La búsqueda de la autenticidad en *Morir por cerrar los ojos*," in *Max Aub y el laberinto español*, vol. 1 (Valencia: Universidad de Valencia–Fundación Max Aub, 1996), 321.

    10. Juan's sentiment is echoed in the words included in the first edition of the play, Aub's dedication: "To the disloyal lackeys who invented nonintervention, Neville Chamberlain, Edouard Daladier, León Blum, whose hands are stained with so much noble Spanish blood. With the contempt of all of us, we submit the evidence of their betrayal, for which their people paid so dearly," *Morir por cerrar los ojos* (Mexico City: Ediciones Tezontle, 1944), 9.

    11. Hitler's wartime propaganda offices published their own sarcastic reference to the so-called impenetrability of the Maginot Line in a 1940 pamphlet, quickly translated into Spanish and reissued as *La campaña de Francia: 10 de mayo–23 de junio de 1940*. The forty-six-page summary of Hitler's triumphant entry into Paris features a photograph of a bombed-out section of the famed fortifications, with the understated caption, "The Maginot Line is broken" (Berlin: E. Zander, 1940), 22.

    12. The play *El rapto de Europa* that Aub published a couple of years after the appearance of *Morir por cerrar los ojos* would develop one of the writer's most enduring themes, the moral duty to act in solidarity on the behalf of others; the subtitle of this 1946 play, *o siempre se puede hacer algo* (Or, You Can Always Do Something) serves as a response to Julio's cowardly excuse for his passivity: "there's nothing we can do" (*Morir*, 110).

    13. Arthur Koestler dedicates his above-cited memoir of the camp of Vernet to the memory of real-life antifascist German writers like the fictitious von Ruhn: "To the memory of my colleagues, the exiled writers of Germany who took their lives when France fell: Walter Benjamin, Carl Einstein, Walter Hasenclever, Irmgard Keun, Otto Pobl, Ernst Weiss," *Scum of the Earth*.

    14. From the collection of short stories *No son cuentos (cuentos)* (Mexico City: Ediciones Tezontle, 1944), published in the same year as the play, see especially "Manuel, el de la Font" and "Yo no invento nada," both of which were written in 1942. From the collection *Ciertos cuentos* (Mexico City: Antigua Librería Robredo, 1955), see "Vernet, 1940"; "Historia de Vidal"; "Los creyentes"; "Un traidor."

    15. See Aub's lyrical document of his experience of the camp of Djelfa, *Diario de Djelfa* (Mexico City, 1944), also published in Mexico City during the same year as *Morir por cerrar los ojos*. For a vigorous early condemnation of the North African camps, see *Le martyre des antifascistes dans les camps de concentration de l'Afrique du Nord*, preface by Virgile Barel (Algiers: Secours Populaire Algerien, 1945), published in Algiers one year after Aub's works.

    16. On the tendency of foreign soldier-memoirists from the International Brigades to idealize Republican Spain and its defenders, see Noël Valis's commentary of George Orwell's *Homage to Catalonia*, a text, she argues, in which the Englishman creates a "new-old myth," "the dream of universal man, founded on the ideals of fraternity, equality and liberty," in "Nostalgia and Exile," *Journal of Spanish Cultural Studies* 1, no. 2 (2000), 125.

17. A twist on Aub's central dramatic trope of *ceguera* to describe the European democracies' attitude toward the implications of Spain's civil war is veteran (and one of the infamous blacklisted "Hollywood ten" of the McCarthy era) Alvah Bessie's 1939 reference to the idealism of fellow foreign *brigadistas* who flocked to the Republic's defense: "You felt: many of these men will never see their friends or families again; they don't know what they're getting into; their idealism has blinded them to the reality of what they will have to face. And you knew immediately that you were wrong; that they were so far from being blind that it might be said of them that they were among the first soldiers in the history of the world who really knew what they were about, what they were going to fight for—and that they were ready and eager to fight. Their very presence on the French frontier was an earnest [*sic*] of their understanding and their clarity . . . ," *Men in Battle* (San Francisco: Chandler & Sharp Publishers, 1985), 13. Bessie repeatedly mentions marching to the "Marseillaise" in his *Men in Battle*, 34, 35, 45. For a recent publication of the diary entries on which Bessie based his 1939 memoir, see his son Dan Bessie's edition of *Alvah Bessie's Spanish Civil War Notebooks* (Lexington: University of Kentucky Press, 2002).

Chapter 5. Imagining Paris

1. Gregorio Marañón, prologue to *Cómo viven los españoles en París*, by Marcial Retuerto (Paris: La Cámara Oficial de Comercio de España, 1941), 7.
2. Ibid., 10.
3. Mistral, *Exilio*, 109, 110.
4. Ibid., 78–79.
5. Ferrer, *Entre alambradas*, 99.
6. Ibid., 107, 124; see also 101, 104, 109, 113, 120, 131, 145, 147.
7. Ibid., 148.
8. For a critical study of Herrera's life and work, see Jesús Gálvez Yagüe's *José Herrera Petere: vida, compromiso político y literatura* (Sigüenza: Ediciones de Librería Rayuela, 2000); for commentary of *Niebla de cuernos* as well as a partial review of the literature about the novel, see 113–24. Gálvez Yagüe, with José Esteban, also published a 2002 edition of the novel, in the Biblioteca del exilio series in Spain (Sada: Ediciós do Castro).
9. Antonio Sánchez Barbudo, *"Niebla de cuernos," Letras de México* 15 (June 1940): 4.
10. Juan Rejano, "A los alcances de la novela," *España Peregrina* (July 15, 1940), facsimile edition (Mexico City: Ed. Alejandro Finisterre, 1977), 261.
11. *Herrera Petere: artículos publicados en* El Nacional-*México*, ed. Narciso Alba (Madrid: Ediciones de la Torre, 1996), 213; José Herrera Petere, *Niebla de cuernos* (Mexico City: Séneca, 1940), 197. Further references to this edition of the novel will be made parenthetically in the text.
12. Certainly the best-known Spanish exile literary text that is formally organized according to the superimposition of the places of civil war Spain with the spaces of 1939 prewar Paris is Herrera Petere's close friend Rafael Alberti's poem, "Vida bilingüe de un refugiado español en Francia (1939–1940)," in *Poesías completas* (Buenos Aires: Editorial Losada, 1961), originally published in 1942; a short fragment of the lengthy poem first appeared in Mexico City in the June 15, 1940, issue of the exile journal *Romance*. Alberti's refugee narrator, like Herrera Petere's, comes face-to-face with France's reluctance to recognize the political implications of Spain's tragedy for its own future:

"—Las cuestiones de España / no interesan, monsieur," [—The matters of Spain / are of no interest, monsieur], "Vida bilingüe," 431.

13. The sumptuous Parisian settings that provide the backdrop for much of Herrera Petere's narrative invite comparisons with those found in Salvador Dalí's novel *Hidden Faces*, published in 1944. Dalí's aristocratic French protagonist, the Count of Grandsailles, maintains one of his houses in Paris's Bois de Boulogne, an exclusive residential area in which Herrera Petere's wealthy Frenchman Jehoel du Bois Sanglant equally finds himself at home. While the world of prewar Parisian decadence and effete aestheticism evoked in Herrera Petere's novel is recreated as well in Dalí's work, the famous painter certainly does not include as counterpoint the anguished plight of the Spanish Republicans in exile that figures so prominently in the earlier novel.

14. It should be noted that several of the civil war songs included in Ernst Busch's edition of *Canciones de las Brigadas Internacionales*, published in Barcelona in 1938, have lyrics penned by Herrera Petere himself; see Santiago Álvarez's 1996 volume on the International Brigades for selected reprints of some of these songs, which include "Marcha del V Regimiento," "Canción del Frente Popular," and "Caballería del Don," *Historia política y militar de las Brigadas Internacionales* (Madrid: Compañía Literaria, 1996). Álvarez himself, a close friend of Herrera Petere throughout the civil war, emigrated to La Habana before returning to Franco's Spain as a resistance fighter, where he was promptly imprisoned. In Mexico in 1945, Herrera Petere published a moving profile of his courageous war companion entitled "Santiago Álvarez," *Herrera Petere*, 299–301. The similarities between the real-life "Santiaguiño" Álvarez, a fearless, even jovial combatant of the Ebro campaign, and the plainspoken, spirited fictionalized Ebro veteran "Saturnino" Fragoso, who accompanies Herrera Petere's narrator in Paris, are noteworthy.

15. Aub, *El rapto de Europa*, 29.

16. Janet Kaplan, *Unexpected Journeys: The Art and Life of Remedios Varo* (New York: Abbeville Press, 1988), 69. Just as Péret has left this record of his memory of that dramatic, emotional separation from Varo in wartime Paris, I suggest that Varo as well documented this poignant moment of farewell in her painting *La despedida* (The Farewell), in *Remedios Varo: Catálogo razonado/catalogue raisonné* (Mexico City: Ediciones Era, 1994), 155; all subsequent references to Varo's paintings cited parenthetically in the text refer to this collection of her work. Two receding silhouettes of a man and a woman disappear through the same brick streets that appear time and again in Bartolí's and Varo's representations of Parisian avenues; the painting is completed during the same period as the other "Paris" paintings analyzed in this chapter. The woman's loyal companion, the cat that keeps her fugitive mistress company in so many of the paintings I attribute to the Paris years of 1939–41, peers out from the safety of a darkened alleyway. The shadows that the separated lovers leave behind seek out one another in memory's embrace.

17. Kaplan, *Unexpected Journeys*, 70.

18. Walter Gruen, "Remedios Varo: A Biographical Sketch," *The Magic of Remedios Varo* (Washington, D.C.: National Museum of Women in the Arts, 2000), 144.

19. A similar street scene is seen in *Banqueros en acción* (Bankers in Action); four identical men in black fly through the air, passing a crouching woman who hides from them on the other side of a walled passageway (*Remedios Varo*, 214). In *Caminos tortuosos* (Torturous Roads), it is the woman who races through the bricked street on a curious kind of unicyle; unfortunately, like her counterpart in *Locomoción capilar*, she too becomes trapped in the tentacle-like whiskers of the sinister black figure lying in wait for her around the corner (138).

20. Victoria Kent, *Cuatro años en París (1940–1944)* (Buenos Aires: Ediciones Sur,

1947); all subsequent references to this edition of the novel will be made parenthetically in the text. Although Victoria Kent did not settle in Mexico like the majority of the other Spanish Republican writers whose work I analyze in this book (she was, however, a member of Mexico City's Ateneo Español de México, according to membership records), I have made the exception of including Kent's novel as a primary text since it provides such a unique document of the Spanish refugee perspective of the world of Paris throughout all the years of World War II.

21. When the SERE offices themselves are the object of a police raid in December 1939, Manuel García Gerpe (a recent escapee from the Septfonds camp) refers to the *razzia* that results in his arrest: "With a big show of it, as if in a film, the 'police' burst into the offices of the SERE," *Alambradas*, 186. A character of Max Aub's 1946 play *El rapto de Europa* similarly describes a fellow character's tale of the police persecution of foreigners in 1941 France in terms of cinematic scenes lifted from the flickering big screen productions of detective stories: "He described it like a plot out a detective film. Escapes. Persecutions. Clandestine departures. A soap opera . . . ," *El rapto de Europa*, 59.

22. Shirley Mangini, *Memories of Resistance: Women's Voices from the Spanish Civil War* (New Haven: Yale University Press, 1995), 159.

23. For historical background and first-person testimony regarding Spanish Republican involvement in both the earliest days of the French Resistance movement as well as World War II military campaigns, see Artís-Gener, *La diáspora republicana*, 131–81; Carrasco, *La odisea*, 179–209; Cuesta and Bermejo, *Emigración y exilio*, 243–77; Alberto Fernández, *Emigración republicana española (1939–1945)* (Madrid: Lee y Discute, 1972); Fillol, *Los perdedores*; Eduardo Pons Prades, *Republicanos españoles en la Segunda Guerra Mundial* (Barcelona: Planeta, 1975); the October 1999 special issue of *Trébede: Mensual Aragonés de Análisis, Opinión y Cultura*, entitled *El maquis, 60 años después*. The most all-encompassing study is Secundino Serrano's excellent *Maquis: Historia de la guerrilla antifranquista* (Madrid: Ediciones Temas de Hoy, 2001). See Neus Catalá's *De la resistencia y la deportación: 50 testimonios de mujeres españolas* (Barcelona: Ediciones Península, 2000), for dozens of Spanish women's personal accounts of their role in the Resistance.

24. Kaplan, *Unexpected Journeys*, 69.

25. Koestler, *Scum of the Earth*, 36, 57, 66–67.

26. Ibid., 94–95. Another foreign national interned in the same camp of Vernet, Bruno Weil, repeatedly refers to the camp as a "League of Nations" in miniature, in his 1941 memoir published the same year as Koestler's, *Francia a través de las alambradas*.

27. Regler, *The Owl of Minerva*, 331.

28. Ibid., 333.

29. *Romance*, 20.

30. Benavides, *Los nuevos profetas*, 202. Further references to the novel will be made parenthetically in the text.

31. Agreeing with President Manuel Azaña's published statement that the Spanish refugees were treated "worse than animals" in France, the historian Javier Rubio has explained that in mid-February 1939 "when the situation of hundreds of thousands of Spaniards in the camps in the Eastern Pyrenees was especially desperate," the French ambassador in London was trying to help arrange the trip of a British medical relief team that was anxious to visit the region. Ironically, the group was comprised of veterinarians sponsored by the Royal Society for the Prevention of Cruelty to Animals; a February 16 letter from the Society to the ambassador indicates that the mission had arrived in Perpignan and was already tending "the great suffering" of the Spanish horses and mules that had crossed the border. Rubio concludes: "Nevertheless, in this stack of French documents concerning the Spanish refugees, we haven't found any evi-

dence that England sent a group of professionals to France in order to alleviate the pain and suffering of other Spanish animals, the rational ones," "Política francesa de acogida," 104.

32. A similar commemorative pattern of paying tribute to the victims of war and exile may be seen in the concluding chapter, "Death," of Max Aub's 1943 civil war novel *Campo cerrado*. In a three-page list dated August 17, 1939, the narrator enumerates the names of personages cited in the novel who figure among the war dead; who were interned in the French refugee camps; who remain in Franco's jail; who have been executed; or who are among the missing. In the final image of the book, reminiscent of the scene cited in Benavides's novel, the echoes of the name of one more disappeared blow in from the sea, "[Marieta] is the only one who sometimes on Saturday nights, when she feels the sea breeze, remembers Rafael López Serrador: What must have become of him? In the distance a dog barks," *Campo cerrado* (Mexico City: Tezontle, 1943), 257.

33. Compare Benavides's 1942 statement with that made by a longtime champion of the Spanish Republicans' cause, the French Nobel laureate Albert Camus, in his 1944 essay "Our Brothers in Spain": "This European war that began in Spain eight years ago, cannot end without Spain" (*¡España Libre!*, 19). This article, published less than two weeks after the Allied forces' liberation of Paris (with Spanish Republican *maquis*' participation), was the first of ten essays published by Camus in the journal *Combat* throughout a one-year period in an impassioned series that urged the Allied governments to work against Franco's regime in order to support the reinstatement of the democratic Spanish Republic now in exile; a December 1944 article, for example, stated: "The day that the Allies publicly recognize that the Spanish Republican government represents the true Spain, that day there will be no more doubt, the nightmare will be over and the liberation of Spain will follow" [32]).

Chapter 6. Luis Suárez's *España comienza en los Pirineos*

1. Giménez Igualada, *Más allá del dolor*, 157. A fellow Spanish refugee, María José de Chopitea, similarly invoked with irony the well-worn slogan of European superiority/Spanish inferiority in her autobiographical novel published in Mexico in 1954, *Sola*. Describing her group's border crossing at Perthus, the narrator referred to the presence of the French colonial troops who unceremoniously received the Spaniards: "Huge black-faced soldiers stopped us . . . 'Africa begins in the Pyrenees?,' I thought, 'Here or there? . . . because as we fled the Moors, we passed through a border checkpoint manned by colossal Senegalese, armed with rifles and bayonets at the ready . . .'" *Sola* (Mexico City: Premiá Editora, 1979), 107.

2. Giménez Igualada, *Más allá*, 157.

3. See Luis Suárez's 2000 memoir, *Puente sin fin* (Mexico City: Grijalbo), for highlights of his illustrious career as an international journalist and political author. The indefatigable Suárez, who served as president of the Federation of Latin American Journalists (headquartered in Mexico City), was completing two books on well-known Mexican politicians Cuauhtémoc Cárdenas and Luis Echeverría at the time of his death in 2003.

4. Suárez, *España comienza en los Pirineos* (1944), 194.

5. Cuauhtémoc Cárdenas, presentación, *España comienza en los Pirineos*, by Luis Suárez (Mexico City: Pangea, 1987), 9.

6. André Simone, *"J'accuse!": The Men Who Betrayed France* (New York: Dial Press, 1940), 180.

7. Ibid., 190.

8. Jacques Maritain, *France My Country: Through the Disaster* (New York: Longmans, Green and Co., 1941), 8.

9. Ibid., 9. Maritain's term "international civil war" for the European conflict brings to mind a phrase made popular by Luis Suárez's fellow exile in the St. Cyprien camp and fellow passenger on board the ship *Sinaia* bound for Mexico, the writer Manuel Andújar. Andújar preferred to refer to the Spanish war as a "guerra incivil-internacional," according to the editor of the reprint of Andújar's 1942 camp memoir, Antonio Mancheño Ferreras; see his "Epílogo. Biobibliografía," in *St. Cyprien, plage . . . campo de concentración*, by Manuel Andújar (Huelva: Diputación Provincial de Huelva, 1990), 124. Mexico's representative to the League of Nations during Spain's war, Isidro Fabela, had long argued against the policy of nonintervention precisely on the grounds of the international dimension of the "civil" war; Fabela remarks in 1940: "The League never acknowledged the undeniable truth of foreign aggression that Spain suffered at the hands of Germany and Italy. It always treated the war on the Peninsula as a civil war, and not both a civil and international war, which it truly was," *Neutralidad. Estudio histórico, jurídico y político: la Sociedad de las Naciones y el continente americano ante la guerra de 1939–1940* (Mexico City: Biblioteca de Estudios Internacionales, 1940), 254.

10. Maritain, *France My Country*, 48. In a review written in 1941 shortly after the appearance of the Spanish edition of Maritain's book (*A través del desastre*, published by Ercilla in Santiago de Chile), Waldo Frank offers his own negative assessment of the moral fiber of the French nation vis-à-vis the Spanish Republic: "In 1938 I came back from Barcelona. I arrived in Perpignan on a Sunday morning: the honorable French people crowded into the cafés, fat and happy, in the shadow of the Spanish tragedy. Everyone knew what was going on, and they said: 'Am I my brother's keeper?' For so many weeks I had been dreaming about white bread, butter, cold beer, a dream that would come true in France. I sat down among some well-nourished Frenchmen and I placed *my dream order* with the waiter. I left without touching the food. At that moment, feeling sick and full of foreboding, I realized that Europe would never match Spain's sacrifice because the French nation wasn't worth saving," *España Peregrina*, 61.

11. Francis Martel, *Pétain: Verdun to Vichy* (New York: E. P. Dutton, 1943), 98.

12. Ibid., 120.

13. Ibid., 134.

14. Henry Torres, *Campaign of Treachery* (New York: Dodd, Mead and Company, 1942), 110.

15. Ibid., 215.

16. Simone, *"J'accuse!,"* 297.

17. David McLellan, *Utopian Pessimist: The Life and Thought of Simone Weil* (New York: Poseidon Press, 1990), 164.

18. René de Chambrun, *I Saw France Fall: Will She Rise Again?* (New York: William Morrow & Company, 1940), 202.

19. Elie Bois, *Truth on the Tragedy of France*, trans. Scarlyn Wilson (London: Hodder and Stoughton Ltd., 1941); Bois's infamous *Petit Parisien* quotation is cited by Luis Suárez, *España comienza en los Pirineos* (1944), 100. Further references to Suárez's memoir (1944) in this chapter will be made parenthetically in the text.

20. Nelken, prólogo, *Los de Collioure*, 9.

21. Suárez's international bridge will soon be traversed—ironically, in the opposite direction—by the very "noninterventionist" French patriots who will have occasion to flee Nazi-threatened France as refugees themselves. René de Chambrun (whose account includes a three-month assignment on the infamous Maginot Line) stubbornly touts France's impenetrability even as he races over the bridge at the Irún—Hendaye border to board a ship in Lisbon on June 9, 1940: "As we crossed France from Paris

to Spain . . . we could not help but feel confident that our army could and would block the Nazi drive into France. . . . I drove with my wife across the bridge and through the ruins of Irún. When we reached the station we got the news that the Battle of France had begun. . . . Two or three days later, at Forges les Eaux, the German tanks and armored cars broke through," *I Saw France Fall*, 187. Staunchly conservative André Maurois reports his wife's border crossing as an unexpectedly eye-opening experience: "On the evening of June seventeenth when she was crossing the international bridge from Hendaye to Irún my wife encountered French *douaniers* who were weeping. 'But why, Madame,' they said, 'have we been beaten?' . . . ," *Tragedy in France*, trans. Denver Lindley (New York: Harper & Bros., 1940), 184. A year before in his 1939 diary, future-exile-to-Mexico Antonio Ros had reported a May 14, 1939, conversation with French dinner companions whose naive, boastful confidence in France's invulnerability to foreign attack is met with this civil war refugee's rueful skepticism: "They believe . . . that if they build, as they are doing, sufficient anti-aircraft artillery, that the swiftly encroaching war won't bring with it aerial bombings beyond the front lines of battle. I bite my tongue and let them fantasize. Poor things!" in *Diario de un refugiado republicano* (Barcelona: Ediciones Grijalbo, 1975), 68–69.

22. Gustav Regler, a commissar in the International Brigades until his near-fatal war injury in June 1937, has described the February 1939 scene at the international bridge ("the no-man's-land between the two republics") in very similar terms. Accompanied by *New York Times* correspondent Herbert Matthews, Regler was an observer as the Republican soldiers relinquished their firearms: "As the first of them laid down his rifle I saw Matthews turn away his head. 'I can't bear to watch it,' he said. But I watched steadily, and I hope to be understood when I say that I have never felt such close feelings of comradeship for any army as I felt for those defeated soldiers of Spain. There was something of tenderness in the man's attitude as he bent down over the rifle which he was relinquishing to the 'friendly hands' of France. . . . Then came the search. . . . The Spaniards did not understand. Until the last moment they persisted in the tragic error of believing in international solidarity. 'Madrid, the capital of anti-Fascism, stronghold of courage high as mountains, and of faith deep as an abyss!' But here there was another kind of abyss. The dirty road on which the disarmed men stood was not merely the frontier between two countries, it was an abyss between two worlds," *The Owl of Minerva*, 322, 323.

23. Like almost every other element of physical adversity—including lice, scarcity of potable water, poor quality of food, inadequate shelter, lack of medical care, etc.—the primitive sleeping accommodations were the source of concentration camp black humor that circulated among the inmates. The following joke was broadcast in Suárez's St. Cyprien on November 26, 1939, as part of a daily radio program called *Altavoz* (Loudspeaker): "'Hey Juanito, where've you been hiding yourself these past few days?' 'Well, I've been standing watch in the sand *[guardando arena]*.' 'Man, I'm happy for you, so you got a job.' 'No, it's not a job, I've had a cold that's kept me from getting up and about.' 'What's that got to do with standing watch *[guardando arena]*?' 'It's simple. Don't people who take to their bed when they're sick say that they stay in bed *[guardan cama]*?*,*" *Plages d'exil*, 97.

24. Juan Negrín, "Actas de la última sesión parlamentaria de la Segunda República Española," in Bravo-Tellado, *El peso de la derrota*, 347.

25. Max Aub, "Segundo aparte," *Morir por cerrar los ojos* (1967), 70.

Chapter 7: Manuel Andújar's *St. Cyprien, plage . . .*

1. Barkan and Shelton, introduction, *Borders, Exiles, Diasporas*, 6–7.
2. Ibid., 7.

3. Ulrich Baer, "To Give Memory a Place: Holocaust Photography and the Landscape Tradition," *Representations* 69 (winter 2000): 38–62; emphasis in the original.

4. Espinar, *Argelès-Sur-Mer*, 80; Artís-Gener, *La diáspora republicana*, 77. Livestock transport trains, most notoriously used to carry millions of victims of the Holocaust to the Nazi death camps, are also used to move groups of Spanish refugees, particularly from one French concentration camp to another. Celso Amieva recalls one such sixty-six-hour journey in February 1940: "There were 750 of us. Destination unknown . . . The train cars were the kind used to transport livestock, with the sign *40 men, 8 horses*. Windowless cars, with a bit of filthy straw," *Asturianos*, 57. In a 1940 letter from the Bram camp, Giménez Igualada describes the transfer of Spanish camp inmates within France: "We created quite a stir when they transported us, like horses, in train cars, whose sign read *8 chevaux, 40 hommes*. Forty men were the equivalent of eight horses, and so it was that they loaded us up and moved us, treating us worse than animals! *Oh, la France!*" *Más allá*, 218. A variation of this term is perhaps first used in print by Spanish exile Manuel Benavides in his 1942 reference to an early wave of civil war Republicans fleeing from the Nationalist zone after the fall of Irún in September 1936: "The first group of refugees left from Hendaye for Barcelona, via Burdeos, in a World War I cargo train. Each car could hold forty men and twenty horses. Thirteen hundred people were on board, some thirty women among them," *Los nuevos profetas*, 117.

5. Palacio, *El éxodo* . . . , 69.

6. Espinar, *Argelès-Sur-Mer*, 23.

7. Vincent Berdoulay, "Place, Meaning, and Discourse in French Language Geography," *The Power of Place: Bringing Together Geographical and Sociological Imaginations*, ed. John Agnew and James Duncan (Cambridge: Unwin Hyman, 1989), 125, 136. Berdoulay, building on the French philosopher Henri Lefebvre's notion of *l'espace vécu*, stresses that meaning embedded in social networks can only unfold within a specific "lived" place: "Place is where meaning is largely being constructed, instead of simply being considered as projected from outside," ibid., 136.

8. Carrasco, *La odisea*, 82–83.

9. Espinar, *Argelès-Sur-Mer*, 26.

10. Renau, *Pasos y sombras*, 416.

11. Artís-Gener, *La diáspora republicana*, 55.

12. Ibid., 76, 77.

13. Espinar, *Argelès-Sur-Mer*, 23, 27.

14. Simon Schama, *Landscape and Memory* (New York: Alfred A. Knopf, 1995), 6.

15. Bravo-Tellado, *El peso de la derrota*, 99–100.

16. Ibid., 109.

17. *Prensa de la Segunda República en el exilio* (Tarancón: Imprenta Antona, 2000), 9.

18. García Gerpe, *Alambradas*, 65.

19. Cruz y Gómez, *Mis campos de concentración*, 134.

20. Celso Amieva, *Poeta en la arena* (Poet in the Sand) (Mexico City: Ecuador O O O, 1964), n. pag.

21. *Plages d'exil*, 54.

22. "Boletines de Argelès-sur-Mer," *Canelobre: Revista del Instituto de Estudios Juan Gil-Albert* 20–21 (1991): 162.

23. Soriano, *Exodos*, 74.

24. Ibid.

25. Kaminsky, *After Exile*, 98.

26. Grando, *Vous avez la mémoire courte*, 123.

27. Ferrer, *Entre alambradas*, 27.

28. Ibid., 195.

29. Antonio Vilanova, *Los olvidados: los exiliados españoles en la segunda guerra mundial* (Paris: Ruedo Ibérico, 1969), 9.

30. Ibid.

31. Ibid., 14. Once actual latrines were constructed in the camps, they continued to inspire and sustain creative political inscriptions. Always a popular site for graffiti, the latrine walls of concentration camps were an especially expressive surface, as Eulalio Ferrer documents in his 1939 diary, referring to the Barcarès camp outhouses: "The inscriptions aren't as common here as in Argelès, but they are certainly more entertaining. An oft-repeated one is 'To the fascists' health.' Another says 'Negrín, wish you were here.' And yet another: *Cagas, pero no la cagues,*" *Entre alambradas* (1988), 88.

32. Espinar, *Argelès-Sur-Mer*, 32. The potentially disruptive power of the refugees' songs was no laughing matter for the French *gendarmerie*, judging from a series of messages sent within the offices of the armed guards in February 1939. Fearing a kind of politically explosive contagion-by-association between the Spaniards and the French people, authorities instruct the gendarmes who escort the refugees to prohibit them from singing "L'Internationale" as they travel within France; see Grando, *Vous avez la mémoire courte . . .* , 70.

33. García Gerpe, *Alambradas*, 50.

34. Vilanova, *Los olvidados*, 11.

35. *Los de Collioure*, 58, 59.

36. Loureiro, *The Ethics of Autobiography*, 157, 151. Jorge Semprún is perhaps the most well-known Spanish Republican to have been interned in a German concentration camp. For a fascinating account of a fellow Spanish internee's incredible photographic record of life in Mauthausen, see Benito Bermejo's *Francisco Boix, el fotógrafo de Mauthausen* (Barcelona: RBA Libros, 2002).

37. As editor of the exile journal *Romance*, Juan Rejano (like Luis Suárez, Rejano was another of Manuel Andújar's fellow passengers on the ship from Sete, France, to Veracruz, Mexico, the *Sinaia*) frequently wrote of the plight of the refugees in his column "Espejo de las horas" featured in each issue; see "Paz . . ." and "Una obra . . ." Luis Zapirain devotes a section of his 1940 study to the refugee question, in which he summarizes the difficulties facing the refugees in the camps, particularly the constant threat of forced repatriation, and concludes: "Solidarity among American nations can stop this deportation as well as open up doors to the Spanish Republicans who are now in France in such dire straits," *Terror sobre España* (Mexico City: Foare, 1940), 37.

38. Manuel Andújar, *St. Cyprien, plage . . . Campo de concentración* (Mexico City: Cuadernos del Destierro, 1942). Subsequent references to this work are taken from the Spanish edition, ed. Antonio Macheño Ferreras (Huelva: Diputación Provincial de Huelva, 1990); page numbers from this edition will be given parenthetically in the text.

39. Baer, "To Give Memory a Place," 59. Michael Ugarte identifies the origin of this term as belonging to David Rousset's 1946 book *L'Univers concentrationnaire*, "Testimonios de exilio," in *El exilio de las Españas de 1939*, 49. The Spanish refugee Pere Vives i Clavé, like Andújar a former inmate of St. Cyprien, and an eventual victim of the Holocaust in the Mauthausen camp, speaks directly to the issue of language and representation in a letter written from France to his family back in Spain on November 22, 1939: "One cannot talk about the camp. You can make an inventory, you can explain what we do, but you can't talk about the camp. My earlier attempts to do so have failed because I refused to recognize my limitations," *Cartes des dels camps de concentració* (Barcelona: Edicions 62, 1972), 63. See Lea Fridman for an analysis that advocates going beyond the "rhetoric of impossibility [of representation]" posited by some scholars of concentration camp literature, and urges the study of "the 'rules' of non-representing in the attempt to gain access to 'unrepresentability'"; she notes that in some cases "the

story told is not that of the particular catastrophe but of the telling of (or failure to tell) its story," *Words and Witness: Narrative and Aesthetic Strategies in the Representation of the Holocaust* (Albany: State University of New York Press, 2000), 1, 6.

40. Naharro-Calderón, "Por los campos de Francia," 313. See also María López-Pozo's 1998 essay on *St. Cyprien, plage*, whose title summarizes the author's theoretical point of departure, "¿Sobrevive el discurso testimonial al que se le niega un referente histórico?" in Manuel Aznar Soler, ed., *El exilio literario español de 1939*, 2 vols. (Barcelona: GEXEL, 1998), 317–23.

41. The *New Yorker* reporter's March 11, 1939, description of the seaside internment camp expresses a similar perplexity about what to call what it is one is seeing in this unreal place: "What we saw was a maze, miles long, of dun-colored shapes which, when viewed close up, turned out to be white men—walking, standing, sitting on sand, sleeping on sand, breathing and eating sand as it blew on food and faces, men living by the thousands on a treeless beach, on the edge of a muddy, soiled sea," Macdonald, *Homage to the Spanish Exiles*, 97.

42. Naharro-Calderón, "Por los campos de Francia," 313.

43. Suárez, *España comienza en los Pirineos*, 193.

44. Ferrer, *Entre alambradas*, 83–84, 82, 83.

45. García Gerpe, *Alambradas*, 50.

46. Michel Foucault, "Of Other Spaces," trans. Jay Miskowiec, *Diacritics* 16, no. 1 (1986): 24. Foucault further classifies types of heterotopias, including the "crisis heterotopias, i.e., there are privileged or sacred or forbidden places, reserved for individuals who are, in relation to society and to the human environment in which they live, in a state of crisis" (24), and "heterotopias of deviation; those in which individuals whose behavior is deviant in relation to the required mean or norm are placed" (25). Foucault stresses that heterotopias "always presuppose a system of opening and closing that both isolates them and makes them penetrable. In general, the heterotopic site is not freely accessible like a public place. Either the entry is compulsory, as in the case of entering a barracks or a prison, or else the individual has to submit to rites and purifications" (26). The concentration camp, in which the "deviant" Spanish Republicans are cordoned off from the French citizens residing just on the other side of the barbed wire, is a Foucauldian heterotopia par excellence.

47. Espinar, *Argelès-Sur-Mer*, 82, 83.

48. Michel Foucault, *The Order of Things: An Archaeology of the Human Sciences* (London: Tavistock, 1970), xviii.

49. Naharro-Calderón, "Por los campos de Francia," 314. The earlier cited reference to Manuel Benavides's novelistic description of the scatologically subversive site, the "wall of shit" of Argelès-sur-Mer, is just such an example of the capacity of the imprisoned body to speak resistance; see Benavides, *Los nuevos profetas*, 280.

50. In his 1947 fictionalized account of St. Cyprien published in Mexico, camp veteran Agustí Cabruja-Auguet also depicts the oral translation of articles in French newspapers for just such a group gathering. In a chapter entitled "Oblivion," he describes the event experienced by the exiled *vencidos* as an episode of intense alterity, as they observe how their own role and point of view in their nation's history has so quickly become elided from official reports: "A young man reads and translates outloud. He goes on and on. When he finishes, a soldier says, 'You see? The papers say nothing, absolutely nothing, about the thousands and thousands of sick and forgotten Spaniards lying here in the sand. They talk about Franco, only Franco. Praise, applause, flattery. Even Pious the Twelfth blesses him and enthusiastically calls him the Phoenix of Peace and of Christianity. . . . On the other hand, not a single word of pity for the suffering, humiliated, starving people.' 'Nobody cares about the defeated. The world always turns

its attention to the great, the powerful, the influential. Now that we've lost the war, we no longer have breasts of bronze or minds guided by an Ideal.' 'We're just the Reds . . . ,' says another, sarcastically," *La ciudad de madera*, 21–22.

51. Isolated inmates' hunger for news from the outside world as illustrated in this scene was so great that even in the German death camps the prisoners put themselves at risk, as Primo Levi has recalled in a work published the year before his death in 1987: "In spite of prohibitions and the danger of being denounced to the Gestapo, on the huge work site [at Monowitz-Auschwitz] . . . in the garbage cans we found newspapers that were a few days old and read them avidly"; one companion even managed to have a German daily newspaper smuggled into the camp: "Every morning, during the long wait of roll call, he gathered us together and gave us an accurate summary of the day's news," *The Drowned and the Saved*, trans. Raymond Rosenthal (New York: Vintage International, 1988), 102.

52. Samblancat, *Caravana nazarena*,137.
53. Giménez Igualada, *Más allá*, 154.
54. Ferrer, *Entre alambradas*, 130.
55. Paul Preston, *Franco: A Biography* (New York: Basic Books, 1994), 320.
56. García Gerpe, *Alambradas*, 147.
57. *Plages d'exil*, 72.
58. Describing one of the art exhibits organized in the camp by the internees, former inmate Juan Renau has referred to the individual creations as the tangible forms of the spirit and the memory of a nation: "The themes are anecdotal. They generally refer to the daily events of a pleasant, normal life before the war; to loved ones; to emotionally charged scenes from a private past. The lost homeland breathes life into those paltry pieces of paper," (*Pasos y sombras*, 422).

59. This incongruous "arco . . . triunfal" that leads into the hellish environs of the civil war *vencidos* was similarly observed by fellow Catalan inmate Roc d'Almenara; writing of his entry into St. Cyprien on September 15, 1939, d'Almenara states: "We went under the monumental entrance into the St. Cyprien concentration camp. The entrance to the camp is in the style of a triumphal arch; there are French flags on each side of the inscription, that stretches from one end to the other: *Camp de concentration de Saint Cyprien*," *Diari d'un refugiat català* (Mexico City: Biblioteca Catalana, 1943), 19.

CHAPTER 8: CELSO AMIEVA'S *LA ALMOHADA DE ARENA*

1. In an entry in her 1982 "Indice biobibliográfico del exilio español en México," Matilde Mantecón de Souto reminds the reader that "Celso Amieva" is a pseudonym for the Asturian writer José María Alvarez Posada, *El exilio español en México, 1939–1982* (Mexico City: FCE, 1982), 724; at different times in his life, the author refers to himself by a variety of other pen names, including Lino Serdal, Corsino Urriel, and Braulio Ríos. After finally leaving France, Amieva resided in Mexico between 1953 and 1969 before transferring from his job as copy editor in the Mexican office of the Agencia de Prensa Nóvosti to the agency's central office in Moscow, *Gran enciclopedia asturiana*, vol. 1 (Gijón: Heraclio Fournier, 1970), 218. After his death in 1988, his remains were brought home to Asturias; he is buried in Llanes, where a street "Celso Amieva" has been named in his honor.

2. Amieva, *Poeta en la arena*; the pages of this slender volume, which includes prose passages as well as poems, are not numbered. Subsequent references to this edition will be cited parenthetically in the text following the abbreviation *(Poeta)*.

3. Apparently Amieva's system of marking each passing year was widespread

among the camp inmates, according to an observation made by the former Republican minister of foreign affairs Julio Alvarez del Vayo in his 1940 book: "Even ten months in the French concentration camps have not been able to break the high morale of the Republican refugees. Just as Spaniards in Franco Spain date their letters: *Primer Año de la Victoria* [first year of victory], so these exiles write: *Primer Año de Espera* [first year of waiting]," *Freedom's Battle*, 369.

4. Amieva, *La almohada de arena*; the pages are not numbered. Subsequent references to this work will be cited parenthetically in the text, following the abbreviation *La almohada*.

5. Amieva, *Asturianos*, 23; subsequent references to this work in this chapter will be made parenthetically in the text, following the abbreviation *Asturianos*. Linguistic variations of this "sand-neurosis" exist; Eulalio Ferrer and his camp comrades referred to the mental/emotional afflictions as *arenitis*, *Entre alambradas*, 129.

6. José Ignacio Cruz, "Los barracones de cultura: noticias sobre las actividades educativas de los exiliados españoles en los campos de refugiados," *Spagna Contemporanea* 5 (1994): 65.

7. Monique Alonso, "Las actividades culturales en los campos de concentración," *El exilio literario español de 1939*, ed. Manuel Aznar Soler (Barcelona: GEXEL, 1998), 134.

8. *Plages d'exil*, 84.

9. Ibid., 87.

10. Cruz, "Los barracones," 66. See also Francisco de Luis Martín, "La FETE y la cultura en los campos de refugiados," in *Emigración y exilio*, ed. Cuesta and Bermejo, 315–29.

11. *Plages d' exil*, 67. For a selection of sample pages from an August 31, 1940, issue of *Rosellón*, a biweekly camp journal also from Argelès-sur-Mer, see *Misión de Luis I. Rodríguez*, 467–72.

12. Ferrer, *Páginas del exilio*, 303.

13. Samblancat, *Caravana nazarena*, 108.

14. Reading the camp poetry of Celso Amieva, fervent admirer of Machado's verse, one cannot help but recall Machado's poem "Al gran Cero" (To the Great Zero) (from the collection *De un Cancionero apócrifo*), that certainly would have resonated prophetically with the younger poet, longtime resident of the isle "O" of Barcarès, *Poesías completas*, 692–93.

15. Alonso, "Las actividades culturales," 137.

16. According to Amaro del Rosal's 1976 account published in Mexico City about the myth and history of "the gold of the Bank of Spain," the besieged Republican government had first transferred the national gold reserves, packed in 10,000 wooden boxes, from Madrid to Cartagena in September 1936. Some 7,800 boxes were subsequently shipped abroad to Moscow in October 1936; three additional shipments from Cartagena were deposited in the Bank of France in Marseilles in April 1937. The final evacuation of the Cartagena reserves destined for Figueras took place in March 1938: "From that moment on, the Figueras castle was the primary stronghold of property and valuables controlled by the Ministry of the Treasury," *El oro del Banco de España y la historia del* Vita, (Mexico City: Grijalbo, 1976), 55. Allusions to the legendary story of Spanish gold had been featured prominently in wartime Nationalist propaganda. In an August 1938 catalog introducing a curious exhibit set up in San Sebastián, *Catálogo del material cogido al enemigo. Exposición de guerra* (Catalog of Material Taken from the Enemy: War Exhibition), the text lauds the Nationalist military campaign as a valiant enterprise undertaken by a scrappy underdog: "Without the gold that the Spanish people had earned through many years of saving and hard work, gold that ended up in the

hands of the Jewish-Marxist-Masonic-Separatists, . . . and without manufacturing . . . without military supplies . . . , Franco's soldiers undertook their heroic efforts to save the Fatherland" (1).

17. Suárez, *España comienza en los Pirineos* (1944), 178–79.
18. Ibid., 180.
19. Mistral, *Exilio*, 58–59.
20. For an eyewitness account of this March 1941 rebellion in the women's camp, see Anita Pujol's testimony first published in 1950: "And it was the women's camp that revolted in a protest so unanimous and so violent, that the authorities in charge of guarding us were frightened. In a matter of minutes, the advancing avalanche of women headed towards the area where they were trying to literally drag the Internationals out of their huts, broke through the barbed-wire fence and ran over everything. . . . With our fingernails, with our teeth, with our mouths, we fought with the Senegalese soldiers and the gendarmes. . . . We grabbed the guards' legs, we bit them, we made them fall to the ground," Montseny, *El éxodo*, 57.
21. León Felipe, *Obras completas* (Buenos Aires: Editorial Losada, 1963), 146, 148. Subsequent references in this chapter to this edition will be made parenthetically following the abbreviation *Obras*.
22. Forty years after Felipe published these verses in *El hacha*, this book was included in the November 1979 museum retropective Obra plástica y obra impresa del exilio español, exhibited in the Museo de San Carlos in Mexico City. A photograph of the title page was featured prominently with a review of the exhibition in a special issue of the Instituto Nacional de Bellas Artes's *La Semana de Bellas Artes* entitled "Cuarenta años de cultura española en el exilio" 109 (January 2, 1980): 4. Felipe's 1939 prophecy about a viable cultural legacy of the *vencidos* is fulfilled decades later in these halls of the San Carlos museum: the exiles' stories and viewpoints are on public display for all to see and for all to remember in this pictorial preservation of a crucial chapter of Spanish history.
23. In a fitting confluence of poetic affiliations between the two exiled Spanish poets, Celso Amieva was the 1974 recipient of the Premio Internacional de Poesía León Felipe, an award presented to Amieva in Moscow, his place of residence at the time. The Alvarez Posada family archives in Spain also include an undated photograph taken in Mexico of León Felipe with his great admirer, Celso Amieva.
24. As one might expect, the place of the camp in this poetry is frequently supplanted by the remembered place of loved ones left in Spain. See especially, "¿Existe todavía . . . ?," "Abrid mi carne con el hierro," "Era la misma . . . ," "Balada de la Peña Benzúa," "Voces," "El tricornio," "Molinera," and "Besos a un retrato."
25. Rafaneau-Boj, *Los campos de concentración*, 179.
26. Cabruja-Auguet, *La ciudad de madera*, 64.
27. Grando, *Vous avez la mémoire courte*, 179.
28. Espinar, *Argelès-Sur-Mer*, 43.
29. Rafaneau-Boj, *Los campos de concentración*, ix.
30. Suárez, *España comienza en los Pirineos*, 110.
31. *Los de Collioure*, 67.
32. Ferrer, *Entre alambradas*, 76–77.
33. *Plages d'exil*, 220.
34. Cabruja-Auguet, *La ciudad de madera*, n. pag.
35. Giménez Igualada, *Más allá*, 147.
36. Ibid., unnumbered page.
37. Alonso, "Las actividades culturales," 136.
38. In his reading of this poem, Michael Ugarte refers to the burial as "a necessary

act that initiates the next step in the long trajectory of exile. It's a ritual, and like all rituals, it's absolutely necessary for the continuation of the nation or the community," "Testimonios de exilio: desde el campo de concentración a América," in *El exilio de las Españas de 1939 en las Américas: "¿A dónde fue la canción?,"* ed. José Naharro-Calderón (Barcelona: Anthropos, 1991), 54.

39. Grando, *Vous avez la mémoire corte*, 89.

CHAPTER 9. AGUSTÍ BARTRA'S *CRISTO DE 200.000 BRAZOS*

1. Manuel Andújar, *La literatura catalana en el destierro* (Mexico City: B. Costa-Amic, 1949), 14. Teresa Férriz Roure accords an equally prominent place to Bartra in her essay published almost fifty years after Andújar's, "Las letras catalanas en el exilio mexicano. Algunas propuestas de estudio," in *El exilio catalán en México (Notas para su estudio)*, by Dolores Pla Brugat, María Magdalena Ordóñez, and Teresa Férriz Roure (Guadalajara: El Colegio de Jalisco–Generalitat de Catalunya, 1997), 43–80.

2. Ibid.

3. Palacio, *El éxodo*, 27.

4. Benavides, *Los nuevos profetas*, 203.

5. Giménez Igualada, *Más allá*, 150.

6. Regler, *The Owl of Minerva*, 321.

7. Montseny, *El éxodo*, 11, 35.

8. Ibid., 63. The image of Christ's crucifixion was coincidentally used during these same years to represent Jewish suffering at the hands of the Germans; see, for example, Stephen Feinstein's essay "Art after Auschwitz," in *Problems Unique to the Holocaust*, ed. Harry Cargas (Lexington: University Press of Kentucky, 1999): "Marc Chagall's *White Crucifixion*, a response to *Kristallnacht* in 1938, remains the icon among many paintings that describe Jewish suffering before 1939. Unlike artists who merely depicted suffering, Chagall used the theme of a crucified 'Jewish' Jesus set against vignettes of Jewish persecution that unfolded in the Nazi era," 157.

9. Bartra, *Cristo de 200.000 brazos*, 11–12. Subsequent references in this chapter to this edition will be made parenthetically in the text, after the abbreviation *Cristo*. The text of the novel's first four pages were reprinted in a 1959 article written by Bartra and illustrated by his close friend in exile, Josep Bartolí; see Bartra, "Arenas de nadie," *Novedades: México en la cultura* (March 3, 1959). I am grateful to Jaume Canyameres for providing me with a copy of this article.

10. Agustí Bartra, *Ecce Homo: Elegías* (Mexico City: Joaquín Mortiz, 1964), 65. According to the biographical account published by Bartra's wife Anna Murià in 1957, he began to write the novel (originally published in Catalan in 1943 as *Xabola*; the current title accompanied the 1958 editions published both in Spanish and Catalan) in February 1940, during the year that the couple resided in the Dominican Republic. He continued work on the novel throughout the five months that they spent in La Habana ("When he comes home, Agustí writes until dawn: he's working on *Chabola*"), completing the book in Mexico City in 1942, "Fragmentos de la *Crónica de Anna*," in *El ojo de Polifemo: visión de la obra de Agustí Bartra*, ed. Cecilia Gironella, (Mexico City: B. Costa-Amic, 1957), 45. The manuscript was awarded a literary prize, the Fastenraht, during the May 3, 1942, session of the Consistorio de los Juegos Florales de la Lengua Catalana, held at the Teatro Ideal in Mexico City; see Foix, *España desgarrada*, 198–99.

11. "Fragmentos de la *Crónica de Anna*," 51; this excerpt is reproduced in the original Catalan in Agustí Bartra's proleg, *Cartes des dels camps de concentració*, by Pere Vives i Clavé (Barcelona: Edicions 62, 1972), 11. Bartra has explained that he did not learn of

Vives's horrendous death, occasioned by an injection of benzine into his aorta while interned in Mauthausen, until August 1946, almost five years after the fact and three years after the publication of his novel; see Bartra, *Ecce homo*, 70; Bartra, proleg, 9; and "Fragmentos de la *Crónica de Anna*," 47.

12. Bartra, proleg, 8.

13. Tzvetan Todorov, *Facing the Extreme: Moral Life in the Concentration Camps*, trans. Arthur Denner and Abigail Pollack (New York: Metropolitan Books, 1996), 40.

14. See Harry Cargas's 1999 edited collection of essays for a book-length treatment of the "moral implications" of a series of "actions or inactions" enacted by the prisoners of "Auschwitz, Dachau, Treblinka, Sobibor, and other death camps," *Problems Unique to the Holocaust*, vii–viii; see especially Didier Pollefeyt for an in-depth review of the literature that addresses the question of ethical behavior among the inmates, "Victims of Evil or Evil of Victims?," Ibid., 67–82.

15. Loureiro, *Ethics of Autobiography*, 179.

16. "Fragmentos de la *Crónica de Anna*," 52.

17. Ibid.

18. The French concentration camp literature written by Spaniards abounds with references to *la manta*, often one of the scant possessions from Spain that the refugees carried with them into the camps, as an almost sacred object laden with powerful emotional and symbolic significance. See, for example, Melitón Bustamante Ortiz's 1960 four-part poem *La manta*, whose sections like "Pasión" and "Transfiguración" chronicle the transformation of dirty, tattered blankets into an enduring emblem of a nation that carries on in exile; Carrasco, *La odisea*, 26.

19. The interpolated text of "Bardo" is not authored by Bartra, but is a translation from the original German of an anonymous prose poem that Pere Vives completed as a gift for the novelist. As Bartra explains in the 1946 letter written to Vives's sister Carme, he carried the text of "Bardo" with him into exile in America, "Fragmentos de la *Crónica de Anna*," 51. As previously indicated, Bartra wrote to Carme Vives that he realizes that at the same time of her brother Pere's death in Mauthausen, that he in Mexico City would have been writing the section of his novel that includes the "Bardo" chapter.

20. Loureiro, *Ethics of Autobiography*, 79.

21. César Vallejo, *The Complete Posthumous Poetry*, trans. Clayton Eshleman and José Rubia Barcia (Berkeley and Los Angeles: University of California Press, 1978), 261.

22. Ibid.

23. The poignant juxtaposition of the ugly barbed wire and the beautiful butterfly is coincidentally replicated in Primo Levi's home office. In Philip Roth's 1986 interview with the famous Auschwitz survivor and author, he describes the office decor: "The most evocative object is one of the smallest: an unobstrusively hung sketch of a half-destroyed barbed-wire fence at Auschwitz. Displayed more prominently on the walls are playful constructions skillfully twisted into shape by Levi himself out of insulated copper wire—that is, wire coated with the varnish developed for that purpose in his own laboratory. There is a big wire butterfly . . .," Primo Levi, "A Conversation with Primo Levi," in *Survival in Auschwitz: The Nazi Assault on Humanity* (New York: Touchstone, 1996), 178.

24. Bartra, *Ecce Homo*, 65.

25. Ibid.

26. Todorov, *Facing the Extreme*, 91.

27. Levi, *Survival in Auschwitz*, 73.

28. Todorov, *Facing the Extreme*, 92, 97.

29. Ibid., 98.

30. Elaine Scarry, *On Beauty and Being Just* (Princeton: Princeton University Press, 1999), 111, 97. Subsequent references to this work will be made parenthetically in the text, following the abbreviation *On Beauty*.
31. Levi, *Survival in Auschwitz*, 73.
32. Bartra, *Ecce Homo*, 72.
33. Homer, *The Odyssey*, trans. Richard Lattimore (New York: Harper Colophon Books, 1975), 106.
34. In his 1993 study of the organizational structures and systems of German concentration camps, Wolfgang Sofsky has used terms like "camp time" and "prisoner's time" to describe the unique aspects of the bizarre temporal dimension of the prisoners' camp experience; the phenomenon he examines shares many of the same features of the "dead time," so widely reported by Spanish witnesses like Bartra, *The Order of Terror: The Concentration Camp*, trans. William Templer (Princeton: Princeton University Press, 1997).
35. According to Bartra's wife Anna, the character of Vives is a composite figure of the novelist and his friend Pere Vives: "In the Vives of *Chabola* the poet fused together his own personality with the real Pere Vives: the thoughts, the reactions of the fictional character could be his friend's, they could be the author's," "Fragmentos de la *Crónica de Anna*," 47.

CHAPTER 10. TELLING STORIES OF GETTING OUT

1. Amieva, *Poeta*.
2. Ibid.
3. Bravo-Tellado, *El peso de la derrota*, 89.
4. Rubio, *La emigración de la guerra civil*, 328.
5. Geneviève Dreyfus-Armand and Emile Temime, *Les camps sur la plage, un exil espagnol* (Paris: Editions Autrement, 1995), 8.
6. Isidoro Fabela, *Cartas al Presidente Cárdenas* (Mexico City, 1947), 127.
7. Ibid., 119–20.
8. Judging from an August 1940 document in the records of another Mexican diplomat's assessment of the French internment camps, the living conditions for Spanish refugees had hardly improved during the eighteen months following Fabela's initial visit. The report from Vichy France entitled "Situación y clasificación de los campos de concentración de refugiados españoles," included in Luis I. Rodríguez's files, chronicles a similarly depressing state of affairs regarding the camps' food, shelter, sanitation, and general health of the inmates. According to the November 10, 1940, evaluation specifically of the Argelès-sur-Mer camp, the situation there is even more dire; the material conditions, says the report, "are absolutely shocking," *Misión de Luis I. Rodríguez*, 453.
9. Fabela, *Cartas*, 126.
10. Ibid., 126–27.
11. These statistics are cited by Clara E. Lida, *Inmigración y exilio: Reflexiones sobre el caso español* (Mexico City: Siglo XXI Editores, 1997), 58.
12. José Antonio Matesanz, *Las raíces del exilio: México ante la guerra civil española, 1936–1939* (Mexico City: El Colegio de México/UNAM, 1999), 322.
13. See Rubio, *La emigración*, 133–34, for a list of the names and political affiliations of the SERE's first executive committee.
14. Ibid., 137.
15. Ibid.
16. Matesanz, *Las raíces*, 401.

17. Despite the impossibility of meeting the needs of the majority of the thousands of refugees petitioning the SERE for emigration, the SERE played a pivotal role in successfully facilitating much of the emigration to America that took place during the first eighteen months after the war, as Alicia Alted Vigil's research makes clear: "Between May of 1939 and June of 1940, the number of refugees who emigrated to Mexico, Chile (as part of the *Winnipeg* expedition) and the Dominican Republic was approximately 13,000. Keeping in mind that the total number of emigrants to America during those months was around 15,000, one may conclude that the SERE was responsible for transporting more than 80%," "Ayuda humanitaria y reorganización institucional en el exilio," in *Emigración y exilio: españoles en Francia (1936–1946)*, 203. The purpose of the following chapters is not to take issue with the fact that the SERE provided invaluable aid and support for thousands of Spanish emigrants to America, but rather to examine how those left behind in the concentration camps of France (and others lucky enough to get out) have portrayed the often embittered, politicized saga of selection for emigration.

18. Matesanz, *Las raíces*, 322.
19. Narciso Bassols, *Cartas* (Mexico City: Instituto Politécnico Nacional, 1986), 364.
20. Ibid., 389.
21. Rojo, *¡Alerta!*, 242.
22. Rubio, *La emigración*, 136.
23. Ferrer, *Páginas*, 242.
24. Espinar, *Argelès*, 29.
25. Ugarte, "Testimonios," 59.
26. Roberto Ruiz, *El último oasis* (Mexico City: Joaquín Mortiz, 1964), 33–34.
27. Vilanova, *Los olvidados*, 13, 14.
28. Amieva, *Asturianos*, 33.
29. Ibid.
30. Ibid., 21.
31. Mauricio Fresco, *La emigración republicana española: una victoria de México* (Mexico City: Editores Asociados, 1950), 40. Subsequent references in this chapter to this work will be made parenthetically in the text.
32. Artís-Gener, *La diáspora*, 85.
33. Ibid., 88.
34. Giménez Igualada, *Más allá*, 165.
35. Ibid., 170.
36. Ibid., 173–74.
37. Ricardo Garibay, "Por aquellos españoles . . . ," *El exilio español en México, 1939–1982* (Mexico City: FCE, 1982), 94.
38. Ibid, 95.
39. Ibid.
40. Sánchez Barbudo, "El Grupo,"101.
41. Mistral, *Éxodo*, 129; 156–157.
42. Ibid., 161.
43. Primo Levi, "The Gray Zone," in *The Drowned and the Saved*, 42.
44. In her descriptive summary of selected passages and illustrations from *Campos de concentración 1939–194* . . . , Eloísa Nos Aldás erroneously identifies the corpulent diner as a Frenchman indifferent to the plight of the refugees, "El exilio español en Francia a través de los trazos de Josep Bartolí: los campos," *Proyecto Clío: Una mirada hispana a la Historia Universal* (http//clio.rediris.es/exilio/loscampos/los%20campos.htm). I am grateful to Professor José Angel Saínz of Mary Washington College for bringing Nos Aldás's work to my attention. I include Bartolí's drawing in my chapter 5.

45. Palacio, *El éxodo*, 76, 77.
46. Ibid., 79, 139.
47. Mistral, *Exodo*, 150–51.
48. Ricardo Baldó García, *Exiliados españoles en el Sahara, 1939–1943* (Alcoy: Imprenta la Victoria, 1977), 48, 49.
49. Bravo-Tellado, *El peso de la derrota*, 157.
50. Mariano Ansó, *Yo fui ministro de Negrín* (Barcelona: Planeta, 1976), 258, 263.
51. Álvarez del Vayo, *Freedom's Battle*, 368.
52. Esteban Vilaró, *El ocaso de los dioses rojos*, 88.
53. Ibid., 103.
54. Ibid., 201.
55. Molins i Fábrega, *Campos*, 55.
56. García Gerpe, *Alambradas*, 99.
57. Mistral, *Éxodo*, 158.
58. Ros, *Diario de un refugiado republicano*, 90. Subsequent references in this chapter to this edition will be made parenthetically in the text.
59. Ros's detailed descriptions of his lavish meals with Republican relief agency officials and the *privilegiados* of exile based in Paris brings to mind Angel Samblancat's novelistic rendering of "the dinner guests of the J.A.R.E. and the moochers of the S.E.R.E., always with a fork at the ready and with a napkin around their necks," *Caravana nazarena*, 151.

Chapter 11: Manuel García Gerpe's *Alambradas*

1. García Gerpe, *Alambradas*, 99–100. Subsequent references in this chapter to this work will be cited parenthetically in the text, following the abbreviation *Alambradas*.
2. Grando, *Vous avez la mémoire courte*, 46.
3. José Antonio de Aguirre, president of the Basque country who crossed the French border into exile on February 5, 1939, in the company of the president of Cataluña, Luis Companys, bitterly recalls that by the spring of 1940 the *vasco francés* Ibernegaray (by then Ministro del Gobierno) campaigned ever more actively against the refugees: "This Basque Quisling, as soon as he entered the Ministry, promised Franco that all the Basque refugees in France would be put in concentration camps.... No one was saved from Ibernegaray's hateful fratricide. Everyone, without exception based on social class or age, was imprisoned in the concentration camp of Gurs. Even Basque priests were taken from their homes at night and carried away in trucks as if they were the most dangerous of enemies," José de Aguirre y Lecube, *De Guernica a Nueva York pasando por Berlín* (Buenos Aires: Editorial Vasca Ekin, 1944), 108–9. Similarly, Spanish exile Diego de Santillán refers in 1940 to Ibernegaray as a "notorious fascist" guilty of placating Franco at the refugees' expense, filling concentration camps with both Basque and Catalonian refugees "to get into General Franco's good graces," prologue, *Cómo terminó la guerra de España*, by José García Pradas (Buenos Aires: Ediciones Iman, 1940), 11.
4. Bessie, *Men in Battle*, 176; 298.
5. Like so many other political episodes of the recent civil war, Casado's coup (which proved to be the death blow for Negrín's politics of continued *resistencia*) became the subject of concentration camp humor. In a July 5, 1939, diary entry, Eulalio Ferrer writes from Barcarès: "Antonio *El Málaga* tells us some jokes to help us fall asleep. Almost all of them have to do with the war. Since he's a confirmed bachelor, he loves this one: 'The North was lost, Aragón was lost, Catalonia was lost, and nothing

happened. But the Center was lost, and that was the end. . . . It got *Casado* [married]," *Entre alambradas*, 100. The wordplay of last phrase rests on the meaning of Colonel Casado's surname, "married"). For an early eyewitness account of the coup penned by one of Casado's supporters, see García Pradas's *Cómo terminó la guerra de España*.

    6. Domínguez, *Los vencedores de Negrín*, 14.
    7. Rojo, *¡Alerta a los pueblos!*, 253.
    8. Ibid., 262, 264.
    9. Palacio, *El éxodo*, 8; *Entre dos fascismos*, 171.
    10. Palacio, *El éxodo*, 35.
    11. Ibid., 79.
    12. Eligio de Mateo Sousa, "México, tierra de promisión," *Historia 16*, 172 (1990): 112.
    13. Mistral, *Éxodo*, 149–50.
    14. Ibid., 151, 152.
    15. Ibid., 153, 154.
    16. María de la Soledad Alonso, et al. *Contribución a la historia de los refugiados españoles en México* (Mexico City: I.N.A.H., 1980), 17.
    17. Salvador Madariaga, *España: ensayo de historia contemporánea* (Madrid: Espasa-Calpe, 1979), 507.
    18. Alted Vigil, "Ayuda humanitaria," 206–7. The intriguing *historia del Vita*, first chronicled like an excerpt from an Ian Fleming novel in Louis Fischer's *Men and Politics: An Autobiography* (New York: Duell, Sloan and Pearce, 1941) in a chapter dramatically entitled "A Yachtful of Diamonds and Pearls," has been the subject of various books. Studies include José Fuentes Mares, *Historia de un conflicto (El tesoro del "Vita")* (Madrid: CUS Ediciones, 1975), as well as Amaro del Rosal's fervently pro-Negrinista account published one year later as a corrective to the earlier text, *El oro del Banco de España*. Indalecio Prieto, Negrín's embittered former minister of defense who was replaced by the prime minister in April 1938, recounts the events surrounding the *Vita* and the founding of the JARE in his 1946 article, "JARE, Rendición de cuentas," in *Convulsiones de España (Pequeños detalles de grandes sucesos)*, vol. 1 (Barcelona: Planeta, 1989), 105–12, as well as the 1955 "Chantaje contra México: la historia del Vita," *Convulsiones*, 113–22. For a fascinating, impassioned exchange between Prieto and Negrín just prior to the establishment of the JARE on July 31, 1939, see their correspondence, "Epistolario Prieto-Negrín," in *Convulsiones*, vol. 4 (Barcelona: Planeta, 1990), originally published in its entirety in Paris in 1939, and even read by the camp inmates, according to Eulalio Ferrer's November 2, 1939, diary entry from St. Cyprien, *Páginas del exilio*, 67. In his June 17, 1939, letter, Prieto holds Negrín responsible not only for the Republic's defeat, but for the "spectacle of half a million Spaniards cast out of their country, struggling in miserable conditions and subjected to the vilest humiliations" ("Epistolario," 24); in his June 23 reply, Negrín pleads for a levelheaded, unified approach to the difficult problem of emigration, for the sake of the most disenfranchised refugees: "We, both you and I, like all Spaniards, should focus our attention on the greater matters at hand. These problems will not be solved if instead of marshaling our forces and setting aside bitter resentments, we become embroiled in fights while the victims who deserve our help are left waiting" ("Epistolario," 29–30).
    19. Prieto, "Epistolario," 14.

CHAPTER 12: EULALIO FERRER'S *ENTRE ALAMBRADAS*

    1. Ferrer, *Páginas del exilio*, 449. Further references in this chapter to this work will be made parenthetically in the text following the abbreviation *Páginas*.

2. Ferrer, *Entre alambradas*, 130. Further references in this chapter to this work will be made parenthetically in the text following the abbreviation *Entre*. I cite from the 1988 Spanish edition of Ferrer's memoir, a revised and lengthier version of the 1987 edition first published in Mexico as *Entre alambradas: Diario de los campos de concentración* (Mexico City: Pangea Editores, 1987). The verses cited are from fellow inmate José Rial's poem "La guitarra en la barraca" (The Guitar in the Hut), subsequently published in Rial's book of poetry *El dolor de la derrota (Notas emocionadas de la emigración española en las cárceles, refugios y campos de concentración de Francia)* (Mexico City: Imprenta Aurora, 1946), 62.

3. In chapter 2, I describe Antonio Rodríguez Luna's painting *Don Quijote en el exilio*, certainly the best-known example from the exilic visual arts of the *Caballero de la Triste Figura*, as an iconic emblem of the Spanish exile of 1939. This painting, not coincidentally, belonged for years in Eulalio Ferrer's extensive personal art collection of Don Quijote iconography in Mexico City; since 1987 (the same year Ferrer published the first edition of his *Entre alambradas* camp diary), it has formed part of the collection donated by Ferrer to the Mexican people, the Museo Iconográfico del Quijote in Guanajuato, Mexico.

4. Alfonso Reyes, elegía, *España Peregrina* 8–9 (October 1940): 55.

5. Eulalio Ferrer, *Santander-México. Presencia de Eulalio Ferrer Rodríguez*, ed. Carlos Galán Lorés, Aurelio García Cantalapiedra, and Valeriano García-Barredo Alonso (Santander: Colección Atarazanas, 1984), 116. Further references in this chapter to this collection of essays written by Ferrer will be made parenthetically in the text following the abbreviation *Santander*.

6. In countless published statements and interviews over the years, Ferrer has emphasized the value of the *Quijote* as a masterful expression of a collective national identity. In a 1945 tribute to his former Argelès comrade and work crew companion Lorenzo Sacristán, who died fighting the Nazis during the liberation of Paris, Ferrer recalls his friend's incisive assessment of the *Quijote*: "the most accurate biography of our people that has ever been written" (*Páginas*, 207). In 1972, Ferrer refers to the novel: "It is a supremely eloquent and moving testimony about a nation's character" (*Santander*, 117); in a 1983 interview, he explains one of the great lessons learned from his repeated camp readings of his favorite book: "It helped me to better understand the character traits of the Hispanic people" (*Santander*, 190). Such is the sentiment shared in a 1947 editorial of the journal *Las Españas*: "Cervantes has meaning for us today because he understood how to live his own life through the life of the people, of his people; because he understood himself by understanding them; because he dreamed himself into existence by dreaming of them," Valender and Rojo, *"Las Españas,"* 164.

7. In a 1940 essay published in *Romance*, Adolfo Sánchez Vázquez also celebrates from the shores of exile in Mexico the spirited example of the marginalized Spanish *pícaro*; as one of Franco's *perdedores* himself, Sánchez Vázquez admires the humble hero of early modern Spanish literature as an antidote to the *triunfalista* rhetoric of Empire that similarly characterized the official discourse of the earlier historical period: "The *pícaro* belonged to a social substratum that did not participate in the pomp and circumstance of the Empire. The light of a Spain made feverish by the fight against the Reformation, did not shine upon him. The warm glow of glory never reached him because his feet were too firmly planted on the ground, rooted to the spot by bloody failures, by reversals of fortune, by hunger," "En torno a la picaresca," *Romance* (May 15, 1940): 6.

8. Rodríguez, *Ballet de sangre*, 45.

9. Gomís Soler, *Cruces sin Cristo*, 376.

10. Ibid., 12, 13.

11. Perhaps no PSOE party official was more inundated by letters from concentra-

tion camp inmates than was Francisco Largo Caballero, who reported in the fall of 1939 that since his arrival in Paris in January, he had received hundreds of letters, especially from camp internees, "And there's not a single letter sent by a fellow emigrant whose questions, proposals, or advice have gone unanswered by me, although I can't say how satisfactorily I've responded"; for a fascinating compilation of his postwar correspondence, see his ¿Qué se puede hacer? (Mexico City, 1940), 10.

12. Eulalio Ferrer is not the only dreamer of freedom and social justice to seek wisdom and sustenance from the pages of the *Quijote*. According to a March 2001 article in the Spanish newspaper *El País*, the constant companion for Mexico's Subcomandante Marcos along his famed *zapatur* (the *Zapatistas'* well-publicized caravan from Chiapas to the halls of the Palacio Nacional in Mexico City during the spring of 2001) was Cervantes's novel; other favorite writers of this revolutionary leader for indigenous rights are reported to have been famous Spanish exiles themselves, "from Antonio Machado to León Felipe," Juan Jesús Aznárez, "Un guerrillero en El corte Inglés," *El País* (March 19, 2001), 80. In translated excerpts of an interview with Gabriel García Márquez that originally appeared in Colombia's *Cambio*, published in *The Nation* as "A Zapatista Reading List," Subcomandante Marcos speaks reverently of the *Quijote*. When asked what he is reading now, he responds: "I have *Don Quijote* by the bedside, and I regularly carry around *Romancero gitano*, by García Lorca. *Don Quijote* is the best book out there on political theory, followed by *Hamlet* and *Macbeth*," *The Nation* 273 (July 2, 2001): 37.

13. The widespread belief on the part of the exiled community generally (particularly during the first years after the end of the civil war) that return to Spain was imminent is captured in the title of Carlos Semprún-Maura's 1975 novel originally published in French, *L'an prochain a Madrid*; a Spanish translation, *El año que viene en Madrid* (Madrid: Musigraf ARABI), was published in Spain in 1978.

14. *Plages d'exil*, 38.

15. Ibid., 107.

16. Ibid., 96.

17. Ibid.

18. Ibid., 98–99.

19. As stated above, in 1946, José Rial published his verses in the book *El dolor de la derrota* (The Pain of Defeat), dedicating the volume to: "All those who are still suffering . . . , to all those who are waiting . . . ; just as I have written *The Pain of Defeat*, I will one day write *The Joy of Victory*." The poem that Ferrer cites, "Arenitis," appears as well, with its concluding verses, "Morir no tiene importancia . . . / Lo difícil es vivir" [Dying doesn't matter . . . / It's the living that's hard].

20. Carrasco's epitaph for Don Quixote that the interned Ferrer finds particularly inspirational is again invoked in the text that accompanies Spanish exile artist Elvira Gascón's painting *Don Quijote, derribado: no vencido* (Don Quixote, Down: But Not Out) in the 1998 illustrated catalog of Ferrer's famed Quixote museum, permanent home to Gascón's portrait: "This idea was endorsed by Elvira Gascón when she wrote the header for her painting, *Don Quijote, derribado: no vencido*," *Museo Iconográfico del Quijote* (Guanajuato: Artes Gráficas, 1998), 54.

21. For a similar story of the far-flung travels of another camp escapee, see Jaime Espinar's *Argelès-Sur-Mer*, 106.

22. In a popular textbook, *El niño republicano* (The Republican Child) used during the years of the Spanish Republic when Ferrer would have been a schoolboy, a couple of chapters are devoted to the history of the beloved French national hymn adopted by the Spanish Republicans ("La Marseillaise," "How the *Marseillaise* came to be"): "All good republicans, whether French, Spanish, Swiss, or American, upon hearing the stir-

ring notes of this song of liberation, experience a profound emotional response at the core of their being. They know that perhaps without this song the French Revolution would have never happened, and without the revolution, the world would never have so quickly and fully embraced the forces of progress and civilization. The *Marseillaise* has influenced the history of men because as it penetrated their hearts and souls, it has made them love the dignity of the free man," Joaquín Seró Sabaté, *El niño republicano*, facsimile edition (Madrid: EDAF, 2000), 144–45.

23. Benjamín Jarnés, "Lanza y estilo," *Romance* 24 (May 31, 1941): 2.
24. "*Don Quijote de la Mancha*," *Romance* 20 (January 15, 1941): 18.
25. Valender and Rojo Leyva, "*Las Españas*," 166–67.
26. Ibid., 510.
27. Cimorra, *El bloqueo del hombre*, 197, 196.
28. Fernando Benítez, presentación, *Entre alambradas*, by Eulalio Ferrer (Barcelona: Grijalbo, 1988), 14.

Epilogue

1. Artís-Gener, *La diáspora*, 111.
2. Ibid., 112
3. Ibid., 114.
4. Ibid.
5. Avery Gordon, *Ghostly Matters: Haunting and the Sociological Imagination* (Minneapolis: University of Minnesota Press, 1997), 18, 8.
6. Ibid., 18, 24.
7. Ibid., 58, 194.
8. Josep Bartolí, *Calibán* (Paris: Ruedo Ibérico, 1972), 138.
9. Ibid., 140.
10. Quoted by Juan Marichal, prólogo, *El archivo de la República española en el exilio 1945–1977 (Inventario del Fondo París)*, by Alicia Alted Vigil (Madrid: Fundación Universitaria Española, 1993), 11.
11. Bartolí, *Calibán*, 154, 156.
12. Gordon, *Ghostly Matters*, 208.
13. Ibid., 195.
14. Bartolí, *Calibán*, 154.
15. José Prat, "Crítica y política," in *El exilio de las Españas de 1939 en las Américas*, ed. José Naharro-Calderón (Barcelona: Anthropos, 1991), 146. For an interesting sampling of the numerous speeches given between 1940 and 1976 on the occasion of the Republic's anniversary, published primarily in the Mexican newspaper *El Nacional*, see the chapter "Una celebración constante: el aniversario de la proclamación de la Segunda República Española, 14 de abril de 1931," José Matesanz, ed., *México y la República española. Antología de documentos, 1931–1977* (Mexico City: Centro Republicano Español de México, 1978), 451–83.
16. Marichal, prólogo, 11. Marichal's words are echoed in the publicity brochure advertising the museum exhibit entitled *Exilio* (organized by the Fundación Pablo Iglesias and the Museo Nacional Centro de Arte Reina Sofía, and on exhibit in the cities of Madrid, Cádiz, and La Coruña between October 2002 and April 2003); the brochure pays homage to the "thousands of Spaniards who, from exile, kept alive the ideal of a constitutional government"; also quoted by Juan Luis Jaén, "Una exposición reúne en el Palacio de Cristal del Retiro 400 objetos de exiliados españoles, una memora viva

de la diáspora republicana," *Madridiario* (2002), http://www.madridiario.es/reportajes/reportaje-exiliados.jsp (May 16, 2003).

17. Zurita Castañer, *Los círculos del exilio*, 51.

18. Marichal, prólogo, 11; emphasis in the original.

19. I am grateful to Leonor Sarmiento Pubillones, president of the Ateneo Español de México, for providing me with a copy of the Ateneo's collection of photographs of Siqueiros's exhibit. The long-lived Ateneo is itself quite literally a "place of history," boasting one of the most significant archives of books, journals, articles, and documents written about the Spanish Republic, the civil war, and the culture and politics of exile. A portion of this outstanding collection was the subject of a 1999 exhibit shown in Valencia, Spain; see the exhibit catalog *Letras del exilio/México, 1939–1949. Biblioteca de Ateneo Español de México*, (Valencia: Universitat de Valencia, 1999).

Works Cited

Abellán, José Luis, ed. *El exilio español de 1939*. 6 vol. Madrid: Taurus, 1976.

——— . *El exilio filosófico en América: Los transterrados de 1939*. Mexico City: FCE, 1998.

"Actas de la última sesión parlamentaria de la Segunda República Española." In *El peso de la derrota, 1939–1944. La tragedia de medio millón de españoles en el exilio*, by Antonio Tellado Vázquez and Antonio Sánchez-Bravo Cenjor, 333–50. Madrid: Edifrans, 1974.

Agnew, John A., and James S. Duncan, eds. *The Power of Place: Bringing Together Geographical and Sociological Imaginations*. Cambridge: Unwin Hyman, 1989.

Aguirre y Lecube, José Antonio de. *De Guernica a Nueva York pasando por Berlín*. Buenos Aires: Editorial Vasca Ekin, 1944.

Agustí Centelles (1909–1985), fotoperiodista. Exhibition Catalog. Barcelona: Fundació Caixa de Cataluña, 1988.

Alberti, Rafael. "Vida bilingüe de un refugiado español en Francia (1939–1940)." In *Poesías completas*. Buenos Aires: Editorial Losada, 1961.

Albornoz, Álvaro de. *Páginas del destierro*. Mexico City: Ediciones Quetzal, 1941.

Almenara, Roc d'. *Diari d'un refugiat català*. Mexico City: Biblioteca Catalana, 1943.

Alonso, María de la Soledad, et al. *Contribución a la historia de los refugiados españoles en México*. Mexico City: I.N.A.H., 1980.

Alonso, María de la Soledad, Elena Aub, and Marta Baranda. *Palabras del exilio: de los que volvieron*. Mexico City: I.N.A.H., 1988.

Alonso, Monique. *Antonio Machado, poeta en el exilio*. Barcelona: Anthropos, 1985.

——— . "Las actividades culturales en los campos de concentración." In *El exilio literario español de 1939*. 2 vols. Edited by Manuel Aznar Soler. Barcelona: GEXEL, 1998.

Alted Vigil, Alicia. "Ayuda humanitaria y reorganización institucional en el exilio." In *Emigración y exilio: españoles en Francia (1936–1946)*. Edited by Josefina Cuesta and Benito Bermejo. Madrid: Eudema, 1996.

Alted Vigil, Alicia, Jean-Pierre Amalric, Benito Bermejo, Lucienne Domergue, Santos Juliá, and Gilbert A. Rigaud. *Exilios: Refugiados españoles en el mediodía de Francia. Guía de comprensión*. Madrid: UNED, 1994.

Alted Vigil, Alicia, and Lucienne Domergue, eds. *El exilio republicano español en Toulouse, 1939–1999*. Madrid: UNED; Toulouse: Presses Universitaires du Mirail, 2003.

Alted Vigil, Alicia, and Manuel Aznar Soler, eds. *Literatura y cultura del exilio español de 1939 en Francia*. Salamanca: AEMIC-GEXEL, 1998.

Altolaguirre, Manuel. "De mis recuerdos." *Hora de España* 5 (1937): 70.

——— . *El caballo griego*. In *Obras completas*. Vol 1. Edited by James Valender. Madrid: Istmo, 1986.

——— . *Obras completas*. Vol. 3. Edited by James Valender. Madrid: Istmo, 1992.

Álvarez, Santiago. *Historia política y militar de las Brigadas Internacionales*. Madrid: Compañía Literaria, 1996.

Álvarez del Vayo, Julio. *Freedom's Battle*. Translated by Eileen E. Brooke. New York: Hill & Wang, 1971.

Amieva, Celso. *Asturianos en el destierro (Francia)*. Gijón: Ayalga Ediciones, 1977.

———. *La almohada de arena*. Mexico City: Suplemento de Ecuador O O O, 1960.

———. *Poeta en la arena*. Mexico City: Ecuador O O O, 1964.

Anderson, Benedict. *Imagined Communities: Reflections on the Origin and Spread of Nationalism*. New York: Verso, 1992.

Andújar, Manuel. *La literatura catalana en el destierro*. Mexico City: B. Costa-Amic, 1949.

———. Prefacio. In *Collioure 1939. Les dernier jours d'Antonio Machado*. Collioure: Foundation Antonio Machado, 1982.

———. *St. Cyprien, plage . . . Campo de concentración*. Huelva: Diputación Provincial de Huelva, 1990.

Ansó, Mariano. *Yo fui ministro de Negrín*. Barcelona: Planeta, 1976.

Artís-Gener, Avel·lí. *La diáspora republicana*. Barcelona: Editorial Euros, 1975.

Aub, Max. *Campo cerrado*. Mexico City: Ediciones Tezontle, 1943.

———. *Ciertos cuentos*. Mexico City: Antigua Librería Robredo, 1955.

———. *Diario de Djelfa*. Mexico City, 1944.

———. *Manuscrito Cuervo: Historia de Jacobo*. Edited by José Antonio Pérez Bowie. Segorbe: Fundación Max Aub, 1999.

———. *Morir por cerrar los ojos*. Mexico City: Ediciones Tezontle, 1944.

———. *Morir por cerrar los ojos*. Barcelona: Aymá, 1967.

———. *No son cuentos (cuentos)*. Mexico City: Ediciones Tezontle, 1944.

———. *El rapto de Europa o siempre se puede hacer algo*. Mexico City: Ediciones Tezontle, 1946.

———. "El turbión metafísico." *Hablo como hombre*. Mexico City: Joaquín Mortiz, 1967.

Aznar Soler, Manuel, ed. *El exilio literario español de 1939*. 2 vols. Barcelona: GEXEL, 1998.

———. "Las literaturas del exilio republicano de 1939: El estado de la cuestión." *Ínsula* 627 (March 1999): 3–5.

Aznárez, Juan Jesús. "Un guerrillero en El Corte Inglés." *El País* (March 19, 2001): 80.

Baer, Ulrich. "To Give Memory a Place: Holocaust Photography and the Landscape Tradition." *Representations* 69 (winter 2000): 38–62.

Balcells, Albert. "Agustí Centelles i el seu temps: Els orígens d'un reporter grafic." In *Agustí Centelles (1909–1985), fotoperiodista*. Exhibit Catalog. Barcelona: Fundació Caixa de Cataluña, 1988.

Baldó García, Ricardo. *Exiliados españoles en el Sahara, 1939–1943*. Alcoy: Imprenta la Victoria, 1977.

Barkan, Elazar, and Marie-Denise Shelton, eds. Introduction. In *Borders, Exiles, Diasporas*. Stanford: Stanford University Press, 1998.

Bartolí, Josep. *Calibán*. Paris: Ruedo Ibérico, 1972.

Bartolí, Josep, and Narcís Molins i Fábrega. *Campos de concentración, 1939–194 . . .* Mexico City: Iberia, 1944.

Bartra, Agustí. "Arenas de nadie." *Novedades: México en la cultura* (March 3, 1959): 6.

———. *Cristo de 200.000 brazos (Campo de Argelès)*. Mexico City: Editorial Novaro-México, 1958.

———. *Ecce Homo: Elegías*. Mexico City: Joaquín Mortiz, 1964.

———. Proleg. In *Cartes des dels camps de concentració*. By Pere Vives i Clavé. Barcelona: Edicions 62, 1972.

Bassols, Narciso. *Cartas*. Mexico City: Instituto Politécnico Nacional, 1986.

Ben-Amos, Dan, and Liliane Weissberg, eds. *Cultural Memory and the Construction of Identity*. Detroit: Wayne State University Press, 1999.

Benavides, Manuel. *Los nuevos profetas*. Mexico City: Colección Luz Sobre España, 1942.

Benítez, Fernando. Presentación. In *Entre alambradas*. By Eulalio Ferrer. Barcelona: Grijalbo, 1988.

Berdoulay, Vincente. "Place, Meaning, and Discourse in French Language Geography." In *The Power of Place: Bringing Together Geographical and Sociological Imaginations*, edited by John Agnew and James Duncan. Cambridge: Unwin Hyman, 1989.

Bermejo, Benito. *Francisco Boix, el fotógrafo de Mauthausen*. Barcelona: RBA Libros, 2002.

Bessie, Alvah. *Men in Battle*. San Francisco: Chandler & Sharp Publishers, 1985.

Bessie, Dan, ed. *Alvah Bessie's Spanish Civil War Notebooks*. Lexington: University Press of Kentucky, 2002.

Bhabha, Homi, ed. *Nation and Narration*. London: Routledge, 1990.

Bois, Elie J. *Truth on the Tragedy of France*. Translated by Scarlyn Wilson. London: Hodder and Stoughton Ltd., 1941.

"Boletines de Argelès-sur-Mer." *Canelobre: Revista del Instituto de Estudios Juan Gil-Albert* 20–21 (1991): 161–68.

Bravo-Tellado, A. A. (Antonio Tellado Vázquez and Antonio Sánchez-Bravo Cenjor). *El peso de la derrota, 1939–1944: La tragedia de medio millón de españoles en el exilio*. Madrid: Edifrans, 1974.

Cabrera Infante, Guillermo. "The Invisible Exile." In *Literature in Exile*, edited by John Glad. Durham: Duke University Press, 1990.

Cabruja-Auguet, Agustí. *La ciudad de madera*. Mexico City: Vértice, 1947.

La campaña de Francia: 10 de mayo–25 de junio de 1940. Berlin: E. Zander, 1940.

Campo, Adelita del. "Camino del exilio, camino de la esclavitud." *Canelobre: Revista del Instituto de Estudios Juan Gil-Albert* 20–21 (1991): 61–70.

Camus, Albert. *¡España Libre! (Artículos, discursos y documentos sobre el problema español)*. Edited and translated Juan M. Molina. Mexico City: Editores Mexicanos Unidos, 1966.

Cárdenas, Cuauhtémoc. Presentación. In *España comienza en los Pirineos*, by Luís Suárez. México: Pangea, 1987.

Cargas, Harry, ed. *Problems Unique to the Holocaust*. Lexington: University Press of Kentucky, 1999.

Carrasco, Juan. *La odisea de los republicanos españoles en Francia (1939–1945)*. Barcelona: Edicions Nova Lletra, 1980.

Castillo Rosas, Rosa. "Comentario sobre la obra literaria del escritor catalán Agustí Cabruja i Auguet." In *El exilio literario español de 1939*, vol. 2., edited by Manuel Aznar Soler. Barcelona: GEXEL, 1998.

Catalá, Neus, ed. *De la resistencia y la deportación: 50 testimonios de mujeres españolas*. Barcelona: Ediciones Península, 2000.

Catálogo del material cogido al enemigo. Exposición de guerra. San Sebastián, 1938.

Caudet, Francisco, ed. *Romance: Revista Popular Hispanoamericana.* Facsimile edition. Madrid: Ediciones Turner, 1989.

Chambrun, René de. *I Saw France Fall: Will She Rise Again?* New York: William Morrow & Company, 1940.

Chopitea, María José de. *Sola.* Mexico City: Premiá Editora, 1979.

Cimorra, Clemente. *El bloqueo del hombre.* Buenos Aires: Editorial Claridad, 1940.

Collioure 1939. Les derniers jours d'Antonio Machado/Ultimos días de Antonio Machado. Edited by Jacques Issorel. Collioure: Fondation Antonio Machado, 1982.

Cowans, Jon. "Visions of the Postwar: The Politics of Memory and Expectation in 1940s France." *History and Memory* 10 (1998): 68–101.

Cruz, José Ignacio. "Los barracones de cultura: noticias sobre las actividades educativas de los exiliados españoles en los campos de refugiados." *Spagna Contemporanea* 5 (1994): 61–78.

Cruz y Gómez, Cesáreo de la. *Mis campos de concentración.* Segovia: CEYDE, 1978.

Cuarenta años de cultura española en el exilio. Spec. issue of *La Semana de Bellas Artes* 109 (January 2, 1980): 1–16.

Cuesta, Josefina, and Benito Bermejo, eds. *Emigración y exilio: españoles en Francia (1936–1946).* Madrid: Eudema, 1996.

Dalí, Salvador. *Hidden Faces.* Translated by Haakon Chevalier. London: Peter Owen, 1990.

"Des dels camps. Cartes de refugiats i internats al Migdia Francès l'any 1939." Edited by Francesc Vilanova i Vila-Abadal. *Quaderns de l'Arxiu Pi i Sunyer* 3 (1998).

Di Febo, Giuliana. "Un espacio de la memoria: el paso de la frontera francesa de los exiliados españoles. La despedida del Presidente Azaña." In *Literatura y cultura del exilio español de 1939 en Francia,* edited by Alicia Alted Vigil and Manuel Aznar Soler. Saint Cugat del Valles: AEMIC-GEXEL, 1998.

Domínguez, Edmundo. *Los vencedores de Negrín.* Mexico City: Editorial Nuestro Pueblo, 1940.

"Don Quijote de la Mancha." *Romance* 20 (January 15, 1941): 18.

Dreyfus-Armand, Geneviève. *L'exil des républicains espagnols en France: De la Guerre civile à la mort de Franco.* Paris: Albin Michel, 1999.

Dreyfus-Armand, Geneviève, and Emile Temime. *Les camps sur la plage, un exil espagnol.* Paris: Editions Autrement, 1995.

Duroux, Rose, and Raquel Thiercelin. "Los niños del exilio: asignatura pendiente." In *Emigración y exilio: españoles en Francia (1936–1946),* edited by Josefina Cuesta and Benito Bermejo. Madrid: Eudema, 1996.

España Peregrina. Facsimile Edition. Mexico City: Ed. Alejandro Finisterre, 1977.

Espinar, Jaime. *Argelès-Sur-Mer (Campo de concentración para españoles).* Caracas: Elite, 1940.

Esteban Vilaró, José. *El ocaso de los dioses rojos. Barcelona, Perthus, Argelès, París, Méjico...* Barcelona: Ediciones Destino, 1939.

El exilio español en México. Madrid: Ministerio de Cultura, 1983.

Fabela, Isidro. *Cartas al Presidente Cárdenas.* Mexico City, 1947.

———. *Neutralidad. Estudio histórico, jurídico y político: la Sociedad de las Naciones y el continente americano ante la guerra de 1939–1940.* Mexico City: Biblioteca de Estudios Internacionales, 1940.

Faber, Sebastiaan. *Exile and Cultural Hegemony: Spanish Intellectuals in Mexico, 1939–1975.* Nashville: Vanderbilt University Press, 2002.

Feinstein, Stephen. "Art after Auschwitz." In *Problems Unique to the Holocaust,* edited by Harry Cargas. Lexington: University Press of Kentucky, 1999.

Felipe, León. *Obras completas.* Buenos Aires: Editorial Losada, 1963.

Fernández, Alberto. *Emigración republicana española (1939–1945).* Madrid: Lee y Discute, 1972.

Ferran de Pol, Lluís *De lluny i de prop.* Barcelona: Selecta, 1973.

Ferrer, Eulalio. *Entre alambradas.* Barcelona: Grijalbo, 1988.

———. *Entre alambradas. Diario de los campos de concentración.* Mexico City: Pangea Editores, 1987.

———. *Páginas del exilio.* Mexico City: Aguilar, 1999.

———. *Santander-México. Presencia de Eulalio Ferrer.* Edited by Carlos Galán Lorés, Aurelio García Cantalapiedra, and Valeriano García-Barredo Alonso. Santander: Colección Atarazanas, 1984.

Férriz, Teresa. "Ejemplaridad y tradición inmediata. (A. Machado y F. García Lorca en el exilio español de 1939)." *Scriptura* 6–7 (1991): 189–96.

———. "Las letras catalanas en el exilio mexicano. Algunas propuestas de estudio." In *El exilio catalán en México (Notas para un estudio),* by Dolores Pla Brugat, María Magdalena Ordoñéz, and Teresa Férriz Roure. Guadalajara: El Colegio de Jalisco–Generalitat de Catalunya, 1997.

Fillol, Vicente. *Los perdedores: memorias de un exiliado español.* Madrid: Ediciones "Gaceta Ilustrada," 1973.

Fischer, Louis. *Men and Politics: An Autobiography.* New York: Duell, Sloan and Pearce, 1941.

Foix, Pedro. *España desgarrada.* Mexico City: Ediciones Ibero-Americanas, 1942.

Fotos Hermanos Mayo. Exhibit Catalog. Valencia: Institut Valencia d' Art Modern, 1992.

Foucault, Michel. "Of Other Spaces." Translated by Jay Miskowiec. *Diacritics* 16, no. 1 (1986): 22–27.

———. *The Order of Things: An Archaeology of the Human Sciences.* London: Tavistock, 1970.

Fresco, Mauricio. *La emigración republicana española: una victoria de México.* Mexico City: Editores Asociados, 1950.

Fridman, Lea. *Words and Witness: Narrative and Aesthetic Strategies in the Representation of the Holocaust.* Albany: State University of New York Press, 2000.

Fuentes Mares, José. *Historia de un conflicto (El tesoro del "Vita").* Madrid: CUS Ediciones, 1975.

Gálvez Yagüe, Jesús. *José Herrera Petere: vida, compromiso político y literatura.* Sigüenza: Ediciones de Librería Rayuela, 2000.

———, ed. *Niebla de cuernos (Entreacto en Europa),* by José Herrera Petere. Sada: Ediciós do Castro, 2002.

García Gerpe, Manuel. *Alambradas: Mis nueve meses por los campos de concentración de Francia.* Buenos Aires: Celta, 1941.

García Lorca, Federico. *Romancero gitano.* Edited by Allen Josephs and Juan Caballero. Madrid: Cátedra, 1987.

García Márquez, Gabriel, and Subcomandante Marcos. "A Zapatista Reading List." *The Nation* 273 (July 2, 2001): 36–37.

García-Moreno, Felipe. "10 Méxicos para 10 españoles." *Viceversa* 61 (June 1998): 8–31.
García Pradas, José. *Cómo terminó la guerra de España*. Buenos Aires: Ediciones Iman, 1940.
Garibay, Ricardo. "Por aquellos españoles . . . " In *El exilio español en México, 1939–1982*. Mexico City: FCE, 1982.
Giménez Igualada, Miguel. *Más allá del dolor*. Mexico City: Tierra y Libertad, 1946.
Giral, Francisco. "Actividad de los gobiernos y de los partidos republicanos (1939–1976)." In *El exilio español de 1939*, vol. 2, edited by José Luis Abellán. Madrid: Taurus, 1976.
———. *La República en el exilio*. Madrid: Ediciones 99, 1977.
Giral, José. "Declaración ministerial del Gobierno Giral ante las Cortes de la República reunidas en México el 7 de noviembre de 1945." In *La emigración de la guerra civil de 1936–1939*, vol. 3, by Javier Rubio. Madrid: Librería Editorial San Martín, 1977.
Gironella, Cecilia, ed. *El ojo de Polifemo: visión de la obra de Agustí Bartra*. Mexico City: B. Costa-Amic, 1957.
Gómez Burón, Joaquín. *Exilio y muerte de Antonio Machado*. Madrid: Ediciones SEDMAY, 1975.
Gómez Molina, Ramón. *Qué son los exiliados*. Barcelona: La Gaya Ciencia, 1977.
Gomís Soler, José. *Cruces sin Cristo*. Mexico City: Compañía General de Ediciones, 1952.
Gran enciclopedia asturiana. Vol. 1. Gijón: Heraclio Fournier, 1970.
Granados, Mariano. *La extradición de los refugiados españoles*. Mexico City: Agrupación de Universitarios Españoles, 1946.
Grando, René, Jacques Queralt, and Xavier Febrés. *Vous avez la mémoire courte . . . 1939: 500.000 républicains venus du Sud 'indésirables' en Roussillon*. Perpignan: Edition du Chiendent, 1981.
Green, Jerald. "Agustí Centelles: La forja de un periodista grafic." *Agustí Centelles (1909–1985), fotoperiodista*. Barcelona: Fundació Caixa de Catalunya, 1988.
Gruen, Walter. "Remedios Varo: A Biographical Sketch." In *The Magic of Remedios Varo*. Washington, D.C.: National Museum of Women in the Arts, 2000.
Halbwachs, Maurice. *On Collective Memory*. Edited and translated by Lewis A. Coser. Chicago: University of Chicago Press, 1992.
Herrera Petere: artículos publicados en El Nacional-*México*. Edited by Narciso Alba. Madrid: Ediciones de la Torre, 1996.
Herrera Petere, José. *Niebla de cuernos (Entreacto en Europa)*. Mexico City: Séneca, 1940.
Issorel, Jacques. "Collioure, 1939. Ultimos días de Antonio Machado (a través de los recuerdos de Jacques Baills, Corpus Barga, Juliette Figueres, José Machado y Matea Monedero de Machado)." In *Collioure, 1939. Les derniers jours d'Antonio Machado/Ultimos días de Antonio Machado*, edited by Jacques Issorel. Collioure: Fondation Antonio Machado, 1982.
———. "Regard critique sur 'un libro en homenaje al gran poeta Antonio Machado.'" *Les langues modernes* 70 (1976): 423.
Jaén, Juan Luis. "Una exposición reúne en el Palacio de Cristal del Retiro 400 objetos de exiliados españoles, una memora viva de la diáspora republicana." *Madridiario* (2002), http://www.madridiario.es/reportajes/reportaje-exiliados.jsp. (May 16, 2003).

Jarnés, Benjamín. "Lanza y estilo." *Romance* 24 (May 31, 1941): 1–2.

Kaminsky, Amy. *After Exile: Writing the Latin American Diaspora*. Minneapolis: University of Minnesota Press, 1999.

Kaplan, Janet. *Unexpected Journeys: The Art and Life of Remedios Varo*. New York: Abbeville Press, 1988.

Kent, Victoria. *Cuatro años en París (1940–1944)*. Buenos Aires: Ediciones Sur, 1947.

Klein, Kerwin. "On the Emergence of *Memory* in Historical Discourse." *Representations* 69 (2000): 127–50.

Koestler, Arthur. *Scum of the Earth*. New York: The Macmillan Company, 1941.

LaCapra, Dominick. *History and Memory after Auschwitz*. Ithaca: Cornell University Press, 1998.

Largo Caballero, Francisco. *¿Qué se puede hacer?* Mexico City, 1940.

Lattimore, Richard, trans. *The Odyssey of Homer*. New York: Harper Colophon Books, 1975.

Letras del exilio/México, 1939–1949. Biblioteca de Ateneo Español de México. Valencia: Universitat de Valencia, 1999.

Levi, Primo. "The Gray Zone." In *The Drowned and the Saved*, translated by Raymond Rosenthal. New York: Vintage International, 1988.

———. *Survival in Auschwitz: The Nazi Assault on Humanity*. 1947. Translated by Stuart Woolf. New York, Touchstone, 1996.

Lida, Clara E. *Inmigración y exilio: Reflexiones sobre el caso español*. Mexico City: Siglo XXI Editores, 1997.

López Barrantes, Ramón. *Mi exilio (1939–1951)*. Madrid: G. Del Toro, 1974.

López-Pozo, María José. "¿Sobrevive el discurso testimonial al que se le niega un referente histórico?" In *El exilio literario español de 1939*, vol. 1., edited by Manuel Aznar Soler. Barcelona: GEXEL, 1998.

Los de Collioure (Relatos de un crimen). Prologue by Margarita Nelken. Mexico City: Editorial Morelos, 1940.

Loureiro, Angel. *The Ethics of Autobiography: Replacing the Subject in Modern Spain*. Nashville: Vanderbilt University Press, 2000.

Macdonald, Nancy. *Homage to the Spanish Exiles: Voices from the Spanish Civil War*. New York: Insight Books, 1987.

Machado, Antonio. *Poesías completas*. Edited by Oreste Macrì. Madrid: Espasa-Calpe and Fundación Antonio Machado, 1989.

Madariaga, Salvador de. *España: ensayo de historia contemporánea*. Madrid: Espasa-Calpe, 1979.

Mancheño Ferreras, Antonio. Epílogo. Biobibliografía. In *St. Cyprien, plage . . .*, by Manuel Andújar. Huelva: Diputación Provincial de Huelva, 1990.

Mangini, Shirley. *Memories of Resistance: Women's Voices from the Spanish Civil War*. New Haven: Yale University Press, 1995.

Mantecón de Souto, Matilde. "Indice biobibliográfico del exilio español en México." In *El exilio español en México, 1939–1982*. Mexico City: Fondo de Cultura Económica, 1982.

El maquis, 60 años después. Special issue of *Trébede: Mensual Aragonés de Análisis, Opinión y Cultura* 31 (October 1999).

Marañón, Gregorio. Prólogo. In *Cómo viven los españoles en París*, by Marcial Retuerto. Paris: La Cámara Oficial de Comercio de España, 1941.

Marichal, Juan. Prólogo. In *El archivo de la República española en el exilio, 1945–1977 (Inventario del Fondo París)*. Madrid: Fundación Universitaria Española, 1993.
Maritain, Jacques. *France My Country: Through the Disaster*. New York: Longmans, Green and Co., 1941.
Martel, Francis. *Pétain: Verdun to Vichy*. New York: E. P. Dutton, 1943.
Martín, Francisco de. "La FETE y la cultura en los campos de refugiados." In *Emigración y exilio: españoles en Francia (1936–1946)*, edited by Josefina Cuesta y Benito Bermejo. Madrid: Eudema, 1996.
Le martyre des antifascistes dans les camps de concentration de l'Afrique du Nord. Preface by Virgile Barel. Algiers: Secours Populaire Algerien, 1945.
Mateo Sousa, Eligio de. "México, tierra de promisión." *Historia 16*, 172 (1990): 112–19.
Matesanz, José Antonio, ed. *México y la República española. Antología de documentos, 1931–1977*. Mexico City: Centro Republicano Español de México, 1978.
———. *Las raíces del exilio: México ante la guerra civil española, 1936–1939*. Mexico City: El Colegio de México/UNAM, 1999.
Maurois, André. *Tragedy in France*. Translated by Denver Lindley. New York: Harper & Bros., 1940.
McLellan, David. *Utopian Pessimist: The Life and Thought of Simone Weil*. New York: Poseidon Press, 1990.
Méndez, Concha. *Memorias habladas, memorias armadas*. Edited by Paloma Ulacia Altolaguirre. Madrid: Mondadori, 1990.
Mije, Antonio. *Los refugiados españoles en Francia y la solidaridad americana*. Mexico City: Editorial Morelos, 1940.
Misión de Luis I. Rodríguez en Francia: La protección de los refugiados españoles, julio a diciembre de 1940. Mexico City: El Colegio de México/Secretaría de Relaciones Exteriores/Consejo Nacional de Ciencia y Tecnología, 2000.
Mistral, Silvia. *Éxodo*. Mexico City: Editorial Minerva, 1940.
Molins i Fábrega, Narcís, and Josep Bartolí. *Campos de concentración, 1939–194 . . .* Mexico City: Iberia, 1944.
Montseny, Federica. *El éxodo: Pasión y muerte de españoles en el exilio*. Barcelona: Galba, 1977.
Museo Iconográfico del Quijote. Guanajuato: Artes Gráficas, 1998.
Naharro-Calderón, José. "De 'Cadahalso 34' a *Manuscrito Cuervo*: el retorno de las alambradas." In *Manuscrito Cuervo: Historia de Jacobo*, by Max Aub, edited by José Antonio Pérez Bowie. Segorbe: Fundación Max Aub, 1999.
———. *Entre el exilio y el interior: el 'entresiglo' y Juan Ramón Jiménez*. Barcelona: Anthropos, 1994.
———, ed. *El exilio de las Españas de 1939 en las Américas: "¿Adónde fue la canción?"* Barcelona: Anthropos, 1991.
———. "Por los campos de Francia: entre el frío de las alambradas y el calor de la memoria." In *Literatura y cultura del exilio español de 1939 en Francia*, edited by Alicia Alted Vigil and Manuel Aznar Soler. Sant Cugat de Valles: AEMIC-GEXEL, 1998.
Nelken, Margarita. Prólogo. In *Los de Collioure (Relatos de un crimen)*. Mexico City: Editorial Morelos, 1940.
Nora, Pierre. "Between Memory and History: *Les Lieux de Mémoire*." Translated by Marc Roudebush. *Representations* 26 (1989): 7–25.
Nos Aldás, Eloísa. "El exilio español en Francia a través de los trazos de Josep Bartolí:

los campos." In *Proyecto Clío: Una mirada hispana a la Historia Universal.* http//clio.rediris.es/exilio/loscampos/los%20campos.htm. (April 29, 2001).

Palacio, Solano. *El éxodo por un refugiado español.* Valparaíso: Editorial Más Allá, 1939.

———. *Entre dos fascismos: Memorias de un voluntario de las Brigadas Internacionales en España.* Valparaíso: Editorial Más Allá, 1940.

Palencia, Isabel de. *Smouldering Freedom: The Story of the Spanish Republicans in Exile.* New York: Longmans, Green and Co., 1945.

Pike, David W. *"Vae Victis!": Los republicanos españoles refugiados en Francia, 1939–1944.* Paris: Ruedo Ibérico, 1969.

Pla Brugat, Dolores. *"Els exiliats catalans": Un estudio de la emigración republicana española en México.* Mexico City: Instituto Nacional de Antropología e Historia, 1999.

Plages d'exil: Les camps de réfugiés espagnols en France, 1939. Edited by Jean-Claude Villegas. Nanterre: BDIC; Dijon: Hispanística XX, 1989.

Pollefeyt, Didier. "Victims of Evil or Evil of Victims?" In *Problems Unique to the Holocaust,* edited by Harry Cargas. Lexington: University Press of Kentucky, 1999.

Pons Prades, Eduardo. *Republicanos españoles en la Segunda Guerra Mundial.* Barcelona: Planeta, 1975.

Prat, José. "Crítica y política." In *El exilio de las Españas de 1939 en las Américas: '¿Adónde fue la canción?,'* edited by José Naharro-Calderón. Barcelona: Anthropos, 1991.

Prensa de la Segunda República en el exilio. Exhibit catalog. Tarancón: Imprenta Antona, 2000.

Preston, Paul. *Franco: A Biography.* New York: Basic Books, 1994.

Prieto, Indalecio. *Convulsiones de España (Pequeños detalles de grandes sucesos).* Vol. 1. Barcelona: Planeta, 1989.

———. Epistolario Prieto-Negrín. In *Convulsiones de España (Pequeños detalles de grandes sucesos).* Vol. 4. Barcelona: Planeta, 1990.

Rafaneau-Boj, Marie-Claude. *Los campos de concentración de los refugiados españoles en Francia (1939–1945).* Barcelona: Editorial Omega, 1995.

Regler, Gustav. *The Owl of Minerva.* Translated by Norman Denny. New York: Farrar, Straus & Cuday, 1959.

Rejano, Juan. "A los alcances de la novela." [July 15, 1940] *España Peregrina.* Facsimile edition. Mexico City: Alejandro Finisterre, 1977.

———. "Paz en la guerra." *Romance* (March 1, 1940): 7.

———. "Recuerdo de Antonio Machado a los 20 años de su muerte." In *A Don Antonio Machado al cumplirse los 20 años de su muerte.* Mexico City, 1961.

———. "Una obra de liberación." *Romance* (June 1, 1940): 7.

Remedios Varo: Catálogo razonado/catalogue raisonné. Mexico City: Ediciones Era, 1994.

Renan, Ernest. "What Is a Nation?" Translated by Martin Thom. In *Nation and Narration,* edited by Homi K. Bhabha. London: Routledge, 1990.

Renau, Juan. *Pasos y sombras. Autopsia.* Mexico City: Colección Aquelarre, 1953.

Retuerto, Marcial. *Cómo viven los españoles en París.* Prologue by Gregorio Marañón. París: La Cámara Oficial de Comercio de España, 1941.

Reyes, Alfonso. Elegía. *España Peregrina* 8–9 (October 1940): 55.

Rial, José. *El dolor de la derrota (Notas emocionadas de la emigración española en las cárceles, refugios y campos de concentración de Francia).* Mexico City: Imprenta Aurora, 1946.

Rioja, Enrique. "Ultimo sol en España." In *'Las Españas': Historia de una revista del exilio*

(1946–1963), edited by James Valender and Gabriel Rojo Leyva. Mexico City: El Colegio de México, 1999.

Rodrigo, Antonina. *Mujer y exilio, 1939*. Madrid: Compañía Literaria, 1999.

Rodríguez, Luis I. *Ballet de sangre: la caída de Francia*. Prologue by Pablo Neruda. Mexico City: Ediciones Nigromante, 1942.

Rojo, Vicente. *¡Alerta a los pueblos! Estudio político-militar del período final de la guerra española*. Buenos Aires: Aniceto López, 1939.

Romance: Revista Popular Hispanoamericana. Facsimile edition. Edited by Francisco Caudet. Madrid: Ediciones Turner, 1989.

Ros, Antonio. *Diario de un refugiado republicano*. Barcelona: Ediciones Grijalbo, 1975.

Rosal, Amaro del. *El oro del Banco de España y la historia del Vita*. Mexico City: Editorial Grijalbo, 1976.

Roth, Philip. "A Conversation with Primo Levi." In *Survival at Auschwitz: The Nazi Assault on Humanity*, by Primo Levi. New York: Touchstone, 1996.

Rowlands, Michael. "Memory, Sacrifice and the Nation." *New Formations* 30 (1996): 8–17.

Rubio, Javier. *La emigración de la guerra civil de 1936–1939*. 3 Vols. Madrid: Librería Editorial San Martín, 1977.

———. "La población española en Francia de 1936 a 1946: flujos y permanencias." In *Emigración y exilio: españoles en Francia (1936–1946)*, edited by Josefina Cuesta and Benito Bermejo. Madrid: Eudema, 1996.

———. "Política francesa de acogida: los campos de internamiento." In *Emigración y exilio: españoles en Francia (1936–1946)*, edited by Josefina Cuesta and Benito Bermejo. Madrid: Eudema, 1996.

Ruiz, Roberto. *El último oasis*. Mexico City: Joaquín Mortiz, 1964.

Said, Edward. "Invention, Memory, Place." *Critical Inquiry* 26, no. 2 (2000): 175–92.

Samblancat, Angel. *Caravana nazarena (Éxodo y odisea de España, 1936–1940 y . . .)*. Mexico City: Ed. Orbe, 1945.

Samblancat Miranda, Neus. "*Éxodo: Diario de una refugiada española*, de Silvia Mistral." In *II Coloquio Internacional: La literatura y la cultura del exilio republicano español de 1939*, edited by Róger González Martel. La Habana: CHE-GEXEL-AEMIC, 2000.

Sampelayo, Carlos. *Los que no volvieron*. Prologue by Manuel Vázquez Montalbán. Barcelona: Los Libros de la Frontera, 1975.

Sánchez, Belén. "'Yo fui esclavo de los nazis.'" *El Semanal* 698 (March 11–17, 2001): 24–32.

Sánchez Barbudo, Antonio. "El Grupo de *Hora de España* en 1939." In *Ensayos y recuerdos*, 89–105. Barcelona: Laia, 1980.

———. "Niebla de cuernos." *Letras de México* 15 (June 1940): 4, 10.

Sánchez Vázquez, Adolfo. "En torno a la picaresca." *Romance* (May 15, 1940): 6.

Scarry, Elaine. *On Beauty and Being Just*. Princeton: Princeton University Press, 1999.

Schama, Simon. *Landscape and Memory*. New York: Alfred A. Knopf, 1995.

Semprún, Jorge. *Viviré con su nombre, morirá con el mío*. Translated by Carlos Pujol. Barcelona: Tusquets Editores, 2001.

Semprún-Maura, Carlos. *El año que viene en Madrid*. Madrid: Musigraf ARABI, 1978.

Seró Sabaté, Joaquín. *El niño republicano*. Facsimile edition. Madrid: EDAF, 2000.

Serra, Pedro. *Memorias de un trashumante: epopeya antinazifascista. Dictadura y exilio.* Mexico City: B. Costa-Amic, 1966.

Serrano, Secundino. *Maquis. Historia de la guerrilla antifranquista.* Madrid: Ediciones Temas de Hoy, 2001.

Shain, Yossi. *The Frontier of Loyalty: Political Exiles in the Age of the Nation-State.* Middletown: Wesleyan University Press, 1989.

Shaw, Donald. "La búsqueda de la autenticidad en *Morir por cerrar los ojos*." In *Max Aub y el laberinto español*, vol. 1, edited by Ignacio Soldevila-Durante. Valencia: Universidad de Valencia–Fundación Max Aub, 1996.

Sherman, Daniel J. *The Construction of Memory in Interwar France.* Chicago: University of Chicago Press, 1999.

Simone, André. *"J'accuse!": The Men Who Betrayed France.* New York: Dial Press, 1940.

Smith, Lois Elwyn. *Mexico and the Spanish Republicans.* Berkeley and Los Angeles: University of California Press, 1955.

Sofsky, Wolfgang. *The Order of Terror: The Concentration Camp.* Translated by William Templer. Princeton: Princeton University Press, 1997,

Soriano, Antonio. *Éxodos: Historia oral del exilio republicano en Francia, 1939–1945.* Barcelona: Editorial Crítica, 1989.

Stein, Louis. *Beyond Death and Exile: The Spanish Republicans in France, 1939–1955.* Cambridge: Harvard University Press, 1979.

Suárez, Luis. *España comienza en los Pirineos.* Mexico City: I.C.D., 1944.

———. *España comienza en los Pirineos.* 2nd ed. Prologue by Cuauhtémoc Cárdenas. Mexico City: Pangea, 1987.

———. *Puente sin fin.* Mexico City: Grijalbo, 2000.

Todorov, Tzvetan. *Facing the Extreme: Moral Life in the Concentration Camps.* Translated by Arthur Denner and Abigail Pollak. New York: Metropolitan Books, 1996.

Torres, Henry. *Campaign of Treachery.* New York: Dodd, Mead and Company, 1942.

Los transterrados españoles del 39. Special issue of *La Gaceta del Fondo de Cultura Económica.* 342 (June 1999).

Ugarte, Michael. *Shifting Ground: Spanish Civil War Exile Literature.* Durham: Duke University Press, 1989.

———. "Testimonios de exilio: desde el campo de concentración a América." In *El exilio de las Españas de 1939 en las Américas: "¿Adónde fue la canción?,"* edited by José Naharro-Calderón. Barcelona: Anthropos, 1991.

Ultramar: Revista mensual de cultura. Facsimile edition. Edited by James Valender. Mexico City: El Colegio de México, 1993.

Valender, James, and Gabriel Rojo Leyva, eds. *"Las Españas": historia de una revista del exilio (1946–1963)*, 161–81. Mexico City: El Colegio de México, 1999.

Valiente, Manolo. *Arena y viento / Du sable et du vient / Sorra i vent. Romance del refugiado, 1939–1940.* Editions du Chiendent, 1986.

Valis, Noël. "Nostalgia and exile." *Journal of Spanish Cultural Studies* 1, no. 2 (2000): 117–33.

Valldeperes, Manuel. *Ombres entre tenebres (L'exode de Catalunya).* Buenos Aires: Edicions de la Revista Catalunya, 1941.

Vallejo, César. *The Complete Posthumous Poetry.* Translated by Clayton Eshleman and José Rubia Barcia. Berkeley and Los Angeles: University of California Press, 1978.

Vázquez Montalbán, Manuel. "Perder la Historia." In *Los que no volvieron*, by Carlos Sampelayo. Barcelona: Los Libros de la Frontera, 1975.

Vilanova, Antonio. *Los olvidados: los exiliados españoles en la segunda guerra mundial*. Paris: Ruedo Ibérico, 1969.

Vives i Clavé, Pere. *Cartes des dels camps de concentració*. Prologue by Agustí Bartra. Barcelona: Edicions 62, 1972.

Weil, Bruno. *Francia a través de las alambradas: La caída de Francia, la vida en los campos de concentración*. Buenos Aires: Editorial Claridad, 1941.

Xirau, Joaquín. "Por una senda clara." 1959. *Diálogos* 19 (July–August 1983): 58–64.

Zambrano, María. "Sentido de la derrota." In *Sentido de la derrota (selección de textos de escritores españoles exiliados en Cuba)*, edited by Jorge Domingo and Róger González. Barcelona: GEXEL, 1998.

Zapata, Mario. *Burgos, 1940–53: Cárcel de la dictadura franquista*. Mexico City: Publicaciones Mexicanas, 1983.

Zapirain, Luis. *Terror sobre España*. Mexico City: Foare, 1940.

Zurita Castañer, Joaquín. *Los círculos del exilio español en Europa (1930–1975)*. Zaragoza: INO-Reproducciones, 1985.

Index

Abellán, José Luis, 37; on language, state control of, 290 n. 5

"Abrid mi carne con el hierro" [Cut My Flesh with a Knife] (Amieva), 184

After Exile: Writing the Latin America Diaspora (Kaminsky), 24

"agrio, El"[The Bitter Wind] (Andújar), 157–58; on acts of naming, 158; elements of nature in, 157–58

Aguirre, José Antonio de, 320 n. 3

Alambradas: Mis nueve meses por los campos de concentración de Francia [Barbed Wire: My Nine Months in the Concentration Camps of France] (García Gerpe), 28, 51, 150, 156, 235–59, 266; death in, 239; early exile experiences in, 240; literary structure of, 241–43; "othering" in, 240; physical treatment in, 238; Septfonds in, 150, 156, 242; Spanish civil war, effect of, 242

Alberti, Rafael, 211

aleluyas (camp-inspired cartoons), 212–13

¡Alerta a los pueblos! (Rojo), 244

almohada de arena, La [Pillow of Sand] (Amieva), 43, 61, 148–49, 169–88; *Don Quijote* (Cervantes): influence on, 185; exile experience in, 148–49; García Lorca, Federico, influence on, 171–73; literary structure of, 169, 173–74; publishing history of, 169; use of text within, 185

Alonso, Monique, 50, 172–73, 184

Alted Vigil, Alicia, 256

Altolaguirre, Manuel, 13, 26

Altolaguirre, Paloma, 28

Alvarez de Vayo, Julio, 225

Alvarez Posada, José María; pen names for, 313 n. 1. *See also* Amieva, Celso

Amieva, Celso, 42–45, 50, 61, 66–67, 69, 150, 167–75, 177–82, 187–88, 235, 285, 310 n. 4; in concentration camps, 42, 150, 167; *Don Quijote*, influence of, 171; on El Dorado mythology, 175; on *El Hacha (Elegía española)* [The Hatchet (A Spanish Elegy)] (Felipe), 177; on exile transportation, 310 n. 4; postwar life of, 187–88

Anderson, Benedict, 16, 23, 31; on exiled nations, 31; on national identity, 16

Andújar, Manuel, 37, 148, 153–66, 189, 295 n. 10; journalist history of, 165; in Mexico City, 154; on national reconstruction, 163; on political exiles, 154; at St. Cyprien, 153–66

Angustia [Anguish] (Varo), 112

Ansó, Mariano, 225

Antonio Machado, poeta en el exilio (Alonso), 50

"Aquella encuesta" [That Survey] (Andújar), 165

"Aquí está el español . . ." [Here Is The Spaniard] (Amieva), 185

Araquistáin, Luis, 287

"Arenosis" (Amieva), 176–80; exile imagery in, 180; Felipe, León, influence on, 177; motifs in, 176; sand imagery in, 180; symbolism in, 179

arenosis (sand-neurosis), 168

Argelès-sur-Mer (concentration camp), 35, 55–56, 145, 164; in *La ciudad de madera* [The City of Wood] (Cabruja-Auguet), 41–42; in *Los nuevos profetas* [The New Prophets] (Benavides), 123; physical environment of, 55–56, 149, 164

Argelès-Sur-Mer (Espinar), 51, 310 n. 4

Artís-Gener, Avel·lí, 14, 25, 60, 147, 285–86; on camp guards, 60; concentration camps, return to, 285–86; on exiles, 14; at Prats-de-Molló, 147

Asturianos en el destierro (Francia) [Asturians in Exile (France)] (Amieva), 42, 168, 175–76; *arenosis* in, 168; El Dorado myth in, 175–76

Aub, Max, 16, 24, 85, 103, 122, 228
Avenida de la Libertad, La 151, 157
Avila Camacho, Manuel, 219
Azaña, Manuel, 214, 235, 306 n. 31; on exile treatment, 306 n. 31; Izquierda Republicana Party and, 214, 235
Aznar Soler, Manuel, 38

Baer, Ulrich, 145, 154
Baeza Medina, Emilio, 229, 257–58; Izquierda Republicana Party and, 257–58
Baills, Jacques, 49–50
Baldó García, Ricardo, 224
"Ballad of the French Mobile Guard" (Amieva), 173–74, 187; García Lorca, Federico, influence on, 173; literary structure of, 173–74
Ballano Bueno, Adolfo, 56, 72; in Argelès-sur-Mer, 72
Ballester, Pepe, 231, 233; SERE and, 233
Ballet de Sangre: la caída de Francia [Ballet of Blood: The Fall of France] (Rodríguez), 86–87, 126, 265; Spanish Republicans in, 87
Barcarès (concentration camp), 35, 170; Amieva, Celso, in, 170; *barracones de cultura* in, 170; exile activity in, 170
Bardes Font, Francisco, 32; on border crossing, 32
Baroja, Pío, 27
Barona, Vicente, 25
barracones de cultura (cultural barracks), 169–70; educational opportunities in, 170; exile activity in, 169
Barrull, José, 243, 254
Bartolí, Josep, 53–54, 72–80, 109, 223, 227, 287–88; illustrations of, 54, 62, 72–80
Bartra, Agustí, 44, 148, 189–92, 198, 316 n. 10; literary aspirations of, 191; post-war life of, 316 n. 10; Vives, Pere, influence of, 192
Bassols, Narciso, 216, 233
Bejarano, Benigno, 220–21; SERE and, 220–21
Benavente, José, 232
Benavides, Manuel: on French political policy, 190
Benitez, Fernando, 284

Berdoulay, Vincent, 146; on process of meaning, 146
Bergamín, José, 48
Bernade, Antonio, 243, 245–47
Bessie, Alvah, 242, 304 n. 17
Bhabha, Homi, 34
Blanch Pita, Hortensia. *See* Mistral, Silvia
Blasco Ibáñez, Vicente, 27
bloqueo del hombre, El: Novela del drama de España (Cimorra), 283
Bois, Elie, 133
Boletín al servicio de la emigración española (journal), 149
Boletín de estudiantes, 150, 272
Boletín de Profesionales de la Enseñanza (camp journal), 170–71
border camps. *See* concentration camps
Borders, Exiles, Diasporas, 85, 145; exile identity in, 85, 145
Bram (concentration camp), 69, 291 n. 2; ingenuity, of exiles, 291 n. 2
Gómez Burón, Joaquín, 49

caballo griego, El (Altolaguirre), 26
Cabrera Infante, Guillermo, 14, 290 n. 5
Cabruja-Auguet, Agustí, 22, 41–42, 61, 69, 72, 180, 183, 312 n. 50
Calibán (Bartolí), 287
Campaign by Treachery (Torres), 132
Campo, Adelita del, 293 n. 30
Campo cerrado (Aub), 307 n. 32
Campos de Castilla, 43
Campos de concentración 1939–194 . . . (Bartolí/Molins i Fábrega), 53–55, 57–59, 62, 64, 70–79, 81, 94–97, 223; Chamberlain, Neville, in, 54; death motifs in, 64; epilogue for, 79; exile assistance, from families, 301 n. 41; fascist iconography in, 57, 59–60; French iconography in, 75; illustrations, importance of, 57–59, 109; literary structure of, 72–79; as "memory album," 55; narrator's role in, 96; religious motifs in, 73; vengeance themes in, 78; violent imagery in, 78
Camus, Albert, 46, 307 n. 33
Cano, Dr. Luis, 228
Caravana nazarena (Exodo y odisea de España, 1936–1940 y . . .) (Samblancat), 51
Cárdenas, Cuauhtémoc, 130
Cárdenas, Lázaro, 130, 212–14, 219; exile correspondence of, 213–14; exile emi-

gration, role in, 212–14, 219; Fabela, Isidro, and, 213–14
Carner, Josep, 193
Carrasco, Juan: at Collioure, 297 n. 41
Carreras, Adela, 150
"Cataclysm, Flood, Fire" (Andújar), 163–64
Caza nocturna [Nocturnal Hunt] (Varo), 112
Centelles, Agustí, 21
Cervantes, Miguel de, 186, 263; literary influence of, 186
CGT (French labor union), 216
Chamberlain, Neville, 54; in *Campos de concentración 1939–194...* (Bartolí/Molins i Fábrega), 54
Chambrun, René de, 133; on exiles, 133
Champlain (ship), 227
Cillán, Luis, 280
Cimorra, Clemente, 25, 283
ciudad de madera, La [The City of Wood] (Cabruja-Auguet), 22, 41–42, 65, 183; Argelès-sur-Mer in, 41–42; imagery in, 41; Machado, Antonio, in, 41–42
CLI (Center for Incurable *Locos*), 266, 268; in *Entre alambradas* (Ferrer), 266
CNT (Confederación Nacional de Trabajadores), 223; Mistral, Silvia, and, 224; SERE, criticism of, 223
collective memory, 34, 85, 294 n. 52; for exiles, 34; Halbwachs, Maurice, and, 294 n. 52; Said, Edward, on, 85
Collioure (concentration camp), 35–36, 38, 48–52, 153, 297 n. 41; Carrasco, Juan, in, 297 n. 41; exile life in, 49; inmate insubordination at, 153; Machado, Antonio, in, 38, 48–49
Cómo viven los españoles en París [The Life of Spaniards in Paris] (Retuerto), 100
Companys, Luis, 234
concentration camps (French): acts of sabotage at, 181–82; anecdotal stories in, 71; Argelès-sur-Mer, 35; Barcarès, 35; Bram, 69; class system within, 225–26; Collioure, 35–36, 38; commemorating the dead in, 72; construction of, 15; French authority in, 152; guards at, 57, 58, 59–62, 299 n. 9; hisory of, 291 n. 8; inhospitability of, 21–22, 296 n. 19; *lieux de mémoire* and, 23; literature about, 22, 148–50; local (French) response to, 238; personal accounts, life in, 16–17; physical environment of, 55–56; Prats-de-Molló, 66, 147; Septfonds, 52; St. Cyprien, 22; as transitional "space," 22–23; *vs.* German, 193; *vs.* local town, disconnection with, 156
concentration camps (German), 192–93; fraternity within, 192–93; *vs.* French, 193
"concentrationary universe," 154, 202
Construction of Memory in Interwar France, The (Sherman), 35; memory site theory in, 35
Cordero, Manuel, 268
"Corona de espinas" [Crown of Thorns] (Amieva), 42–45, 50, 172; genesis for, 172; Machado, Antonio, in, 43–45, 172
Cristo de 200.000 brazos (Campo de Argelés) (Bartra), 148–49, 189–207, 316 n. 8; beauty, function of, 204; "Ciudad de derrota" [City of Defeat] in, 191; exile experience in, 148–49; expressions of creativity in, 200; fraternal themes in, 191; Homeric allusions in, 205–6; literary reality in, 201; literary structure of, 194–99, 206; religious imagery in, 189–90, 316 n. 8; seasonal imagery in, 199–200; Vives, Pere, influence in, 192
Cruz, José, 170; on *barracones de cultura*, 170
Cruz y Gómez, Cesáreo de la, 47, 150; Machado, Antonio, and, 47
Cuatro años en París (1940–1944) (Kent), 101, 114–20; French themes in, 119; "In The Street" in, 115–16; literary structure of, 114–15; narrator, role in, 118, 120; political motifs in, 116–17; "The Four Walls" in, 114–15; "Towards Freedom" in, 117–18
Cuba: in Spanish Civil War, 152
Cuba (ship), 259

"Death of the Poet, The" (Mistral), 45–46; Machado, Antonio, in, 45–46
Descamisao, El, 263
Diario de un refugiado republicano [Diary of a Republican Refugee] (Ros), 227, 235
diáspora republicana, La (Artís-Gener), 287, 299 n. 11
"Dichosos los que cayeron" [Fortunate Are the Fallen] (Méndez), 212

Domínguez, Edmundo, 243, 298 n. 2
Don Quijote de la Mancha (Cervantes), 45, 171, 261; *La almohada de arena* [Pillow of Sand] (Amieva), influence on, 185; exile literature, influence on, 262; motifs in, 171
Don Quijote en el Exilio (Rodríguez Luna), 171
Dorado, El (myth), 174–75, 314 n. 16; exiles, effect on, 174
Drowned and the Saved, The (Levi), 222
Duroux, Rose, 31

Emigración y exilio: españoles en Francia (1936–1946), 294 n. 42
emigration (for exiles), 212, 214; Martínez Barrio, Diego, role in, 214; Matesanz, José Antonio, on, 215; SERE, role of, 212; tactics for, 251
Entre alambradas (Ferrer), 45, 262–67, 270–84; celebrations, importance of, 279; CLI in, 266; emigration hopes in, 266; exile trauma, examples of, 267, 274; on *la libertad*, 270; literary aspirations of, 264; Mexico, symbolism of, 267; solidarity themes in, 278; themes in, 266
Entre alambradas [Inside the Barbed Wire] (Ferrer), 227
Entre dos fascismos: Memorias de un voluntario de las Brigadas Internacionales en España [Between Two Fascisms: Memoir of a Volunteer in the International Brigades in Spain] (Palacio), 29
"Era la misma . . ." [She Was the Same] (Amieva), 184–85; war symbolism in, 184–85
"Esclava, La" [The Slave] (Felipe), 178
España, aparta de mí este cáliz [Spain, Take This Cup from me] (Vallejo), 198
España comienza en los Pirineos [Spain Begins in the Pyrenees] (Suárez Lopez), 38, 48, 129, 134–41, 151, 156; concentration camps, symbolic role in, 136; emotional motifs in, 137–38; geopolitical lessons of, 138–39; literary structure of, 134; on naming the camps, 151; visual metaphors in, 135
España Peregrina (magazine), 38, 48; Machado, Antonio, in, 48
Españas, Las (exile journal), 36, 165, 281

Español del éxodo y del llanto [Spaniard of Exodus and Grief] (Felipe), 177; exile experience in, 177–78
Espinar, Jaime, 22, 29, 31, 51, 145–46, 152, 156, 180, 217; on exile journey, 145–47; at St. Cyprien, 146
Esteban Vilaró, José, 14, 225–26
exiles, 14–15, 31, 34; activity in *barracones de cultura*, 169; collective memory for, 34; cultural importance of, 288; El Dorado myth, effect on, 174–75; forced repatriation of, 66–68; under Franco, Francisco, 14; French nationalist response to, 31; ingenuity of, in camps, 150, 301 n. 43; language, state control of, 290 n. 5, 311 n. 39; loss of self for, 168; nationalist identity for, 34, 85; political protest and, 162; population (in France), 51; SERE and, 212; Spanish Republicans and, 15
treatment, in France, 299 n. 10
Exilio y muerte de Antonio Machado (Gómez Buron), 297 n. 42
exilio español de 1939, El (Abellan), 37
Exodo (Mistral), 49, 293 n. 21
éxodo, por un refugiado español, El (Palacio), 26, 214

Fabela, Isidro, 213–15, 308 n. 9; on camp environment, 214; Cárdenas, Lázaro, and, 213–14; on emigration, to Mexico, 214–15; on non-intervention policy, for exiles, 308 n. 9
Facing the Extreme: Moral Life in the Concentration Camps (Todorov), 192–93; concentration camps, fraternity within, 192–93
FAI (Federación Anarquista Ibérica), 223; SERE, criticism of, 223
Falcón, César, 283
fascism: images in *Campos de concentración 1939–194 . . .* (Bartolí/Molins i Fábrega), 57, 59–60; in Spain, 53
Febo, Giuliana Di, 24–25, 30, 292 n. 13; on border crossing, symbolism of, 292 n. 13
Felipe, León, 167, 171, 176–78, 182, 186–87; "Arenosis" (Amieva), influence on, 177; on exile emigrants, 178; Machado, Antonio, and, 182

Fenómeno [Phenomenon] (Varo), 113; imagery in, 113
Fernández, Miguel Angel, 231
Ferran de Pol, Lluís, 146–47; camp experience of, 147
Ferreiro, José, 243
Ferrer, Eulalio, 17, 45, 68, 101, 129, 151, 156, 162, 217, 260–61, 268–69, 273–75, 282, 322 n. 6, 323 n. 12; camp diary of, 260–61, 267, 274, 282; *Don Quijote de la Mancha* (Cervantes), influence on, 261, 270, 275, 322 n. 6, 323 n. 12; emotional survival for, in camp, 272–74; on exile repatriation, 162, 217; Mexico, importance for, 268–69; on naming camps, 151; postwar life of, 296 n. 29; Rial, José, and, 273; SERE and, 268
Férriz, Teresa, 36
fichas de emigabilidad (application for emigration), 246
Flandre (ship), 221
Flores, Sánchez, 231
Foix, Pedro, 30
Foucault, Michel, 156–57, 312 n. 46; on heterotopias, 156, 312 n. 46
Fournier, Claudio, 14–15; on exiles, 14–15
France: exile escape into, 24–25; nationalist response in, to exiles, 31; Spanish Civil War, literary response to, 130–32; Spanish Civil War, role in, 31, 87, 131–32
France My Country: Through the Disaster (Maritain), 131
Franco, Francisco, 13–14, 131–32, 287; death of, 287; exiles under, 14; Law of Political Responsibility and, 162; Pétain, Marshal, and, 131–32
Franco's Spain (Bartolí), 63
Frankl, Victor, 202
Fresco, Mauricio, 218; role in exile emigration, 218

Gabor, Zsa Zsa, 231
Gaceta del Fondo de Cultura Económica, La, 38
Gallegos Rocafull, José, 281
Gamboa, Fernando, 216, 221, 249–50; exile emigration and, 249–50
Gamboa, Susana, 221

Ganarás la luz [You Will Reach the Light] (Felipe), 178
García, Delegado, 249; emigration experience of, 249
García Gerpe, Manuel, 28, 51, 61, 68, 150, 152, 156, 162, 226, 235–37, 245, 259, 269; on camp guards, 61; emigration of, 259; on Law of Political Responsibility, 162; Panadero Caballero, Esperanza, and, 237, 245; at Septfonds, 152, 156, 162, 235–38; SERE and, 306 n. 21
García Lorca, Federico, 61. *See also* Lorca, Federico García
García Mella, Moisés, 231, 233
Garibay, Ricardo, 221
Ghostly Matters: Haunting and Sociological Imagination (Gordon), 286
Giménez Igualada, Miguel, 32, 56, 68, 161–62, 183–84, 190; on border crossing, 32; Mexican emigration of, 220; threatened repatriation of, 68
Giner de los Ríos, Don Francisco, 40, 47
Giral, Francisco, 37
Giral, José, 37
Gómez Molina, Ramón, 290 n. 5
Gomís Soler, José, 265, 302 n. 48
González, Alfonso, 129; at Septfonds, 129
González, Felipe, 284
Gordon, Avery, 286, 288
grand voyage, Le (Semprún), 192
"Gray Zone, The" (Levi), 222
Gross, Berta, 24
Gruen, Walter: on Varo, Remedios, 112
Gypsy Ballads (Lorca), 173; *La almohada de arena* [Pillow of Sand] (Amieva), influence on, 173; at Bacarès, 173

hacha, El (Elegia española) [The Hatchet (A Spanish Elegy)] (Felipe), 176–77, 315 n. 22; Amieva, Celso, on, 177; exile experience, role of, 177; symbolism in, 176
Halbwachs, Maurice: on collective memory, 294 n. 52
Herce, Abel, 277
Hernández, Angel, 52
Herrera Petere, José, 16, 101–2, 122, 228, 305 n. 14; on war exiles, 103
Hervás, Mariano, 243, 251–52; on repatriation, for exiles, 252

heterotopias, 156–57, 312 n. 46; definition of, 157; Foucault, Michel, on, 156
Historia del refugiado, 212
History and Memory after Auschwitz (LaCapra), 35
Hitler, Adolf, 120, 303 n. 11; propaganda machine of, 303 n. 11
Horas de angustia y esperanza [Time of Hope and Anguish] (Ros), 227
"hurry-up streets," 151
Hutton, Barbara, 231

Ibáñez, Paco, 21
Infame cancerbero del infierno [Monstrous Gatekeeper of Hell] (Bartolí), 58f
"La insignia" (Felipe), 182–83; literary relevance of, 183
"Invention, Memory, Place" (Said), 23
Ipanema (ship), 222, 249–50
Izquierda Republicana Party, 228–29, 235; Azaña, Manuel, and, 214, 235; Baeza Medina, Emilio, and, 257

J'Accuse!": The Men Who Betrayed France (Simone), 130
JARE (Junto de Auxilio a los Republicanos Españoles), 233, 256–58, 269, 271; genesis of, 257; SERE, conflicts with, 257–58, 269, 271
Jarnés, Benjamin, 280–81; *Don Quijote de la Mancha* (Cervantes), influence on, 280–81
Jiménez de Asúa, 228
Jouhaux, León, 216
Juvé, Teresa, 181

Kaminsky, Amy, 24, 151; on language, power of, 151
Kaplan, Janet, 109
Kent, Victoria, 16, 101, 119, 122, 228
Kérillis, Henri de, 132
Koestler, Arthur, 120, 122–23, 303 n. 13

LaCapra, Dominick, 35, 295 n. 2
Lamoneda, Ramón, 268
Laviña, Rosa, 67
Law of Political Responsibility, 162, 243–44; Franco, Francisco, and, 162; García Gerpe, Manuel, on, 162; parameters of, 162
ecriture ou la vie, L' (Semprún), 193
León, María Teresa, 35

Letras de México, 102
Levi, Primo, 193, 202, 204, 222, 313 n. 51; on survivor guilt, 222
Humanité, L, 239
"Lice and Other Niceties" (Andújar), 159–60
lieux de mémoire (place of memory), 15; concentration camps and, 23; Nora, Pierre, on, 15
Lillo Pérez, Elenterio, 272
Indépendant, L, 42, 168, 180
"Lines, The" (Andújar), 160
Lizarraga, Gerardo, 109; Varo, Remedios, and, 109
Locomoción capilar [Hairy Locomotion] (Varo), 112
"Un loco," (Amieva), 43
López Barrantes, Ramón, 69
López Rodríguez, Manuel, 66
Lorca, Federico García, 61, 171–73, 175–76, 264; *La almohada de arena* [Pillow of Sand] (Amieva), influence on, 173
Los de Collioure [The Men of Collioure] (Nelken), 50, 65, 134; French political policy in, 134
Los que no volvieron [The Ones Who Never Returned] (Sampelayo), 13
Loureiro, Angel, 35, 153, 193; on reality, psychological adjustment to, 153
Luis Suárez, 16, 62, 103

Macdonald, Nancy, 32
Machado, Antonio, 16, 36–42, 45–50, 171, 280, 295 n. 10; Andújar, Manuel, on, 295 n. 10; in *La ciudad de madera* [The City of Wood] (Cabruja Auguet), 41–42; in Collioure, 48–49; in "Corona de espinas" [Crown of Thorns] (Amieva), 43–45; death of, 42, 296 n. 31; in "The Death of the Poet" (Mistral), 45–46; exile history of, 38–41; Felipe, León, and, 182; literary legacy of, 36–37; memorialization of, 45–50; and *vencidos* (war veterans), 42; Xirau, Joaquín, on, 38–41, 48
"macuto, El" [The Knapsack] (Amieva), 186–87; literary structure of, 186–87
Madariaga, Salvador, 256
Madrid (Falcón), 283
Madrid, Miguel de la, 284
manta, la, 317 n. 18

Manuscrito Cuervo (Aub/Naharro-Calderón), 86
"manuscrito, El" [The manuscript] (Amieva), 185
Marañón, Gregorio, 100, 228–29; on Spanish war history, 100
Marichal, Juan, 288
Marinos del Báltico, 27
Maritain, Jacques, 131
"Marseillaise, La," 279
Martel, Francis, 131–32; Spanish Civil War, French involvement in, 131–32
Martí, José, 27
Martínez Barrio, Diego, 214–15; on exile emigration, 215
Martínez, Salvador, 230
Martorell, Joan, 27
Más allá del dolor (Giménez Igualada), 56, 307 n. 1
Mateo Sousa, Eligio de, 250
Matesanz, José Antonio, 215–16; on exile emigration, 215
"memory album," 53, 55; *Campos de concentración 1939–194...* (Bartolí/Molins i Fábrega) as, 55
"Memory, Sacrifice, and the Nation" (Rowlands), 35
memory site, 35
"memory text," 40
Men in Battle (Bessie), 242
Méndez, Angel, 211, 213, 218
Méndez, Concha, 28
Mexico: exiles and, 17, 167, 212, 293 n. 23; guidelines for refugee response, 212; symbolism of, for exiles, 212–13, 218–20
Mexique (ship), 218, 220, 254–55
Mije, Antonio, 67, 154
Mimetismo [Mimetism] (Varo), 113; imagery in, 113
Miñana, Federico, 231, 257–58
Mingarro, Pepe, 232
Miró, Antonio, 30
"De mis recuerdos" [From My Memories] (Altolaguirre), 26
Mistral, Silvia, 26–27, 29, 45–46, 49, 56, 59–60, 67, 69–70, 101, 175, 226; border crossing of, 27; on camp guards, 59–60; CNT and, 224; diary entries of, 27, 29; threatened repatriation for, 67
Molins i Fábrega, Narcís, 53, 60, 71–72, 226

Montseny, Federica, 32, 56, 190; on border crossing, 32
Morales, Ramón, 231
Morir por cerrar los ojos [Death by Blindness] (Aub), 86–96, 98–99, 126, 141; character identity in, 90; character symbolism in, 89, 92; conflict themes in, 91; international politics within, 92–93; literary structure of, 88–95; memory album imagery in, 95; Spanish Civil War, French involvement in, 87; violence in, 97–98
"muertos vuelven, Los" [The Return of the Dead] (Felipe), 178
Mundo: socialismo y libertad, 62
Muñoz, Manolo, 233–34
Murià, Anna, 193

Naharro-Calderón, José, 22, 86, 154, 158–59; on language, for exiles, 154; on *St. Cyprien, plage... Campo de concentración* (Andújar), 155
Nation and Narration (Bhabha), 34
national identity, 16; Anderson, Benedict, on, 16
National Socialist [Nazi] party, 121
Negrín, Juan, 140, 215, 217, 243–44; exile emigration, role in, 215; on Spanish Republicans, 140
Nelken, Margarita, 50, 154
Neruda, Pablo, 34, 86
Niebla de cuernos (Herrera Petere), 101–10; France *vs.* Spain in, 106; French symbolism in, 104; literary structure of, 103–8; publishing history of, 102; violence in, 105; war motifs in, 104–5
Nora, Pierre, 15–16, 35, 292 n. 7; on *lieux de mémoire*, 15, 35, 292 n. 7
nuevo venció Atila, De [Attila has Conquered Again] (Bartolí), 58
nuevos profetas, Los (Benavides), 101, 119–28
nuevos profetas, Los [The New Prophets] (Benavides), 122–28; Argelès-sur-Mer in, 123; internationalism as part of, 123, 128; literary structure of, 122–25; Spanish Republicans in, 127

ocaso de los dioses rojos: Barcelona, Perthus, Argelés, París, Méjico... El [The Twilight of the Red Gods] (Vilaró), 14, 225

Odyssey, The (Homer), 205; *Cristo de 200.000 brazos (Campo de Argelès)* (Bartra), allusions in, 205
Oeuvre, L', 239
Oficina de la Ficha Antropométrica, 241
Oliva, Julián, 21, 154; illustrations of, 154; in *St. Cyprien, plage . . . Campo de concentración* (Andújar), 154–55
Ombres entre tenebres (L'exode de Catalunya) (Men Among the Shadows) [The Exodus From Catalonia]) (Valldeperes), 55–56
On Beauty and Being Just (Scarry), 204
Ortega y Gasset, Eduardo, 229
Otros se fueron: tú quedaste [The Others Left: You Stayed Behind] (Bartolí), 80f
Owl of Minerva, The (Regler), 121

"Padre Nuestro" (Valiente), 260
Palacio de Velázquez del Retiro (museum), 21
Palacio, Solano, 26, 29, 51, 189, 213–14, 244; SERE, criticism of, 213–14
Panadero Caballero, Esperanza, 65, 237, 245; García Gerpe, Manuel, and, 237, 245
París 1939–1940 (Bartolí), 110f
Paris-Soir, 239
"Paris-Soir" (Andújar), 160
Pellicer, Carlos, 48
Péret, Benjamin, 109, 112; Varo, Remedios, and, 109, 112
Perujo Echevarría, Agapito, 51, 66
peso de la derrota, El (Sánchez-Bravo/Tellado), 85
Pétain, Marshal, 117, 131–32, 298 n. 8; Franco, Francisco, and, 131–32
Pétain: Verdun to Vichy (Martel), 131
Petit Parisien, 133
Pike, David, 31
Plages d'exil: Les Camps de réfugiés espagnols en France, 1939 (Villegas), 183, 291 n. 8
"Plebiscite" (Andújar), 160, 162; political protest in, 162
Poemas humanos (Vallejo), 198
Poeta en la arena (Amieva), 184
"Por una senda clara" [Along a Clear Path] (Xirau), 38
Prat, José, 288, 324 n. 15
Prats-de-Molló (concentration camp), 66, 147; Artís-Gener, Avel·lí at, 147

Prensa, La, 46
Presencia inquietante [Unsettling Presence] (Varo), 113; imagery in, 113
Preston, Paul, 162; on Law of Political Responsibility, 162
Prieto, Indalecio, 233
"Proverbios y cantares" (Machado), 44
PSOE (Socialist Party of Spanish Workers), 268, 322 n. 11
Puche, José, 48
Puigverd, Joan, 29
Pujol, José, 56, 315 n. 20

Quijano, Alonso, 281
Quintana, Pauline, 49

Radio Chabola (radio shack), 270
Rafaneau-Boj, Marie, 152, 180; on camp punishment, 180
Ramón Jiménez, Juan, 46, 171
rapto de Europa, El (Aub), 24, 100, 109
rebeldes españoles no hacen una guerra santa, Los [The Spanish Rebels are not Fighting a Holy War] (Maritain), 131
Regler, Gustav, 120, 122–23, 190, 302 n. 49, 309 n. 22
Rejano, Juan, 47–48, 103, 154, 311 n. 37; Machado, Antonio, and, 47–48
Renan, Ernest, 34–35
Renau, Juan, 27, 147, 313 n. 58; exile experience of, 147; on memory, for exiles, 313 n. 58
repatriation, 66–68, 252–53; for exiles, 66–68; for Giménez Igualada, Miguel, threats of, 68; Hervás, Mariano, on, 252; for Mistral, Silvia, threats of, 67; for Sánchez Ramírez, Angel, 67
Republican Party (Spain), 15, 53, 87; in *Ballet de Sangre: la caída de Francia* [Ballet of Blood: The Fall of France] (Rodríguez), 87; exiles and, 15, 33; Negrín, Juan, on, 140
Retuerto, Marcial, 100
Reyes, Alfonso, 48, 262
Rial, José, 273; Ferrer, Eulalio, influence on, 273
Ridruejo, Dionisio, 42
Rioja, Enrique, 27
Rodríguez, Luis I., 86, 265, 302 n. 6; exile aid from, 302 n. 6
Rodríguez Luna, Antonio, 171

Rodríguez, Marcial, 250
Rojo Leyva, Gabriel, 36, 281
Rojo, Vicente, 32, 216–17, 244; on border crossing, 32
Romance (exile journal), 36, 47, 121, 280–81
"Romance de la Guardia Civil Espanola" (Lorca), 61, 172
"Romance de la Guardia Móvil Francesa" (Amieva), 61, 172–73; García Lorca, Federico, influence on, 172–73
Romancero español (Lorca), 173–74
Ros, Antonio: on exile emigration, 228–29, 237; on exile experience, 227; in Paris, 235–38; SERE and, 229
Roussillon, Le, 238
Rowlands, Michael, 35–36, 52; on exile memorialization, 52
Rubio, Javier, 51, 78, 212, 215, 217, 302; on exile emigration, 212, 215; on exile population, 51
Rubirosa, Porfirio, 230–31; SERE and, 230–31
Ruhn, Gerhard von, 93
Ruiz, Cristóbal, 36
Ruiz, Roberto, 217
Ruiz-Funes, Mariano, 229; exile emigration and, 229

Said, Edward, 23, 85; on collective memory, 85; on geography and nationalism, relationship of, 23–24
Sale étranger! [Dirty Foreigner!] (Bartolí), 111
Salido, Cruz, 234
Samblancat, Angel, 51, 161, 172; on exile repatriation, 161
Sampelayo, Carlos, 13
Sánchez Barbudo, Antonio, 22, 102, 222; on Mexican emigration, 222
Sánchez, Liqui, 275
Sánchez Ramírez, Angel, 65–67, 153, 181; at Collioure, 65, 153, 181; repatriation and, 67
Sánchez Vázquez, Adolfo, 322 n. 7
Sánchez-Bravo Cenjor, Antonio, 25, 28, 71, 212
Scarry, Elaine, 203–4; on beauty and ethics, 203–4
Schama, Simon, 148; on Jewish diaspora, 148

Scum of the Earth (Koestler), 120
Sée, Jean, 233
Semprún, Jorge, 153, 192–93
"Sentido de la derrota" (Zambrano), 13
Septfonds (concentration camp), 52, 61, 129, 152; ceremony at, 152; González, Alfonso, at, 129
SERE (Servicio de Evacuación de Republicanos Españoles), 212, 215, 220–21, 223, 228–29, 247, 257–58, 269, 271, 319 n. 17; Bejarano, Benigno, and, 220–21; CNT and, 213; criteria for release for, 216; criticism of, 213; emigration rates, to America, 319 n. 17; FAI and, 213; Ferrer, Eulalio, and, 268; financial aid, for exiles, 217; García Gerpe, Manuel, and, 248; JARE, conflicts with, 257–58, 269, 271; political demographic of, 215; quota systems and, 215; role in exile emigration, 212; Ros, Antonio, and, 228–29; Rubirosa, Porfirio, and, 230–31; Templado, Félix, and, 230
Serpa Pinto (ship), 109
Serra, Manuel, 220; at Collioure, 220; emigration for, 220
Serra, Pedro, 28, 60
Servicio de Evacuación de Republicanos Españoles. *See* SERE
Shain, Yossi, 85
Shaw, Donald, 88
Sherman, Daniel, 35
Simone, André, 130, 132
Sinaia (ship), 140, 222, 250
Siqueiros, Jorge, 289
Solar, Ramón, 268
"sombra, La" (Amieva), 285
Soriano, Antonio, 27, 32, 45
Souza, Cándido, 66
Spain: exile history of, 100; fascism in, 53, 140–41; language, state control of, 290 n. 5, 311 n. 39; Republican party in, 53
Spanish Civil War: Cuban soldiers in, 152; France, role in, 31, 87, 131–32; French literary response to, 130–33; museum exhibits for, 21; Nationalists during, 23; veterans after, 13
Spanish Refugee Aid, 290 n. 2
Specters of Marx (Derrida), 287
St. Cyprien (concentration camp), 22,

134, 139; in *España comienza en los Pirineos* [Spain Begins in the Pyrenees] (Suárez López), 134, 139, 145; Espinar, Jaime, at, 146; Suárez López, Luis, at, 181

St. Cyprien, plage... *Campo de concentración* (Andújar), 148–49, 154–66; "collective memory" as part of, 158; exile experience in, 148–49; as historical chronicle, 158; illustrations in, 154–55; language in, role of, 155; literary structure of, 159–60; Naharro-Calderón, José, on, 155; punctuation in, role of, 156; purpose of, 154; transformative markers in, 164

"Stroll Down the Avenue, A" (Suárez López), 139; symbolism in, 139

Suárez López, Luis, 129, 133–41, 156, 174–75; on El Dorado myth, 174–75; on French political policy, 133–34; on Spanish identity, 129–30; at St. Cyprien, 181

survivor guilt, 222; Levi, Primo, on, 222

Tanning, Dorothea, 119
Tellado Vázquez, Antonio, 25, 28, 71, 212
Templado, Félix: SERE and, 230
Todorov, Tzvetan, 192–93, 203
"Todos tendremos para pagar la entrada" [We'll All Be Able to Afford the Cost of Admission] (Felipe), 178
Torre, Guillermo de, 182
Torres, Henry, 132
Toyos, Joaquín, 275, 281
"Tremblinka: Death Camp in Poland," 62
Truth on the Tragedy of France (Bois), 133

Ugarte, Michael, 217, 296 n. 21, 299 n. 9
"Ultima muerte" (Altolaguirre), 13
Ultramar (journal), 17
Urogallo, El (journal), 165; Andújar, Manuel, and, 165

Valender, James, 36, 281
Valera, Fernando, 233
Valiente, Manolo, 32, 150, 180, 260
Valldeperes, Manuel, 55–56
Vallejo, César, 189, 198
Varo, Remedios, 109–14; exile history of, 109–10, 112; Gruen, Walter, on, 112;

Lizarraga, Gerardo, and, 109; paintings of, 112–14; Péret, Benjamin, and, 109, 112

Vázquez Montalbán, Manuel, 13–14, 290 n. 2; on *vencidos*, 14

Velo, Carlos, 221–22; on Mexican emigration, 222

vencidos ('the vanquished'), 14, 36; Machado, Antonio, and, 42; Vázquez Montalbán, Manuel, on, 14

Vernet d'Ariège (concentration camp), 35, 86, 120–21; exiles in, 120–21

"Vida bilingüe de un refugiado español en Francia" (Alberti), 211, 304 n. 12; literary significance of, 304 n. 12

Vilanova, Antonio, 57, 151–52, 218; on "hurry-up streets," 151

Villaurrutia, Xavier, 48
Villela, Agustín, 49
Visita inesperada [Unexpected Visitor] (Varo), 113–14; imagery in, 113–14
visitante, El [The Visitor] (Varo), 114; imagery in, 114
Vita (ship), 269
Vives, Pere, 192; Bartra, Agustí, influence on, 192; *Cristo de 200.000 brazos (Campo de Argelés)* (Bartra), influence on, 192
"Voces" (Voices) (Amieva), 62
Vogue Magazine, 260–61

War Heroes (Bartolí), 76
Weil, Simone, 203
"What is a Nation?" (Renan), 34
Winnipeg (ship), 255
Winnipeg y otros poemas, El (Neruda), 34

Xabola (Hut) (Bartra), 44
Xirau, Joaquín, 36, 38–39, 47; on Machado, Antonio, 38–41, 48; "memory text" of, 40

Yo fui ministro de Negrín [I Was Negrín's Cabinet Minister] (Ansó), 225
Yuglá Mariné, Enric, 69

Zambrano, María, 13
Zapirain, Luis, 154
Zugazagoitia, Julián, 234
Zurita Castañer, Joaquín, 15; on exiles, 15